CRUELTY AND SILENCE

War, Tyranny, Uprising, and the Arab World

CRUELTY AND SILENCE

War, Tyranny, Uprising, and the Arab World

KANAN MAKIYA

W · W · Norton & Company

New York   London

Copyright © 1993 by Kanan Makiya
All rights reserved
Printed in the United States of America
First Edition

The text of this book is composed in 12/13.5 Bembo 270
with the display set in Gill Sans Bold Extra Condensed at 180% horizontal scale
Composition and manufacturing by the Haddon Craftsmen, Inc.

Library of Congress Cataloging-in-Publication Data
Makiya, Kanan.
Cruelty and silence : war, tyranny, uprising and the Arab World /
by Kanan Makiya.
p. cm.
Includes bibliographical references and index.
1. Political atrocities—Iraq. 2. Iraq—Politics and government.
3. Intellectuals—Arab countries—Attitudes. I. Title.
DS79.736.M35 1993
956.704′4—dc20   92-42667

ISBN 0-393-03108-X

W.W. Norton & Company, Inc., 500 Fifth Avenue, New York, N.Y. 10110
W.W. Norton & Company Ltd., 10 Coptic Street, London WC1A 1PU

1 2 3 4 5 6 7 8 9 0

To Afsaneh

Contents

Acknowledgments

A handful of dear friends have always read everything that I wrote. They are Afsaneh Najmabadi, Mai Ghoussoub, and Emmanuel Farjoun. What they have contributed to all my books goes beyond comments and suggestions for improvement; I take nourishment from their spirit. To Mai, who never wanted me to dwell so much on the violence of our world even as her example taught me how to grasp only what was most essential about it, I dedicated *Republic of Fear* in 1986. Things being what they were under the Iraqi Ba'th, that dedication remained a secret between us. No longer.

Cruelty and Silence could never have been written in that 1980s atmosphere of mistrust and personal isolation. This is a book of Arab and Kurdish voices. In the nature of things I have a large number of people to thank. Homes were opened up to me, personal letters were passed on, newspapers were clipped and complicated interviews arranged. I was entrusted with sensitive government documents, with names that were not to be revealed, with family secrets, with the stories of terrible things that people were compelled to do. In Cambridge, Massachusetts, where much of the writing was done, and in London and Iraqi Kurdistan where most of the information was obtained, Iraqis took care of my children, collected information, introduced me to people, and told me what to look for and where. They commented on chapter drafts, took me to places, and provided me with protection inside Iraq. This is their book. Being able to say this gives me great pleasure. Nonetheless, I alone am responsible for errors or for controversial ideas. Nor, it must be stressed, does appearance in the book involve any kind of responsibility for it.

9

Aside from the "characters" in this book, I am grateful to Haydar Hamoodi, Ghanim Jewad, Nabaz Kamal, Dhia Kashi, Muwaffaq al-Rubaie, Zuhair Hamadi, Rend Rahim, Shoresh Rasoul, Tamara Daghistani, Muhammad al-Hakim, Faleh 'Abdel-Jabbar, Mustafa al-Kadhimi, Bushra Rahim, Amin al-'Issa, Ahmad Chalabi, Latif Rashid, Barham Saleh, Hoshyar Zibari, Jawhar Namiq Salem, Burhan al-Jaf, and the members of the Iraqi-American Forum for Peace and Democracy. There remain many other Iraqis spread across the world whose personal circumstances preclude my naming them. I hope that one day, in an edition of this book issued from Baghdad, their contribution can be properly acknowledged.

My friends Andre Gaspard, Paula Hajar, Lawrence Weschler, Greg Singer, Cliff Wright, Kenneth Roth, Stephen Howe, and Hazim Saghiyeh kindly read through various early drafts of part or the whole of this manuscript. It has been greatly improved by their comments. I would also like to express my appreciation for the confidence placed in me by John Blake, the producer of *Everyman* at the BBC, Marty Smith and David Fanning of "Frontline" at WGBH, and Gwynne Roberts in whose company I traveled to northern Iraq in the winter of 1991. Gwynne also kindly provided me with translated transcripts of interviews conducted in Kurdistan in November 1991. Neil Conan of National Public Radio and Tony Horowitz of the *Wall Street Journal* very graciously gave me transcripts of interviews they had conducted inside Iraq, both of which have found their way into the text. Sarah Zaidi and Aliza Farjoun drew my attention to the important fieldwork done by Pakistani and Palestinian women on political rape. Jacqueline Williams put together an invaluable chronology of the Iraqi intifada. I feel greatly indebted to all of them. I am also grateful to Nabaz Kamal for helping with translations from Kurdish. As for the translations from French, I am indebted to Donald Stone, Eric Evans, and a very dear Iraqi friend who prefers not to be named. Translations from the Arabic are my own unless otherwise noted.

The Center for Middle East Studies at Harvard University provided an environment most conducive to writing. In particular, I would like to thank Roy Mottahedeh and William Graham for their support and for inviting me to be a part of that community while working on this book.

My publishers, Mary Cunnane at W.W. Norton and Neil Belton at Jonathan Cape, have provided support at every step of the way.

They followed the twists and turns of this book from its inception in June 1991 to its completion in December 1992. I have lost count of the number of different drafts I forwarded on to them for comment. No author could ask for more.

I published an article in the May 1992 issue of *Harper's* Magazine which was based on the material in Chapter 5, Taimour. I am very grateful to Jerry Mazaratti for his editorial insights during the writing of that article; they remained invaluable in shaping the enormous mass of material that ended up as Chapter 5. A less-developed version of the argument in Chapter 7, Who Am I?, was published in Arabic by Saqi Books in a pamphlet entitled *Al-Harb Alati Lam Tuktamal*. Throughout, many of the ideas put forth were explored in the form of lectures given at Oxford University, the University of Utah, Harvard University, the School for Advanced International Studies at Princeton University, the University of Washington in Seattle, and the Massachusetts Institute of Technology.

Finally, there are three special people who did something much more than just work on or help out with this book: they left a piece of their hearts inside its pages. Naghmeh Sohrabi, from Iran, combed libraries and edited transcripts. Rena Fonseca, from India, read and reread chapters when I could no longer see the forest for the trees. Ayad Rahim, from Iraq, did a little bit of everything. No task was too big or too small for him, and he was always there. I met Ayad accidentally in October 1990 in the Old City of Jerusalem shortly after the killings on the *Haram al-Sharif*. He was working on the human rights abuses endured by Palestinians under Israeli occupation; from there we began a return journey into the cruel world of Ba'thi Iraq. Together, we worked and laughed and cried for the year and a half that it took to finish this book.

A Note on Transliteration

I have kept in mind the general reader, not the specialist, in transcribing Arabic into English. Arabic names which have entered into English, such as Cairo, Mosul, Omar, and intifada, have been kept in their widely accepted form. Where Arab writers or publications have a common rendition of their name, I have opted for these (for example, Hisham Djaïet, Edward Said, *an-Naqid*). The definite article "the" has been rendered *al-* with the exception of the construction " 'Abd al-," which has been rendered " 'Abdel-" because that is what most people with that construction in their name seem to prefer (for example, 'Abdel-Rahman Munif). Otherwise I have used a simplified version of the English transliteration system employed in the *International Journal of Middle East Studies (IJMES),* leaving out all diacritical marks with the exception of (') for the Arabic guttural consonant *'ain* and (') for the *hamza,* an unvoiced glottal stop. I have also used "dh" for the three Arabic letters *dhal, dhad,* and *dha',* the sounds of which range from the English "th" (as in "the") to an emphatic muffled "d." The long vowel sound produced by a *dhamma* and a *waw* is transliterated as "ou" (as in Mahmoud). The long *e* sound is transliterated as "ee" (as in *Khaleej* and Sa'eed). The intent is to provide a better sense of the pronunciation to the general reader. A particular problem for which there is no ready solution is the rendition of Iraqi colloquial and Kurdish words. Where, in such cases, the above rules broke down, I improvised.

Introduction

ON AUGUST 2, 1990, when I heard that Saddam Husain had just invaded Kuwait, I felt sick. The instinctive thought was that he was going to get away with it. The Arab world was in a moribund, fragmented state and Saddam Husain knew his world, however little he may have understood anyone else's. Had he been allowed to get away with the annexation of the whole or part of Kuwait, everything that he stood for in politics would have been projected outward, shaping the Arab world for generations to come. For each one of us, the most important moments in politics begin with the kind of raw feeling that overcame me as I sat in my living room listening to the news. All the complex analyses and fancy formulations—which are a writer's trade—fall into line behind such feelings. Writing and thinking turn into mere elaboration of elemental instinct.

"Saddam Husain has to be stopped," I wrote that same August. "The major flaw in the American-led effort against him is that the shock troops in the front lines are not Arabs. The old nationalist, anti-imperialist formulas are therefore already being trotted out, to terrible effect. For the sake of the future of the Arab world itself, Arab must be seen to be fighting Arab in the sands of Arabia for the sake of the restoration of the sovereignty of Kuwait and against the principle of violence in human affairs which is what Ba'thi politics is all about."[1]

ON JANUARY 17, 1991, the day the Allied forces began bombing Iraq, I was in Cairo to attend the twenty-second annual Arabic language

1 5

book fair. Stepping out of the taxi that had brought me from the airport to my hotel the week before, I saw spread out on the pavement of Tal'at Harb Street a host of cheap mass-market paperbacks, among which was a pirated Arabic edition of *Republic of Fear.* An Egyptian friend claimed it had been put out by a man who worked for the Saudi intelligence services. Thumbing through the pirated edition of my book, I asked the eager bookseller if he knew anything about who had written it. "He used to be one of them," he replied. "Then he broke with his comrades just before the invasion of Kuwait and spilled the beans." The book was flanked by two spy memoirs. One was Peter Wright's *Spycatcher,* and the other was by a former member of Mossad, entitled *By Way of Deception.* These had appeared in Arabic in time to make a big hit at the book fair. Cloak and dagger spy stories are popular in Egypt, and it seems *Republic of Fear* was deemed by Egyptian book distributors to be of the same genre.

Lying on the same pavement on Tal'at Harb Street, just outside the front entrance to my hotel, was one of the half dozen or so scurrilous attacks on Salman Rushdie which can be found all over Cairo. This one had a Satanic caricature of Rushdie on the front cover with horns protruding from his head two inches above the ears. Elsewhere, spread out on the pavement, was a collection of everyone's favorite Egyptian love stories, and the most ubiquitous book in the whole of Cairo, *The End of the World,* written by the Billy Graham of Egypt, the "Shaikh and Imam" Muhammad Mutawwali al-Sha'rawi. Apocalyptic scenarios, magical events, astrological predictions, conspiratorial machinations, and cloak and dagger politics were very much the rage in Cairo on the eve of the Gulf war in January 1991.

At the fair there were also books which argued for the separation of mosque from state by Muslim rationalist thinkers like Fouad Zakariyya and liberal secularists such as the writer Farag Fouda. I was fortunate enough to be able to attend a public talk by Fouda on his latest book. After the talk, Fouda passionately debated hundreds of angry opponents. It took enormous courage to defend secularism in public like that. For that courage, on June 9, 1992, less than a week after Fouda had publicly criticized President Hosni Mubarak for restricting civil liberties in Egypt, he was gunned down by Muslim extremists.[2]

Another new book on the Gulf crisis, *Oil and Blood,* pseudonymously written and virulently hostile to Saddam in its rhetoric, fur-

nished alleged secret documents of the Iraqi regime, including lists
of the names of all Jews in the Ba'th Party and an account of their
"real role" in Iraqi politics. This is the methodology utilized by the
Ba'th themselves. In the 1980s, Fadhil al-Barak, the director-general
of internal security in Iraq, wrote a book which attempted to document how "evil expansionist forces" worked by planting spies and
saboteurs in Iraqi Jewish and Iranian schools.[3] The lists he provided
in his book are the very same ones that the unknown authors of *Oil
and Blood* have replicated in theirs. Mr. al-Barak's fortunes changed
after the Gulf war. He fell out of favor with his Ba'thi employers.
Under torture, he confessed to being a spy for Russia and Germany.
In the summer of 1992, his body was returned to his family in Takrit
in a sealed box.[4]

EXTRAORDINARY times do strange things to a book. *Republic of Fear*
was finished in 1986. It took a long time to get published. Strange as
it may seem now, only a short while ago very few people were
willing to believe that things were that bad inside Iraq. Many a
reader or editor found the manuscript "biased and one-sided," not
scholarly enough, or excessively polemical. I still wince from the
memory of being rejected by one publisher because the most emi-
nent Arab scholar of modern Iraq in the United States reported that
the book "insults" the people of Iraq. Because of Saddam Husain,
however, I ended up with something as close to a best-seller as a
specialist book on one country of the Middle East (barring Israel)
can be in the English language.

I counted fifteen new titles on the Gulf crisis in Cairo's book fair,
fifteen "instant" books, as the phrase goes in the trade. Among them
were two different Arabic editions of the first four chapters of *Republic of Fear*. I think the second half of the book was considered too
academic for Saddam's demonization. One edition was published by
Dar al-Thaqafa, a tiny, respectable, secular publishing house. The
second pirated version was the one I found on the pavement of
Tal'at Harb Street. Later, I found out that another pirated edition, a
terrible translation of all eight chapters, had been published by an
Islamic publishing house called Dar al-Zahra'. All of this sudden
interest should be set against the fact that no Arabic language publisher would touch the manuscript from the time it was completed
until Saddam Husain's invasion of Kuwait.[5]

Macabre and terrible though the circumstances were, I was

pleased by all the attention. What writer wouldn't take pleasure in seeing his book spread out on the pavement of Tal'at Harb Street in Cairo, especially beside a manual with red hearts plastered all over it on how to write love letters? The rest of my company on the pavement, I could do without. For example, *The Butcher,* an instant book on Iraq with a grotesque caricature on the cover of the Iraqi leader stitching the map of Kuwait to Iraq. Ironically, my book was becoming redundant at exactly the moment it was becoming popular. I was trying to draw attention to the importance of taking the violence of the Ba'th very seriously. No one needed to read 300 pages to find that out after August 2, 1990.

Serious doubts about the meaning of all of this attention, however, do creep in when one realizes that by being published and distributed in the manner I have described, *Republic of Fear* was not going to be taken seriously by some of the very people it was written for, namely, in this case, the Egyptian intelligentsia. Instant books have the same reputation in Cairo as they do in London or in New York. If one considers the argument of *Republic of Fear* as having implications for the state of contemporary Arab politics, then the likelihood is that this argument would be ignored through association with *The War Between Islam and the Devil,* another dusty companion on the pavement of Tal'at Harb Street whose cover depicts Dracula-like fangs coming out of Saddam's mouth and blood dripping from a dagger in his hand pointed at the Ka'ba in Mecca. True, many Egyptian and Gulf Arab intellectuals were now critical of the Iraqi regime. But they had become so only after August 2, 1990, and everyone's inclination in January 1991 was to focus all blame on Saddam Husain, as though the brutishness of his person was all that had gone wrong in the Arab world in the past twenty years.

The real catastrophe, however, was not the intellectual scene in Egypt or the state of Egyptian publishing; it was the mind-set exhibited by the intelligentsia of the Arab world, particularly those originating in countries east of Egypt. The support for Saddam among the most cosmopolitan, secular, and westernized stratum of Arab intellectuals—in particular the most sophisticated group among them, the Palestinians—was extraordinary in its breadth and depth. It is one thing for a Palestinian in the Occupied Territories who is being humiliated daily by the Israeli military authorities to feel a sudden surge of sympathy for "the dark-skinned knight on his white horse," as that wonderful exception, the Palestinian writer Emile

Habibi, satirized Saddam; it is something else entirely for the growing number of journalists, writers, or professors in Western universities who think of themselves as "Arab" or "pro-Arab" to be uttering the same sentiments in support of a brutal tyrant and in the full knowledge of what he was doing to fellow Arabs.[6] During the first flush of the Gulf crisis, an Arab cultural malaise which has been many years in the making, and which is best symbolized by the emergence of Saddam Husain himself, erupted forcefully onto the center stage of Arab politics.

Like many Iraqis, especially those with a record of activism on the Palestinian question, I had some very unpleasant personal experiences with this Arab reaction. I was attacked for writing *Republic of Fear* under a false name. To some, the pseudonym Samir al-Khalil was confirmation that I could only be a Mossad agent, or "an Iraqi Jew." The facts are more prosaic: neither I nor anyone from my family has been hurt by the Iraqi Ba'th, and writing under a pseudonym was the most practical way of ensuring that things stayed that way.

Much has been made of pseudonyms and political positions; far too little of what actually happened inside Iraq. *Republic of Fear* tries to build a case that Ba'thi Iraq should not be dismissed as a run-of-the-mill dictatorship with equally nasty counterparts all over the Third World. In the course of the 1970s it developed into a totalitarian state, one that bore a greater resemblance to the Soviet Union under Stalin in the 1930s and Hitler's Germany than it did to Jordan or Saudi Arabia. Does the evidence marshaled in the book confirm such conclusions? For that matter, does the enormously expanded body of documentation on Iraq now available confirm or refute that characterization of the Ba'thi state? What actually happened in Iraq over the last twenty years? Accepting the broad lines of the argument in *Republic of Fear* has implications which go far beyond Iraq, extending to the whole Arab world. Arab intellectuals wanted to avoid those implications during the Gulf crisis.

ON MARCH 7, 1991, during the Iraqi uprising against Saddam Husain, I went public at a symposium organized by Harvard University's Center for Middle Eastern Studies. At that forum, and in the others that followed, I called on the Allied forces to finish the war and take upon themselves the task of replacing the Ba'th regime with a transitional government:

The scale of the Iraqi defeat carries with it a historic opportunity for a new beginning, one likely to shape the region's politics in less than a generation. But first the allied forces must openly recognize and work with the Iraqi insurgents . . . and march into Baghdad. . . . [A] strategic political leap equal to the scale of the war itself is required. What would have happened if the US had withdrawn from Europe after World War II, with no commitment to democracy and economic reconstruction?[7]

The United States was not obligated to come halfway across the world with 443,000 soldiers to sort out the problems of the Middle East. Saddam Husain was no threat to American citizens. American presidents had dealt with him before and they could certainly deal with him again. George Bush, in particular, was comfortable doing business with Saddam Husain.[8] But once the United States chose to shoulder that responsibility, and once the fighting began, then it acquired an obligation to the people of Iraq to end things differently, an obligation which it did not have before all those Americans were sent to fight in the Gulf.

After I went public with this position, the non–Iraqi Arab reaction that I had experienced earlier got worse. For example, the Arabic daily Al-Quds al-'Arabi decided to publish an "Exposition and Discussion of the Ideas of Kanan Makiya" following the U.K. showing of the documentary The Road to Hell, in which I reported on the organized mass murder of more than 100,000 Kurdish civilians between February and September 1988 (see chapters 4 and 5 of this book).[9] The article, written by the Syrian Subhi Hadidi, appeared under two subheadings: "How Did the Book 'Republic of Fear' Became a Legend?" and "Out of Despair Comes Mental Pandemonium."[10] Hadidi's purpose was to show that Samir al-Khalil, this "rising star of the Iraqi opposition" who called on the Allied forces to finish the war and take out the Iraqi dictator, was a creation of the Western media. His light will fade, the article implied, as his true Shi'ite sectarian colors become pronounced.

Although the article's banner headline proclaimed it to be an exposition of ideas, at no point did it address the argument of Republic of Fear. Hadidi wrote that he did not have the space to go into it. But a lot of things can be said in two whole pages of a daily newspaper (approximately 3,200 words). What else, one might reasonably ask, was there to write about? Moreover, there was not one word in

Hadidi's two-part article on the terrible allegations made in that documentary. How important is the fact that at least 100,000 innocent Iraqi men, women, and children were trucked from their villages to their deaths over a six-month period in 1988? How important is it that since 1975, no less than 3,500 Kurdish villages have been demolished by the Iraqi government in the name of Arabism?

On the other side of the Atlantic, Edward Said, University Professor at Columbia and probably the most prominent Arab intellectual in the Western hemisphere, criticized *Republic of Fear* as a project serving to "advance the thesis that the feuds and violence in the Middle East are due to, relatively speaking, prehistoric causes, inscribed in the very genes of these people [Arabs]." Samir al-Khalil, he said in an interview on the role of intellectuals during the Gulf war, is a "guinea pig witness," who functioned as a "native informant" serving the interests of American policymakers.[11]

There is more despair and hopelessness buried in such words than there is in a whole library of books devoted to the brutality of Middle Eastern dictatorships and the terrible human costs of their wars. To be political, and to want to reclaim the meaning of political action in the Arab world, is to refuse to become a prisoner of this kind of language. Decades of unremitting violence in the region have allowed skepticism, cynicism, and absolute distrust to grow alarmingly among us. No one can say what might have happened had the Arab world reacted to Saddam Husain's invasion of Kuwait *the way it should have*. To expect too much (as I did in August 1990, when I called on Arabs to lead the fight against other Arabs over the issue of Kuwait, and none did so, preferring to leave it to the United States) is better than to be ensnared in bitterness and despair. On the other hand, insisting upon what is right—finishing the war and taking out the tyrant—is not the same as believing that it is going to happen; it is about projecting into the world an attitude of hope. Things don't have to be as bad as they actually are. If I am preoccupied with the cruelty and violence that has grown so alarmingly in the Arab world, it is in the belief that there is no other way of making that cruelty recede from our lives. No one can know what tomorrow will bring, and so everything and nothing are always possibilities in moments of great crisis. This political stance is at bottom a refusal to give up on the Arab world from which I originate, and it is a refusal to give up on the West where I now choose to reside. There is no politics, no future, and no hope without such acts of acknowledgment and refusal.

THE GULF CRISIS was never simply a matter of foreign manipulation or of the evil man playing the demagogue; it was at bottom an Arab moral failure of historic proportions, for which everyone who cares for the future of this part of the world must feel personally responsible. Something, somewhere along the line, has gone profoundly wrong in the Arab world; Saddam Husain merely typified it and acted it out. In this book, I do not claim to have fully explained what went wrong; my purpose is to acknowledge and describe it. Amidst the tempest of emotions released by the Gulf war, *Cruelty and Silence* was conceived with this in mind.

While cruelty and violence overlap, they are not the same. Violence can be justified according to the ends that it pursues (for instance, as an act of self-defense). There can be violence between equals. Cruelty, on the other hand, can never be justified because it is the intentional infliction of physical pain on individuals who are in a position of weakness. For there to be cruelty, there has to be subjugation and powerlessness in some form. Psychological or social cruelty is beyond the scope of this book, but to a large extent both follow from—and feed into—physical cruelty. The violation of the human body by force or with an instrument of some kind has a visceral, irrational, and irrevocable quality about it. It is the bedrock under all the layers of horrible things that human beings do to one another.

The cruelty that I am concerned with has nothing to do with "genes" or "prehistoric causes"; it is political in cause and universal in effect. Its mere occurrence is an affront to everyone's humanity and this makes it cut across national and religious boundaries and sensibilities. Cruelty of such a universal kind has grown in many parts of the world in recent years, at faster or slower rates (one has only to think of the break-up of Yugoslavia and the daily death toll in Sarajevo). One of the key questions posed in the second part of this book is: Has cruelty grown in the Arab world in the last two or so decades? And if so, what forms has it taken?

Certainly it grew in Iraq during the decade of the 1980s. The latest cycle of invasion, occupation, war, and uprising that Saddam Husain unleashed on the region ended cataclysmically with the Ba'thi regime still in place. In the course of the uprising, Iraqi hopes were raised and then dashed. Yet nothing could ever be the same again. One of the most closed countries in the world had been opened up, and virtually every Arab, for a brief moment, had something urgent to say on the subject. Most importantly, the victims of cruelty were beginning to speak, and to tell stories, as they had never done before. I wanted all those new words that were tumbling out to write this book for me. The first part of the book, therefore, is by far the most important; it is a journey through that cruelty told in the words of individuals who experienced it at first hand. My role was to turn the words of the heroes of this book—Khalil, Abu Haydar, Omar, Mustafa, and Taimour—into stories, tales of the otherwise impossible-to-believe things that we human beings are capable of doing to one another.

Khalil is a remarkable Kuwaiti who stayed in Kuwait during the occupation, and was changed by the experience. Painful though that experience was, it taught him who he was. He searched me out in the summer of 1991, and we discovered a deep bond, out of which emerged the first chapter of this book.

Abu Haydar is a former officer in the Iraqi army, born in the holy city of Najaf. He decided on March 1, 1991, that he had had enough, and took his life into his hands to revolt against Saddam Husain. The story of his *intifada* is told in the form of a collage of Iraqi voices. The rebels were cruel to their erstwhile tormentors. In their own words, they tell of the things that they did. Still, I believe they struck a blow for freedom in Iraq. In the wake of their failure, Najaf and Kerbala were sacked as no Iraqi city has been sacked since the Mongols took Baghdad in 1258. Even as I write, the Ba'th are trying to rebuild them, as they rebuilt Babylon, in their own image.

Omar is a young engineer from al-A'dhamiyya in Baghdad. He spent forty-two days in a Baghdad prison. Although he was not tortured, he entered a world of unimaginable horror which has become a kind of norm inside Iraq.

I met Mustafa in Iraqi Kurdistan in November 1991. He took me to see a monument he had built to memorialize the deaths of sixty-eight of his fellow Kurds from the village of Guptapa, wiped out in a chemical gas attack in 1988. Twenty-five of them were members of his family.

I first saw the Kurdish boy Taimour in a videotape clip passed on to me in August 1991. He was sitting cross-legged on the floor, talking about how he had survived execution by a firing squad in August 1988. His father, mother, and three sisters were not so lucky. Thirteen months after the Iraqi invasion of Kuwait, like everyone else, I was growing immune to Ba'thi atrocity stories. But there was something different about this one. Maybe the difference registered because of a wad of paperwork which I had been given a few days before seeing the tape. These were copies of official documents captured by Kurdish insurgents during the March 1991 uprising. Their significance had hitherto been ignored. The paperwork and the videotape became inextricably connected in my mind. The connection had a name: the campaign of mass murder (mentioned earlier) conducted by the Iraqi army between February and September 1988.[12]

The greater a crime, the harder it is to eliminate all of its traces. Taimour was somewhere out there in the mountains of Kurdistan, willing to bear witness. I entered Iraq on November 11, 1991, to interview Taimour and to see those captured documents. I came out with many terrible bits and pieces of evidence, not all of which have been woven into the stories that comprise the first part of this book.

Cruelty is private, directed at individual human bodies; it is profoundly personal in its implications for the rest of a victim's life. Taimour gets dressed up to look like a big, brave guerrilla fighter these days and trotted out to be interviewed by all and sundry. But he is still just a little boy who was as old as my daughter is now when the world collapsed in on him.

I am a writer, not a human rights worker, and I do not claim to have done justice to the terrible things that have happened to the people whose names appear as chapter headings in Part One. If I have done my best and stuck to the facts as far as it was possible to establish them, I still know that in the case of the people whose stories I have tried to tell, no one's best is ever good enough. To restore Khalil, Abu Haydar, Omar, Mustafa, and Taimour at the center, I had to turn them into metaphors for gross cruelty. Inevitably, real flesh and blood individuals have been written into a new kind of Arab archetype.

IN HIS last dark meditation, just before taking his own life, Primo Levi wrote of the people who have survived unfathomable acts of cruelty:

Almost all the survivors [of the Holocaust], orally or in their written memoirs, remember a dream which frequently recurred during the nights of imprisonment, varied in its detail but uniform in its substance: they had returned home and with passion and relief were describing their past sufferings, addressing themselves to a loved one, and were not believed, indeed were not even listened to. In the most typical (and cruellest) form, the interlocutor turned and left in silence.[13]

If cruelty is individual, then silence is collective. It arises from the actions of many individuals working, consciously or unconsciously, as a group. Breaking with silence as a way of dealing with the legacy of cruelty is thus itself necessarily a collective act. While the cruelties that are talked about in Part One were going on, the Arab intellectuals who could have made a difference if they had put their minds to it were silent.

Like cruelty, the silence of Arab intellectuals is not immutable. Many sensitive Arab minds are profoundly aware of how deep the intellectual and cultural malaise inside the Arab world became during the 1980s. I will constantly be referring to what they have to say. The main point of this book is that the collective Arab silence toward the cruelties that are so often perpetrated in the name of all Arabs originates from many years of thinking in a certain way; it is, therefore, not an essentialist or an unchangeable condition; it is *a politics of silence*. During the Gulf crisis, the form that this politics of silence took was the myth of Saddam as some kind of saviour, and its mirror image, the idea that the crisis and ensuing war grew out of the machinations of Western racism or imperialism.

There was a time when an all-powerful West meddled with and shaped the destiny of the world. A fair amount of that still goes on. The point of the second part of this book is not to deny the obvious; it is to show how "history" has been internalized by the intelligentsia of the Arab world into a profoundly unhealthy political mind-set, one which is at variance with the actual condition of Arabs. Many Arabs knew that something had gone terribly wrong inside the Arab world, but they chose not to speak out, especially not before a Western audience. This kind of intellectual thus became part of the problem, instead of spearheading its solution. In times of moral crisis, silence turns into acquiescence. The abdication of intellectual responsibility is greater among such Arabs than it is among those who don't see the problem in the first place; it is greater precisely because they know better.

The flood of articles and statements written by these intellectuals in the first year and a half of the crisis, elaborating upon the myth, are therefore my prime source in depicting this politics of silence. Pseudo-scientific generalizations and abstractions hide too many sins; silence has its own concrete language, which needs to be illustrated. In any case, by naming names, and quoting what people said and thought, I expose myself as much as I expose those I am criticizing. Some people changed or moderated their opinions after the full scale of the Iraqi military debacle became clear. Some are today talking out of both sides of their mouth at the same time, which suggests that the passions that led to those articles and statements in the first place did not always change. Those emotional wellsprings, not the individuals themselves, lie at the center of my critique.

People are endowed with the gift of being able to change their minds. I bank on that gift because I have seen it at work in so many young Arabs. I write for them. With them in mind, this book appears in three languages at the same time (English, Arabic, and Kurdish). These young people of the Middle East urgently need to break with the heroes who have failed them. They need to invent a different language by which to examine who they are and what it is they want out of this world. The truths that I am dealing in are not cast in stone. They are made by human beings. They are choices which can just as easily be unchosen. There is no general truth that is not particular and individual; that is what hurts so much. But, then, so does cruelty and the language of those Arab intellectuals who have labored to justify it.

We will never stop debating what is truth, but no one should ever have to be in any doubt over what is cruelty. This book is a polemic in favor of calling things by their rightful names; of recognizing failure and of taking responsibility for it. Unlike the satisfaction I felt in telling the stories of Khalil, Abu Haydar, Omar, Mustafa, and Taimour, I found no pleasure in dissecting the words of Arab intellectuals. But it had to be done. Things have gone too far now and there is no turning back from the road that Saddam Husain himself first opened up when he entered Kuwait on August 2, 1990. The stakes are very high because in the end this is a fight over the kind of future the Arab world wants, a struggle over that persistent Middle Eastern question: "Who is an Arab?" In this fight, I seek to be fair, but I do not claim to be impartial. My purpose is not personal, but my style is. I want to tap at the roots. I want to reach into the emotional heart of things instead of staring uselessly at intellectual mirrors. In the meantime, the graves of the dead are still open in the Arab world.

London
December 1992

CRUELTY

1 ′ Khalil

The Importance of a Name

Would that my mother had not brought me into this world to have to live through the anguish of these times.[1]
—Abu Haydar, *January 17, 1991*

KHALIL, a Kuwaiti in his early thirties, discovered these words on one of the walls of the living-room annex in what used to be his luxurious family home. They had been carefully scripted in "wrenchingly exquisite calligraphy," so he told me, by an Iraqi soldier stationed in occupied Kuwait who called himself Abu Haydar.[2] Khalil had lived through the seven-month occupation of his country by adopting a false name, and was reentering his house for the first time since the Iraqi army took it over. On another wall, with equal care, Abu Haydar had written: "To my son and daughter, who are dearer to me than anything else in this world." Nothing else is known about Abu Haydar, not even whether or not he survived the mad rush out of Kuwait City when the order finally came from Baghdad to withdraw on Monday night, February 25, 1991. I would guess, however, that he is—or maybe I should say he was—a literate and educated man.

Khalil found his house looted. "They took anything they could to get out," said a Kuwaiti resident. "If they didn't have a car they stole one. They just wanted to get out as fast as possible."[3] Nonetheless, some unknown Iraqi, before going, took the time to write on the back of a photograph of Khalil's sister: "Dear Kuwaiti sister: Please forgive us for what we have done." Was it Abu Haydar? In fact, it could have been any one of a number of different soldiers. So many of them had bivouacked in Khalil's house since it was first confiscated on September 21, 1990.

Along with the graffiti and the photograph, Khalil found a half-eaten sheep's carcass on the living-room floor. Its skin and bones were littered about and the blood had soaked through the plush carpet. The animal had been slaughtered on the second floor, cooked, and then brought downstairs to be eaten. In spite of the numerous toilets in the house, soldiers—presumably not all that different from Abu Haydar, and maybe even including Abu Haydar himself—had defecated on the carpet around the partially consumed carcass. The whole house, Khalil recalled, exuded a putrid, sickening odor.

> Some of these memories are really horrible. So revolting, my subconscious just wants to suppress them. Before even dealing with them, I need to come up with a mechanism, a system, for bringing them out. It is as though I need to seduce this information to come out. In a sense I need to find a way of telling the memories: "It is okay to come out. I can face up to you again. You are unable to harm me."

Men like Abu Haydar had lived, eaten, and emptied their bowels in the same room, at the same time, possibly even in front of one another. They had done this occupying someone else's house in someone else's city. What kind of men are these? I thought to myself. Khalil must have had a similar thought because he looked at me with an intensity that left me feeling distinctly uncomfortable. "They did the same all over Kuwait," he said.

> The whole thing was violence for the sake of violence, destruction for the sake of destruction and killing for the sake of killing. The country has been literally sodomized. A new word should be coined for what was done to Kuwait: "Saddamized." Yes, Kuwait has been Saddamized.

> Imagine a surrealistic painting by Salvador Dali of death and violence. We human beings have these brutal deposits in our minds, tens of thousands of years old. Primeval forces still subliminally there, which act upon us from time to time. How could a human being think up something like that, I ask myself, in front of Dali's paintings. Some of the images can really hit you in the stomach. As much as there is creativity, there is also sickness. Sick creativity. Yes, that was the force that was at work in Kuwait during the occupation.

I recall walking into the London flat of a friend and finding the place burgled—the contents of every drawer strewn all over the floor. A five-gallon can of white paint had been neatly upturned in the middle of the living-room carpet. The paint had dried in a thick, white, turdlike whorl. A mixing stick poked obscenely into the air. How it managed to stay up in that ridiculous position while the paint dried, I shall never understand.

Khalil found his house violated far more thoroughly than this Kensington flat. No occupation is normal, but some are even less normal than others. The transformation of a family living room into a butcher's shambles and an outhouse is not open to a simple interpretation. The strange thing is that Khalil's house had not "merely" been vandalized like many other houses in Kuwait; it had been occupied, looted, and ransacked. "The branch has returned to the original tree," or the wayward son to his family's bosom. That is how Ba'thi propaganda liked to explain what its army was doing in Kuwait. But what of the words Abu Haydar wrote on Khalil's living-room walls? What kind of an occupation was this?

The more one digs into this particular story—who Khalil is and what happened to Abu Haydar—the more complicated the whole phenomenon of the invasion of Kuwait and the Gulf crisis appears. Abu Haydar clearly didn't want to be there. Yet he did some terrible things. And he knew that he had done them. That knowledge turned into the force behind an uprising against Saddam Husain inside Iraq which began on the day after Khalil took back his house. The spark that lit the fuse of that rebellion was ignited by returning soldiers like Abu Haydar who, although they had seen their comrades bombed, riddled, and roasted in their thousands by American firepower, nonetheless chose to turn their wrath against the tyrant who had sent them into Kuwait in the first place.[4]

And what of young Khalil? He left Kuwait for the first time since the Iraqi occupation in the summer of 1991, and searched me out in London. He wanted to meet the author of *Republic of Fear*. I was going to write a book about the Iraqi *intifada,* or uprising, and at that time had no intention of interviewing Kuwaitis or incorporating their stories into my new book. A cordial social exchange turned into a long formal interview, which ended up reshaping the way I had intended to write this book. During the interview I came to realize just how much the experience of occupation can change a person. Khalil is no longer the man he was.

Working through the individual stories of people like Khalil and Abu Haydar complicates the future, making it more resistant to generalization. For one thing, the dust has not yet settled. But then nothing is as it seems in an occupation, during a war, or in an uprising. My own views on the Iraqi intifada changed in the course of interviewing some of the people who participated in it. Nurtured by twenty years of appalling dictatorship, pent-up hatreds and pain exploded in an orgy of violence across Iraq in March 1991. Poring over the brutally frank descriptions of the terrible things that people did to one another, I often found myself nauseated, even estranged from an uprising that I had thrown myself into supporting heart and soul while it was going on. Victims imitated the regime that had created them and their revolt failed. Does it have to be like this?

Still, I was mesmerized by the words coming from the participants. These were as raw and harsh as the actions they described. The tired metaphors and melodramatic sentimentality of Arab political discourse was absent. In its place came a new kind of truth-telling with which I wanted to identify. Iraqis were stripping themselves naked and they were speaking to me because they wanted the outside world to know what had happened. For a brief while, the victims themselves were refusing to buy into that deadly argument that all problems can be attributed to the evil machinations of the West and Israel. Instead, as we saw in those few words which Abu Haydar wrote on Khalil's living-room wall, some Iraqis looked inward. In extreme circumstances, the obscene and the sublime can combine in human behavior; individuals emerge who rise above the stereotypes we so often insist on assigning to them.

SOLDIERS like Abu Haydar fled Kuwait by way of the main highway to Basra. On the approach to Mutla' Ridge, a sandy hill a couple of hundred feet high twenty miles or so northwest of Kuwait City, near the town of Jahra, American Marines of the Second Armored Division, Tiger Brigade—known as the "Hounds of Hell"—attacked the retreating column. A pool reporter attached to the Tiger Brigade said, "Most Iraqis just gave up—or tried to. It was a bizarre scene. The advance was like a giant hunt. The Iraqis were driven ahead of us like animals . . . [they] looked like spectators caught on a demolition derby." Soldiers who tried to take cover off the road ran into their own minefields. In desperation, some Iraqis opened fire on fellow soldiers blocking their way. The Allied intention was to grab whatever was left of the Iraqi army and hang onto it "like a junkyard dog," as one senior U.S. officer put it. "It was a turkey shoot for several hours, then the weather turned sour," said Major-General Moore, commander of Marine Air Wing 3. To the more pastoral British imagination, what happened at the Mutla' resembled "herding sheep."[5] These phrases describe how a ramshackle, panic-stricken convoy of stolen cars, buses, vans, and armored vehicles was turned into a ghoulish traffic jam of scrap metal and roasted occupants, filling all four lanes of a sixty-mile stretch of highway from Jahra to the Iraqi border. The operation was conducted in darkness, at a distance of half a mile, and incurred only one U.S. casualty.

An unfamiliar heat is generated by the kind of high-tech weaponry tested out upon Iraqis during the Gulf war. Along the Mutla' road, the intensity of this heat melted windshield glass into silicone droplets and caused otherwise harmless objects to explode. It also did peculiar things to bodies.

One man who was trying to escape in a Kawasaki front-end loader ended up with only half of his body "hanging upside down and out of his exposed seat, the left side and bottom blown away to tatters, with the charred leg fully 15 feet away." Nine men in "a flat-sided supply truck were killed and flash-burned so swiftly that they remained naked—skinned and blackened wrecks in the vulnerable positions of the moment of first impact. One man's body lay face down with his rear high in the air, as if he had been trying to burrow through the truckbed. His legs ended in fluttery charcoaled remnants at mid-thigh. He had a young, pretty face, slightly cherubic, with a pointed little chin; you could still see that even though it was mummified. Another man had been butterflied by the bomb; the cavity of his body was cut wide open and his intestines and viscera were still coiled in their proper places, but cooked to ebony."[6] When the journalist Robert Fisk visited the scene a few days later, he saw wild dogs gnawing away at the remains of Iraqi soldiers.[7]

One Kuwaiti who went out to see what had happened at the Mutla', after liberation, felt "very happy" at the sight and expressed a view widely held among Kuwaitis at the time: "I am pleased to see this death and destruction because they did more than this to us."[8] Khalil, on the other hand, reacted differently when he walked up the Mutla' Pass less than twenty-four hours after the killing had stopped. It was 5:30 P.M. and the sun was just about to set. He went looking for his childhood friend Humoud, who had been picked up as a hostage by the Iraqi army four days before liberation. Khalil, like

thousands of other Kuwaitis, had good reason to fear that what was
left of Humoud might be on that road:

> The first thing that hit me as soon as I got out of the car was the smell.
> Something like napalm, like burning. Organic and not organic at the
> same time. During the entire occupation, even before the oil fields
> were set on fire, there was a foul smell pervading the country. I remem-
> ber it being particularly strong during the months of January and Febru-
> ary, to the point that I took to using large quantities of aftershave lotion
> to get rid of it. Here in the Mutla', this smell slapped you like a heat-
> wave in the face. Something rancid and decaying. A mixture of burning
> tires, rotting corpses, a stench too powerful for words.
>
> You had to be very careful. Ammunition and weapons were littered all
> over the place. I was quite literally threading my way up the road,
> picking each step, one at a time. There came a point when you had no
> other option but to go off the road, or to climb over a car. Finally I
> decided to walk on the knee-high narrow concrete divide which sepa-
> rated the lanes going north from those going south. That made things a
> little bit easier.
>
> In spite of the stillness you could see the tumult and turmoil frozen as it
> were in space and time. Raw panic had stricken these people to the
> exclusion of everything else. They were petrified with terror. You have
> to understand the cars were all over the place, pointing every which
> way. Doors, tailgates, and bonnets opening up at all sorts of angles.
> Some vehicles were pointing to Subiyya, others due east, or northeast
> or west, and halfway up the shoulder, or even totally off the road. Some
> had even swiveled around a full 180 degrees to end up pointing back
> again to Kuwait City. It had all happened so fast. I walked by cars which
> still had their radios and tape recorders on, the sounds of music or a
> weather report faintly playing in the distance.
>
> There was a red fire engine from the Kuwaiti fire-fighting department
> with its ladders and hoses all rolled up. It had smashed into a blue and
> white civilian bus, the kind that would have been used to transport
> Humoud to Iraq. He wasn't there. The bus was empty, ghostlike. No
> people in it at all. I remember a huge tanker and a dairy van. Then there
> was this Toyota Corona passenger car which had crumpled up against
> an army tank. Lots of tanks. You can't imagine the strangeness of the
> ensemble.
>
> But what really blows my mind is what was inside these vehicles. I
> thought I knew Iraq. I thought I knew the people. They are not so

different from us, from anyone else. Soldiers are expected to fight and to die. This, one understands. But why does this same soldier steal a plastic tray, for instance? Or a box of Q-tips? Or tubes of toothpaste?

Barbie dolls. Can you imagine! They stole Barbie dolls! Not just one doll, but lots of them. Dressed like brides in white lace. Ladies' underwear, wall calendars, watches, cartons of cigarettes, piles upon piles of a silly magazine for Kuwaiti ladies called *Mir'at al-Umma* [*The Mirror of the Nation*]. Not to mention boxes of oranges and bags of rice and onions. Generally, the most trivial and silly things were taken. It was like a junk market. The stuff was spilling out of suitcases thrown into armored personnel carriers and the like. Iraqi soldiers had died amidst piles and piles of this stolen junk. It is bizarre and makes you start to think about your own life, to reflect about material things and their value. There was gold and jewelry in Kuwaiti houses; instead, look at what these men took with them while running away for their lives. What was more precious, I ask you, their life or these trinkets? What an ugly death! Regardless of whether or not you think this war was just, these men died cheap thieves.

Ba'th Party pamphlets and Iraqi intelligence files were strewn about inside another army vehicle. I collected them and saved twenty-eight files in all. They were about al-Farwaniyya district in Kuwait. I recall one of them reported on the finding of a typewriter in someone's house. Others were about missing or stolen cars in the district. I gave them all to the resistance. I picked up a Mawrid English-Arabic dictionary which was lying on the tarmac with the name of its owner on the inside front cover. I have kept it with me and intend one day to look up its owner to return it to him. I would like to know who he is. The name is Egyptian. . . .

What stands out the most for me, however, from this experience of walking up the Mutla', is this one Iraqi soldier; I shall never forget him for as long as I live. He was dead of course. I was walking up north and he was lying face down on the road at an angle, in a small clearing of asphalt surrounded by wrecked cars. He was pointing northwest, toward Fao, I believe. He had his fists clenched and two arms symmetrically in an arc on either side of his forehead. You couldn't see any facial features, only the back of the head. He looked like someone about to have a massage, or lying straight on his stomach in order to give his back a good suntan.

Two things about him: first, he was all black, burned, with no uniform, no hair. A piece of charcoal. From a distance I couldn't distinguish the body from the tarmac because its color and that of the asphalt was one and the same. Second, the lower part of his body, from the navel on down, was not there. Literally, it looked like it had been sheared off, with a giant pair of very sharp scissors. But you could tell this man must have been very muscular and strong. With big shoulders and long arms.

I felt that he was taking refuge in the asphalt from the tempestuous fury of the battle going on around him. He had been unable to find a softer ground on the sand nearby, for instance, to hide his face. Like a child who has been scolded or who has done something wrong and goes running to his bedroom, slamming the door behind him, throwing himself on the bed and burying his face in the pillow as though to keep his sorrow, his fears, his anguish all to himself—this soldier was burying his face on the hard ground because there was no other exit, nowhere left to run away from, nowhere left to head toward.

The way this man must have died brought to my mind something unrelated. About a cousin of mine who died just before the war started, on January 5. My cousin was an epileptic, so very young, in his late twenties. It was all so unexpected. Around 9:00 A.M., the maid rushed into my aunt's house where I was staying with tears in her eyes. She kept repeating his name and telling me to go and see him. I knew something must have happened because he is an epileptic and has been under constant treatment since being involved in an automobile accident. I thought he had had a fit. So I rushed over there.

He was a heavy smoker. He must have tried to release the discharge from his lungs during the night without getting out of bed. He would have rolled over onto his left side trying to reach the oval metal dustbin beside the bed to spit into it. While he was trying to do this I think he slid accidentally off the bed and got his head stuck in the bin. That is how I found him.

My cousin always reacted strongly to things, raising his voice even when he talked. Probably he had an epileptic fit as his head got stuck in the bin. He couldn't free himself and the discharge blocked his breathing passages. He died of suffocation with his head inside the bin. I tried to give him first aid by forcing air into the lungs. But the body was cold. The oval shape of the rim had left a mark on the neck. His face was bluish and bruised. His tongue, thicker than usual, was forced out. His hands were frozen and in the same position as that of the corpse I found on the asphalt at the Mutla'. What a horrible way to die, I remember thinking over and over to myself. Just like the Iraqi soldier on the Mutla'. The last picture he had of this world was looking into the bottom of a dustbin. This is how he said goodbye. It made me think about my own death. I would want to die while making love, or in my sleep. Something pleasant and beautiful. Not like this.

Prejudice

WHEN I gave the tapes of this interview to my assistant Firyal to transcribe, she became extremely upset. Did I seriously intend to use the words "just as they are"? She thought they ought to be changed in some way. Her feelings as an Iraqi had been hurt. I had the impression she was asking for permission to change them even as she worked. Naturally I insisted that they not be tampered with in any way. Instead, Firyal should write down her feelings, which is what she did. What was it about Khalil's description of his walk up the Mutla' that so upset her?

The smell. Firyal was shaken and deeply offended because even "professional and very educated Kuwaiti people accuse us Iraqis that we smell." She reminded me of the Kuwaiti women who used to call in to Spectrum International, the Arabic broadcasting station in London established after the occupation of Kuwait. They would go on and on about the "horrible Iraqi smell" that was pervading their country. The stench got worse as the occupation proceeded, and it came "from the Iraqi invaders themselves." Firyal was convinced that Khalil was not really talking about rotting corpses or burning tires. Nothing I could say would change her mind. Khalil was talking about "us," she insisted, looking me right in the eye. In effect, he was saying "we" smelled. Was I aware of the fact that Kuwaitis were forever crossing over the border to pick up Iraqi women in Basra? Their sole purpose in coming was to "mess about" with Iraqi women. Such issues were on many Iraqi minds in the immediate aftermath of the invasion. Men in particular felt that their honor was at stake, especially after Saddam said in a speech, by way of justifying his action, *"al-'Iraqiyya al-majida saret ib-dirham lil-Kuwaiti"* (To the Kuwaiti, the glorious Iraqi woman goes for a nickel).[9]

I remember feeling as uncomfortable as I had felt when Khalil was telling me about the human excrement lying around the half-eaten sheep's carcass he found on his living-room carpet the day after liberation. Firyal had suffered under the Iraqi Ba'th. She did not want to gloss over the terrible things they had done. Yet she was worked up about the interview. Obviously a great deal was at stake here, so much so that she had gone to the trouble of checking her own memory of what those Kuwaiti women from the radio call-in program had said, only to be confirmed in her impressions by the recollections of friends. Firyal became so upset by Khalil's interview she could no longer work on it.

Khalil's account of the atrocities he experienced during seven months of occupation brought home for me the full horror of what had been visited upon the city of Kuwait in ways that no newspaper or television account had been able to do.[10] For instance, he told the story of the three brothers suspected of being members of the Kuwaiti resistance because they were found with cellular telephones on them. They were shot and left out in the street, piled up one on top of the other as an example to others. I had heard such stories before. But not the way Khalil was telling them:

> I was struck the most by the one on the top. He was very dark-skinned. A red and pinkish-white blob covered his head. But you couldn't tell exactly where it was coming from. Eventually I realized it was his brains which must have slowly oozed out. The problem was I couldn't take my mind off the contrast between the pinkish-white and the almost black skin color; it reminded me of the rosy cheeks in a Renoir painting and the way they always seem to jump out at you from the background. But how could I think of a Renoir painting at a time like this! It probably says something terrible about me. I don't know.

A kind of malignancy was at work during the Ba'thi occupation of Kuwait, which went beyond the killing of Kuwaitis and the looting of houses. Specific violations were in the end attributable to it. Imagine Kuwait being visited by a foul-smelling kind of plague, one that could not be seen but that secreted deadly humors in its wake. These came seeping out of pus-filled sores whose very existence no one had been aware of before. The most tangible thing about this malignancy was that it exuded a stench. An Israeli novel imagines a former soldier in the Occupied Territories who returns from his job only to find that he cannot rid himself of a foul odor that has begun to emanate from his body, becoming an ineradicable part of his constitution. "The smell covered us like a heavy cloud, attacking the senses. It was hard to sit there. . . . Maybe it is a punishment for cruelty."[11] The truth in such fiction is that occupation—whether on the West Bank of the Jordan River or in Kuwait—is always foul-smelling.

A similar kind of truth is present in the observation that a new rotten odor was in the air in Kuwait after August 2, 1990. The smell was unusually bad, permeating everything. It grew more and more unbearable. The garbage, after all, was not collected, and decomposed to release a stew of organic odors. The bodies of Kuwaitis who resisted and were caught—like the three brothers—were left out in the streets. There was nothing to hinder the bacteria from working on their human remains and their work naturally smelled. Both Iraqis and Kuwaitis would have sweated more profusely, and they would have cleaned themselves less often than before. Water, after all, was scarce. Soiled clothes remained unwashed. Electricity was intermittent. Maintenance standards in the desalination and water-purification plants had plummeted. Crude oil was pumping out into the ocean and finding its way back into the city by mysterious pathways. Marine life was dying and decomposing.

So it was true that the rank odors of refuse, vile-smelling fish, dirty water, and sweaty, filthy, rotting bodies filled the air of Kuwait with a pungent and offensive aroma, to say nothing of the later effects of six hundred burning oil fields and children who now took to coughing up soot-laced mucus. The truth of the matter, whether physically tangible or fictional and literary, is the same: occupation seeps into the body. Kuwait smelled differently under Iraqi occupation, and maybe it will never smell the same again.

Occupation, war, tyranny, and uprising remain abstractions until you have lived through them. They can remain without embodiment in flesh and blood and real human feeling, even in spite of such powerful evocations as Khalil was able to pass on through his words. The obscene reality of the Iraqi occupation only overwhelmed me after Firyal reacted in the way that she did to Khalil's interview. It was then that I came to realize that Khalil's compelling sincerity and Firyal's seething preoccupation with the prejudices of Kuwaitis did not negate each other. Quite the contrary: they explained each other, and smell was the key.

A bad smell suggests that something is not clean, which would make it impure in the eyes of a practicing Muslim. Ablutions before prayer are obligatory, and ritual washing is prescribed following intercourse, during menstruation and childbirth, and after death in preparation for burial. The idea is not so much sound hygiene as protection from defilement. When the Iraqi regime refuses to allow those it executes to be washed ritually in the way prescribed by Islam, it is imposing damnation on those souls in perpetuity. The *Tilkeyf*, an Iraqi Christian Chaldean minority named after the town of Tilkeyf, are probably the most looked-down-upon community in Iraq. They are called the *nazzaheen,* or "cleaners of sewers." The association of a Christian community with smelly and dirty work in a Muslim culture is no accident. On the other hand, exotic and particularly pungent-smelling perfumes and incenses, so loved in the East, suppress smell, thereby suggesting cleanliness, purity, and sanctity. According to Arab customs of hospitality, guests are expected to make appreciative noises at the dinner table that greatly please their hosts. Belching, on the other hand, is the pinnacle of rudeness when seated at a formal English dinner. Yet the one thing that an Arab man must not do in public is the very thing that in a Western setting is considered involuntary and excusable: fart.

The worst thing that a bodily fluid can do is to exude an unpleasant odor. Firyal was seeing through the apparent neutrality of physical biology into the complicated world of cultural meanings and hidden connotations. I, on the other hand, had become too westernized and no longer appreciated a whole symbolic language, capable of very fine degrees of differentiation, all to do with the importance of how something smells. Khalil's bodily reactions had summoned up the whole range of complicated feelings that eat away at all occupying and occupied peoples: humiliating justifications, threatened identities, wounded pride, feelings of shame and guilt, the desire to get even. His taped words had evoked the prejudices associated with these feelings, not the mere biological fact of an olfactory sense.

Poetry and Prejudice

IN "all the demonstrations that have shaken (and that will shake) the Arab world, no slogan is shouted more violently than that which targets the monarchies and principalities of the Gulf," wrote Moncef Marzouki, president of the Tunisian Human Rights League. Even though Kuwait was under occupation, "90 percent of all Arabs, Egyptians included, profoundly hate these dictatorial and archaic regimes that have squandered Arab resources and honor and have always treated Arab citizens as despised party crashers. It is this deep aversion that explains the global and massive character of the pro-Iraqi demonstrations, notably in the Maghrib,* where Saddam is less

★The Maghrib is that group of North African Arab countries west of Egypt (Morocco, Algeria, Tunisia, Libya).

acclaimed than Fahd is vituperated. Here we have the most anti-democratic and anti-human rights of regimes that goes so far as to refuse women their right to drive, carried at arm's length by the noble Western democracies. . . ."[12] These words are from the president of the oldest, most highly developed and outspoken human rights organization in the Arab world, with 4,000 members in 1989 (grown from 1,000 in 1982) organized into some 40 local sections.[13]

Politics aside, there was an extraordinary lack of empathy on the part of many Arab intellectuals with the plight of the Kuwaitis during the Gulf crisis. "Kuwait is not important," wrote 'Abdel-Rahman Munif, an important Arab novelist most famous for his *Cities of Salt,* which is about the very Gulf Arabs he thinks are not important.[14] Others waxed eloquent about how Kuwaitis were "wastrels" and "corrupt," their state an "imperialist creation," "archaic" and "historically illegitimate," even though these same Kuwaitis had not yet killed in such large numbers as the supposedly more cultured Arabs of Syria, Iraq, and the Lebanon. Kuwait was pilloried and ridiculed as if every other state in the region were more legitimate and less corrupt. "Prejudice" is the only word to describe how many Arabs felt toward Kuwaitis even as their country was being invaded and sacked.[15]

The roots of this kind of prejudice run very deep in the Arab tradition. One way of thinking about its origins is as a style of discourse, the target of which can effortlessly switch, depending on circumstances. The best examples of this style can be found in the art of *hija',* or invective diatribe, designed to impugn the honor of individuals or groups for all time. *Hija'* is more likely to be practiced in verse than in prose; it accompanies war, or any kind of serious rift between two parties, and was widely cultivated as a highly regarded poetic form among Arab tribes from pre-Islamic times. Abu al-Tayyib al-Mutanabbi (A.D. 915–965), often thought of as the prince of Arabic poetry, wrote a very famous example of *hija'* in the shape of a virulent attack on the ruler of Egypt and one-time slave, Kafour, followed by another on the servility of all Egyptians. When the Egyptian ruler did not give the penniless poet who had gone to beg at his door everything that he expected, Mutanabbi sought his revenge through poetry. His style was to set the highest standards of nobility and breeding—invariably himself—against "this black man with his pierced camel lips," who is "pot-bellied" and a "woman-like slave." So unworthy is the eunuch Kafour that not even death will bother to take him away, "unless his hand has a trace of its stink.

With loosened belt, the flabby belly breaks wind; / Neither counted among men nor yet among women."[16]

This poetic tradition, which thrives on scorn, derision, insult, and abuse, and whose purpose is the humiliation and dishonoring of its victims in the eyes of the poet's own supporters, has lived on in modern Arabic cultural discourse, including poetry.[17] Consider, for instance, the work of one of the Arab world's most popular poets, Nizar Qabbani, the son of a well-to-do merchant from Damascus who started publishing in the late 1940s. In the poetic revival that accompanied modernity in the Arab world, Qabbani did more than any of his contemporaries to bring the classical language of poetry closer to the current written and vernacular Arabic of the Fertile Crescent.[18] He has the largest audience of any Arab poet and seeks an immediate emotive effect in his work, which he often achieves in an uncanny way through choice of words and short, sharp, cutting phrases.

Eighteen months before the invasion of Kuwait, Qabbani published a poem entitled "Abu Jahl Buys Fleet Street." *Abu Jahl* means "the father of ignorance," and is a reference to a contemporary of the Prophet Muhammad's who, Muslim tradition has it, tried to have him murdered. It also evokes *'asr al-Jahiliyya*, the age of ignorance, the phrase used to describe the state of the Arabian peninsula before the advent of Islam. The reference is to "Bedouins" who have been "infiltrating Buckingham palace," "sleeping in the Queen's bed," and substituting their camels for those "beautiful red buses" of London which are consequently disappearing. The poem combines simple language, customary idioms, arabized English words, and derisively scornful images in the style of al-Mutanabbi. The imagery is always taut and evocative (Bedouin buffoons in Soho, the tails of their long white robes flailing around as they dance jazz—an image rendered in a mere five words). The four-page diatribe on Gulf Arabs concludes:

> Oh Shaikh of much longevity:
> Ye who purchase women by the pound,
> And literary talent by the pound,
> We want nothing from you.
> Go on fucking your concubines as you will,
> And killing your subjects as you will,
> And besieging the nation with fire and steel.

Nobody wants your happy kingdom.
Nobody wants to steal your royal gown.
Drink the wine of your petroleum to its lees,
Only leave culture to us.[19]

Poetry is the most revered and the most developed art form of the Arab peoples, occupying pride of place in a classical literary heritage which, along with Islam, provides the only persistent tie Arabs have with the past. No matter how much conflict there may actually be among Arabs, constant invocation of this tradition in modern times—whether literary or religious—has become a powerful basis for asserting Arab identity. The answer to the question that haunts all Arabs—Who am I?—has thus increasingly taken on the form of a move toward tradition—Islam—or, as in the case of Qabbani, a revolt against facts. Qabbani tells us that he writes "in order to explode things."[20] He has the wounded, angry sensibility of the archetypal modern Arab Poet who sees history as one of permanent revolt and heart-wrenching disappointment. His poetry, which used to be revolutionary, is always militantly rejectionist—an affirmation of unity through denial by way of invective. He has, as a result, often been banned in Arab countries and has been led to adopt courageous positions in public, especially with regard to sexual freedoms, against polygamy, and for women's rights.

On the other hand, he is very much a platform poet—a style much loved by the Arabs—who throws words and sounds back at his audience, not meanings. He has the gift of poetical forms and rhythms, not ideas. This virtue, grossly inflated, turns into the poet's principal vice, and into the vice of the modern cultural-political tradition which he represents better than most. Qabbani thus becomes a victim of the traditions of his own language and a mirror of everything that is—in my opinion—no longer worth preserving from that tradition. He thinks of himself as a revolutionary, for instance, when all that he is really doing is hurling abuse into the wind—being angry but providing no reasons, no rationalizations, no intellectual connections. In an age when Arabs want their poets to be political and to avenge them against the outside world, Qabbani fitted the bill perfectly. He writes against the Saudis, but he gets published by their newspapers. In fact it no longer matters what he says because the subject is no longer actually Zionism, imperialism, the Palestinian question, or the disgusting kings and presidents of the

Arab world; it is the mindless permanent anger of the poet himself.

The problem of culture in the Arab world is that it has remained in the hands of poets like Nizar Qabbani. Contrast his style with Khalil's account of what he saw and how it smelled, and Firyal's reaction to his words. The hard, definite, self-reflective descriptions and precisely targeted personal reactions of Khalil and Firyal are lacking in much of modern Arab poetry. Few of the famous names of Arabic letters will attempt the task. Painstakingly accurate visual recall is not considered a legitimate poetic enterprise for an angry, rejectionist poet like Nizar Qabbani. Namecalling, stereotyping, and bigotry is.[21]

The damnable thing is that there are always half-truths in stereotypes. Moreover, everyone uses them. Black Americans applied them to Korean Americans during the Los Angeles riots, just as white Americans have been doing to blacks for centuries. Arabs and Israelis do it to each other all the time. The extremes of wealth and poverty and the profligate nouveau-riche lifestyle of many Gulf Arabs have made them targets of resentment. I am not trying to deny the obvious, which, in part, helps to explain why the phenomenon persists the way it does. No Arab, including myself, likes to talk about such ugly things as racial prejudice, anti-Semitism, and the lampooning of whole populations. Compared to the other problems of this part of the world, it seems a marginal and unedifying preoccupation. But the moral credibility of Arabness—whatever that word might be taken to mean—and the desire for a less violent and more tolerant Arab world are at stake. The phenomenon today has gotten completely out of hand, as the reaction of a majority of Arabs to what Saddam did in Kuwait shows. Arabs before anyone else are today called upon to take a stand against the racist stereotyping that is everywhere rampant amongst them, just as black American intellectuals should be to the fore in the struggle against anti-Semitism among blacks.[22]

Bigotry in the hands of prominent Arab intellectuals like Qabbani rationalizes and legitimates petty or parochial jealousies, acting as a stimulus for their transformation into something ultimately more ominous. It feeds on the anxiety of the times, attacking like a deadly virus the whole body politic precisely when it is most riddled with crisis. The extent of the prejudice against Kuwaitis unleashed by Saddam Husain's action on August 2, 1990, was truly alarming, and suggests a deep cultural malaise. Moreover, one can see it everywhere in the Arab world. One can see it in reverse, for instance, in the post–liberation attitude of Kuwaitis toward Palestinians, of Lebanese toward Syrians, of Sunni Arabs toward Shi'i Arabs, and so on. To his personal credit, Qabbani himself stood by the people of Kuwait during their tribulations (unlike the majority of Arab intellectuals). But political positions are not what I am trying to grapple with here; they will be considered in the second half of this book. Qabbani's honorable stand during the crisis highlights the very issue I am trying to focus on now: namely, the fact that his language—the very peculiarities of his style and the kind of imagery that he has spent a lifetime perfecting—ultimately served the purpose of fueling the tide of bigotry and prejudice in the Arab world. The secrets of the peculiar kinds of horrors which the Iraqi occupation of Kuwait gave rise to, Qabbani's example suggests, lie hidden somewhere inside the shadowy realm of sensibilities that even someone like Qabbani has come to represent inside the culture.

Khalil, on the other hand, is one of those "uncultured," "uncouth" Gulf Arabs that Qabbani was writing about. He did not, it is true, speak to me in the name of Arab culture and poetry. He was talking like an ordinary human being who just happened to be very sensitive to those microscopic details that make up the way real life is felt and experienced. He told his story as it had happened, and the way he told it was true to his own feelings. Both Firyal and Khalil felt the world around them intensely, and they felt it deeply. In point of fact, they smelled it and they both sensed it smelled rotten. Maybe they blamed one another for the way it smelled. That is a separate issue. But at least they knew what was important and what was not.

Poets like Qabbani are no longer in touch with their world in the same sort of way. Consider this extract from a poem written during the Gulf crisis entitled *"La Budda an Asta'dhina al-Watan"* (I Must Ask the Nation's Permission):

I wish to see you my lady,
But I am afraid to scratch the feelings of the nation.
I wish to shout out to you every night my lady,
But I am afraid of being overheard through the windows of the nation.
I wish to make love to you in my own way,
But . . . I am ashamed of my folly
Before the sorrows of the nation.[23]

I choose this poem precisely because of its ambiguity on the question of the hour, the Gulf war, which was looming while the poem was being written. You cannot tell from anything in the poem whether Qabbani is for or against the war. The poem is critical about the general state of things without saying explicitly what they are. It ignores all frontiers, all the really divisive issues that were tearing Arabs apart at the time it was being written. Its fatherland is the general, not the concrete. The appeal is to a mood, a feeling of discontent, uprootedness, disintegration, anxiety, and general loss of identity which was widespread at the time. The tone develops into one of anguish, of despair, even of disgust. Finally, the poet concludes with the question: "Are we Arabs one big lie?" And the implication of his conclusion is, Yes, we are. Why are we one big lie? For having got into this mess, this mess of the Gulf crisis.

But I am not as interested in this conclusion as I am in the remarkable fact that the poet goes on allowing the lie to dictate the terms of his discourse; he will not let go of it. In fact, it is providing him with an artistic agenda. You might even conclude that the poet has chosen the lie over life—life as represented by the woman he is in love with and whom he is addressing in the poem. He cannot see, or call out, or even make love to this woman, the flesh and blood of his affections. Something else, something supra-human, is always hovering over him, holding him back, making him hesitate. That something is *al-watan*, the poet's whole Arab homeland, which he himself is totally fed up with and which, in disgust, he ends up calling a lie. Yet still the lie—and the anxiety at having to live a lie—remains uppermost in his consciousness. The most interesting thing becomes the fact that the poet is unable or unwilling to let go of the lie; it has become a part of him.

Qabbani wants to see, to call out to, and to make love to the lady he is addressing in the poem, but can no longer do so. Indeed, he goes on in the poem to bemoan: "This is the age of prose my beloved. . . . It has no poetry. No love. No clouds. And no rain." For him, the world also "has no smell." The problem, of course, is that it does have a smell and he is running away from how it smells. Khalil, Abu Haydar, and Firyal know that it smells, and their words—spoken in prose—teach us how important is the fact that it smells.

Real life as men like Khalil and Abu Haydar lived it on the ground, as they saw it with their eyes, as they heard it through their eyes, and as they experienced it in the flesh, with all its trials and tribulations, all this Qabbani puts aside. He puts it aside to wrestle with an abstraction, *al-watan,* the Arab nation or homeland. But whose *watan* are we talking about? Saddam Husain's or the Emir of Kuwait's? Or maybe even Hafiz Asad's or Husni Mubarak's? Nizar Qabbani would be horrified at the thought that any of these people might represent his *watan.* His *watan* is not Iraq or Kuwait; it is not even Syria, and it is certainly not Egypt. Qabbani's *watan* is a romantic idea suspended above concrete political leaders with all their overarching vulgarity. That romance and that suspension from one's own reality is the source of the poet's cruelty toward the woman he loves. And in the end, that cruelty is the problem with this poem. Ultimately, even as Qabbani rejects all of the nastiness around him, he is not addressing himself to the problems of Khalil and Abu Haydar. He is, instead, subordinating real life as it is lived, with all its terrible contradictions and disastrous ills, for the sweet lie, for his reassuring myth of the *watan.*

Nizar Qabbani's career as a poet is consistent with this poem. It is even consistent with a later poem written in April 1991, this time attacking Saddam Husain directly and in the most sarcastic and bitter language imaginable. The April poem is entitled *"Hawamish 'ala Daftar al-Hazima"* (Marginal Notes on the Notebook of Defeat).[24] The title is a direct reference to another very famous and influential poem written by Qabbani after the 1967 war, *"Hawamish 'ala Daftar al-Naksa"* (Marginal Notes on the Notebook of the Setback). Things have gotten worse because a *naksa* has turned into a *hazima,* a setback in 1967 to a full-fledged defeat in 1991. But not much else has changed in the meantime; certainly not the style of writing and of thinking associated with the Arab world in 1967. The two poems are interchangeable—in this fact are summed up the failings of a whole generation.

In April 1984, Qabbani wrote an interesting letter to none other than Saddam Husain. The letter was published in his own handwriting in the Iraqi periodical *Alef-Ba.* The most popular poet in the Arab world, a Syrian not resident in Baghdad and under no obligation to the Iraqi regime, wrote these words:

> I came to Baghdad a broken man . . . only to find that Saddam Husain stuck together my parts . . . I came an atheist cursing the practices of

the Arabs . . . only to find that Saddam Husain gave me back my faith and tightened up my shattered nerves . . . And so it is that I return from Baghdad filled with the sun . . . Thanks be to Saddam Husain . . . who let gently drop into my eyes the color of green. . . .[25]

Green is of course the color of Islam. This letter is dated April 25, 1984, and the Iraq-Iran War was well into its fourth year. That war was what Qabbani's visit was all about.

People do, however, change their minds. That is the proof of their freedom. There is nothing wrong with that. Moreover, I believe Nizar Qabbani to have been as sincere in 1991 as he was in 1984 and as he was in 1967. I am not trying to score cheap points but to get at a bigger issue which arises from the observation that although everything changes, yet still there is something in the poems themselves that is unchanging. And the problem lies here; it lies in that which is constant in the work itself, not in political positions, which change a lot in the Middle East.

Qabbani's freedom to decry authority, to rail against the failure of his world, is haunted by ghosts. These ghosts come in the form of the images he uses, not the ideas he either accepts or rejects. The ideas, like political things in general, are constantly in flux. But the imagery, and what it evokes in the minds of readers, stays the same. The problem is one of style, not ideological position. It is one of language, of how that language is written and how it is meant to be read. One has the sense that Qabbani's poems are last-ditch attempts to restore through art that which he freely acknowledges has been lost in politics. They therefore operate within the same ground rules as the politics they reject. They call for sexual freedom and women's liberation, but do not break, for instance, with accepted traditional codes of honor and shame, of what constitutes a so-called manly act or a cowardly one. Instead, they work through those codes and through nostalgia, extreme lyricism, romanticism, and rejectionism. This was the style of the young Michel 'Aflaq in the late 1930s and 1940s. 'Aflaq, the founding father of the Ba'th Party, rejected reason as the basis for his Arabism, and called instead on the forces of "faith" and "love." Ironically, therefore, whatever may be the political intent of a poem like *"La Budda an Asta'dhina al-Watan"* (I Must Ask the Nation's Permission), its flowery romantic style is that of early Ba'thism.

Qabbani's poetry of bravado and tragic pessimism culminating in deep anxiety appeals to an amorphous community which is fickle and unsure of itself. It appeals to *al-jamaheer al-'arabiyya,* the Arab masses who came of age in politics after World War II. This is not a poetry designed for a modern, cultivated, individualized public, based on competing and interacting aristocracies of developed tastes and sensibilities. For the reality is that such a cultural aristocracy barely exists any longer as a cohesive force in the Mashriq;* it is locked away in suffocating isolation or fragmented and scattered in exile. This cultural elite has had its independence wiped out throughout the Mashriq by a combination of tyranny, tribalism, and corruption. And this in spite of the fact that there are more highly educated Arabs today than there have ever been in the past, and that such educated Arabs are present in all Arab countries.

Khalil is such an Arab. He is a Kuwaiti whose sensibilities do not match up to the stereotype of a Gulf Arab, a stereotype that lives on in the sensibilities of a cosmopolitan and forward-looking Arab intellectual like Nizar Qabbani. The romantic or heroic style in modern Arabic culture, as exemplified by Qabbani's poetry, is the attempt to unite the culture of the intellect with the emotions of the multitude, not with the sensibilities of a quintessentially modern Arab like Khalil. But in the wake of the mountain of bodies created by the Lebanese civil war, the Iranian revolution, the Iraq-Iran War, and the Gulf war, there can be no more romance and no more false heroics in the Arab world. There is only a legacy of pain which must be grappled with by a new language and in a new style. Hence, while intellectuals like Qabbani write verses to bemoan the departure of poetry from their world, people like Khalil and Abu Haydar today speak to us in a language that so engages with their world as to turn their words into a new kind of poetry.

Who Is Khalil?

KHALIL is a young Kuwaiti, widely read in both Arabic and English. He is curious, perceptive, and open to the outside world in ways that one does not often find among intellectuals from the Mashriq these days. It became clear during our conversation that he had grown more in touch with his feelings, more aware of himself, in

*The Mashriq is the group of Arab countries east of Egypt.

the course of the Iraqi occupation. He is a mathematician by education, an artist by disposition, and an investment banker by profession, who, through the experience of occupation, got to know his
own body and what it was capable of better than at any time in the
past.

> My body weight dropped by fifteen kilos in the first weeks of occupa-
> tion. During the whole seven months, feelings of violence were rising
> up in me. The sexual urge multiplied maybe tenfold over what it was
> before. On February 26, 1991, the day Kuwait was liberated, I experi-
> enced other new emotions all at the same time and at the same high
> pitch of intensity: happiness, anger, revenge, sorrow, hatred, euphoria,
> extreme pleasure. I don't think there will be in the future, in my per-
> sonal experience, another moment in time to match the concentration
> and number of emotions which I felt in al-'Alam Square on that day, a
> day I will never forget for the rest of my life.

Khaled Nasser al-Sabah, not Khalil, is his real name. Khalil was
the pseudonym adopted by Khaled under occupation, and forged on
various identity papers to hide the fact that he was a member of
Kuwait's ruling family. Judging by his real name, Khaled is the
archetypal Gulf Arab stereotyped by Nizar Qabbani. There was no
more valuable hostage for the Iraqi regime during the occupation of
Kuwait than a member of the ruling family. Ironically, Khaled was
saved in the first days after August 2, 1990, by the fact that he had
hitherto consistently avoided using his full surname, preferring to
carry identification papers in the name of Khaled Nasser, not Khaled
Nasser al-Sabah. "Because I didn't want to stand out," as he put it to
me.

But there had to be more to it than that. A leftist political activist
at university, Khaled was formed, like my whole generation, on the
basis of a romance with the post-1967 organizations of the Palestinian Resistance movement. He had many close Palestinian friends
and worked hard in Arab student organizations and on Palestine
solidarity campaigns while he was studying in the West, just as I had
done ten years earlier. You didn't do that sort of thing while adver-
tising a family surname like al-Sabah.

In 1989, Khaled/Khalil came across a copy of *Republic of Fear* soon
after it was published. He read the book and passed it around to his
friends, knowing that it was written by an Iraqi under the pseudo-

nym Samir al-Khalil. Only a handful of people were interested in the book in those days. When the tanks of the Iraqi regime rolled into his city on August 2, 1990, he, like thousands of others, knew his very life depended on the speed with which he could forge a new identity. Khaled Nasser would inevitably be found out to be a Sabah. Khaled had to do something with his name. "I kept on thinking what name I should pick. I wasn't going to use any old name. Finally I decided on Khalil as a first name. I couldn't use the whole of Samir al-Khalil; that would have been too conspicuous. For me it was a sign of protest." I cherish Khaled's choice as the single greatest compliment ever paid to me for something I have done.

THE very same Arab intellectuals who, in their writings and senti-ments, pillory "feudal" and "archaic" Gulf Arabs like Khaled, and "artificial" "imperialist" creations like Kuwait, are responsible for having elevated "Palestinianness" to the status of a myth of victim-hood in Arab culture. Palestinians are no longer real people in the Arab imagination; they have been turned into symbols of Arab suf-fering in all its manifold forms. No other Arab has suffered as much, the myth reads, and so all other varieties of suffering—Iraqi, Kuwaiti, Kurdish—are subordinate to it. I will be returning to the consequences of this kind of mythmaking later on in this book. After August 2, 1990, and during the occupation, Palestinians in Jordan and the West Bank in particular acted out this myth by finding their salvation in the person of Saddam Husain; in Kuwait some even collaborated with the Iraqi regime in their "liberation." This episode left behind new layers of prejudice and pent-up hatreds for which many people, especially Palestinians, are still paying the price. A new stereotype was born: that of the Palestinian-as-collaborator. Real life, however, is always more complicated.

Khaled Nasser al-Sabah told me this story of a Palestinian water tank driver whose name he does not know, who probably saved his life. The occupation was in its last month and the Gulf war was in full swing:

I went out to get some water. There was a severe shortage. The tanker's driver was a Palestinian. He seemed to be a religious man for he sud-denly started praying in the middle of the street. It was two weeks before liberation. The man said, "Please, get inside right now. Don't ever come out into the street." I asked why he was saying this. "I heard that the Iraqi army has orders to pick up young Kuwaitis. You'll fit the bill. Don't tell anybody I said this." Later, I found out what the man said was true. My friend, Humoud, was picked up on February 21.

Khaled, you will recall, went on that grisly walk up the Mutla' Pass looking for his childhood friend, Humoud.

ANOTHER Palestinian, Hanan, a young woman who was born and brought up in Kuwait, stood by Khaled even more forcefully. In the panic that accompanied Saddam Husain's initial invasion, Hanan kept on recalling the stories of her grandmother in 1948 scrambling up and down Palestinian hills escaping from the Haganah—the Jewish underground army—carrying her daughter, Hanan's mother.[26] Those memories fortified her, because when Khaled, who was in love with her, wanted to know if she was going to flee Kuwait, her first thought was: The Iraqi army is not going to make me run away. Like Khaled, Hanan is a Palestinian who breaks down stereotypes. Her attachment to Kuwait, and to Khaled, grew with the occupation. "For the first time in my life, I felt that this was my country. In the first days of occupation, I was in a state of pure love with the place. Khaled would not think of leaving it, and day by day I could see him metamorphosing into Khalil. The Palestinian in me felt herself identifying intensely with a raped land and falling in love at the same time with Khalil. That love made me capable of anything."

Under occupation, the couple shared everything and tore away at the barriers of prejudice built upon ignorance and self-isolation. "It was amazing," she told me, "to find out how much the Palestinian community in Kuwait and the Kuwaitis did not know about each other, even though we had lived together for decades. I saw a partial explanation for this in the strong Palestinian sense of identity which makes them stick to their own 'kind' wherever they go in the diaspora. I also found it in the fact that Kuwaiti society is very closed. During the occupation, when the population shrank because of the exodus outside the country, poor communication and rumor-mongering made things even worse."

In November, Hanan's family left Kuwait for good. Kuwait was no longer their home. But Hanan had to go back "one last time," she said. "My heart was there. I had to smuggle gas masks for Khalil and his family. I managed to get four: for him, his uncle Ahmad, his aunt Sarah, and his brother Abdallah. I hid the masks on my body and in the icebox with my food. When an Iraqi soldier asked us to get out of the bus and stand in line for inspection, I was terrified. Luckily they did not do a thorough search." At great personal risk, traveling alone through Jordan and war-torn southern Iraq, Hanan succeeded in smuggling the gas masks into Kuwait. "The first thing I did was call Khalil. The minute he heard my voice, he became elated and very emotional. He could not believe I had come back. We exchanged coded messages over the phone, as we had accustomed ourselves to do. I found out his latest hiding place and went to him with the masks. The last time I saw him was December 31, 1990. He gave me a flower which survived the trip back to my family, and which I still have pressed in a book."

But, after the liberation of Kuwait, things were not the same between Khaled and Hanan. Both had changed during the occupation, and they kept on changing after it. They began blaming one another for the way things had turned out. Khaled grew angry and bitter toward those Palestinians resident in Kuwait whom, he felt, supported the Iraqi occupation and turned on Kuwaitis in their hour of need. They had betrayed him. For even the most thoughtful of Kuwaitis there was no longer any romance in being a Palestinian. His feelings in this regard far exceeded those he expressed toward Iraqis, the former occupiers of his country. He spoke of Abu Haydar, for instance (whoever he might be), with empathy and curiosity. As Kuwait brutally expelled the remnants of its resident Palestinians in retaliation for the collaboration of some of them with the Iraqi army, Hanan, for her part, rediscovered her Palestinian roots. She came to the conclusion that her only true home lay in a future Palestinian state.

> With the liberation of Kuwait, and the terrible things that the Kuwaitis now began doing to Palestinians, I felt that the story of Khalil was coming to an end for me. When Khaled called me in the summer of 1991, right after he first left Kuwait, I saw a man more intent on revenge than on love. Rightly or wrongly, I became convinced that Khaled killed Khalil, the man I truly loved.

In different ways, Hanan and Khaled/Khalil found out who they were as a consequence of what Saddam Husain did to Kuwait. They acquired this knowledge painfully, by violent means, and both ended up being hurt by it. Nonetheless, they acquired it, and the knowledge reshaped them.

IT WAS Khaled, not Khalil, who searched me out in London on his first visit outside Kuwait after liberation. The day was hot and we talked for hours. After we finished, he asked me to autograph his copy of *Republic of Fear*. In Arabic I wrote: "From one Khalil to another; To Khaled Nasser from Kanan Makiya." He read the inscription as we were walking to the door. Clearly unhappy and embarrassed about something, with the door half open, he paused and asked if I wouldn't mind humoring him with a small, insignificant favor. "Of course not," I assured him, quite taken aback. Then Khaled asked me if I wouldn't mind adding "al-Sabah" to his name in the inscription.

I realized immediately that I had made a terrible mistake and fumbled for a pen. But I couldn't locate the exact same pen used for the original dedication. Embarrassed though he was, Khaled insisted upon it; his name in the inscription had to look seamless. This was a man who was not going to hide his identity ever again. Eventually I found the right pen after a confused search, my mind racing over the meaning of what was going on. The mistake was corrected and shall not be made again. But the nagging question remains: What associations had I subliminally been trying to suppress by dropping al-Sabah from Khaled's name?

2 / Abu Haydar

The Uprising in Najaf

WHO is Abu Haydar? There was an Abu Haydar in the Iraqi army who was bivouacked in Khalil's house. *Haydar* means "lion" in Arabic, and the name is associated in the Islamic tradition with the fourth Caliph of Islam, 'Ali ibn Abi Talib, the cousin and son-in-law of the Prophet Muhammad and the patron saint of Shi'ism. We know, therefore, that Abu Haydar is—or was—an Iraqi Shi'ite Muslim.

We know this man's feelings on January 17, 1991, because he wrote them down on the living-room wall. Guilt (or was it shame?) also led someone—perhaps Abu Haydar—to write on the back of a photograph of Khalil's sister: "Dear Kuwaiti sister: Please forgive us for what we have done." Khalil's house smelled rotten after people like Abu Haydar had lived in it for 154 days. Occupation exudes foul odors, which, it seems, Abu Haydar did not like. Along with Khalil, Abu Haydar changed under occupation. He began to make up his own mind about what is right and what is wrong. This Iraqi Shi'ite called Abu Haydar even plucked up the courage to make his feelings known, using the walls of Khalil's house and a photograph of Khalil's sister. Abu Haydar was probably brought up on the same stereotypes about corrupt Gulf Arabs and their wastrel children as the rest of the Arab world. He might even have burned with resentment at uncouth Bedouin potentates who spend all their time frequenting casinos and sleeping with the women of more cultured Arabs from the Fertile Crescent like himself. But for a moment at least he regained his self-respect, rose above bigotry, and honestly faced up to what he had done.

We know all these things about Abu Haydar, but the fact remains we don't know what he looked like, or who he really was.

WALKING up the Mutla' the day after the Allied "turkey shoot" of February 25, 1991, Khalil stumbled upon the diary of an Iraqi police officer who had been stationed in Kuwait on the first day of the invasion. He came across it while rummaging through a heap of half-charred papers strewn all around the stolen van in which they had been stowed. The last entry in the diary was made late at night on February 21, 1991. The author, an apparently loyal Shi'i Ba'thi, originally from the marshes area of southern Iraq, had composed some verses about his birthplace alongside an account of his assignment to Kuwait, daily routine items, and a nostalgic reminiscence on the great failed love affair of his life. "In 1989 I cut relations with her completely for reasons that cannot be written down here." Yet the diary entry makes it obvious that he loved her still.

The marshes the officer was born and brought up in span a triangle between the cities of Basra, 'Amara, and Nasiriyya. Marsh Arabs are descendants of the ancient Sumerians and one of the oldest peoples in the world. They persist largely because of a unique way of life, rooted in the special ecology of the marshes—a vast area of lagoons, islands, and reedbeds. Official government policy is to drain the marshes "for security reasons."[1] The operation is cloaked in secrecy, but the evidence suggests that it has been under way since 1989. The sad verses in the police officer's diary reminisce over the loss of this unique world and the wonderful times he used to have fishing there as a young boy with his brother. This would-be poet, who says he fought and maybe even killed Kuwaiti resisters in the performance of his duties, recorded his name and address in the diary; he was not Abu Haydar. But, like Abu Haydar, he could be dead.

Whose was that neatly shorn-off upper torso which Khalil saw at the Mutla', lying face down with arms wrapped around his head and fists clenched as though trying to burrow into the asphalt surface? Was he all that was left of the policeman-poet who got separated from his diary? If Khalil is really Khaled Nasser al-Sabah, maybe that black piece of charcoal on the Mutla' is all that is left of the Abu Haydar who wrote on Khalil's living-room wall: "Would that my mother had not brought me into this world to have to live through the anguish of these times."

Let us suppose that Abu Haydar survived the "turkey shoot" at the Mutla'. He would then have ended up in the southern Iraqi city of Basra, like hundreds of thousands of other tired and starving Iraqi soldiers. None of them wanted to fight in Kuwait. "We counted the hours when we would see the Americans coming," said one officer. With tears running down his face, another soldier from Basra said, "If only I could live until they came, and then live long enough to see the [American] soldiers face to face, then I knew I would be all right. I would see my family again." His face creased up, and he became unable to speak.[2]

Trapped by geography and the Allied forces, desperate and exhausted men like Abu Haydar poured into the devastated city with their stolen cars and armored vehicles. An old woman from Basra told me she saw her conscripted neighbors returning from Kuwait "running away barefoot this way and that. They had dropped all their weapons." Habeeb, a young Iraqi close to the top Ba'thi command, was told by someone close to 'Izzat al-Douri, a key member of the Revolutionary Command Council, that "when the cease-fire was announced, many officers and soldiers came back from Kuwait in their underwear. They threw away their military insignias and clothes to look like civilians. They were ashamed of being soldiers. Many of them walked five days from Kuwait and Basra to Baghdad."[3] These were the very same soldiers who started the nationwide uprising all over Iraq known as the *intifada*.

The First Spark

THE spark that touched off the intifada began in the predominantly Shi'i city of Basra, the largest city of southern Iraq. It seems to have started around the time that the formal cease-fire in the Gulf war came into effect at 5:00 A.M. on February 28, 1991. A column of tanks fleeing from Kuwait rolled into Sa'ad Square, a huge rectangular open space in downtown Basra. The commander at the head of the column positioned his vehicle in front of a gigantic mural of Saddam in military uniform located next to the Ba'th Party Headquarters Building in the square. Standing on the chassis of his vehicle and addressing the portrait, he denounced the dictator in a blistering speech: "What has befallen us of defeat, shame, and humiliation, Saddam, is the result of your follies, your miscalculations, and your irresponsible actions."[4]

A crowd assembled. The atmosphere became highly charged. The commander jumped back into his tank and swiveled the gun turret to take aim at the portrait. He blasted away with several shells. A delirious crowd cheered him, chanting, "Saddam is finished. All the army is dead." None of the other tanks or soldiers in the square intervened. Soon they were joining in the demonstration that was fast developing. "They were all shooting in the air," recalled 'Abdallah al-Badran, a twenty-four-year-old Kuwaiti who had been taken hostage and was a witness to what was going on.[5] Guns were handed out to eager grasping hands and the crowd stormed the Ba'th Party headquarters. They burned the palatial residence of the governor of Basra and attacked police stations wherever they could find them. They looted the security offices, destroying all files. The rebellion spread like wildfire, and within hours of those first shots in Sa'ad Square, the local residents from Basra and the returning soldiers from Kuwait had set up roadblocks and were in control of the city. It was a classic revolutionary moment.

THE first time I heard the story in any kind of detail was from Sayyid Muhammad Bahr al-'Uloum, a longtime opponent of the regime in Iraq, when he spoke at Harvard University on March 7, 1991. It filled me with enthusiasm. I probed Bahr al-'Uloum for little details. The same story, in different variations, was repeated by refugees who had escaped to Iran or else it came back indirectly from other participants who had been inspired by it but who came from other cities. Clearly, it had become a metaphor for the whole uprising. But was it true? During the summer of 1991 I searched for eyewitnesses to those crucial first hours in Basra and tried to reconstruct the exact sequence of events from that first spark in Sa'ad Square to the wholesale conflagration of southern and northern Iraq. In the end, this proved impossible. I was not even able to discover the name of the commander who jumped on the tank and fired at Saddam Husain's portrait. Nor was I able to establish whether he survived the massive government retaliation that followed the uprising. But there was such a man, and what he did in Basra in the early hours of February 28, 1991, has already become an Iraqi legend. I like to think that man was the same Abu Haydar who wrote his feelings down on the walls of Khalil's house, but the fact is I do not know.

The story of what happened in Sa'ad Square leapfrogged into

Kurdistan, and reached Iran, Syria, and London. Before reaching these faraway places, however, it had lit a fire in every city of southern Iraq. Kadhum al-Raysan, a notable from the town of al-Nasiriyya, told me he saw fourteen young men carrying light weapons like those issued to Iraqi soldiers, emerge from the surrounding marshes, heading straight for the town center.[6] Authority dissolved as they entered al-Nasiriyya, chanting, *"Allahu Akbar, Allahu Akbar"* (God is Great, God is Great). Soon hundreds had joined them. Nizar al-Khazraji, the former army chief of staff, on his way back to Baghdad from Kuwait, got caught in the fighting. He holed up in a government building with sixty or seventy loyalists. The fighting raged for hours, and everyone in Khazraji's group was killed except the general himself. Severely wounded, he was taken by rebels to the local hospital. Why was Khazraji spared, I wanted to know. Less illustrious fellow travelers of the regime were killed on the spot. Raysan, who participated in the fighting, did not know. At any rate, a few days later Khazraji was snatched out of rebel hands by a government helicopter assault team.

Like the Abu Haydar I imagine, Kadhum al-Raysan is not an ideologue or a confessional sectarian. He protected Na'im Haddad, a former member of the Revolutionary Command Council and speaker of the Iraqi National Assembly, from the wild, uncontrollable anger of young rebels during the first days of the uprising. Haddad and his family were concealed in Raysan's house even as the latter was fighting the Ba'thists in the streets of Nasiriyya, and trying to bring a semblance of order to the administration and protection of his city from inevitable government reprisal. He negotiated with nearby Shi'ite tribes, trying to convince them to join in the uprising. But they wouldn't take the risk, preferring to wait and see which way the wind was blowing. On the other hand, Raysan told me emphatically, many Sunni Arabs did join the rebellion. Eventually he fled to Saudi Arabia along with his family and fellow tribesmen. He lives in the Rafha refugee camp, a good 10 percent of whose population are Sunni Arabs. I asked him why he, a Shi'ite notable from Nasiriyya, chose to escape to Saudi Arabia when Iran would have been easier to reach. "What am I to do in Iran, a country whose language I do not speak and with which I have no connections? Sure, it is a Muslim country, but we spent eight years fighting it."

Fatma, a deeply religious woman in her early forties, witnessed the intifada in her hometown, Samawa, which sits on the Euphrates River some thirty miles to the west of al-Nasiriyya. She married in 1975, but had not seen her husband, Abbas, since 1980 because he was evicted from Iraq for being "of Iranian origin."[7] In point of fact, Abbas was a Communist, who had previously spent several years in one of Iraq's most notorious prisons, Nugrat Salman, a black hole in the desert near the Iraqi-Saudi border, where tens of thousands of Kurdish victims of the *Anfal* operations are probably buried.[8] Fatma and Abbas had just been reunited after twelve years of separation when I spoke with her about the first hours of the intifada:

> The first thing I heard was sharp crackling sounds coming from the roofs of houses. It was a Thursday night in Ramadhan. All through the night, the shooting went on making an unbelievable racket. You didn't know where the bullets were coming from. "Oh my, what is this!" I shouted. They said an intifada is happening. "What kind of a thing is this intifada?" I wanted to know. They said it was coming from Kerbala, from Najaf, and that 'Amara and Nasiriyya had just fallen into the hands of our young boys. They said the intifada was going to spread to all the governorates. Now it was Samawa's turn.
>
> Many of the Ba'thists were already gone. Fear had been building up inside them and they had either taken official leave or fled to Baghdad. So I said to myself, "By God, I must go out." And I did. We all did, men and women. The first thing I saw at the head of our side street was some twenty young men. They were in their white *dishdashas* and heading straight for the big police station on the right hand side. I tell you, the oldest one there couldn't have been more than twenty! They were our boys, all from the neighborhood. I know every one of them. Even my cousin was among them. These boys were sick to the teeth of going from one war to the next. Their souls just exploded from frustration.[9]

The March 1991 intifada marks a watershed in the modern history of Iraq. As Iraqis like to put it, *hajiz al-khawf inkiser,* the barrier of fear was broken. The officer who jumped on top of his tank in Sa'ad Square began the business of tearing down that barrier. Whoever he is, and wherever he might now be, that officer's initiative signaled the beginning of a future for a country which was in effect brain-dead, living in a time warp of absolutist dictatorship. Those days are now gone and all Iraqis owe the fact that today they have the possibility of a future to a nameless officer, the hero of their intifada.

The First Day in Najaf

EVENTUALLY I got to interview an actual army officer, one who joined the rebellion and led the defence of the city of Najaf against the onslaught of the Republican Guard. As the tanks and helicopter gunships were closing in on his city in the middle of March, he escaped through French-controlled lines carrying a message from the leadership of the intifada in Najaf to the Allied forces, pleading for help. He was ignored, or not taken seriously, and then there was no going back. The Allies didn't trust Shi'ites. The officer still has a large family in Iraq and must be given a pseudonym. He was not the tank commander in Sa'ad Square and Abu Haydar is not his real name, but that is the name I choose to give him.[10]

We met in a miserable little London bed-sit. Abu Haydar used to be a Ba'thi, who joined the party out of conviction in the 1960s while still in high school in Najaf. But "the party died in 1979. In party cells we stopped educating on political matters. All discussion began to revolve around the person of Saddam. My hatred of Saddam goes back a long way. You see, he killed within my family." Whatever was left of his youthful idealism after that killing (about which Abu Haydar did not want to talk) was certainly wiped out in the eight grinding years of the Iraq-Iran War, all of which he served on the front lines. When I asked him why he had been against the invasion of Kuwait on August 2, he answered with the characteristic fatalism of Iraqi Shi'ism: "Because I am a realist. The world was imposing something on us and I accepted what it was imposing. One must accept what reality imposes. Saddam used to say: 'Each Kuwaiti is served by five people.' What about you, Mr. Saddam, I ask! How many people serve you? The whole regime serves him. Everyone does. I don't believe in politics anymore. I want people to be left alone. After January 17 I was just waiting for the Allied attack to come."

Cautious by necessity, not temperament, with pale blue eyes and the beginnings of a middle-aged spread, Abu Haydar is a disciplined professional man. To his military mind, the Iraqi retreat from Kuwait was "a full-fledged rout, not a withdrawal." Najaf, the city he

was born and brought up in, grew around the burial place of Imam
'Ali ibn Abi Talib, the divinely ordained sovereign of the Shi'a, also
known as *Amir al-Mu'mineen,* the Commander of the Faithful. Of all
the holy Shi'i cities of Iraq, Najaf is the one with the most religious
significance, and the weakest Iranian influence. The first structure to
have been erected over what the vast majority of Shi'is accept as the
place of 'Ali's burial was commissioned by the Abbasid caliph Ha-
roun al-Rashid during the golden age of Islamic civilization. At the
heart of the city today, as it has metamorphosed in its thousand-year
history, lies the imposing gold dome of 'Ali's Shrine, built in the
seventeenth century, and made even more prominent by the un-
relievedly flat surrounding landscape and the twisted lanes and alleyways which abut the arcade enclosing the quietness of the shrine.
The building sits, shielded from the hustle and hubbub of the surrounding city, in the middle of a large *sahan,* or open-air courtyard,
enclosed by an arcade of rooms. Abu Haydar was a witness to this
visual and spiritual center of the city turning into the headquarters of
revolutionary operations during the intifada.

We talked for several hours about what happened there on that
first crucial day. For a man with a price on his head, who still has a
big family inside Iraq, he seemed relaxed and matter-of-fact in describing the things he had seen and done.

It was around noontime on Thursday [February 28] when I heard from
people on the street about what had happened in Basra. "Bravo to
you," I remember saying to myself about that tank commander who
blew the wallposter of Saddam away in Sa'ad Square. "This Saddam is a
criminal and he has led us all to destruction."

You see, I had an image of Najaf, the city I was born and brought up in.
I knew this city, whether through my experience with the party and
party members, or through the people I grew to know over the years.
The image I had was that even if what had happened in Basra were to
result in the whole of Iraq exploding in revolution, from the north to
the south, the city of Najaf would never revolt. Najafis would be too
afraid of the kind of vengeance that Saddam would wreak on this city in
particular if it rose up against him. There is after all a reality here; this is
the city of Shi'i *marja'iyya* [of Shi'i learning and religious reference]. Of
course the state takes special precautions in a city like this. These
precautions were more than in any other city in Iraq. Saddam has a
tendency to make mountains out of molehills. He likes to have absolute

control of every event, no matter how minuscule. The *mukhabarat* [the secret police of the Ba'th Party and probably the most feared branch of the state intelligence system] are present in unimaginable numbers in Najaf. For all of these reasons, you have to understand, I was really taken aback by what happened.

Allied bombing had destroyed nearly 60 percent of the strength of the Jerusalem units of the Republican Guard, which were based on the city outskirts. Much of the heavier weaponry which we later used to defend the city came from what they had left behind. The Allies had also bombed the al-Amir residential district with about fourteen rockets. Three houses were completely demolished, wiped out, flattened to the ground. Four were hit, but only partly destroyed. They of course are no longer suitable for residence. Dozens of houses were affected by the bombing. But the holy places were not hit at all. As for the residents who died, I can tell you that thirteen alone died from the house of Sayyid Rahim Haboubi and his brother 'Aziz. One rocket wiped them all out. Sayyid Rahim himself is the only one that survived. Someone died from the Zwain household, I recall, and four unknown occupants of an automobile, a Super model 90 I think it was, all got killed. Oh and there was that taxi driver who was blown to bits by a bomb. Three F-15s bombed Najaf. At least I think they were F-15s. They destroyed the airport and the radar station and hit the gas plant and the cement factory four times.

On the Friday morning of March 1, I returned with the shopping. I began to meet up and talk about the situation with some doctors, engineers, teachers. Everyone shared my feeling that nothing could happen here in Najaf. The news came that some youths were planning a demonstration against the regime in the center of the city, in the al-Maidan area near the Great Souq, on the following day. Just the idea of having a demonstration affected me greatly; my heart filled with enthusiasm, even desire. But I tell you I still didn't believe it would happen.

Late in the morning of the following day I went scouting around to see what was going on. A couple of youths told me that the demonstration had been postponed until 2:30 P.M. the next day [i.e., March 3]. That was when the people were supposed to gather. Why did they postpone it? The security forces already knew that it was supposed to happen. Everyone knew about the demonstration. I was deeply depressed when I heard that the demonstration had been delayed. It confirmed my belief that nothing was ever going to happen in this city. But the barrier of fear was coming down. I could see it in the streets. How so? For instance, I saw a car driver shouting curses at Saddam from his window.

In front of a huge crowd of people someone spat on the portrait of Saddam. It was astounding. Still I remained unconvinced. You have to remember a kilo of flour was 7.5 dinars. Who can pay such prices? To be making a revolution in these circumstances seemed unimaginable.

I heard Basra was completely in the hands of the rebels and that they had taken over the city the previous day. The word had been that the demonstration in Najaf would start from the tunnel in Maidan Square in the direction facing the Great Souq and the holy *sahan* [the enclosed courtyard containing 'Ali's golden-domed shrine]. I was there at exactly 2:30 P.M. on Sunday, March 3, chatting with a friend from Baghdad. This is what I saw:

Young men, fifteen to twenty-four years old. Not older. In fact I would say the majority were fifteen- to eighteen-year-olds. *Shabab,* youth, that sums it up. They came running out of the alleyways and back streets in groups; they came from 'Aqd Khaniyya, from Khawarnaq Street, and from Sadir Street, which is partially demolished. Some groups came running out of Sadiq Street, and from 'Aqd 'Abd 'Abtan. They were all running out of these small side streets in the direction of al-Maidan. About a hundred persons at most in each group, all carrying clubs and *qamat* [swords]. Two or three had pistols. I remember one was a Webley. They were chanting, *"Saddam sheel iydak; sha'b al-Najaf ma yridak"* (Saddam remove your hands; the people of Najaf don't want you). Also they were shouting out, *"maku wali illa 'Ali; inreed hakim ja'fari"* (There is no governor except 'Ali; we want a Shi'i ruler).[11]

The security men were close to the *sahan.* They started shooting in the air from the Souq al-Kabeer in the direction of Maidan. They were therefore drawn out of the *sahan,* which is where they originally thought the demonstration was going to be heading toward. The first security man to be killed was a party man named Radhi 'Abdel-Shaheed. He was shot with a pistol. On Rasoul Street, Officer 'Ali al-Husain was killed, as were some five or six demonstrators. But the youths kept on coming. Suddenly they wheeled around onto Zain al-'Abideen Street and Sadiq Street, which the security men were not expecting. From a hundred, the numbers swelled to a thousand. They were all Najafis. Young men from good, well-off, and comfortable families. Their fathers were merchants, goldsmiths, carpet dealers, or managed car showrooms and the like. Not civil servants. I could see happiness written on their faces.

Then the demonstration started toward the *sahan* of the holy shrine. Large numbers of security men were there. In the thousands. Most of them, however, were just watching. Waiting to see which way the wind would blow. The young men headed now deadly serious straight for the *sahan*. When they saw this, the security men fled. At the main entrance gate to the *sahan* there was fighting. Several security men were killed. The first one to die had his throat slit; someone grabbed him from behind while he was shooting away. Several of the young rebels were killed at that gate. Until they took the *sahan*, some twenty to thirty youths were killed and many more security men. By sunset the shrine and its courtyard were completely in the hands of the revolutionaries.

I was very excited throughout, but remained unconvinced that this thing was going to succeed. With all the shooting, it was getting dangerous. So I decided to head back to my family. They are calling it an *intifada*. But I tell you the whole thing was a demonstration to start off with. Saddam's cronies are responsible for turning it into something else.

Once the battle for control of Shi'ism's holiest mosque was over, the rebels switched their attention to the main police headquarters building. Here the fighting went on all night, the young men of Najaf pounding away at the building using 82mm artillery abandoned by the Jerusalem units of the Republican Guard. By 4:30 A.M. on Monday morning, March 4, all police resistance inside the building collapsed and the rebels swarmed in, burning all the papers and files. There was some attempt made to stop the destruction. "But," Abu Haydar recalled, "it was useless. Everything was destroyed: car records, property registers, police files, court proceedings."

Abu Haydar's account of the beginning of the intifada in Najaf is borne out by other participants. One group of Najafi males, former soldiers or army deserters, started off as sixty young men, all relatives or close friends from the same neighborhood. The sixty swelled to six hundred within hours after the outbreak of fighting around the *sahan*. Acting under no authority whatsoever, this snowballing crowd of young men stormed six police and Ba'thi strongpoints, suffering many casualties. They seem to have killed everyone who resisted them, releasing only soldiers or policemen who surrendered without a fight or who announced a switch of loyalties. A leading participant described a battle that raged for two hours around a secondary school: "If you could have but seen the sight. By the Qur'an, I tell you there has been nothing like it since the days of the Islamic revolution in Iran. They were spraying us with bullets. We ran out of hand grenades and started yelling, 'Bottles of benzene! Bring bottles of benzene!' The women made us Molotov cocktails out of Pepsi-Cola bottles. An assembly line was set in motion. The women were ululating and taking care of the wounded, carrying them off to houses in the neighborhood. Finally we stormed the place, like worms we crawled up the walls and came at them out of everywhere.''[12]

With the collapse of all police resistance inside Najaf, the action shifted to the remnants of army units on the outskirts of the city. The soldiers hardly put up a fight before fleeing, leaving open the road to Kufa, the second holiest city of Shi'ism. The same pattern was repeated, with a heavy battle outside the Security Headquarters Building in Kufa that went on until the white flag of surrender was raised. Yunis al-Shammari, a commander of the security police, was put on trial for ordering the police to resist. He was told his life would be spared in return for information on the location of secret arms and ammunition caches. al-Shammari refused. Abu Haydar heard his defiant taunt to the rebels just before he was executed: "I have lived a Ba'thi all my life and I will die one."

Not many senior Ba'this died like this. Most fled. Najaf's deputy head of security, Colonel 'Ali, did so by disguising himself as a woman with an 'abaya (a black cloak that traditionally covers all but the woman's face) over his body, and a pooshiyya (a thin cotton cloth that screens the entire female face so that no skin remains visible) over his face. He left men like Lieutenant Mahmoud behind to take the brunt of the people's anger. A young Najafi rebel stumbled upon the lieutenant from Ramadi, whom he knew quite well. Mahmoud had his ankles and feet all shot up and had crawled to hide in a rubbish dump. The rebel was returning home for a bite to eat and was drawn by the moans of someone in great pain. Mahmoud pleaded for his life. Unfortunately, the lieutenant was known to drink alcohol in the holy sahan of 'Ali's Shrine where he worked, so he didn't stand much of a chance. "This man wanted to damage the reputation of the Imam 'Ali, and of the Shi'a of Iraq. When an ordinary visitor comes to the sahan and sees alcohol there, he doesn't say this is the work of Lieutenant Mahmoud, he says the servants of the Haram [the holy grounds containing the shrine] and the holy men of Najaf must be engaging in this corruption." That was the reason the young rebel gave to several of his friends for executing Mahmoud, whose body was left to rot in the dump.[13]

Nouri Farhoud, Khalid al-Garawi, a senior Ba'thist called Bol-boli, and the popular poet Falah 'Askar, who used to work as a lowly traffic policeman in Hilla, were among those "formally" executed in Najaf during the uprising, along with Yunis al-Shammari. As one young man put it, "We could not stop the revolutionaries from getting at them." Rebel sources have put the number of Ba'this killed during the twenty-five hours of fighting that it took to capture the city of Najaf at over four hundred.

Who were these people? Torturers and top Ba'this like al-Shammari made up a part. But many were ordinary fellow Shi'ites like Falah 'Askar, who originally came to the attention of the Ba'th because he had a gift for coining sad and revolutionary rhymes. 'Askar became famous for tunes like *kull al-sha'ab shaddat warid, wa al-riha Ba'thiyya''* (The whole people is a bouquet of flowers and the smell is Ba'thi), or *bil-rouh, bil-dam, nifdeek ya Saddam''* (With our souls, with our blood, we will die for you, oh Saddam). In the traditional Arabic mode, such lines could be sung or recited in a very emotive way, even when they were not written out of conviction or were intrinsically empty of content. In popular Arabic rhymemaking, form evokes emotions more than content; 'Askar excelled at this.

'Askar's balladlike poetical skills are largely of Shi'ite inspiration in Iraq, deriving their sources from the annual *ta'ziyya* and *latmiyyat,* or "consolation through mourning" ceremonies, which dramatize the tragic events surrounding the death of Husain the son of 'Ali on the plains of Kerbala in A.D. 680. Talented poets like Falah 'Askar, Ridha al-Fahham, Kareem al-'Iraqi, and Hasan 'Amara were brought up on these stories and then grew up to become associated with leftist politics. After the collapse of the Iraqi Communist Party in the late 1970s, they were assiduously courted by the Ba'th; they were the 1980s equivalents of 'Aziz 'Ali, the great popular satirist and social critic of the 1940s.[14]

The story is told that when Hasan 'Amara (a pseudonym) was getting married, the wedding was broken up by goons from the security police. They beat up his bride, mauled her father, and smashed the whole place up. The next day, a dejected would-be groom got a call from Saddam on the eve of his becoming president. Saddam indicated to 'Amara that he knew what had happened during his wedding, and he wanted to strike a deal with the poet, one that he knew he would not refuse. He promised to punish those responsible if 'Amara would show his gratitude by writing a few verses on the achievements of the great Ba'thist revolution. Thus was launched, in the style of *The Godfather,* a new and illustrious career in Iraqi popular music.

Popular poets like Falah 'Askar, Ridha al-Fahham, and Hasan 'Amara were targeted during the intifada although they were by and large broken men who, like most Iraqis living under twenty years of Ba'thi rule, no longer had any real commitment to anything. Some had switched from communism to Shi'i Islamic underground politics in the early 1980s. Others had switched to writing Ba'thi verses because, like Hasan 'Amara, they were afraid not to. They did what ordinary people and the bulk of the Iraqi intelligentsia were doing regularly—and for much the same reasons. Modern Ba'thi Iraq has been built on circles of complicity which left no one untouched.

The story of how Falah 'Askar died is typical. He was held overnight in the *sahan* of 'Ali's Shrine, pending his "trial," along with about five hundred or so other prisoners. One of the rebels who was in charge of these prisoners tells the tale of what happened that night: "You know all these popular poets switched sides. I remember that Falah 'Askar organized five poems during the night we held him in the Sahan praising Sayyiduna al-Husain and the Imam 'Ali, and, may God's blessing be upon him, the late Imam Khomeini. All the prisoners began chanting *latmiyyat* and beating their breasts because they had switched against the Saddamist reality. So I said to Falah, 'Where are your beliefs, you who used to say all those things about Saddam?' He said to me, 'That man is a criminal, I was fooled by him.' "[15]

Poor 'Askar's luck had run out. He didn't believe in Saddam Husain or in anything any longer. But not even the verbal skills that had put him in this predicament could save him now. It is unclear how many people like Falah 'Askar were put to death by the rebels. Certainly, nothing the Iraqi government has to say on the subject can be considered reliable. Not everyone was killed. In a village near Samawa, rebels captured a local portrait artist who made his living, like hundreds of others, painting the Great Leader's pictures. "The man begs for mercy," Tony Horwitz of *The Wall Street Journal* reports, "assuming the rebels will kill him. Instead, they fine him 50 dinars and make him say Saddam Husain is the 'son of a dog.' "[16]

Many Ba'this or so-called Ba'this were spared if there was a well-placed relative to intercede on their behalf or if they declared their repentance and returned to God.[17] Fatik al-Safi, for instance, a high-ranking Ba'thi during the 1950s who had escaped to Syria with Saddam Husain after a failed 1959 assassination attempt against the then president of the country, was captured by the rebels during the uprising and released on such conditions. Men who had acquired considerable influence and wealth under the Ba'th were released, while others like Falah 'Askar were killed. Two Shi'ite clerics, both of them *sayyids* (descendants of the Prophet Muhammad and men of religious learning), who had appeared in the past as active Ba'thist supporters and cheerleaders, were also released. A rebel denounced one of them as "an illiterate and a pretender to religious scholarship," whom he clearly regretted having to let go. The *sayyid* was after all captured with a pistol and two grenades in his hand, fighting against the intifada. But he had to be released because of the intervention of other clerics, who, I suspect, did so not out of any love for the man or because they believed in the principle of not killing collaborators. It is more likely that they did not want a precedent of clerical executions to be set, which might one day rebound against them.[18]

Where did the people of Najaf get their weapons from? Saddam's government seems to have convinced itself that American soldiers were going to be parachuted into Iraqi cities. Thus police stations and the buildings of the Ba'th Party in every city and town were turned into centers for the distribution of light armaments. Someone in the highest echelons of the Ba'th had come up with the bizarre idea of turning the Iraqi masses into an urban guerrilla force which was going to impose huge casualties on the Allied forces. Fatma from Samawa told me that all a young boy of fifteen or sixteen had to do to get a machine gun was show up and say he wanted to fight the Americans when they started falling from the sky.[19] A Najafi rebel said, "Saddam was so pleased with himself, he was so sure he would succeed in his battle with the Allies, he put guns in all the schools just in case the Americans dropped in on us." An older man listening to the young man piped up with this telling story of what became of these weapons on the eve of the intifada: "A well-known *sayyid* asked me one day, discreetly, if I could manage to get him a machine gun and a pistol or two because he needed to have them around the house. I did so and carried them over in a suitcase. There I noticed he already had a collection of guns. What was going on, I wondered. Someone else came to visit him while I was still there.

"Where are the weapons you promised me?" the cleric asked his visitor. He was given yet another two machine guns and some pistols. So I asked the *sayyid* what he intended to do with all of these. "They will come in handy, they will come in handy," he muttered quietly.[20]

Not all the *saadeh* (plural of *sayyid*) of Najaf were as calculating or as primed to become urban guerrilla fighters against the regime as this particular gentleman. Another *sayyid* played a leading role in the intifada, but reluctantly and from an entirely different vantage point. Unfortunately, his identity must be concealed because he "committed" an act of compassion involving personal courage which, in the atmosphere of hate and sectarianism that followed the intifada, might still be held against him.

I got sucked into the intifada because the eight-year-old son of my neighbor, a widow, went missing. Ahmad had been sent off shopping to the *souq* before anyone knew something was going on in the city. He hadn't returned by the time the shooting started. Ahmad's mother went all hysterical, pleading with me to go looking for her son. She sat in the courtyard of my house screaming and pulling at her hair. So I set off in the afternoon of March 3 with a party of friends in two cars. We slowly threaded our way to the *al-Maidan* area, in the heart of the city. The city was in the hands of young rebels from local neighborhoods who had set up blockades everywhere. Bodies and corpses were littered all over the place. We reached a point when the car couldn't move amidst the crowds and the confusion and so we pulled into a side street. A friend had a house nearby.

Hiding near where we parked the car—you wouldn't believe it—was a wounded Ba'thist intelligence officer. I knew him from before. The man had seven bullets in him, including a gaping hole in the palm of his hand which was bleeding all over the place. He told me he had managed to get one shot off before being riddled with bullets. He begged me to save him. What could I do? I dressed him up in the black *'abaya* [Iraqi style of veil] of a woman and bundled him up into the car. We got him to the hospital. He wanted me to stay with him because the hospital was being run by revolutionaries, but I couldn't. I don't know what happened to him in the end. Eventually we found the little boy and returned him to his mother.[21]

The Role of Ayatollah Khoei

THE highest spiritual authority of Shi'ism in the world, the Ayatollah Sayyid Abu al-Qasim al-Khoei, lived in Najaf during the intifada. Born in 1899 in the town of Khoy, in Iranian Azerbaijan, Khoei came to Najaf at the age of twelve to study at the city's religious academies. Considered the pontiff for many of the world's Shi'a Muslims, Khoei has taught in Najaf for seventy years, written more than forty volumes on Islamic jurisprudence, and is the spiritual head of a worldwide foundation bearing his name with strong support in the Indian subcontinent. Khoei opposed the involvement of Shi'a jurists in politics long before this was turned into a central issue by the success of the Iranian revolution in 1979 (indeed, Khomeini had formulated his doctrine of *velayet-e-faqih,* or rule of the jurist, in Najaf as a series of lectures in 1970 designed to counter earlier teachings by Khoei). He did so on the grounds that this involved unacceptable compromises which would be bound in the end to besmirch and devalue religious authority.

All through the Iraq-Iran War, Khoei succeeded in the Herculean task of remaining aloof from political influences, whether directed from Baghdad or Tehran. But, in the aftermath of the Gulf war, the tragedy of Iraq finally caught up with him. Acting under the pressure of large numbers of Najafi notables who had come streaming in to see him, the Ayatollah issued a *fatwa* on March 5, the third day of the uprising. A *fatwa* is a legal opinion issued by a religious scholar who, under the Ottomans, might have acted as a court adviser. With the advent of the modern Arab state, *fatwas* declined in importance, only to revive in recent years with the politicization of Islam. In Najaf, the holiest city of Shi'ism, al-Khoei's opinions took on the status of the only law there was for the chaotic nine days that the city was in rebel hands.

Khoei's *fatwa* was issued reluctantly and under the pressure of events. The city was being ransacked and the unclaimed corpses of security men and officials were lying about everywhere. At the time his *fatwa* was issued, the *sahan* of the Shrine of 'Ali was surrounded by tanks captured by the rebels, and was packed with thousands of heavily armed and very excitable young men who were holding hundreds of prisoners inside. These prisoners, like Falah 'Askar, were being tried and executed. Looting was widespread in the city and almost completely out of control.

Hameed, a young schoolteacher who supplements his meager income by driving a battered orange and white taxi, first heard about the uprising on the Voice of America, "when they told about what happened in Basra." Hameed joined in the demonstrations at the Shrine of 'Ali, and his job during the intifada was to listen to foreign news broadcasts and translate them because "I wasn't accustomed to shooting guns." He refused to believe what he was hearing at first. But then he got excited and tore up his teacher's certificate. "You see, the school where I teach is named after Saddam Husain." He insists it wasn't "a religious rebellion. It was against our treatment by Saddam Husain. At first, we were a little crazy. We believed even the traffic lights represented Saddam Husain so we wrecked them. People broke into schools, which the army used for storing weapons, and they distributed the weapons. By nine that night, the rebels controlled the center of the city. Some people whose fathers were killed in the war with Iran saw the officials who had drafted them. Many officials were hung in the basement of the Islamic school next to the mosque. People dragged officials into the street and shot them. They were so angry they cut them up and burned them. Others came and spat on the bodies."[22]

These are the chaotic conditions under which the Khoei *fatwa* appeared. As was the custom, the document was stamped with the Ayatollah's seal and neatly written out by hand in the *naskhi* script, quite likely by a professional clerk. It was brought to public attention by Majid al-Khoei, one of the Ayatollah's sons. On the third day of the uprising, addressing a packed assembly of thousands of Najafis gathered in the huge enclosed expanse of the *sahan,* and using a microphone from the roof of the mosque, Majid al-Khoei read out the *fatwa:*

In the name of God, the Compassionate, the Merciful
My dear devout sons

May peace be upon you, and God's mercy and blessings.

Praise be to God for his boons and bounties, and prayers and peace upon
  the noblest of his apostles, Muhammad, and his holy family.

There is no doubt that preserving the heart of Islam and safeguarding its
  sanctity is the duty of every Muslim. For my part, I pray to God

Almighty to bestow success upon you in upholding all that is good for the Islamic Umma [the community of all Muslims].

I urge you to be exemplars of noble Islamic values by observing precisely the laws of the Islamic *shari'a* in all your actions. You should never lose sight of God's presence whenever you embark on any action. You are obligated to protect people's property, money, and honor, likewise all public institutions, for they are the property of all. Depriving anyone of these institutions is depriving everybody.

I also urge you to bury all the corpses in the streets, according to *shari'a* rites, to refrain from maiming anybody, for these are foreign to our Islamic morals; and to not be hasty in taking individual decisions that have not been thought out and that go against the *shari'a* and the public interest.

May God preserve and guide you in His right path, for He is the All-Hearing and the All-Giving.

May peace be upon you and God's mercy and blessings

On the 18th of Sha'ban, 1411.[23]

The fundamental intent of the *fatwa* was to stem the descent into anarchy and introduce order into the affairs of the city. The very fact that the Ayatollah felt it had to be issued is proof of how much the situation had deteriorated. On March 8, a second *fatwa* appeared, which appointed "a Supreme Committee" to act in "society's public interest." It was made up of nine *mujtahids,* Shi'i religious scholars, most of whom were heads of different seminaries in Najaf. The Supreme Committee was authorized to act in Ayatollah Khoei's name in everything. They were for all practical purposes a government. But government of what? Was the committee a temporary emergency administration restricted to the holy city of Najaf, or was it the embryo of an alternative government for the whole of Iraq? This question, not surprisingly, was avoided during the intifada.

To a considerable degree the Ayatollah, working through his sons and entourage, succeeded in his purpose. The evidence is incontrovertible that his personal intervention saved many Iraqi lives and curbed the tendency among the young men of the intifada toward mindless butchery rooted in pent-up hatreds and a desire for vengeance. Consider, for instance, the case of the five hundred prisoners inside the *sahan.* The order came from the Ayatollah to get them safely out of there and into Dar al-Hikma, a seminary some 100 yards (300 meters) away belonging to the al-Hakim family. One of Khoei's sons oversaw the formation of a loyal group of twenty-five heavily armed men, who then took the terrified prisoners out from under "the glittering eyes of the *mujahideen*," in the words of one of the members of that elite group. The hearts of the fighters milling around the *sahan* and watching this operation, he went on to recall, were like "red-hot coals filled with anger at these Ba'this who had hurt, executed, and raped people." The prisoners were escorted on foot, or carried in stretchers, in small groups, and the operation continued through the night until the small hours of the morning. "The Sayyid asked of us," said the man who was responsible for this operation, "to fight the *mujahideen* in the *sahan* if we had to."[24]

The Supreme Committee also formed subcommittees to organize the distribution of food and the reopening of essential services to the city. Public officials, doctors, engineers were all assured of their safety and urged to resume their work. The subcommittees functioned for a few days before the city fell to the forces of the Republican Guard. A military subcommittee of six officers had also been appointed. Its job was to organize the defense of Najaf and to coordinate with other liberated cities. One of the six officers, who was appointed upon the direct instructions of Ayatollah Khoei and dispatched through French lines to plead for Allied help on his behalf, was Abu Haydar. "When I got asked to join, I told my wife: 'I am going, woman, I am going to my death.' You see, I never expected the intifada to succeed. But what gave me a tiny spark of hope was that Najaf, the city I was born and brought up in, which I least expected to revolt, had risen up against tyranny. I acted because of that."

The View from Baghdad

UNTIL the Gulf war, Habeeb lived with his parents in a wealthy, high-security area of Baghdad. As a young university graduate with ambitions to develop the family business, Habeeb's career was full of promise. His complacent and comfortable existence was shattered at 2:30 A.M. on January 17, 1991. "I was just going to sleep when the war started. The sky went brilliant red pierced by bright streaks of light. Aircraft noise came crashing through the night. I cannot explain to you the sound of the bombing blasts. It was like the end of the world. I switched on the radio and heard Saddam broadcasting a speech. 'The Americans are attacking us. . . .' No one could believe what was happening. Even Saddam Husain did not believe it. When he broadcast to the public, his voice was faint and it sounded like he had just had a rod rammed down his throat.''[25]

While Baghdad Radio was broadcasting the love songs of the singer Majida al-Roumi, more than a million of the 4 million residents were stampeding out of the city. This mad rush at the start of the war out of the cities brought more immediate and direct physical hardship to people than the bombing campaign itself (which in Baghdad at least was as precisely executed as the Allied forces claimed it to be). As soon as he realized that the bombing was not indiscriminate, Habeeb, like most people, returned to watch over his house and business. Through his many high-ranking Ba'thi and Takriti friends, he got to visit the infamous 'Amiriyya shelter before and after it was hit by an Allied missile, killing some four hundred civilians.

> The families of Ba'th Party members were taking refuge there at the time. Every single member of Jameel Shanshal's family was burnt alive. But there were other families who lived nearby who had sought refuge there. I visited the scene on the day it was bombed, before they sealed the whole place up. I was told by my friends that the government took important documents out in crates before dealing with the people inside. Some bodies had turned into charcoal; others looked like they had melted or were fused onto one another. Arms and legs fused into torsos. You could not tell one human being from another. In fact, they didn't look human any longer. The remains were put into trucks with no attempt made at identification. Anyway, it was hopeless. I can still see the images. Often I wake up in the middle of the night. Whatever I say, you cannot imagine what it meant unless you go through what we went through.

Habeeb's sentiments on the Gulf war closely reflect those of the Sunni Arab community of Baghdad, as does his state of mind on the eve of the intifada that began the moment the war ended. They are the fears of a beleaguered minority which, while not supporting the dictator, rallied around him during the intifada because they felt their very existence was threatened by the unfolding situation. Regardless of whether or not those fears were justified, Habeeb's words make it obvious that the issue as far as he was concerned was one of survival, not preservation of privilege.

We heard about the intifada in the south from Western broadcasts. Do you realize that a small battery for a portable radio was 10 dinars in Baghdad? And you couldn't find any at that price! There was, of course, no more television. I used to have to listen to my car radio to hear the news and important speeches. There were all kinds of new radio stations, some I had never heard of before. The government didn't call it an *intifada,* they called it sedition, *fitna.* The rebels were wild mobs, *ghogha'iyeen.* They only started to talk about what had happened in the south after government troops were controlling the cities once again. There was no news about the Shi'a uprising when it first began. But word soon spread.

I was told about a Shi'a commander of an army unit of about four thousand soldiers which reached the outskirts of Najaf and Kerbala. One of the *sayyids* welcomed him, and gave his men food free of charge. All this food came from Iran. Meanwhile we were starving in Baghdad. Together they changed the Governorate of Kerbala and Najaf into an Islamic Republic. Also, the Iraqis who were thrown out of the country during the Iraq-Iran War all came to Kerbala and Najaf to fight. People were chanting in the streets, *"maku wali illa 'Ali, inreed hakim Ja'fari"* (There is no governor except 'Ali; we want to be ruled by a Shi'i).

We were frightened because the Shi'a almost reached Baghdad. Iraqis are good at ransacking, they are experts in *farhoud* [the looting of Jewish homes and shops during the 1941 pogrom is called *farhoud;* the term was widely used all over Iraq during the intifada]. I tell you, if the Shi'a unrest had reached Baghdad, it would have been a bloodbath *(al-dhabih ib-filis).* Naturally, they would have entered any house, and once they found out who the occupants were, they would have ransacked its contents and massacred us. Nobody would have found out who was killed by whom. The Christians were very frightened, many of them fled the country. Who gets caught in the middle when it is a matter of Shi'a Muslims killing Sunni Muslims, both of whom are Arabs? Not to mention Sunni Kurds killing Sunni Arabs! Why, Christians and Jews, of course.

Let me tell you a story. People were queuing one day for food when a Muslim woman wanted to jump the queue in front of a Christian woman. She pushed her aside saying: "You're Bush's daughter; go to him, he'll give you food." The Christian woman took off her slipper and hit the Muslim woman, shouting at her: "My husband was at the front defending our country, like every other Iraqi. My brothers died in the Iraq-Iran War. How dare you call me Bush's daughter!" Many fights like this happened in Baghdad. Christians were called British and American allies because America, a Christian country, bombed Iraq. I tell you, there is no love lost between Iraqis—everyone hates everyone else.

The government sent its Special Forces to deal with the situation in the south. They are very fierce and vicious. All of them are Sunni. The soldiers came from Ramadi, Hit, Sammara, Mosul, and Takrit, and they erased the two cities—the cemeteries, everything. They wiped the place clean. Dogs were eating people's corpses in the streets.

Now, there is a great enmity between Shi'i and Sunni; no matter what happens, it will not be reconciled, the hatred is there. Not just that—revenge was spreading between ordinary Iraqis. In the midst of the unrest, people who hated each other surfaced. This was going to be the right time to take revenge.

When the Kurds started their uprising, a woman who lives in my neighborhood came from the north with her children and told us the atrocities. The Kurds killed her husband, a member of the party, and told her, "We are not like Arabs, we will only kill your husband. Take your children and go home." She said, when the Kurds controlled the area, they caught the Ba'this, displayed them in the town, and asked the people to say who did what to whom. Each person began to tell a story. How this person harmed that person, and so on. When the Kurdish leader of the group holding the prisoners agreed upon an execution, people would jump at the prisoner with knives before the sentence could even be carried out. People were beheaded; their bodies were cut into pieces. All was revenge and settling accounts; it was a slaughter-house. The Kurds killed thousands of Ba'this. Nonetheless they did not kill indiscriminately—only Ba'this and collaborators with the regime. While the Kurds were in control of Kirkuk, some Iraqis were not allowed to enter the city. They were told that this is Kurdistan. It was as if you now needed a visa to get in to your own country.

Habeeb has a sense of humor. He recounted what happened when Saddam visited Najaf and Kerbala, after the uprising had been crushed. In the Arab tradition of victory and celebration, the president of Iraq yanked out his pistol and emptied it into the air. "The next day we heard on Radio Monte Carlo that this was considered a violation of the cease-fire agreement and Saddam was fined $1,000, which was going to be added on to the reparations bill."

Habeeb, however, is not a Sunni Arab; he is a Baghdadi Jew, born and brought up in Saddam Husain's Iraq. People often mistake him for a Ba'thi "because of my mustache, and because I am so dark-skinned. Because of this I was asked many times to join the Ba'ath Party. I did join when I was sixteen years old, but I was expelled because of a fear that I might go up the ladder in the party and give information to Israel." Whenever Western delegations came to Baghdad, they would want to pay a visit to Habeeb's synagogue.

> One day this American crew was excitedly filming us in the Synagogue, as though we were some long lost Jewish relics from Babylonian times. The cameraman was concentrating on my Torah, filming it and me from every conceivable angle. I was doing my best to look very serious and devout, focusing intently on the page in front of me as though nothing else in the whole world mattered. It was very hard to keep a straight face. At one point I had to turn and ask an old Jewish man next to me whether I was on the right page. He looked at my Torah, and then at me, and said, "You are holding it upside down." To be frank, I can't read Hebrew.

Jews are not only one of the oldest minorities in Iraq, they have also been turned into one of the tiniest—a few hundred people. They know better than most what it means to live under the threat of persecution. When the Ba'th first came to power in 1968, they sought to legitimize themselves by whipping up an anti-Semitic campaign—complete with public hangings—which turned out to be the thin end of the wedge in a generalized campaign of terror that finally touched every Iraqi. An upsettingly common reaction among some Arabs to my book *Republic of Fear* was "Why did you give so much space to the plight of a handful of Jews in 1968? Didn't every Iraqi suffer?" But the persecution of every Iraqi under the Ba'th began with that of the most helpless amongst them. Habeeb therefore speaks for the fears of all minorities in Iraq better than most because he speaks from a deeply instilled experience of what it means to be persecuted by a majority culture. In particular, he speaks for the new fears of the historically most privileged Iraqi community, the Sunni Arabs of Baghdad.

The Intifada's Other Face

RUMORS and sightings of strangers are rife during an uprising. Hameed, the young schoolteacher quoted earlier, was a witness to the takeover of the *sahan* of 'Ali's Shrine in Najaf. On Sunday, March 3, he heard people whispering to each other that "forces were flooding in from Iran," and then he saw about fifteen to twenty men who called themselves *mujahideen,* or holy warriors, "march out of the main mosque, shouting, 'God is Great,' and carrying small weapons." They were chanting, *"la sharqiyya, la gharbiyya, jumhouriyya Islamiyya"* (No East, no West, we want an Islamic republic), a slogan associated with the Iranian Islamic revolution.

> They also called out, "Islam is our religion, Hakim is our Leader."[26] I didn't recognize one of the men—he looked unfamiliar. He had an Islamic beard and wore a green headband. Some people said these men had already taken care of the secret service men inside the mosque. At the mosque, people gathered to hear instructions over the loudspeakers. They were distributing food, asking for medicine. There was a rumor that food had been poisoned. One wealthy pharmacist, who later fled to Saudi Arabia, made his storehouse available for everyone. They asked for men who could drive tanks or operate strella missiles. The mosque loudspeakers warned people about which cars or persons might be undercover police. To identify ourselves at the checkpoints on the road, we'd have a picture of Imam Ali or Ayatollah Khoei on the dashboard or a green banner on the aerial of the car. There were rumors everywhere—that we'd meet up with the Kurds in Baghdad, that the Iraqi opposition was going to meet with Dan Quayle.[27]

Hameed's account of what happened introduces new elements, which conflict with his own assertion that "this wasn't a religious rebellion." The regime and many upper-middle-class Sunni Iraqis also firmly believe that everything that happened was the work of "outsiders." Another interpretation of the intifada, one consistent with the presence of strangers in the city of Najaf, is that it was not spontaneous but organized and planned in advance. Such was the opinion of a senior commander in the Kurdistan Front. He led the first organized *peshmerga* attacks on Iraqi army positions and played a key role inside northern Iraq during the uprising.

We made the news inside Iraq. Maybe the uprising was a spontaneous event in some places, but in the Kurdish region it was organized and planned by the Kurdistan Front. We lit the fire of the uprising, which began in the town of Raniyah near the Iraqi–Iranian border and the housing settlements attached to it. There was nothing spontaneous about it. Right after the Iraqi invasion of Kuwait, various scenarios of what might transpire were discussed inside the leadership of the Kurdistan Front together with the leadership of the Supreme Islamic Assembly over many different meetings. A kind of coordination between the Kurdish movement and the Shi'ite opposition in Iraq was reached and a number of principles agreed, among which was military and political coordination. Our Shi'ite brothers promised not to announce their desire to establish an Islamic republic in Iraq and not to talk about a Shi'ite or an Islamic revolution in Iraq because this would immediately create hostility on the regional and international level toward the intifada.

KM: But slogans calling for an Islamic state appeared during the uprising?

Yes, and this was one of the main reasons for its defeat. If those promises had not been broken, and if the slogans you refer to had not spread around, the intifada would not have reached the tragic end that it did.

I realize that it is not to the benefit of the Iraqi people and the Iraqi opposition to say that this uprising was coordinated between the Kurdish movement and the Supreme Islamic Assembley over several months in the course of many pre-planned meetings. But I tell you these meetings went on continuously via a coordinating committee based in Bakhtaran. Meetings were also held in Tehran. There were military, political, and public relations subcommittees between us. The Iranians were witnesses to all this. They recorded the sessions on tape and wrote notes during the meetings. You have to remember the Supreme Assembly of the Islamic Revolution of Iraq had a large force known as the Badr Brigade with some ten thousand men. The Kurdish movement also had armed forces. These were distributed according to agreed arrangements in the north and south of the country.

KM: But is the story of the tank commander in Sa'ad Square true?

Yes, it is true.

KM: What was his name?

I don't know, unfortunately.[28]

I have no reason to doubt that meetings of the sort mentioned by the Kurdish commander, attended by official representatives of the

Iranian government, did take place. The Iranians appear to have pressured the Kurdistan Front into attending, and the Tehran meetings took place at the highest political levels of both the Front and the Supreme Islamic Assembly. Their significance, however, is a different matter.

Non-party-affiliated Kurds believe that the uprising was as spontaneous in the north as it was in the south, and that the Kurdish parties entered only after ordinary Kurdish citizens inside Iraq began taking matters into their own hands. Early in the morning of March 3, for instance, in Khabat, a residential complex built to house Kurds forcibly resettled by the government during the 1980s, students from the main secondary school confronted a unit of the Emergency Forces which was searching for army deserters. Fighting broke out and several were killed. But the incident was contained.[29]

On March 6, special instructions were issued to the Dohuk Security Police by the Central Security Directorate in Baghdad with orders to suppress popular demonstrations—as distinguished from fighting armed Kurdish guerrilla fighters (also called *peshmerga*). The document, captured by insurgents during the uprising, is headed by the traditional Islamic *basmallah* ("in the name of God the Compassionate, the Merciful"). The focus is entirely on "hostile demonstrations" and the measures that need to be taken like "sealing all roads" and "controlling the elevated areas that overlook them." The fourth item is the most crucial: "After taking the above measures and encircling the hostile elements, use armed force under central command instructions with a view to killing 95 percent of them, leaving the remainder for interrogation."[30]

An electrician, Sarwar, witnessed the fall of Dohuk in spite of these extraordinary instructions. "The emphasis was on the security offices, which resisted fiercely until 6:30 A.M. on the morning of March 17, 1991. The governor was in there giving instructions and encouraging his men to keep on fighting. He was saying to them, 'Don't be afraid, these are not *peshmerga.*' He was right. The hundred and fifty or so people attacking the building were from the general public and Kurdish advisers. When I left my house, I actually saw some of these advisers wearing *peshmerga* clothes even though they were not really *peshmerga.*" The following day, Sarwar recounts, a contingent of sixty *peshmerga* arrived in Dohuk, after the town had been completely liberated by its own citizens and former so-called advisers."[31]

"Advisers" are influential Kurds, often tribal leaders, who receive enormous benefits from Baghdad in return for pacifying and controlling the Kurds through military units headed by them and attached to the Iraqi army. These "advisers," known locally as the *Jahsh* (the word, originally coined as an insult, means "little donkey" in Arabic and Kurdish), commanded all-Kurdish units which varied from a few hundred to a few thousand men. In the late 1980s there were between 300 and 350 such units, making up a total of more than a quarter of a million Kurdish irregulars. The organizations of the Kurdistan Front in the north acted only after the defection of several hundred of these so-called advisers. The near-simultaneous defections of so many *Jahsh* Kurdish officers/advisers, with the men under their command, paralleled what was going on in the south. The defections seem to have begun several days after the outbreak of the uprising in Basra, although the groundwork for them was laid earlier in the shape of a joint decision taken by all the Kurdish political organizations to grant amnesty to all Kurdish "collaborators" with the Ba'th. This decision was communicated to the advisers through secret contacts and radio broadcasts beamed into Iraq in the winter of 1990. The defections which ensued provided the incentive for the two main Kurdish political parties—the Kurdish Democratic Party and the Patriotic Union of Kurdistan—to act militarily. On March 6, the town of Raniyah, close to the Iranian border, became the point of entry of the Kurdish *peshmerga,* who then spread out to other areas. In coordination with armed cells and units already placed in the towns and cities, the forces of the Front quickly dealt with the security centers and Ba'th Party headquarters. Towns like Dohuk, 'Amadiyya, Zakho, and Acre were liberated by *Jahsh* officers with no help from the *peshmerga* of the Kurdistan Front. The fiercest resistance to the advance of the rebel forces pouring in from Iran did not come from the Iraqi army, which was everywhere crumbling; it came from the People's Mujahideen, a sectarian, anti-Khomeini, Iranian Islamic group based in Iraq and led by Mas'oud Rajavi.[32] Using tanks and artillery supplied by the Iraqi government, Rajavi's forces held up the Kurdish advance to Sulaimaniyya for two days. With the liberation of Kirkuk on March 20, the whole of northern Iraq was in Kurdish hands for the first time in Iraqi history.

The spontaneity of the uprising in the north is a matter of interpretation as much as it is a question of fact. However, the evidence is overwhelming that in its origins the intifada as a whole event began in the Iraqi army and was sparked off by a junior officer, who probably took even himself by surprise when he jumped up on that tank and denounced the regime. He certainly took the organized Iraqi opposition based in Iran—Shi'ite and Kurdish—by surprise. This officer's example spread like wildfire, but it was followed up very differently in the north versus the south of the country.

Support for the intifada, even among the Kurds, was not as solid as many in the Iraqi opposition have since claimed. Not all the Kurdish *Jahsh* leaders, for instance, defected. One wealthy land-owner and tribal chief, who was involved in business dealings all over Iraq, fought with the regime against his own relatives all through the uprising, changing his mind only after it was all over. He was, in his own words, "a close friend of Saddam's family," and maintained close relations with high-ranking members of the Ba'thi command for many years. It started some time in the mid-1980s, when "I, with a group of people, went to receive these medals for bravery. We were about twenty. We went to the Presidential Palace and when Saddam appeared, none of us clapped hands for him. We were the chiefs of tribes and felt ashamed to clap hands like babies." But something happened, because when he and the other tribal leaders went back for their second visit, "we agreed among our-selves to clap hands for Saddam because we realized that he liked that sort of reception." The remarkably frank reasons given by this *Jahsh* leader for his behavior during the uprising could, with appro-priate modifications, be applied to all those Iraqis who benefited materially during the 1980s:

Yes, in 1975, when the Kurds were repressed, I stood by. In 1988, when chemical weapons were used against the Kurds, I stood by. In 1991, when the Kurds were driven to the mountains and many thou-sands died, I stood by. How could I do these things? I just didn't have confidence in the opposition forces at that time. The other Kurdish advisers and I have been brought up in towns and cities. We're accus-tomed to a luxurious life. We have lands and relatives. I have about seven thousand donums of land behind the mountains over there. Sad-dam confiscated them, and instead bought my loyalty for one hundred thousand dinars a month. Some of our relatives have been subjected to oppression. . . . I know that. But, as I said before, we didn't trust the opposition forces at the time of the uprising.

We saw that the Kurdish problem was connected with the Iranians. But whenever Iranians gave something to Iraqis, they would let the Kurds down. Had America or Britain or France adopted the Kurdish cause, we would have joined the Kurdish revolution. But, as I must again repeat, we had no trust in the opposition forces. So, we stayed loyal to the regime.

I was forced to come back with the army to retake my own home town. And when we came, we found that our relatives were fighting against us, blocking the way in. Three days before we retook it, we advanced towards a nearby town. We took the town, and with it three armed *peshmergas*. When night fell, I secretly released them, telling them to go and tell the people what they had seen with their own eyes. Tell them that the army was coming again.

Even when I was injured, I was pleased that the Kurds were fighting back. I wanted them to continue defending the town. My brother, my cousin, and some other relatives were fighting in the surrounding mountains. They wounded me . . . but I was happy. Although I had been injured, I refused to go to the hospital. The reason I stayed on with the army was to prevent any harm being done to the people or the town. Afterwards we went on to the next town which we found abandoned. That was when I realized that the Kurds were getting wise and that this time around they would achieve their goals.

The question now is what will happen when the Allies leave. Ten days ago [May 1991], 'Izzat al-Douri sent for me and the other Kurdish dignitaries who hadn't joined the rebellion. He had prepared for each one of us a case full of money. He said to us, "You're worried . . . you feel afraid because we are about to compromise with the Kurds." We answered that we are not afraid because all our relatives, all our possessions, had gone to the mountains. We were left alone. He said that they would give us the province of Dohuk. We said that these days even our children don't agree with us. He answered, "Well, you know you have influence, and we could install you as representatives of the government in Dohuk." I said, "Now all Kurds wouldn't agree to appoint us as their representatives." Douri then said, "Sometimes we deal with the Kurds peacefully, other times we go to war with them. Now is the time for negotiations. But when this is done and the Americans withdraw, three days will be enough to tackle the Kurdish problem."

By tackle, he meant going to war with the Kurds. The difference this time is that the army will not necessarily engage in a wide-scale attack. Saddam will use other means. It wouldn't bother him to assassinate me, and then go to the Kurds and accuse them of this deed, asking for my blood. He's gambling for time. So he will keep us until he makes an agreement with the opposition. Then he will hand us over to them. He will motivate other Kurds to kill us.

I think the time has come to change sides. Now I have connected my fate with my people. We all trust America to stand by us, to defend us. It is true that America sold out the Kurds in 1975, but now it is different because the United States will lose its credibility. Either because of its humanitarianism or because the Kurds are lucky, America is trapped. It's facing a de facto situation as far as the Kurdish case goes. It is unlikely that a civilized world, like the West and America, the defenders of human rights throughout the world, would give hope to the Kurds and then let them face an enemy like Saddam. If it weren't for Saddam's fatal mistake in invading Kuwait, all the Arabs would have gone on hating the Kurds, and the Kurdish problem would have remained unknown to the world.[33]

From Euphoria to Burlesque

IF REVOLUTION is a kind of theater, then the most theatric and deeply symbolic event in the first days of the intifada, enacted in every city of the country south and north, was the tearing down of Saddam Husain's portrait. Hana' (a pseudonym), an engineer and the mother of two young children, described the scene in Sulaimaniyya:

When we heard that the battle for the Central Security Headquarters Building had ended, everyone went out to the street. About five children between five and seven years old came running up to a group of men and women who were standing before a wooden portrait of Saddam glued to a concrete slab. The children threw stones at it. Then they attacked it with knives and other implements. The older people looked on quietly. To tell you the truth, we were afraid. Then the children piled up the bits and pieces of wood. A Kurdish woman passer-by, carrying a container with fuel in it, splashed her fuel on the pile of wood and set it on fire. The fire flared up in Saddam's face, and everybody started clapping. People gathered around the children and the woman to see how the fire was actually igniting Saddam's picture.

After it was burned, people headed for one of the slogans on the road. But it was too high. They threw stones at it, but it wouldn't fall. So they moved on toward the center of Sulaimaniyya, where there were other pictures of Saddam. I didn't stay with them, but the next day we went by foot and saw the burned pictures all over the place. There was blood on some of them. Such moments were deeply moving to those of us who were there. They broke the barrier of fear.[34]

By contrast with events in southern Iraq, a measure of organization and discipline was quickly brought to the Iraqi cities and towns that fell into the hands of the Kurdistan Front. In a crucially important political move, the Front announced in November 1990 a general amnesty for all collaborators with the Saddam regime (which of course included the *Jahsh*). The amnesty, first broadcast over the radio, was rigorously implemented and has lasted until this very day. It reassured most of the *Jahsh,* and introduced unity and clarity of purpose to the Kurdish response. In a stirring address delivered at a rally in the town of Koi Sinjak at the height of the Kurdish intifada, Mas'oud Barazani, son of the legendary nationalist leader Mulla Mustafa Barazani and leader of the Kurdistan Democratic Party, captured the rapturous mood of all Iraqi Kurds with these words:

> One second of this day is worth all the wealth in the world.

> It is seventy-one years since the Iraqi state was founded. . . . We have lost one martyr after another, village after village has been burnt, all for the sake of liberating the Kurds and Kurdistan. But, because there was a lack of unity, for seventy-one years we weren't able to fulfill our hopes. Today we are united. In one week we liberated this land from Zakho to Khanaqin. The *peshmerga* and the people took the army bases as easily as if they were going on a picnic.[35]

Nonetheless, the degree of control that the Kurdish organizations were able to bring to the situation should not be exaggerated. In Raniyah, a crowd dragged police and Ba'thi officials being detained in the town mosque onto the roof of the local hotel; their names were read out. "Shall we throw him over or not?" the men holding the Ba'this would shout out to the crowd below. The huge crowd gathered below gave its verdict, and one by one the men were pushed off the three-story building. An angry crowd, including young women, rushed at the broken bodies and shredded what was left with knives. One old man, horrified by the sight, tried to stop them. A woman turned on him, her eyes burning. "They deserve more than this," she said. He backed away. In the end, Kurdish *peshmerga* intervened to drag people off the mangled corpses.[36]

An extraordinary letter, written by a young Sunni Arab from Baghdad to his brother Omar (pseudonym), describes the unforgettable scene at the Central Security Building in Sulaimaniyya on March 8, 1991. Written shortly after the events it describes, the writer gives the impression of being still in a state of shock.

My Dear Brother Omar,   *April 24*

. . . I don't know how to start telling you of the painful tragedies that have befallen our people, both Arabs and Kurds. We have been through ordeals surpassing those one sees in films or reads about in fiction. Death, death, and more death was everywhere. . . .

I took the family to Sulaimaniyya. . . . Within days events began to move with astonishing speed. At first Saddam's men were in control of everything and no one expected what happened next. In the evening of March 6, the radio station [of the Kurdish Front] began calling on the people to take to the streets. On the morning of March 8, the people started coming out on the streets and attacking the police centers, the intelligence services, and the *mukhabarat* [party security]. They got hold of weapons. There were no more than two hundred *peshmerga* fighters in the whole of Sulaimaniyya and the rest were people from all walks of life. It was, I tell you, a genuine popular revolution! The bodies of security agents, intelligence officers, and Ba'th Party men were torn to shreds. The people revenged themselves on what was done in Halabja and other places. The cries of the cowards penetrated into the skies, but there was no mercy shown to these despicable and deviant men. I tell you, dear brother, it was a magnificent epic that no human being will ever forget.

The real battle was waged around the well-fortified Central Security Headquarters Building in Sulaimaniyya, which held out for forty-eight hours. All the senior officials had fled into this building. Finally their impregnable fortress fell and the masses swarmed in, destroying and killing everything that stood in their way. I saw torture chambers and instruments like you wouldn't believe. Seven hundred security and party men died here and we had to walk on top of their corpses. Those who had survived the fighting were tried and executed on the spot by the people using iron saws and knives even as they screamed and sobbed.[37]

In the south of the country there were no organizations with either the credibility or the maturity to provide even the minimal level of political leadership that existed among the Kurds. Chaos ruled the land. Five to ten thousand armed Iraqi Shi'ites, organized in small bands and recruited from refugees expelled by the Ba'th during the late 1970s and early 1980s, entered the country through the marshlands around Basra on the second or third day of the uprising. They were units from the Badr Brigade, organized by the Supreme Islamic Council headed by Muhammad Baqir al-Hakim (the Badr Brigade is named after the first battle of Islam between the forces of the Prophet Muhammad and the Meccan army which had assembled to fight them in A.D. 653). The first action of these angry young men pouring in from Iran seems to have been the storming of the Sheraton Hotel and the burning of the bars and casinos of the city of Basra. They then proclaimed the establishment of a Shi'i Islamic Republic in Basra.[38] Surrendering or captured army personnel were executed, occasionally in "trials" presided over by clerics. These judgments were implemented on men who were in the eyes of the rebels "enemies of God" (the notion of "enemies of God," although a very old one with biblical and classical roots, was revived in the course of the Iranian revolution and has come into wide use in political polemics all over the Middle East; it is the Islamic equivalent of the Ba'thi idea of being a "traitor to the Arab nation"). Slogans like "Kill the Betrayers of Islam!" and "Death to Saddam the Apostate!" were shouted out in the streets or painted on the walls of southern Iraqi cities.

The idea of apostasy, *kufr,* the enemy within, was very widespread during the intifada. The whole Ba'thist regime was declared *kafir,* apostate, and all those who continued to perform their former duties for whatever reason, or did not declare their repentance—or were simply not believed by the rebels to have returned "to the ways of God" even if they had repented, like Falah 'Askar—became apostates. Apostasy in Islamic law is a much worse offence than the Christian notion of heresy because Islam perceives itself as a political community, not just a religious community. It follows that apostasy is a form of treason against a very basic and all-encompassing group identity and loyalty, the penalty for which, according to Islamic law, is invariably death.[39]

Such violence, justified in the name of Islam, but more often than not motivated by the desire for vengeance, promptly terminated the lifeblood of the intifada: the flow of defections from the army. This explains the ability of the regime to regroup its shattered forces and strike back. In Najaf, as we have seen, attempts were made to check the descent into anarchy by resident notables and *'ulema',* learned religious men, acting through the prestige of Ayatollah Khoei. But in Basra and Kerbala, whatever leadership there was came from Iraqis based in Tehran. These are also the cities where some of the worst rebel excesses occurred. According to Um Husain, a traditional veiled Shi'i housewife from Basra, the pattern for every government building was the same: kill every official you could get your hands on, loot everything inside, spread some kerosene around the building, light a match, and get the hell out of the place fast. "There were no courts," she said, just roving bands. "For example, I have a relative who was in the party. They came for him to his family's house. They would say, 'Bring out so-and-so for us, we want to kill him.' Some people were brought out, and killed. Now this man, my relative, he leaped from his house to the house next door and he crossed the street and fled. But I have two relatives who were killed this way in al-Nasiriyya. Every higher-up, they killed." But what infuriated Um Husain more than anything was what the Iraqi government was saying. "It's blasphemous the government saying it's Islamic. Those who came from outside were heathens, too. They're not good people, the ones who came—they destroyed, burned, demolished. They killed and fled. Is Islam like this?"[40]

Members of the security police and the city's crime prevention unit in Basra tied a green band around their head and joined the intifada. Um Husain's brother ran into a couple of these born-again Muslims playing dice behind his garden wall. He asked them what was going on. "It's an Islamic Republic—it's freedom," one of them answered. Um Husain recalled the story of the sniper perched on top of a nearby building who spent a whole week taking pot shots at anything that moved within his firing range. She was one of his targets.

I was sitting in the garden, shortly after the war ended, and leaned over to pick up this metal cup from the table. I was holding it like this in my hand. The bullet came zinging right over my shoulder. It came for me. I didn't see anybody, I didn't hear a bullet, or anything. At first I didn't even know it was a bullet. The children were playing in the street. They came running. I told them, "Kids, what did you throw at me?" You see, I thought they had thrown an onion or something at me which had knocked the cup out of my hand. They said, "Grandma, why are you

saying we shot you with an onion? That's not an onion, that's a bullet."
This really bowled me over. Where did the bullet come from? The
children looked for the cup, and found it. I have brought it with me
because I wanted to show it to my son in London. [She holds up the
metal cup with its bullet entry and exit holes to show me as evidence.]

While the looting was going on in Basra, my sister took a wagon and
came back to her house with an air conditioner. I said to her, "Hey,
where did you get that?" She answered, there's *farhoud* going on. She
used the word *farhoud* for looting and ransacking [Habeeb had also used
the word *farhoud,* which refers to the looting that went on during the
pogrom against Iraqi Jewry in 1941]. Then I saw this woman whom I
knew on the street. I asked her, "Where's your brother-in-law?" Very
coolly she answered me, "They took him." She just said, "They took
him," and went on calmly with her looting as though nothing had
happened! The police, or the army, or some other government forces,
had picked up her brother-in-law and all she could coldly say was:
"They took him," and then go back to her stealing. I tell you, that's the
level people have sunk to in Iraq.[41]

The energy that the rebels ought to have put into organizing
themselves was put into stealing. The looting was on a scale that is
impossible to exaggerate and painfully sums up the depths to which
public morality seems to have sunk inside Iraq. Indeed, the phenomenon deserves a sociological study of its own. The official precursor was of course government policy toward Kuwait. That part
of it at least is understandable. However, private initiative also got
into the act. Fatma told me that a taxi service into the occupied
"nineteenth province" of Iraq was set up in Samawa for the sole
purpose of carrying back Kuwaiti "booty." People would go
empty-handed, be taken on a tour of the shops and Kuwaiti houses
for a mere ten Iraqi dinars each way, and come back with televisions,
videos, clothes, chocolates, and other delicacies. During the intifada,
the situation got worse. One man was seen hauling a kidney dialysis
machine out of a Sulaimaniyya hospital. Another was driving along
an asphalted road with his car and roof rack crammed full of things
and an oven tied to his rear bumper shooting sparks as it scraped
along. Metal frame hospital beds on roller castors were popular because they could be trundled up and down streets carrying stolen
goods like a grand supermarket cart. "You know what they did in
the military hospital," Saman, a civil engineer from Sulaimaniyya,

said. "They took out a bed with the patient still on it shouting, 'I am sick! I am sick!' But they kept on pushing it along as though he didn't exist. They wanted the bed, you see."[42]

The basic nihilistic impulse, north and south of the country, was everywhere the same. But it went unchecked in southern Iraq. Some rebels led the way, genuinely thinking that looting was what revolution was all about. Whatever the reasoning, the situation soon got completely out of hand. Every kind of public building, including museums, was pillaged and burned. The brave curator of the Museum of Nasiriyya refused to budge from her museum's gate until finally she succeeded in talking the looters out of their purpose.[43] But such people were rare. In a town like Samawa, there was a complete vacuum of authority—no Muhammad Baqir al-Hakim and no Ayatollah Khoei. Naji Hamid al-Sarraj, a local Ba'thi thug who was responsible for bringing in his own sister's teenage son on charges of being a member of the underground Islamic Da'wa Party, was crucified on the walls of the local *husainiyya* in Samawa.[44] Then his arms, legs, and head were chopped off, and the pieces left on top of the town rubbish dump until the smell became unbearable.[45] In the cities or districts that the bands of gun-toting young men controlled, every Ba'thi or Sunni, regardless of whether they were for or against the intifada, was in imminent danger of being killed. Men like Abu Haydar, Kadhum al-Raysan, and Hameed, the schoolteacher, all of whom had lived through the years of the Ba'th inside Iraq, were not ideologues or fanatics; invariably such people showed a more human face. These were the kind of men who appealed to the Allied forces for help during the uprising.

There were many Abu Haydars at first, but as the help was not forthcoming, they eventually got swamped by the militiamen pouring in from Iran and their supporters inside Iraq. They came with three truckloads of color portraits of Khomeini, 'Ali Khamanei, and Muhammad Baqir al-Hakim. The idea of the Supreme Islamic Assembly seems to have been to replicate the experience of the Iranian revolution by attaching the insurrectionary fervor inside Iraq to new symbols. A key motif in revolutionary Shi'ism, to which the Islamic Assembly was appealing, is the idea of the "hidden Imam" who, in a saying attributed to the Prophet, will return at the appropriate moment to "fill the earth with justice and equity as it is now filled with injustice and tyranny."[46] In March 1991, Iraq needed its Imam Khomeini, and if he didn't exist, he would have to be invented by pasting up lots of poster portraits, freshly minted in Tehran, on Iraqi city streets. This happens to be how Saddam thinks as well. As fast as ordinary citizens inside Iraq, like those witnessed by Hana', were tearing down Saddam's portraits, ideologically driven Islamic militants pouring in from Iran were putting up new ones.

Iranians themselves do not seem to have entered the country during the intifada—contrary to what the regime in Baghdad has claimed—apart from one exception that I can confirm: a film crew from the Iranian information ministry, which was seen in a Toyota patrol car driving around the streets of Najaf while the uprising was in full swing.[47] Unfortunately for Iraqis, they had not come to record for posterity and the outside world this historic moment in Iraqi history; they had come to film the house on Rasoul Street which the Ayatollah Khomeini lived in for fifteen years before his departure to Paris and greater things. Iranians now have their own Islamic state with its mass media bureaucracies, and these people's job, like their counterparts in Ba'thi Iraq, is to reinforce and reinvent—through television—their own symbols and allusions to the past. Revolution is a kind of theater. Burlesque, however, is the form that it sometimes takes.

What kind of men were these Iraqis pouring in from Iran? There is the story of one militiaman, an illiterate teenager who calls himself Tha'ir (clearly a pseudonym that means "revolutionary" in Arabic). The account was handwritten and dictated to a scribe. Many like it were generated by Iraqi refugees in Iran after the collapse of the uprising. Often, such documents are indigestible ideological tracts with no evidentiary value. Tha'ir's adventures do in fact read like something Fouad Matar could have written about Saddam Husain.[48] But whereas Matar's hagiographic biography oozes insincerity, Tha'ir's testimony reads like the account of a poor, confused, yet earthy soul, who in fact never killed anyone and maybe never even got to fire his gun. The will was certainly there, but probably the spirit was weak, and then the accidents of life conveniently intervened to result in this would-be "revolutionary" wandering Iraq like a child vagrant for weeks on end, miraculously surviving the anarchy and violence swirling all around him.[49]

Tha'ir claims that his unit of seventeen armed men, only five of whom survived, was the first to enter Iraq from Iran. Before entering, Tha'ir says, "my comrades and I girdled ourselves with an explosive belt." The idea was to blow himself up, killing as many Ba'thists as possible, in the event of being captured alive. Tha'ir says his unit undertook a few operations and succeeded in linking up with rebels from the inside. They holed up in a building in Basra. Tha'ir got sent off to fetch some ammunition as supplies were running low. When he came back, he found his unit under fierce attack by government forces and virtually destroyed. "By a miracle I survived, after reading my prayers and many verses from the Qur'an." He then discarded his explosive belt, "because if they were to see it on me, I would be executed in public, to say nothing of how they might defile my body." The terrified boy crawled to safety during the night, eventually reaching what looked to him like a pool of water. There he washed and drank, only to find out in the morning that he was at the exit point of a disgustingly filthy sewer.

I left cursing the age in which I lived until some villagers found me and washed my feet. Then they gave me a short *dishdasha* [the traditional long gown] and some bread. My *dishdasha* used to belong to a fat man. Eating that bread was the tastiest and most enjoyable experience of my life because it invigorated me with life. I started to cry as soon as I remembered my comrades. What could have happened to them? So I decided to cross the river and head toward Baghdad where my sister lived. But the villagers told me that first of all you don't know how to swim, secondly, the bridges are all blown up, and thirdly, the waters are at their highest. They said it was a suicidal operation, but I did it, crawling and clinging as though I was in another world. Mercy be to God I reached the other side and started walking in my bare feet toward Baghdad from Basra. There must have been 150 search points along the way. Sometimes I got through by pretending to be a beggar, other times by pretending to be mad. Once I said that my house was destroyed in Basra and I was going to my sister in Baghdad. Days passed like this.

Penniless, living by his wits from day to day, Tha'ir finally made it to the house of one of his sisters. "Her son, a childhood friend, opened the door. When I said who I was, he began to laugh at me. He was right to laugh. I was in an unbelievable state." Tha'ir had been out of Iraq for twelve years. Yet his family reunion was very short. He was given clothes, a wash, and 400 dinars, and sent quickly on his way—his very presence a death warrant to every member of the household. After more adventures, Tha'ir eventually reached Safwan and was flown back to safety in Iran in an Allied Canadian plane.

The Aftermath

THE Allied forces left four Republican Guard divisions intact during the Gulf war. These were the backbone of the force that Saddam Husain dispatched to suppress the intifada in the south. When these divisions, supported by tank and artillery units, made a three-pronged entry into the city of Najaf on Wednesday morning, March 20, 1991, the tanks had the words *"la shi'a ba'da al-yawm"* painted on them: "No more Shi'a after today."[50]

Napalm and cluster bombs had already been dropped on residential areas, and as many as thirty-five SCUD missiles fired into the city, to soften up the resistance.[51] Fired from far away, these inaccurate ballistic missiles struck without pattern or warning. Among many others, they killed Sayyid Basi Abu al-Tananir and everyone else in his house; Hasan Kamouna's wife and daughter; and Hilal Gashoosh's wife, two sons, and daughter-in-law. These missiles, whose proclaimed purpose was to "eat up half of Israel," according to Saddam Husain, demolished the homes of Abu Hameed al-Shukri, Salim Hashim, Sayyid Yousuf, Sayyid Salman, and Kadhum al-Naddaf, among others.[52] The bombing, shelling, and ballistic missile attacks were designed to sow terror, with the intention of letting every Najafi know that this regime had the means and the will to demolish the entire city and kill every individual in it if necessary.

The ground assault was supported by a fleet of helicopter gunships, which began operations by encircling the residential area of Ayatollah Khoei and bombing the neighboring houses. Hundreds gathered around the house to protect him, many of whom were killed. The surrounding area was flattened. A unit of heliborne commandos then descended upon the house of the Ayatollah and kidnapped him and his companions. Walking over the bodies of the defenders littered around the house, the pontiff of Shi'ism, and all his relatives and entourage, were loaded into helicopters and transported to a specially prepared detention center in Baghdad.[53] "They forced the Imam," said an eyewitness, "to walk without assistance, and since he cannot, he fell to the ground. Then his son helped him up and all were taken away."[54] The next day, the ninety-two-year-old cleric, who had done more than anyone else to curb the wild men of the intifada, was put on television with Saddam Husain, whose audience, it was alleged, he had "sought" so that he could denounce the intifada. A video tape of that appearance shows an old man wearing a flowing brown wool cape and a black turban as is the custom of all *sayyids* (descendants of the Prophet). A long white beard hung from a roundish face marked by brown spots around the temples. His demeanor was gentle and critically distressed; his voice breathless and the barest of whispers. After that appearance, he was kept under house arrest in Kufa for the next seventeen months. On August 8, 1992, Ayatollah Khoei (the embodiment of the history of the Shi'a from the Ottomans through the regime of the Ba'th) died in Kufa, Iraq.[55]

The soldiers deployed in the attack on Najaf (and in southern Iraq generally) appear to have been selected from the Sunni towns of Hit, Mosul, Shirkat, Beigi, and from the Yazeedi community, a tiny sect based in northern Iraq which has a history of conflict with Shi'a Muslims.[56] Iraqi soldiers who managed to escape from these units and reach the American post at Checkpoint 5 Alfa reported that they were offered a reward of 250 Iraqi dinars for each woman or child they killed and as much as 5,000 dinars for adult males.[57] However, each soldier was only entitled to claim on an upper limit of one hundred dead people a day. The slogan painted on the tanks of the Republican Guard, "No more Shi'a after today," was clearly not a local initiative; it was official policy.

In the course of entering the city, troops used women and children as human shields, forcing them to walk in front of infantry patrols and tanks so that the rebels would be unable to fire without killing innocent civilians.[58] Soldiers also forced women and children to remain in buildings which the army had turned into strongpoints. These hostages were sometimes placed on the roof of the building in full view, so the rebels would know that any attack on the building would result in their deaths.[59] Civilians who had survived the initial artillery and aerial bombardment found themselves in even greater danger from the advancing Republican Guard and the security police who followed in their wake. A favorite army tactic was to send a loudspeaker-equipped helicopter over an area of a city to announce that the citizens would be given time to evacuate before the army attacked. Leaflets were also dropped containing threats to use chemical weapons, but advising the populace to leave by specified safe routes reserved for them. For example, in Kerbala, people were advised to leave by the Hindiyya road. Along this road queues several kilometers long of civilians desperate to escape the fighting formed. Helicopter gunships then strafed them with machine guns, creating scenes of horror that have been described by several eyewitnesses. On other occasions, the army opened fire on mobs of fleeing refugees with artillery.[60]

Government forces paid special attention to those doctors who had kept their hospitals open during the uprising. Many stories of what happened to medical people have emerged. One doctor who managed to escape to the American lines reported that the security forces threw his wife, children, and brother out of a helicopter to punish him for treating wounded insurgents. Another surgeon reported that fifteen doctors at the Jumhouri Hospital in Basra were executed on the spot and then artillery was fired at the building, even though four thousand civilians—patients and their families—were still being held there.[61] Um Husain told me of one doctor who was "made to look like a sieve" in full view of all the employees working at the central hospital in Basra, who had to stand around in a huge circle and watch.[62] At Saddam Hospital in Najaf, army troops molested female doctors, murdered men with knives, and threw injured patients out of windows. Dr. Muhammad al-Khilkhali was paraded on television to set an example, and has since disappeared. Drs. Muhammad 'Ali Qraidi and Qays Hilal al-Jilawi, on the other hand, were among those executed in public by firing squads.[63]

The families of insurgents and suspected insurgents suffered particularly hideous fates. Security forces routinely murdered relatives to punish rebels. In one case, security forces surrounding the Shrine of 'Ali recognized a fighter inside. A squad then raided the man's house and "captured" his infant son. They returned to the shrine with the boy. When the father appeared, the infant was flung at the shrine and perished on impact. On another occasion, a refugee in Iran reported that army troops surrounding the Shrine of 'Ali threw severed human limbs at the fighters inside.[64]

Children who would not give their parents' names to soldiers were doused with gasoline and set on fire. Some were tied to moving tanks to discourage sniper fire from the rebels. Security forces also burned entire families in their houses when they would not give or did not know the location of the head of the household. One hundred and fifty people in Amara were tossed into the river with concrete blocks tied to their legs; thirty people suffered the same fate in Basra. The army made liberal use of "necklacing"—a form of punishment made famous in South Africa. In one incident, three children belonging to the Turfi family, the oldest of whom was nine, had tires soaked in gasoline placed around their necks and set alight. Some rebels, it has been alleged, were forced to drink gasoline before being shot. It appears that instead of crumpling into an undramatic lifeless heap, the victim explodes and burns like a torch for a short while. Executions of this sort had more impact on onlookers than lining people up against walls and mowing them down.[65]

More routine atrocities included summary executions of any man caught with his face covered. Families that returned to their homes after the fighting suffered a similar fate. "The families that had fled the fighting returned with their children. They lined them up and executed them."[66] If an army patrol was fired on from a house or neighborhood, the entire area was held accountable. In one case, a sniper firing from a hotel along Zain al-'Abideen Street killed a soldier. In reprisal, the army emptied all of the houses on the surrounding streets, gathered the residents together, and demanded that they produce the sniper. When they could not do so, the men and women were separated. The women were released after a day in uncomfortable detention. The men disappeared.[67]

The initial military assault forces were followed by units of the security police, the Intelligence services, the Special Security, the local police force, and even the traffic police. These forces ranged through the cities, snatching young men for questioning and arresting suspected opposition leaders. House-to-house searches produced new levels of outrage. According to interviews conducted by the Organisation of Human Rights in Iraq, the forces making the sweeps had a standard modus operandi: They would search all houses in a given area, confiscating anything that looked like a weapon and arresting every able-bodied male. If the sweep found no one in a house, the soldiers looted and ransacked it. Women in the houses were often abused, raped, and forbidden to wear their veils (as a way of impugning the family's honor). Following one such sweep, on March 15, 1991, Muhammad 'Ali al-Rumahi, a fifty-five-year-old man from Najaf, set himself on fire and burned to death after being forced to witness Republican Guard soldiers raping his three daughters.[68]

Men and boys picked up in such sweeps had little or no chance of survival. Iraqi refugees arriving in Iran in early April reported that more than four thousand people had been executed in the previous ten days in Najaf.[69] Indiscriminate arrests and executions were the order of the day. A survivor interviewed by Middle East Watch reports that "the army started sealing up area after area, looking for men. Everyone they found—youths, men, foreigners—they took to the sports stadiums, and from there, in large convoys, to Baghdad. These operations went on until [April 10]. . . . We don't know what has happened to them since."[70]

Organized rebel resistance first collapsed in Basra, sometime between March 7 and March 9. Bands of rebels continued to engage in hit-and-run operations with government forces, but the city never passed out of government hands. Samawa held out the longest, falling on March 29, after local tribal leaders switched their allegiances back to the government. Najaf fell around March 16, 1991, and Kerbala followed suit shortly afterwards. A senior figure in the Ba'th Party told the foreign correspondent of the BBC, John Simpson, that he thought four times as many people lost their lives in the uprising as from the Allied bombing.[71] By the middle of April 1991, some five thousand religious scholars and students from Najaf alone had been arrested. With all of their students and faculty in police custody, the religious schools shut down.[72] Entire families disappeared into the hands of the regime. Sayyid Muhammad Bahr al-'Uloum, who first told me about the tank commander in Sa'ad Square, lost dozens of members of his extended family. They were seized in an army sweep on March 22. All are still missing, presumed dead. The Iraqi security forces detained or killed all of the religious scholars of Najaf who did not escape from the country. According to one member of the Bahr al-'Uloum family who managed to avoid death or arrest, "Every turbaned person has been killed or arrested."[73]

Everything that set the Shi'a apart, and that gave them their identity, became for the first time in modern Iraqi history a target. In Najaf, the Imam 'Ali Mosque in the Amir district, the Baqee'a and Imam Sadiq mosques in Medina Street, and the Murad Mosque on Tusi Street have all been leveled. Government bulldozers have flattened portions of the vast cemeteries of Najaf with their monumental family tombs, some of which are centuries old, in order that they be concreted over.[74] About fifteen hundred Najafis had fled into the extensive catacombs underneath these cemeteries, hoping to avoid napalm attacks. Many were buried alive as the tunnels collapsed in on them. One survivor made his way to Saudi Arabia and told the tale.[75] During the intifada, the golden dome of the Shrine of 'Ali took several direct artillery hits; its main gate was destroyed; the interior was ravaged. Husain's shrine in Kerbala was much more extensively damaged. But the government's cultural offensive against holy sites, religious buildings, seminaries, and libraries continued long after the fighting in the cities was over.[76] All the palm groves surrounding Kerbala were cut down and the city center around the two shrines leveled, in the first stage of what the penniless regime claims is a massive urban renewal program for Kerbala. Ancient treasuries that have survived centuries were looted or transported to Baghdad. The "jewels, gold, [and] manuscripts, all invaluable," that were stored in the Shrine of 'Ali in Najaf, representing "gifts made over a thousand years by princes and kings," were gone. An enormous diamond which Ottoman Sultan Murad I gave to the shrine in 1634 is missing.[77]

Physical destruction is at least reparable. The same cannot be said for the burning of the libraries of the religious schools and seminaries of Najaf, Kufa, and Kerbala containing ancient manuscripts, most of which have never been properly studied or catalogued by modern methods. The Dar al-Hikma Library established by the late Ayatollah Muhsin al-Hakim and the public library run by the Hakim family on Rasoul Street (containing some 60,000 books and 20,000 manuscripts) were both burnt and ransacked. So was the Dar al-'Ilm Library belonging to the late Ayatollah Khoei, which is estimated to have contained some 38,000 books and 7,500 manuscripts. Even a proper inventory of these priceless treasures may now never be made since so many of the people who were in charge of them have either been arrested or murdered. The very real danger exists that the scale and organized character of the assault launched by the regime in Baghdad has ended a thousand-year tradition of religious scholarship and learning in Najaf, with unpredictable future consequences.

By way of making a balance sheet of all of this, *al-Thawra,* the official mouthpiece of the Ba'th, ran a series of six unsigned major articles in April 1991.[78] These mark a sea-change in Baghdad's official position on its Shi'a citizens. As was to be expected, the regime described the intifada in the south as "a dirty foreign conspiracy." The novelty came in the idea that the perpetrators were not only "foreign by virtue of their identity and nationality," but were "alien to Iraq by virtue of their mentality, conscience, and feelings." Instead of loyal Iraqis, working for the good of the Ba'th revolution and the Arab nation, which is how the Shi'a were extolled in official propaganda all through the Iraq-Iran War, they became degenerate subhumans, who observed a debased religion that had no proper moral code. This kind of language has never been used in Ba'thi publications before, and it was followed up by a stream of articles in the Iraqi press and reports of "doctoral dissertations" through the summer of 1992, all denigrating the Shi'a and their religion.

The *al-Thawra* articles went to great lengths to "prove" that Iraq's Shi'a were actually "un-Iraqi." Iranian influence over southern Iraq, it was claimed, has debased the culture and especially the religion of the Shi'a. They have lost the self-respect and close understanding of Islam that is a characteristic of the true Arab. The Shi'a are presented as a primitive and superstitious people, who worship the descendants of the Prophet—so-called *sayyids*—with a fawning adoration that disgusts the true Arab: "The adulation sometimes reaches a point where some people kiss the feet or the footmarks of the *sayyid* on the ground. . . ." Such habits, introduced by the Iranian clergy into Iraq, border on heresy and "reveal how foreigners try to belittle the Iraqis and . . . to subject them to their own will through practices which they dishonestly call religious." True Arabs "are not used to bowing down before other people."

The articles go on to attack the Marsh Arabs for their poverty, backwardness, and immorality. They are referred to as a naturally vicious, slatternly, and dirty people, descendants of Indian slaves and not true Arabs at all. Their sexual practices are disgusting and their women sluttish and immodest. "One often hears stories of perversion that would make your mouth drop," writes *al-Thawra*. Nonetheless, the unnamed author concludes, Saddam Husain treats these people "humanely, in accordance with . . . pure Arab traditions and proper Islamic principles. Whereas the *sayyid* scarcely mixes with his followers, except on big occasions, to maintain his authority and influence on an ignorant people, Saddam Husain mixes with ordinary people in the marshes without the trappings of authority, sleeps and eats with them, and shares their joy and sadness."

ARAB intellectual, religious, and official opinion ignored what was going on in Iraq during March and April 1991. Not one of the intellectuals whose ideas I will be criticizing in Part Two of this book, or who fulminated against the West for getting itself involved over Kuwait, wrote or spoke up in defense of a people that had finally gathered the courage to rise against the regime that had napalmed, gassed, tortured, and terrorized them for twenty-three years. Distinguished Arab professors speculated across dinner tables in the West about how much better off Iraqis would be if Saddam survived. Others made the rounds with American legislators and policymakers, urging them not to intervene in the relentless mass killing of Iraqis that was under way, ostensibly because of the dire consequences to the region of doing so.[79] Such reactions are a proof of moral bankruptcy; sadly, they are not even founded upon ignorance. Rather, they are founded upon a complete lack of empathy with the suffering of fellow human beings who happen—in this case—to be fellow Arabs. I can do no better than to close this chapter with the moving response of the Shi'i cleric Sayyid Mustafa Jamal al-Din, a poet and man of letters from Najaf, to the silence of the whole Arab-Muslim world:

> Let us suppose that the intifada was a southern Shi'i phenomenon, and not a generalized Iraqi one. And let us suppose that the Islamic allegiances of the Shi'a are the object of suspicion—as some Sunni extremists contend. Do not these Holy Shrines and mosques belong to Islam? Are not the fourth caliph of Islam, 'Ali ibn Abi Talib (may God's blessings be upon his face), and his sons (God's blessings be upon them), buried here? Does the bombardment of their tombs with scud missiles . . . not deserve one leaflet, one denunciatory statement coming out of some Arab or Islamic source—even if it is non-governmental—like the al-Azhar in Egypt for instance, or the Zaytouna Mosque in Tunis, or the Mosque of the Qaraween in Morocco, or the Islamic League in Saudi Arabia, or any other mosque, group, Islamic party, or man of religion. . . .

> Is the sanctity of all these holy shrines to be defiled, only because we Shi'a live beside them?

> I am not a sectarian, and there is nothing in my literary or political history which would show that. On the contrary, I have always emphasized our own ignorance, we Muslims, of the true nobility of spirit in Islam. We let confessional sectarianism overrule the tolerance and humanity of this religion. We Arabs are ignorant of the tolerance and humanity of our own Arabism. We have let it move in the direction of chauvinism.

These are my beliefs in Islam and in Arabism and they can be summarized in the fact that I consider the greatest sickness of Muslims in the current period to be religious sectarianism and racism.

We are all Arabs because we live in one part of the world and share in the feelings of all Arabs, wherever they may be. We speak their tongue and we feel their feelings, and we are bound to one another by a common fate. Arabism is not the blood that flows in some people's veins and not in others—it is these feelings, this common fate.[80]

3 ' Omar

Inside a Baghdad Prison

OMAR, a cheerful, well-groomed, ambitious young man in his early thirties, was detained for forty-two days in the Military Intelligence Services Building, located near the fountains in the al-Kadhum district of Baghdad and destroyed during the Gulf war.[1] We first met because his brother, Basil, who was in Sulaimaniyya during the intifada, had written him a long description of events in a personal letter. Omar gave me permission to use extracts from Basil's letter, written as a refugee in Iran while he was still in a state of shock from the tempestuous violence he was inadvertently swept up in.[2]

In the course of our conversation, however, I realized that Omar also had an incredible story to tell. His detention in Baghdad precedes what his brother went through in March 1991 by over two years, and looks, superficially, as though it has nothing to do with it. But Omar's story is incredible—and indispensable to understanding what happened to Basil—precisely because it is so commonplace. The prison in which Omar was incarcerated is a microcosm of that much bigger prison called Ba'thi Iraq. Untold thousands of Iraqis experienced what Omar experienced during the 1980s in Iraq; they did not have to have done anything and it did not always matter who or what they were. Omar is a Sunni Arab from al-A'dhamiyya, who was informed upon by a Kurd, and whose chief interrogator was a Shi'i. He was lucky because he was deemed innocent by the standards of the Ba'th. Nor was he tortured in the technical sense of the term. Yet from the very ordinariness of what Omar went through was born the violence of Abu Haydar's intifada.

The youngest of a family of three brothers and three sisters, Omar left Iraq the moment travel restrictions were lifted in 1990, arriving in the United States in June. We met for the first time in Cambridge, Massachusetts, in the company of two other Iraqi friends, and talked through the small hours of

*the morning. Omar is a natural storyteller with a remarkable eye for detail
and a prodigious recollection of his period of detention. He has a gift for seeing
the funny side of cruelty. I will never forget the uproariously hilarious way in
which he described his release. It was three o'clock in the morning and we had
been through hours of harrowing detail. Everyone laughed uncontrollably.
Suddenly, following some telepathic cue from Omar himself, we burst into
tears in perfect unison. In retrospect I realized that it was necessary to laugh
as hard as we did in order for us all to cry the way we did.*

*I have converted those hours of dialogue and recollections (and other later
sessions) into this first-person narrative, verified by Omar. Names, dates,
and numbers have all been changed to protect those involved, police agent,
jailor, torturer, interrogator, informer, and prisoner alike. The substituted
names come from the same ethnic or confessional background as the original—Kurd, Arab, Sunni, or Shi'i—thus preserving the democratic way in
which Iraqi prisons, like the Iraqi army, exercise violence.*[3]

I WAS born in the *al-A'dhamiyya* district of Baghdad, a hothouse of
Arab nationalism in the old days. My father was an engineer in the
Iraqi navy back in the days when it used to be called the "River
Force."[4] He took part in the 1941 coup of Rashid 'Ali against the
British which the Ba'th call the first Arab revolution. All through
the 1950s, he used to adopt a close-cropped, Hitler-style mustache.

On September 2, 1979, right after my graduation as a civil engineer from Baghdad University, I was called up for service in the
Iraqi army. I was released on April 7, 1985, the anniversary of the
foundation of the Arab Ba'th Socialist Leader Party. I put in five
years, seven months, and five days worth of service. My father and I
share some odd parallels in our lives—and some differences. For one
thing, we are both engineers. But whereas I was a soldier during the
Iraq-Iran War, and hated every second of it, he was a dedicated
nationalist officer who took part in a failed coup d'état. The price
my father paid for his political passion was dismissal from army
service and four years' imprisonment. The price I paid for being a
happy-go-lucky easygoing type of guy who just likes to have a good
time was forty-two days in an Iraqi prison. The point is, my forty-
two days in that dreadful place and his four years are whole worlds
apart.

I used to work as a site engineer in the construction of a government guest residence complex. This was a very important building.

As a result, I had excellent contacts with some of the really big Ba'thi names. I hobnobbed with their kids in parties and at the clubs. Not out of choice, you understand, but out of necessity—like everyone else.

One cold winter night in 1987, the last year of the Iraq-Iran War, I stayed up late working on some calculations to do with materials supplied to the building. But it got too exhausting and I had had a bit too much to drink after a sixteen-hour working day. It was around 1:00 A.M. by the time I got home and parked in the garage. No sooner had I dragged myself out of the driver's seat when four men jumped me in the dark like wild beasts. "Are you Omar who works in the government guest complex?" one of the men barked out.

I was so startled. Two of them had guns pointed at me. It was dark. I couldn't see anything clearly. Was I in a dream? I reached for my identification papers, which were in my wallet in the glove compartment of the car. The man barked out, "Hold it! Hold it! Don't stretch your hand! Don't move!" They must have thought I was going for a gun. They pulled me out violently. The sharpest recollection I have is that they were nervous, hysterically so.

No one showed an ID. They were shouting all the time, which added to my confusion. "What's the matter?" I asked. They yelled back, "Shut up. Not a word. Turn around." This lasted for about ten seconds. Meanwhile my mother had come running into the garage through the garden. She was pale and I remember noticing that she looked very tired. Her hair was uncovered, which was very unusual. She screamed, "Omar, Omar! Watch out! Your brother has already been taken." I didn't know what she was talking about. The moment my mother reached us, one of the four men, a tall, ugly-looking son of a bitch with hollowed-out pockmarked cheeks, gave her a strong push. She lost her balance and almost fell on the floor of the garage. He shouted at her to keep quiet in a thick hoarse voice, and then for no apparent reason began hurling abuse at her.

Is this real? I thought to myself. Outside the garage, my hands were handcuffed behind my back. I heard screaming and crying, and my mother's voice saying, "Please don't hurt him, please, please." A white Toyota Land Cruiser with civilian number plates appeared out of nowhere. These are standard issue to all of the Intelligence and secret police services. I was bundled into it. My mother stood outside screaming and saying, "Watch out. Please don't hurt him.

May God keep you safe. By God, my son has done nothing wrong!''
She was shoved into the house by the men and the door slammed
shut in her face.

Before getting into the car, they had taken my sweater off—it was
terribly cold that night—and used it to blindfold me with. As the
sweater was made of wool, I could see through the stretched
stitches. That is when I saw my brother being bundled into the back
seat of the Land Cruiser with me. The car reversed and took off.
Behind us was a second Land Cruiser.

They had been lurking around the house, it turned out, for three
hours, waiting for me to show up. The assumption was that I was
very dangerous. My brother reached for my hand from behind and
squeezed it hard as if to say, "We are really in the shit now."

Inside our car, they started a tirade. "Where have you been? You
dog and son of a dog, where the hell have you been? We've been
waiting here for hours. Don't you think we have anything better to
do? Have you been with your friend, Kifah?" It is true, I have a
friend called Kifah. They knew his name. How did they know?

"Who is Kifah?" I asked, trying to be smart. They were trying to
trick me into saying yes, so they could go after him. He lived nearby.
One of the security men turned to my brother and asked, "Has he
been to see Kifah?" "Who is Kifah?" my brother replied. For the
time being they seemed inclined to believe that Kifah, my friend,
was not involved. But not involved in what? I still had no idea. Had
I admitted that I was working with him, Kifah would be a dead man
today. Kifah, you see, was an army officer, and officers are very
severely dealt with.

Every now and then the cars would stop to pick somebody else
up. When I first got in, I noticed someone lying in the back of the
car all covered up in a blanket. I found out later that he was the
informer responsible for our arrest and that he had led the way to my
house. They didn't want my brother and I to know who he was
right away. Now the man was starting to talk. But I couldn't identify
his voice even though I felt sure that I had heard it before. I was in a
stupor, unable to think clearly, overwhelmed by the size of the
calamity that seemed to have come tumbling down on my head.
They went on picking people up. More and more people were
squeezed into the two Land Cruisers.

I can still recall the music that was being played in the Cruiser—a
tape of Um Kulthoum [the most popular female vocalist in the Arab

world]. The men were singing and clapping to it. And they were shouting and chanting at the same time. "I went out with my girl-friend yesterday," one of them told the other. It was as if we didn't exist. Suddenly he would stop chatting to his friend and turn on me, "Do you know the hairdresser Riadh?" I replied that I didn't know anyone by that name. This time I was telling the truth. "You pimp! You son of a whore! You don't want to confess. Wait until we get you there. We'll make you talk." I was shaking with fear. I had no idea why they had arrested me. They picked up yet another person. At one point we had to wait an hour at somebody's house. I heard screaming and through the stitch holes in my sweater I could see guns being pointed.

The two cars that had been parked outside my house were now packed. In our car there were my brother and myself to begin with, plus the informer. Three security men were sitting in the front, including the driver. And we were joined by one more person on the back seat. So it was a full house.

We drove for what felt like hours until the vehicle started to rise gently up an incline which I realized was a bridge. I could smell the river, although it was freezing cold outside and the windows were closed. Shortly after the bridge, the car rolled to a stop in front of a barrier. Voices were shouting out: "Stop!" The barrier was lifted. I heard the guards and the driver greeting each other. We went in.

When the car stopped and the engine was switched off, I found myself praying like I never had before. *"Ya satir, ya hafidh"* (Oh Saviour, oh Protector). Now we were ordered to get out. We were like blind people, clinging to one another like the carriages of a train. When we were being brought in, one of the guards stuck his leg out and I stumbled over it and fell. They found it very funny. I could hear the noise of the walkie-talkies as we groped our way through the darkness. *"Mawt illi kurafak! Tah hadhak"* (Let death scrape you up! You luckless sod!), they yelled as I struggled to regain my balance. Every now and then they would abuse or spit on us. We took a few steps forward, then we were told to climb, one step, two steps, three steps. I still remember the exact number. We climbed, still clutching one another in a state of complete blindness.

Being blind was very important to them. I don't know why ex-actly. They did not want us to know where we were. Probably it was for psychological reasons. When you don't know where you are, you feel forgotten, more afraid, and more inclined to confess.

Fear of the unknown is the greatest fear of all. They made sure that we didn't know where we were or who all these people around us were. Even after I got to know where I was, I kept the information strictly to myself. Had I let on that I knew, I would have been harmed by them. Those who hit, beat, and yelled questions at me gave me their names: Abbas, Husain, and so on. But all of them were fictitious, of course. That's normal.[5]

We were organized into a queue with a lot of pushing and jostling. It was freezing cold. Then the handcuffs were released and the blindfolds taken off. We were instructed to open our eyes. We were in a square building with a courtyard in the middle. The windows all looked onto the courtyard; there were no windows on the outside. Imagine a square inside a bigger one. The inside square is a concrete courtyard overlooked by windows; the rest was all rooms. The place looked like a hotel.

The first thing I saw was something like a hall with a mosaic floor and windows. There were three wooden doors on my left; the courtyard was on my right. Nothing fierce-looking about these doors. We were herded into an interrogation room in the center of which was this clerk sitting at a desk. He ordered us to undress. "Hey you! Take off your clothes." He looked like the kind of jerk you see in any government office. *Zmal allah, ib ardh allah* (God's donkey in God's land), as the saying goes.

I took off my shirt, then my trousers, and waited for him to say, "That's enough." I was too afraid to ask how far down I should strip. Since he didn't say a thing, we kept on going until all five of us were completely naked. The windows had been left open, deliberately. It was freezing cold. The guards were all warmly wrapped up in thick military jackets. You have no idea how cold it was. "Why are you shivering, you coward? What are you doing here if you can't take it?" one of them screamed at me. As though I had come here of my own accord.

Five people had been arrested that night, including Ja'far, a recent friend of mine and top soccer player who lived in Madinat al-Thawra.[6] The other two guys I had never seen before. My brother, Ja'far, and I looked at each other every now and then. They walked us down a long corridor, making us stand straight like little machines, each facing a different cell door with a tiny barred window. I heard the clanking of what sounded like a hundred locks. The iron door opened. I was shoved inside with a kick in the rear.

Never in my wildest nightmare could I have encountered such a sight. Frightfully skinny people, with piercing black eyes and bleached skins blotched in pale blue and yellow patches. Zombies. Their heads were shaven and they were dressed in rags, torn *dishdashas*. One had exactly half a *dishdasha,* another was dressed in one which covered only half his ass. I walked in nude. Nobody said a word. They stared at me with their mouths hanging open as if they had never seen a human being before. It was as if I had come from a different planet. They started to feel me, touch me with their hands. I thought they were no longer human beings as I understood the word. For five whole minutes nobody spoke one word to me. I was terrified out of my wits.

"Allah, the smell of *'arak!* How glorious," one of them finally said, taking a deep sniff.[7] That was the first thing anyone said to me.

"Come, sit down," the most handsome one among them said in a friendly tone of voice. He was kind of foreign-looking. You could have mistaken him for an American: blond, with a tattoo on his arm, he was wearing the cleanest *dishdasha* in the group.

"What's your name?" he asked.

"Omar."

"What have you done?"

"By God, I don't know."

"Don't pretend to be innocent. If you've done something wrong, say so. I can be helpful to you. I can teach you what to say to them when they come for you."

Looking back on it now, I am deeply grateful to this man. At the time, of course, I was suspicious of him. Why was he so clean and tidy? He made me sit and lie down next to him. They had a cloth in the cell which was used to wipe the floor or clean up people's vomit. It stank and was flea-ridden. Once upon a time it used to be a *dishdasha*. The blond guy gave it to me to cover myself up. Stench and fleas notwithstanding, it was better than nothing. I put it on. Anyway, how could I refuse? These men were like my seniors. I felt I must obey them.

The silence broken, questions began to come at me from every direction. Always the same subject. Why was I here? What had I done? How many of us were involved? Had I been drinking at the Sheraton? I kept on swearing to them on the Qur'an that I didn't know. They didn't believe me. Or rather, some did and others didn't. You have to understand, these men weren't mentally defective or anything. On the contrary, I found out gradually that they were all pretty smart. Cleverer than you would think the first time you set eyes on them. They had simply adapted, like animals, to the new environment.

I sensed that blondie was the smartest and most experienced one among them. He started talking to me, with the purpose of figuring out why I had been brought in.

"Did you get together a lot with friends to drink, have fun, that kind of thing?"

"Yes," I said.

"What kind of people do you mix with?"

I told him.

"Okay. Now I know why you are here."

"Why?" I asked, "I don't know myself."

"You must have said something."

He told me his name was Sa'ad al-Samarra'i. "If I tell you my story, you won't believe me."

"What's your story?" I asked.

"I am Spanish."

"What?" I exclaimed.

"I am married to a Spanish woman and became a Spanish citizen. I was active among the opposition in Spain," he said. "One day, I received a phone call from the embassy asking me to call on them. I went and they gave me a drink of tea. When I next opened my eyes, I found myself in this place."

This is exactly what the man said. I don't know whether he was telling the truth or not. He had been inside for two years and was in his late thirties.

He said he was going to teach me a number of important rules and procedures for surviving in this place. He was going to tell me about these things whether I wanted to hear them or not. You see, in every cell there was an inmate known as *al-aqdam,* the senior one. The jailors themselves designated him, not on the basis of his length of detention but because of his leadership qualities. He was not chosen to spy for them, but to organize and fix things, which made their life easier. For example, the guards didn't want to waste time teaching me to address them as *sayyidi,* my Lord. Sa'ad taught me what I was supposed to say and the proper tone of voice to adopt.

He also taught me the toilet procedures. When a cell's turn came, the door would be opened, everyone would crouch down waiting for the signal, and then run for it. By the count of ten you had to have finished everything and be back in the cell. If you went past ten, you got kicked or slapped around. I remember this old man who didn't make it once. He started crying. Weakness in a person could make a guard go berserk. They undressed the poor man and laid him flat on his stomach. The ground, I remember, was wet and freezing cold. Then the guard stepped onto his back and began walking over him, literally, backwards and forwards. The old man shook all over and cried like a baby. When the guard had had enough, he said, "I've forgiven you this time. Get up, go!"

Nor were you allowed to run to the toilet normally. Each inmate had to run doubled up, with his arms dangling to touch the floor. They called it *rikdhet al-quroud,* the Monkey Run. It happened three times a day—after breakfast, lunch, and dinner (incidentally, you had to rinse out the pot they had brought you food in at the same time). We all ran to the toilet this way, with our eyes cast downward, looking neither to left nor right, and especially not up into anyone's face. The toilet, when you got to it, was not a proper water closet; it was more like a puddle in the ground into which you relieved yourself. Sa'ad filled me in on these vital routines without my asking him. They were absolutely essential to getting along without a beating.

Later on I picked up the nuances myself. Depending on the guard, for instance, and the prevailing level of tension in the prison at the time, you might find a way to bend the rules. Some guards were more lenient than others. A few bastards took real pleasure in counting fast, or at an intermittent rate, so you would never know how much time you had left. Others hated what they did and counted slowly. It takes heroism to count slowly among such colleagues. Just because a man works in such a place, he is not necessarily a brute.

Sa'ad also prepared me for my interrogation, which was to commence in the morning. He realized how scared I was and just talked quietly and slowly without expecting anything from me.

"I give you this advice. Firstly, you are going to be blindfolded and made to wait for hours before you face the interrogator. You will be scared. You will hear shouts and screams—ignore them.

"Secondly, when you walk in and they remove the blindfold, you will see a tape recorder. You will also see ropes, chains, truncheons, and cables for whipping. They are there to scare you. They will tell you that in the recorder there is a taped conversation of yours. You will be told that you will be dangled from the ceiling and flailed with truncheons. Don't believe it. Don't be afraid. This is all play-acting. Just don't confess to something you haven't done.

"Above all, don't mention a lot of names and specific events. Even if they suggest names, try not to confirm them. Don't introduce more details into the picture. The more names you involve, the longer your own interrogation will be. The longer the interrogation, the more the damage to yourself."

Such things were easier said than done! Sa'ad was giving me an insight into the tricks of the security men. I could tell he wasn't scared himself. He had nothing to lose, as they say. I certainly had my suspicions of Sa'ad in the beginning. These lasted until what he had said turned out to be true and I realized that he could not have been acting for the security men themselves. Sa'ad was a good man, as good as they come in this world. This was his way of struggling against the system. "Any Iraqi you save is a service to the country," he said. What had he to gain from saying something like that to me?

I was in Sa'ad al-Samarra'i's cell for only one day and never saw the man again after that. But I will forever be grateful to him.

Of the other people with me in the cell, I still remember this unbelievably skinny twenty-four- or twenty-five-year-old guy who was sitting in a corner all by himself. He wasn't sure, but thought he had to have been about four years in this same room, in this same place, accused of raising money for an opposition party while serving as a soldier in the Iraqi army.

Others in the room had not been sentenced, nor had they been interrogated or anything. They were suspended in a kind of time warp. Like hostages. For instance, I saw an old man who had nothing to do with politics. His sons had been politically active and they had fled. He was being held pending their giving themselves up or getting captured.

Our cell, which was about 2.5 m by 2.5 m [8 ft by 8 ft], already had eighteen people in it; I was number 19. Everyone slept sideways, not on their backs or their stomachs. People arranged themselves in two rows, with two sets of heads pointing to the wall and two sets of feet toward the middle. Feet would get entangled and people would start kicking each other in their sleep, without waking up. Fierce kicks they were, too! One person turned a bucket upside down, sat on it, and went to sleep leaning against the door. The light was kept on all night, and every ten or twenty minutes somebody would quietly peer through to check on us. I got sandwiched in the middle and had problems breathing, my nose being squashed against the back of the inmate in front. I was the only one in the room who was completely unable to fall asleep for what remained of that night. Everyone else had adapted to the situation.

In the morning, the door was given a great big kick. No one ever knocks in this place. It slammed open, and the guard standing in the doorway called out my name. I was blindfolded, which, let me tell you, I hated more than anything else. Proper custom-made blind-folds this time. The guard ordered me to walk, stop, proceed, take a left, and so on. Finally, I was told to sit. That meant squat, because sitting on chairs was not allowed. One must always squat when a guard orders you to sit. I squatted, blind as a bat, facing the wall, for five hours at least.

I didn't know where I was. I think I was in a corridor or hallway of some sort, but I cannot be certain. He had placed me directly opposite an open window, deliberately, I am sure. The freezing air blew hard over my naked body. I only had that torn-up rag of a *dishdasha*. Practically naked, blindfolded, facing a wall, squatting with bare feet on a mosaic floor in December—try to imagine what that was like! The cold air cut through me like a knife. The cold was the worst thing. In an adjoining room I could hear vigorous sounds of an interrogation going on. When would it be my turn?

There was no torture during an interrogation, just talk and every now and then a beating—not what I call torture. There is a differ-ence between slapping, kicking, punching, even flogging, and actual torture. I call all such things beating. The guards were calling out "Muhammad!", "Ali!", "Mahdi!" I recognized the names of people who had been arrested with me or whom I knew. In the interroga-tion room they must have started on our case, whatever the case was—asking questions, kicking butts, slapping faces, barking com-mands, flogging backs. I heard it all.

It felt like I was alone in this hallway with people coming and going, doors opening and closing. Was there a guard looking over me the whole time? I don't even know. There must have been other prisoners squatting around, but I was not aware of them. That is what is so terrifying about being blindfolded. Every now and then I would get a slap on the head or a kick or a punch in the side. I wasn't allowed to stand up or make a move. Or I would hear, "You son of a bitch!" and I wouldn't even know whether I was being spoken to or not.

Then a voice from inside called out to the guards, "Bring Ayad in." Ayad is my brother. I could hear the interrogator's voice very clearly every time the door opened. Then I heard the interrogator saying, "Welcome. Who do we have here? Abu Raya." My brother's daughter is called Raya. He wanted him to know that he knew he had a daughter. Psychologically very effective. "How are you, Abu Raya? Tell us." Then the door closed and I could no longer hear what was being said. I could only hear muffled sounds, as if coming across a long distance. It must have been an hour at least after my brother was taken in that I was finally summoned.

The interrogation room was carpeted and warm. The heater was on. I was ordered to squat. "How are you, Omar?" asked a low voice coming from somewhere in front of me. "Tell me, how did you guys arrange your political meetings?"

I was totally taken aback at this and didn't answer. This was the one question that had not entered my mind during all those hours squatting blindfolded trying to reconstruct what was going to happen next. The best way to handle the situation, I thought, was to keep quiet. Maybe I was too nervous to say anything and needed to take things in. Resisting the temptation to affirm or deny things would give me time to organize my thoughts. Anyway, I hadn't the faintest idea what he was talking about. So I didn't say a word.

He went on, "You are anti-party and anti-revolution."[8] This accusation was more standard. "You have hateful feelings toward the regime and you've called Saddam names," he added.[9] He did not use the address *sayyidi al-ra'ees,* "My Master, the President," which even the big shots have to use when mentioning Saddam: he simply said, "Saddam." Now, anywhere else in Iraq it is an insult if you drop "My Master, the President" before mentioning Saddam's name. But not in this place. The man had the great privilege of just saying, "Saddam." I was terrified, because this was a sign of the enormity of his power. Never have I been so frightened in my life as I was at that point. I was trembling all over and he could see every muscle on my body moving.

"I have not said such things, *sayyidi,*" I replied.

"Yes, you have!" he suddenly shouted fiercely. "And we have the tape to prove it. Remove your blindfold!" I struggled to undo the damn knot in vain. He got extremely angry with me. "Undo the blindfold, you ass!" He was shrieking this time. Two or three voices started to order me around all at once.

"Undo the front bit first."

"Push it up a little bit."

"Hurry up, we don't have all day!"

I was totally confused. When I eventually succeeded in taking the thing off, I couldn't believe my eyes. This was the interrogator! Having heard him shouting and screeching abuse, I had formed a totally false impression of what he was going to look like. You wouldn't think he was an interrogator if you saw him in the street. He didn't even have a mustache—you expect a man in this kind of a job to sport a Saddam-style mustache! His hair was thinning at the front and long at the back. He was wearing a pair of jeans, and a colorful jacket on top of a plain T-shirt. A thin man, and much younger than you would expect. His speech was a mixture of standard newspaper Arabic and slang, spoken in a southern Iraqi Shi'i accent. You wouldn't believe that such a pleasant-looking person could have such a horrible voice. The first thing I saw when I opened my eyes was this man, my interrogator, sitting at a desk with his finger on the play button of a tape recorder sitting before him.

It was incredible—everything was happening just as Sa'ad had said it would. Deep inside, however, I believed that he did have a tape. He was, after all, the authority. Would you take a fellow prisoner's word over this man's word? But there is no question about it—what Sa'ad had said stayed in my mind, and it proved to be very useful. Sa'ad's advice had made me reluctant to respond to the interrogator's statement quickly. Had I not been warned, I might have blurted things out to the interrogator that I would later regret, and then how would I have gotten out of that mess! Life is separated from death by the breadth of a hair in a place like this. Sa'ad had given me an edge.

I paused again, and then said, "No, *sayyidi,* I haven't said anything."

"We've got the person who recorded what you said."

But he did not play the tape. Had he been telling the truth, he would have played it. But he didn't.

"Who is he, *sayyidi?*"

All this time I had been looking straight ahead and up at my interrogator from my squatting position, never turning my head, not even fractionally. This was expected of me. "Turn your face left," the man ordered.

To my left, suddenly, appeared the familiar shape of my friend

Nabeel, clean-shaven, and very smartly dressed in the special blue military uniform of the Iraqi air force. Even as I am speaking to you now I can visualize his navy blue beret, sitting cockily slightly off to one side. My scalp began to tingle. What was I supposed to make of this? Nabeel was their agent and had informed on me. What else could it mean?

At this critical point, barely aware of what I was doing, I made a very smart move. I think it saved me. Instead of denying or showing anger, or any other kind of ill-feeling toward Nabeel, I smiled sweetly at him.

"Hello, Nabeel. How are you?"

"So you know him," said the interrogator in a loud voice.

"Why, of course I do. Nabeel is my friend."

I sensed that Nabeel had become all confused.

"Nabeel, what do you have to say. Did Omar insult Saddam or didn't he?" snapped the interrogator.

"Yes, *sayyidi*. He did. He did talk," said Nabeel in a subservient tone, with a transparently false sickly smile plastered all over his face. But the color was draining away. Things had changed. I continued denying I had said any such thing without attacking Nabeel in any way. But inside I was boiling over with hatred, especially after I found out that he had told the interrogator all kinds of personal details about my girlfriend.

"Tell me, Omar, do you fuck her in her father's house? I want to know how you do it. Speak up! You know we were watching you that time you did it in the car. We have it on tape!"

I said nothing. Then he started on my father, who was half paralyzed because of a stroke. The stroke had descended on us during one of the big battles of the war when my brother was at the front and the whole family was keyed up with worry over him. The doctor said that tension had precipitated it. From then on my father and I developed a special relationship. I was the one who shaved him. I was the one who took him to the toilet and cleaned up after him every day. And I was the only one who could understand his speech after his voice went all funny from the paralysis.

"This father of yours is obviously a despicable bastard to have brought sons into the world like you and your brother. He deserves to be punished."

Up to this point my interrogator had been speaking very quietly. Then he suddenly screamed in a voice that almost brought the roof down.

"I shall bring him this instant and hang him up here! GUARDS! Bring his father, *Bring that bastard of a father of his!*"

The tears almost drowned me out when he said this. I couldn't see a thing and felt like a complete degenerate for having brought such pain on the man who brought me up.

"*Sayyidi,* God preserve you, please, *sayyidi,* my father is paralyzed. He was one of Iraq's nationalist officers in 1941. He is a sick man. Please, *sayyidi,* God preserve and watch over you, he is a great Arab nationalist."

My breakdown and nationalist appeal seemed to impress the interrogator. I felt he respected me for the fact that I was trying to protect my father. Maybe he hadn't known that my father had spent four years in the prisons of the ancien régime because of his role in 1941. The Rashid 'Ali affair of 1941 is a big thing with the Ba'thists.

He told the guards to go away and that was the end of my first interrogation. I was sent off to a new cell that had only two other inmates in it. The following day, when I was on my ten-second Monkey Run to the toilet, I saw Nabeel, half naked, in filthy rags, just like everyone else. Nabeel had been playing the role of informer in a big charade prepared for my benefit. He was in the same boat as I was! Worse in fact. In the end, I spent forty-two days inside and was decreed innocent, whereas he, poor chap, got life imprisonment.

I make no claims to saintliness. Saints are dead men in Iraq. The important thing is to be smart and know how to adapt. I was put in Nabeel's position once, long before I got arrested. I had this friend, Hashim, who came from 'Amara. In other words, he was a Shi'ite from the south like my interrogator. He was in the same army unit with me and was a great fan of Khomeini's, as so many Iraqis were in the early 1980s. Unfortunately, he was also not very smart. He talked too loosely about Islamic revolutions, without doing anything about it, mind you; he just talked. One day the intelligence officer of our unit summoned me to his room. Upon entering, the door was locked behind me. There were three or four people inside who immediately started heaping praise on me. "You are such a good man. From such a good family." All that kind of rubbish. Intelligence people praising me. Naturally I got scared. I smelled trouble, but there was no exit. The bastards were all around. What's this about? I wondered. Suddenly, a remark slipped in, along with all the pandering and bantering, about "my friend" Hashim. They were onto him.

"Oh, him," I said, before they had a chance to say what they wanted. "He is not really a friend. I just give him a lift from time to time." If I refused to work for them, I would automatically become suspect. In an inspired flash, I went on in the same breath, "Why on earth didn't you ask me to spy on him earlier?" "What do you mean?" the senior officer asked. "You see, on a couple of occasions I praised the government in front of Hashim and he has by now got the firm impression that I am a committed Ba'thist. I am sure he doesn't trust me any longer." It was a clever move on my part, even if I do say so myself. You wouldn't believe what happened next! The imbeciles actually started blaming one another for failing to ask me to spy on Hashim earlier. Shortly afterwards they got to him through somebody else.

That time, I was quick on my feet. But in this predicament I knew I was not going to slip out so easily. I had several more interrogation sessions after that initial one, then finally they left me alone; they were too busy sorting out new batches of people all brought in on the same charge. What was the whole thing about? Play-acting and games! Believe me, that is the be all and end all of the whole business. I ended up in these sessions informing on two acquaintances, both of whom were already implicated.

The first person was Husain Halbous, the man who started the whole nightmare.

Husain was an unsuccessful second-rate TV actor, who was planning to flee Iraq. He was incredibly naive—not dangerous at all, a heavy drinker who moaned constantly about his years of military service and his work. I had no idea he was planning an escape. But can you blame him? Every young Iraqi man I know thinks about it. Husain had convinced himself that he had to flee via the Kurdish areas to Iran. He claimed to like the Islamic regime of Khomeini even though he drank a bottle of 'arak a day. He stumbled upon a Kurd who promised to make all the arrangements. The guy asked Husain for some letters which would convince the Iranians he was genuine. Husain was dumb enough to write those letters. Can you imagine? Naturally, the Kurd turned out to be an agent for Military Intelligence.

Shortly afterwards Husain got a phone call from a woman who started flirting with him, claiming she fancied him. The poor sod got all worked up. Earlier, he had been living with his cousin who was a lieutenant. A nice, quiet man who never involved himself in anything controversial. The telephone caller told Husain that she fancied him and that her sister fancied his cousin. They fixed up to meet near al-Mustansiriyya University. The date turned out to be a trap set by Military Intelligence. Husain and his cousin were both arrested.

None of us knew anything about all of this. Husain simply stopped showing up at our weekly evening get-togethers. They tortured the living daylights out of him, probably thinking that he was a genuine Iranian agent. They never realized that the poor man was too much of a deadbeat to spy for anyone. Well, of course, he started feeding them with names; the more names he spewed out, the deeper he sank into the shit. I saw him only once, halfway through my detention, thin as a rake and all doubled up as though structurally deformed. He was hobbling to the toilet with his hands and feet in chains. Husain was used to inform on my brother during his interrogation. My brother told me Husain's poor cousin was also pulled up and forced to beat Husain over the head with a shoe in front of him and the interrogator. Can you imagine how that humiliates and destroys a human being?

Husain confessed to anything you care to think of. He implicated me, my brother, Nabeel, and many others. Husain was the informer lying on the floor of the white Toyota Land Cruiser wrapped in a blanket the night they picked me up. Then those whom he named brought up new names, and so on. Imagine a huge ball of string which begins to unravel the moment you find a loose end. Husain was that loose end. Forty-five people were eventually implicated on this one case. I knew eight of them at the most. When I informed on Husain, all I actually said was that I knew him to be "anti-party" and "anti-revolution," and this was what they wanted to hear. It took months before they executed him and his cousins and delivered their broken bodies to their families in sealed boxes. It is of course against the law in Iraq to open a coffin delivered in such circumstances, and therefore to wash it and prepare it for burial in the way prescribed by Islam. Nor can the family announce the burial, as is the custom in Iraq, and arrange for ceremonies in the traditional way. Everything has to be secret. Even the coffin has to be taken to a special location especially designated "for traitors." Crudely painted on the box, with the paint streaking down the sides, is the word "Coward."

Along with the secrecy come the lies. There was a standing joke in the prison about a group of prisoners who were called *jama'at al-'afo,* the pardoned ones. The Iraqi government, as everyone knows, was constantly issuing amnesties or pardons to deserters or to people who had fled from the country. Some poor suckers actually fell for it and returned or gave themselves up. Apart from a handful who got displayed on television, the rest of these "pardoned ones" were with us in jail awaiting execution.

Why do you think Nabeel got life imprisonment? Because he displayed weakness and said too much. He believed them when they said that the more information he volunteered, the easier things would go for him. Things don't work that way in the Iraqi prison system. There was absolutely no need to give any details about my girlfriend. The Ba'th despise weakness in a person, and crush him even more fiercely when it gets obviously displayed. My older brother Ayad got sentenced to five years because he implicated himself. The mistake that Ayad made was to attempt to please his interrogator by admitting that he knew Husain was an army deserter. I simply confessed that two men I knew hated the regime. When they didn't get any additional details from me, they assumed that since I had already proven my loyalty, I didn't know any more. My interrogation was therefore shorter and less painful, just as Sa'ad had said it would be. My God, how much I owe that man!

Ayad used to be a dissident Ba'thist. My other brother was a leftist who grew up in the fifties. We were not all influenced by my father's Arab nationalism, you know. Those who grew up in the sixties became Ba'thists. People forget, but being a Ba'thi was the most normal thing in the world to be in those days. Shi'ites were doing it as much as Sunnis. I am younger than my brothers and came of age in the 1970s under the Ba'th. To my way of seeing things, there is not much difference between being a Ba'thist, being a Communist, being a Pan-Arabist, or nowadays being an Islamicist in politics. You think they are so different? Bullshit! Everybody has his own ideology. I don't even hate what the Ba'th stand for, in spite of all they have done to me. They want the unity of the Arab nation. Fine. No problem at all. You are free to think what you like. Just don't hurt someone else while doing it. That is all I want out of life these days. But in Iraq, people believe in things fiercely until death, until other people's deaths, that is. They go on believing this in spite of the fact that everything depends on how old you were when you got politicized!

The interrogator, who seemed to be a religious man himself, took a real dislike to Ayad. I could tell from the way he treated him during sessions when they would bring us in together. He constantly said things like, "By my prayers, I will make you talk!"[10] He could be speaking softly and calmly, and then all of a sudden he'd shriek so loudly you'd jump out of your skin. He would start banging the desk and screeching until you thought he was having a fit. The guards would come rushing in as soon as they heard him; they were just as afraid of him as we were. This interrogator conveyed enormous authority through his terrible voice. He would order them to beat Ayad (once or twice he did it himself). They would rain down blows on my brother, jumping on him, kicking him in the ribs, punching him in the face. These guards, emulating their boss, would turn into wild animals out of sheer anxiety to please him. "Stop! Get out," he would suddenly order, abruptly dismissing them as if they were pieces of dirt. All of a sudden he'd switch to being a different person—now he was your saviour. You'd actually start to like him. This was a very strange man.

Of course you hated his guts, because you realized that he was playing with you, exploiting your weakness. But during the interrogation, you would feel that he was capable of kindnesses. It was up to you to reach for them. However weird the man may have been, he was very able and professional about his job. He had to go through all of this with forty-five people, fishing for information, checking and cross-checking it with different detainees. In the end, he had to produce a report which pieced together the whole complicated business. And then he was going to be judged by that report. Could he afford to conclude that Husain Halbous was just a deadbeat? That all the effort that had gone into arresting and interrogating forty-five people was for no very big reason at all? Of course not. Interrogation in Iraq is no longer about information extracted by thugs wielding cables and flailing away with their fists.[11] It is about psychology and play-acting. Everybody is playing games.

I got my fair share of slaps, kicks, and punches, not what I call torture. Real torture began around midnight. I couldn't tell you the time exactly. But I did hear the screaming every night. My brother told me about a special room, a little bigger than an ordinary cell, with ropes hanging from it. I am not claiming anyone hung me upside down or flayed the skin off my back with weird instruments and stuff like that. One night I woke up with a start from the sound of a metal door getting hit repeatedly. I peeked out of the window overlooking the corridor and saw somebody in pajamas being held by four men who were banging his head against a cell door as though he was a battering ram. They'd just brought him in. He was already lost to the world. My forty-two days in detention is nothing when you compare it with what that man went through.

Still, I have to tell you about every memory, every image of those days. I want you to know. I want you to believe me when I tell you all these stories. Wanting others to know what it was like burns inside me like a red-hot iron. I don't really expect anyone to understand what I am talking about. I have seen what happens to Iraqis who spend too long in the West. They go soft. They haven't even the stomach to see nasty things on television. I saw them turn their heads away from the sight of other Iraqis who had fled Saddam's helicopter gunships during the intifada and were exhibiting their gaping big open wounds on television. As they turned their heads away from the pictures in disgust, I got all twisted up with anger inside. How can they understand what Iraqis are going through if they are unable to watch such things? Maybe something is wrong with me. I don't know any longer.

In prison we had only one source of contact with the outside world: the call to prayer. We used to hear it done twice each time: in the Sunni way and in the Shi'i way. On the wall of my cell, prisoners used to feel the urge to commune with God or pass messages. With what, you might ask. They used the very lead pencils we were all issued with to write down our confessions. They would write things like "Oh, God!", or "Oh, 'Ali, Oh, Husain, save me!" Or there would be something like "I am going to be executed on such-and-such a day. Please you who may read this let my family know."

I cried a lot in prison. One of the guards was a mean son of a bitch who developed an intense dislike of my brother. He picked on him one day for the way he had washed his pot. Ayad got spreadeagled against the wall of the corridor and whipped with cables. I could hear him screaming without being able to see a thing. I started banging my own head against the wall. My cellmates stopped me from doing damage to myself. But I couldn't stop crying for the rest of the day. I just crouched in a corner and cried and cried.

One of my crying bouts was brought on by two guards studying English together. One of them was apparently looking at a book and asked the other what the word "school" meant. "I don't know," his friend answered. I had been blindfolded for hours, and could hear them talking in the background. Suddenly one of them said, "Let's ask this bastard. He looks educated." I told them what I thought the word "school" meant. "Hey, are you really an engineer?" the guard shouted at me. I said yes. *"Tah hadhak, ya ghabi"* (Curse your luck for coming here, you idiot), he said. I told him, "Yes, *sayyidi,* I am an idiot."

Those words affected me more than all the hits and the slaps to which I had become accustomed. Suddenly, I was overwhelmed with emotion. When you're inside a place like this, you forget the outside. This guard had reminded me that I was an engineer, that I had an education. Why, I even spoke English. Yet here I was, squatting blindfolded facing the wall, just waiting for the next blow. My luck was running out. I felt an intense self-pity and began to cry. I have cried before but never like this. Don't think I was weak. Many inmates broke down regularly. One of my later cellmates would start crying for no obvious reason at the same time as he would slap his head with his hands over and over again. Because of all this the guards were absolutely terrified that someone might commit suicide. You wouldn't believe the fuss that was made when one of them lost a razor blade.

Along with self-pity comes hate. While in detention I felt that I was forgotten by everybody, including my mother. She cried when I told her this after I came out. Instead of resenting Saddam, I started to resent all the people who were enjoying themselves while I was rotting away. It was as if they were responsible for my plight and I had a right to resent them. I don't know why I blamed the whole of society, but I did. That's the truth. The Intelligence services understand this selfishness in all human beings—the tendency to start hating others who are as innocent as you are. They reinforce it skillfully by increasing your humiliation in every little way possible.

The guards patrolled the hallways or sat in the corridors wearing masks on their faces and gloves on their hands. Scabies and other diseases were widespread. A half-naked man on his haunches, before a fully dressed, cable-wielding masked guard, is quite a sight. Every hour somebody died from some disease or other. That was the reason for the masks and gloves. Not that they worked perfectly. Our guards were always very thin men, their faces yellow and sickly, exuding wickedness. They had lived and worked in the place too long; their lives stank. I got scabies and scratched myself until I drew blood. But I never knew what scabies were while I was in prison. Lice were widespread. Guards generally did not like prisoners to come into any kind of physical contact with them, but once one of them asked a cellmate of mine to shave the hair in his armpits and around his penis. Do you know how humiliating that is? You feel vile, and end up hating yourself, which is of course what they want.

When they shaved my head bald, they made me walk out of the cell on all fours like a dog and stick my head between the legs of this guard sitting on a chair who was holding an electrical shaving machine. All the time I thought I was being prepared for execution. When my brother saw me bald like that, he cried for days on end. Having given up all hope of getting out himself, he had been hoping that I would. After scabies became widespread, they instituted new washing and shaving procedures. The guards shaved us using old blades. Everyone's face was crisscrossed with cuts.

Our food was often just thrown into the cell by demented inmates who accompanied the guards. There were a lot of crazy or demented people around in prison. When you hear the sound of locks opening, you get ready, and rush for the food sitting outside the door the same way you rush for the toilet: on all fours. You try to pull the food into the cell very quickly before receiving a kick. The guards peer in every few minutes while you are eating. If you don't eat, they force-feed you. The crazy inmate walks in front of the guards passing out the bread and the pail with lentil soup or some kind of stew. Behind him two guards saunter, swinging their cables. In the morning they throw one hard-boiled egg each and a piece of bread through the tiny barred window. Everyone dashes around trying to catch his before it hits the floor.

Not all of the guards were like the man who whipped my brother. One of the guards who was in charge of our toilet routine caught me trying to peek into my brother's cell. "Who is it that you are looking for in the cell?" he asked. I was afraid to answer because of how it could be interpreted. You see, none of the guards knew that Ayad was my brother. But this man spoke softly, "Omar, you're a good boy, I want to help you." I told him, "I am looking out for my brother." That night he woke me up, opening the door carefully. Clearly worried at the risk he was taking, he led me to Ayad's cell next door. I went delirious with delight. I couldn't imagine anyone doing such a kindness for me. If he'd let me kiss his shoe to express my gratitude, I'd have done it gladly. From when I first set eyes on this man, I could feel he was different. There was a distant reflective look about his eyes.

He moved a little way back so I could have the pretense of privacy with my brother. I took Ayad's hand through the small barred window on the cell door and started kissing it all over. We both did. Neither one of us could speak. Finally I had to tell the guard, "Take me back, *sayyidi,* I can't take this anymore." It gave him pleasure that I had been able to see my brother. Suddenly he blurted out: "This job is contemptible. Only dogs do it; I'm a dog." I began to become afraid that somebody would hear him and then I would get blamed.

I also informed upon a second man, as I told you before—a very different kind of a person from Husain Halbous. Have I been trying to put off telling you? Maybe.

There was a group of us who used to get together and have fun. We drank like fish, played the *'oud* [Arab lute], made up songs, and chatted. Husain Halbous, Nabeel, my brother and I, and a whole lot of other people, were all part of the group. Drinking had a lot to do with loosening people's tongues during these parties. Iraqis have taken to drinking very heavily, especially soldiers, who often spent their entire leave during the Iraq-Iran War drinking. Many soldiers had serious family and sexual problems. Impotence, or general inability to perform sexually, was common. We talked about such things during our parties. The stories were either very sad or very funny. Men became alcoholics as a way out of their problems. We drank a lot during our evening get-togethers—the basic impulse being to have a good time, to forget everyday life.

Inevitably, politics came into the picture. You couldn't help it. What do I mean by politics? Exchanging news and gossip. Scandals were a favorite subject. "Have you heard the latest? Saddam was supposed to have gone somewhere but he sent his double instead and the idiot messed it up. . . . Ha, ha! Isn't that funny?" That kind of thing. Occasionally we got serious talking about what should or shouldn't happen, and how it would be wonderful not to have a dictatorship. Let the best man rise to the top in every profession, that was our motto. The army was the richest source of jokes. Every young Iraqi wants the institution abolished. It goes beyond hatred even; the word "army" has become unbearable to young men who experienced what it was like in the 1980s. What benefit has it brought to the country? Even the 1941 revolution which my father took part in and which the Iraqi army is so proud of was supported by Nazi Germany.

The life and soul of these gatherings was a friend of my brother's, a man in his early forties called 'Ali al-Nasiri. He would introduce new people and prompt most of the venting of frustration. When they failed to bring him in along with the rest of us, my suspicions were aroused. I thought he was the one who had reported us to the authorities. He was picked up a few days after us. After they pulled 'Ali in, the intensity of my own interrogation declined dramatically. You have to understand that no one knew what had happened to Husain Halbous at the time, or that he had informed on all of us.

No one knows much about 'Ali. He is a mysterious ex-Communist with a long political history. I met him through my brother. 'Ali was wounded in the skull during the heyday of the Islamicists in the early 1980s. A bullet chipped off a bit of the bone of his skull and he almost died. He let me feel the hole, now covered up by skin. He had been driving to his home in Madinat al-Thawra, in an official car—a white Toyota Land Cruiser, no less. The official story is that militants from the Islamic Da'wa Party, assuming that he was working for the security police because he was in that kind of a vehicle, attempted to assassinate him. "Did the Da'wa Party really fire at you?" I asked him once. He laughed as though to indicate that the story was more complicated than that, but said nothing. In Iraq, you never go on pushing on something so sensitive. The story has a further twist. Rumor has it that Saddam phoned 'Ali personally in the hospital and paid for him to be sent to Germany for treatment. You see, he used to be an embassy official stationed abroad before the shooting and went on to run an import-export agency after it. That is a privileged thing to be doing in Iraq. They don't give anyone off the street a license for doing it. His partner in the business was a high-ranking intelligence officer. 'Ali no longer takes part in any political activity, at least so far as I am aware. But like any educated Iraqi, he used to talk and criticize the government. He was a highly educated man, a marvelous singer and a great entertainer.

My mother and my brother's wife kept a vigil by the door of our house for three days after Ayad and I were arrested. 'Ali came by and she told him what had happened. She remembers him laughing and saying to her, "They are coming for me too, then. I had better prepare myself." He told me once how in his youth the police were waiting for him while he was sitting for his baccalaureate exams.

After finishing the exam, he calmly walked over to them. They pulled the pencil out of his hand and dumped him in prison.

Upon hearing about our arrest, 'Ali went to Najaf and Kerbala to pray. Then he returned to his Baghdad house; he knew that it was hopeless to run away. There are seven search points on the 70-kilometer stretch between Baghdad and the town of Falouja alone. If you hide in someone else's house, they'll hurt everyone in the house as much as you. 'Ali could never put a friend in such a position. The whole of Iraq is a prison. So 'Ali went home, had a shave, put on a clean white *dishdasha,* and started drinking. This was a remarkable man, with nerves of steel. That is how they found him when they came.

They brought 'Ali into a small interrogation room. Of course he was blindfolded. The interrogator was sitting at the table. 'Ali was told to squat on the floor, in his clean *dishdasha.* Ayad and I were standing in the corner, having been instructed to keep absolutely still and silent.

"You're still a Communist, aren't you?"

'Ali replied that he wasn't. Both men were Shi'ites and spoke to each other in a southern accent. I had the impression that 'Ali was being treated in a special way, as though the interrogator sensed that he was the key to the whole affair.

"I want to know all about the structure of your organization. Who is its head?"

'Ali had his back straight, his head raised high as though he could see through the blindfold, and he was talking normally. He did not look in the least bit afraid. I was trembling all over, uncontrollably.

Suddenly 'Ali said, "I would like to have a cigarette." A cigarette is a very big thing in prison. When they give you one, that's a terrific day. The interrogator put one in his mouth and lit it.

"Now we have given you a cigarette," the interrogator said, his voice dripping with sarcasm, "is there anything else you want?"

"Some water."

This was the first time I had seen my interrogator struggling to keep his temper under control. 'Ali had got to him. The guard was ordered to fetch some water.

"You have been criticizing the government."

"We have nothing to do with politics; I am a man who likes to fool around and have some fun."

He said it in such a funny, gutsy way that even I, in my pathetic state, felt a laugh start bubbling up from inside. The man was as cool as a cucumber, as if he did this sort of thing every day. Now the interrogator really lost his temper. He leaped out of his chair and bowled 'Ali over on the ground with a kick in the chest. 'Ali got verbally abused and slapped and shoved around quite a bit. But on the whole they treated him all right and they got nothing that they didn't already know out of him. At the very end of the whole thing, 'Ali was ordered to take off his blindfold and look in our direction.

"These people informed on you."

He took it very coolly, confirmed that we were his friends and denied everything all over again. But I could see the anger in his eyes. 'Ali never informed on me, or, as far as I can tell, on anyone else. I found out later that he had praised me to the interrogator and denied that I was present when anti-government things were being said at our parties. I tried, unsuccessfully, to visit him in prison where he and my brother were serving their five-year sentences. The intelligence officer who was his business partner eventually got him out of prison in less than a year. 'Ali remains a big enigma for me. I respect him enormously, but I don't know what to make of him.

On the forty-second day of my arrest, a group of five of us were brought into a room and had our blindfolds released. "You're going out," someone said. Instantly the five of us started crying, as though we were in mourning. We hugged and kissed one another.

A guard directed us to a room with a huge pile of clothes rising like a hill in the middle of the floor. I grabbed a pair of ripped trousers, a shirt that did not have a single button on it, and some torn slippers. Their owner might very well have just been executed for all I knew. The ring and necklace I was wearing at the time of my arrest were officially returned to me.

Then we got a lecture. The five of us had to stand up. The officials were all smiles. I was holding my oversized trousers with one hand and my buttonless shirt with the other. A senior-looking man instructed us to tell anyone who asked that we had been away on holiday. He went on, "If they ask you whether you saw Jamal, or Muhammad, or 'Adnan, just deny seeing anyone." One of the five whom I don't know asked in the most obsequious way imaginable: "*Sayyidi,* I'm a government employee. Will I need a paper for my department?" You could tell from the smiles that it was no longer a risk to ask such a question. Things had changed. He was told that everything was taken care of and there was no need for any papers. Everybody should just show up at work as though nothing had happened.

Then the guards came to shake our hands, one by one. One of them said: "I hope we didn't bother you or hurt you in any way?" The chief guard I remember particularly well. He was wearing a red sweat suit and took the business of making up very seriously, hugging each one of us, like we're supposed to be friends leaving to go on a long trip. I gathered up the courage to ask one of the guards if I could see my brother. He agreed on condition that I did not say a word. I was very emotional when I saw Ayad. The guard let me into his cell. Ayad started kissing my hand. I whispered that I had been released. We both began to cry. Then he cried out to the guard, *"Sayyidi, sayyidi,* what have I done that I have to stay here?" He was pleading like a broken man. There are no words to describe how terribly guilty that made me feel. I was leaving him behind. He was so unbelievably skinny and had been really hurt. I felt that my brother was on the edge of breaking down.

They blindfolded us once again, put us in a Land Cruiser, and asked us to keep our heads down tightly between our legs. We were not supposed to see where we were going. The car could not have driven more than half a kilometer when, suddenly, came the last command: "Open your eyes." I won't forget that instant until the day I die. In unison, like one man, all five of us said: "Sun! The sun!" The guard sitting in the front said, "So what's the big deal? Don't overdo it." The sun was so bright. For forty-two days I hadn't seen it.

They dropped us off next to Kadhumiyya Hospital, to grab the nearest taxi. The chief guard who had kissed each one of us in the prison then asked, "Do you need money?" I said, "No, *sayyidi,* I don't." He knew of course that we didn't have a penny. Not one of the five took money from him.

Whichever taxi we stopped fled the moment the driver got a chance to look at us. Finally, a car stopped, not a taxi. Three of us hitched a ride. My heart was on fire—I just wanted to get home. Along the way, I saw a girl I knew from college days. She didn't recognize me. I ran to the door of the house. I had missed seeing my mother most of all. She wasn't there. My nephew came rushing out. We were crying, hugging, and kissing. I entered the hall and there was my father on a chair. He began to kiss my hand and I fell into his arms. He had lost so much weight. Five months later he died.

My mother, I was told, would be back later in the evening. I picked up the telephone, which felt as if it came from a different world. It was like using it for the first time. I called my best friend; his sister answered. The phone dropped from her hands and joyous cries could be heard from their house. They came rushing over in their nightgowns and barefoot, even though we were seven houses away. They thought I had died. Everyone was crying and passing around chocolates. I phoned for some alcohol. When it came, I drank whisky and ate a salad.

I looked at myself in the mirror. Long scraggly mustache, bald-headed, with a bluish complexion. Blue, not yellow. Black circles around my eyes. I was as thin as a stick. I was shocked at how I looked. I had a bath and changed into decent clothes. Now I felt like a king. My mother arrived, accompanied by one of my sisters. I went out into the front patio so I could see her. She didn't see me at first. "Mother, this is Omar." She couldn't believe it and fainted on the garage floor. I thought she had died. I rushed up and kissed her face all over. Then she reached out for me from the floor, hugging me, crying and shaking all over. She couldn't look at me without trembling. My sister came out of the car. I recognized her and called out, but it was dark. She seemed bewildered. Also I looked so different, bald and sticklike. Then she realized who it was and she too collapsed. I rushed over to her; she was screaming at the top of her lungs: *"Omar, Omar, is it you? Is it really you?"* My brother's wife the same. I was running back and forth between them like a crazy man.

WHAT were we arrested for? What was it about the forty-five of us that made the intelligence people think we were so dangerous? I have told you about Husain Halbous's predicament, which started the whole thing off, and about the enigmatic 'Ali al-Nasiri, who was the driving spirit of our whole group. Husain and three others were executed. One of the other three executed was my friend Ja'far, who was picked up on the same night in the same Land Cruiser as I was. He used to play for Iraq's soccer team. For a while we shared a cell. He was married to two women, both of whom he was very fond of. This was a real family man. He used to cry every day over his four-year-old daughter, to whom he was very attached. He was sure that he would get out, because he had really done nothing.

Ja'far had too many other things on his mind to joke or make fun of anything, much less the government or Saddam Husain. But he got executed. Why, I don't know. It is all arbitrary. There was no rhyme or reason for anything. However, like 'Ali al-Nasiri, Ja'far lived in Madinat al-Thawra. That's never a good sign. This suburb of Baghdad has a long history of political militancy and it is teeming with people. Maybe that's what got him in the end. Who knows?

Three people including myself were not charged with anything and let out. Everyone else was sentenced, from nine months to life. So, what was all of this about?

Well, in the course of my interrogation, it became clear that Iraqi Intelligence had somehow developed the idea that our wild drinking and singing parties with their gossip, songs, and jokes were actually meetings of a secret new anti-government political party. That is why the very first question the interrogator asked of me, and later of 'Ali, was, "How did you guys arrange your meetings?" He was talking about clandestine meetings of a secret organization that never existed. The case was deemed to be about state security at the highest levels, and that is why they assigned it to the sixteenth division in Military Intelligence. By the end of the investigation, however, they seem to have come to the conclusion that no such party was in the works. So they executed only four people, and let five of us out.

In Iraq, words can kill. Words are what got us in the end, not anything we did. I know a woman who wanted a divorce. Her husband was a real asshole who refused to give it to her. She secretly taped him cursing Saddam, and the man was executed. She inherited his property and lives today in my own neighborhood in *al-A'd-hamiyya*. That is the power of words. Suppose, on the other hand, I had drunk too much and instead of making a joke about the Iraq-Iran War, had run over a pedestrian and killed him while driving back home. This would not be a big deal. Don't get me wrong. Drunken drivers get arrested in Iraq like everywhere else in the world. But with the proper connections, they get released on bail and later on tried in ever so normal court proceedings attended by a lawyer of their own choice. With a sharp lawyer, a bit of luck, and a few connections, one can get away lightly from the whole thing, like anywhere else in the world. Words are a different matter all together. Words get you into more shit in Iraq than anything else.

I don't know exactly what Husain Halbous said we said when

they began torturing him. But I do know he told them about all sorts of different things that got said at our parties. I know for a fact that they got particularly worked up about a joke which someone made up at one of 'Ali's evenings of partying and fun. Husain told them about the joke, although they had no tape recording or any other kind of evidence that it had been said—a line from a song which I only dimly recollect myself. Shortly before my release, in the presence of a smartly dressed official whom I had never seen before, I got to see the line carefully written into my file, underlined, in parentheses. I don't recall who composed the song, but it was about the town of Fao in southern Iraq, which the Iranians had captured and hung onto with enormous loss of life. They rained more shells on Fao than anywhere else, and still the Iranians wouldn't budge. Then they gassed them, and that did it. They were so proud of recapturing Fao that they installed a plaque at the entrance to the flattened town, which announced that 53,000 Iraqis had died here. At the time of our arrest, Fao was a big issue in Iraq.

The implication of the line from the song was that Fao would not return to Iraq. Nothing made my interrogator go so absolutely berserk as that line. He made one scene after another. I kept on telling him that I genuinely and deeply believed that Fao would return to Iraq, that it ought to return to Iraq, that it was an integral part of the country, and so on. Anyway, all of this was beside the point because Fao had after all been won back. I don't remember the whole song now; we were very drunk when it got composed. But the line that got underlined in my report is correct: *"Rahat al-Fao. Min tizi tirja'"* (Fao has gone. Out of my asshole it will come back)."

4 · Mustafa

Building a Monument

'ABDALLAH 'Abdel-Qadir al-'Askari and his elderly father live in Sulaimaniyya with 'Abdallah's cousin, Mustafa al-'Askari. I met them in Mustafa's house during a trip to Kurdistan in November 1991. Like Omar's once carefully concealed story, this trip was only possible because the March 1991 intifada, following on the heels of the devastation of the Gulf war, has opened up Iraq's secrets to the kind of scrutiny that was not possible for twenty-three years. The visit was also my first to the country of my birth in the same number of years. 'Abdallah lives in Sulaimaniyya today because of the chemical attack on his village, Guptapa, which he witnessed.[1]

On the evening of May 3 [1988] the situation in my village, Guptapa, was not normal. We had heard that the regime was preparing a chemical attack, but we didn't know when they would strike. It felt like there were unusual army maneuvers. Late in the afternoon with my brother-in-law and two friends—both teachers like myself—I climbed from our farm, which is on lower ground, to the highest point of the village. We wanted to see what was going on.

Two inspection planes flew over. They threw out flares to determine the direction of the wind. Then another group of planes came, we think about eighteen of them. These were divided into three groups, one of which was directed at our village, Guptapa, and the second at the nearby village of 'Askar. The third group of planes headed for an area where *peshmerga* lived. Eight planes were intended for Guptapa. . . . They circled twice and came back the third time to bomb the village.

The explosions were not very loud, which made me guess they were chemical bombs. When we raised our heads, we saw the sandy brown and gray clouds billowing upward. My background as a chemist left me in no doubt this was a chemical attack.

We climbed to the highest spot possible even though the wind was taking the gas away in the opposite direction. From there I shouted down to the people in the village: "This is a chemical attack! Try to escape! Come up the hill, come up here!" A lot of people did come to where we were and were saved. But a lot remained in the areas affected by the chemicals.

We discussed what to do. I thought we should wait ten or fifteen minutes, then go down. If we went at once, we too would be in danger and unable to help the others. But my friends wouldn't listen. So, we went down to the back of the village where the gases had not permeated and a lot of people were gathered. Some were very disturbed; one man shouted at me, "You have lost everybody; they are all killed. They have been bombing your house." This made me worried; I wanted to go back to my house but we hadn't waited long enough. Only three minutes had passed of the time I had fixed in my mind as the minimum. Nonetheless, some of us set out for my house right away: my brother-in-law, Diyar, Fayeq, and me.

Before we set out, I told them they should wet their sash or turban and use it to cover their faces to reduce the effect of the chemicals. My brother-in-law had all his weapons on his sash, so he couldn't undo it. I told him to use his turban instead. But he wouldn't. He just washed his face with a little bit of water. Diyar also didn't prepare well. He was so upset, I don't think he even heard me. He just put a wet handkerchief over his face. Then we went to the river that flowed past our village. Again, I told Fayeq, "Wet your sash!" I put my own sash in the river and covered my face to protect my eyes as well. Then I headed back toward my home; the others went to their own homes.

Instead of walking by the river, as they ought to have done, Diyar and Fayeq found themselves in a field of tall bean plants. As they walked through these plants, the poison on the leaves blew up into their faces and they shouted for help. But I couldn't do anything—I was too upset and far away. Fayeq shouted out, " 'Abdallah, I am dying. Help me!" I could see he still had the sash around his waist and shouted at him, angrily, "But I told you to tie it around your head." He did so, but too late.

All I could do was pull him out of the affected area by the legs. On the way we met a boy of seven or eight who was lying on the ground, his body shaking. He also said, " 'Abdallah, what can you do for me!" I told Fayeq to hold tightly onto the child's legs as I pulled his. We were like a train until we reached a small stream where we could wash our faces and the child's. We pulled him up a little bit but he lost his strength and fell down. At the time I didn't know if he had survived or not. Later I found out he was alive because the *Jahsh* had come the next day and saved him, along with others.

I took Fayeq to a place further off and gave him two injections of an antidote (since [the March 1988 massacre at] Halabja, I had kept a supply hidden). I knew it to work against the kind of gas that affects the brain and the nervous system. He was shouting, "Leave me," as his nervous system was obviously affected. The poison used in Guptapa in my opinion wasn't a single gas; it was composed of several gases. The combination affects the muscles, making them rigid and inflexible. In two minutes it can kill a person. After the injections, I found a car for Fayeq, handed him over to my friends, and told them I was going to my house.

Finally I could run to my house. It was twenty minutes before sunset. When I got there it was entirely dark, but I found a small flashlight. First I put on a gas mask to protect myself. Then I went to the shelter which I had prepared for just such an eventuality. My wife knew that this was where the family should hide in case of a chemical attack. Nobody was there. I became really afraid—convinced that nobody had survived. I climbed up from the shelter to a cave nearby, thinking they might have taken refuge there. There was nobody there, either. But when I went to the small stream near our house, I found my mother. She had fallen by the river; her mouth was biting into the mudbank.

All the members of my family had been running toward this stream because I had told them that water is good against chemical weapons. By the time they reached the stream, a lot of them had fainted and fallen into the water. Most of them had drowned. I turned my mother over; she was dead. I wanted to kiss her but I knew that if I did, the chemicals would be passed on. Even now I deeply regret not kissing my beloved mother.

I continued along the river. I found the body of my nine-year-old daughter hugging her cousin, who had also choked to death in the water. Then I found the dead body of another niece, with her father. I continued along the stream. I found a woman who wasn't from our family and heard a child groan under her. Turning the woman over, I found the child; the water had almost reached him. I took the boy's clothes off, took him inside, and bundled him up in other clothes.

Then I went around our house. In the space of 200–300 square meters I saw the bodies of dozens of people from my family. Among them were my children, my brothers, my father, and my nieces and nephews. Some of them were still alive, but I couldn't tell one from the other. I was trying to see if the children were dead. At that point I lost my feelings. I didn't know who to cry for anymore and I didn't know who to go to first. I was all alone at night.

I saw one of my brothers: his head was tilted down a slope. My wife was still alive beside him, and my other brother was on the other side. My two daughters, the six-month-old baby and the four-year-old, were on either side of my wife and they were both dead . . . They were both dead. I tried to move them, to shake them. There was no response. They were both dead. I just knew they were dead.

My brothers and my wife had blood and vomit running from their noses and mouths. Their heads were tilted to one side. They were groaning. I couldn't do much, just clean the blood and vomit from their mouths and noses and try in every way to make them breathe again. I did artificial respiration on them and then I gave them two injections each. I also rubbed creams on my wife and two brothers. After injecting them, I had a feeling they were not going to die.

Our family has forty members. I mean, it did. Now, of that big family we have only fifteen left. Twenty-five of the beloved people of our family are dead. Among those were my five children. There were two boys—Twana 'Abdallah 'Abdel-Qadir, who was sixteen years old, and Tishko 'Abdallah 'Abdel-Qadir, who was six years old. There were also three daughters; the big one, Taban, was nine years old, Tavga was four years old, and Shokhan was six months. This was my personal family. But of our extended family, my mother 'A'isha 'Abdel-Kareem is dead; my cousin, who was the wife of my brother, and the two wives of my brothers: 'Atiya 'Abdel-Rahman, and Parwin Sayyid Ahmad, the wife of Mr. Lati, who was a teacher. They are all dead now, they aren't in life. I mean, twenty-five members of my family are dead.

Actually, as I am telling you this, I don't know what to say; my feelings are not dead, but we are not able any more to be sad for that time when all this happened. No more tears are left. We were so very sad and we have spilled so many tears. We are not capable of feeling anything more.

As fate would have it, 'Abdallah, now a secondary school teacher in Sulaimaniyya in his thirties, is a qualified chemist. He was especially eager to talk about the chemistry of the attack on that day. After the first chemical attack on a Kurdish village in Shaikh Wisan in 1987, and especially after the Halabja bombardment in April

1988, 'Abdallah began using his background to research the various gases that are part of the Ba'thi arsenal. He suspects that a combination of gases, not one gas, was dropped on Guptapa. The combination included some very strange chemicals, he thinks. Why? Because the bodies of some of the children he had seen were blue. There had to be cyanide, he said, because the plumes of smoke slowly rising above the village contained a certain shade of brown, uniquely associated with that poison. He had assembled what he thought might be antidotes to those gases and hidden them in his family home in Guptapa. Over twenty antidotes that could be injected had been obtained from his contacts in Sulaimaniyya, along with ointments and smelling salts. His wife and brothers had been given in-depth instructions on what to do. But to little avail.

'Abdallah's words poured out like a torrential flood. He wasn't looking at me as he went on and on about the properties of poisonous gases and their antidotes. The sentences came out in one big jumble of little details. He spoke in a staccato tone, his hollowed-out cheeks spitting out the words. He spoke like a man possessed, a man for whom there was no longer any tomorrow. I did not get to ask a question.

I had precisely the opposite experience when I eventually got to interview another Kurdish survivor, the boy Taimour.[2] Taimour spoke in gentle monosyllables, calmly, as though nothing out of the ordinary had happened. Unlike 'Abdallah, he was reluctant to dwell on details, which had to be dug out of him, one excruciating question after the other. He was speaking because he had to, not because he wanted to. Taimour wanted those memories excised out of him, not relived. Those who have been scarred by cruelty of this kind seem to fall into one or the other of the two extremes represented by Taimour and 'Abdallah. For as long as I live, I will never forget the different ways in which these two survivors spoke about what had happened to them.

'Abdallah's father, who also lived through the attack on Guptapa, is a thin wisp of a man with large bulging eyes. He has to be coached before he can say anything. 'Abdallah, when he is not talking about what happened on the evening of May 3, 1988, says nothing and just fades away into the background. He brings the tea on a large silver tray, and runs backward and forward doing little household errands. He becomes shy, often looking down at the ground for no apparent reason. Mustafa, a proud, older man with a round and owlish face, treats him with a trace of contempt. His cousin 'Abdallah, you see, has not taken what happened to him as a Kurdish man should. He lives in the past, acts like a servant, and comes alive only when talking about what happened in Guptapa. The future has collapsed for him into the events of a few hours that took place over three years ago but which have now become the absolute center of his life. 'Abdallah is a marked man; he is no longer a hardy Kurdish fighter for the greater cause of his people. Mustafa cannot handle what 'Abdallah has become.

History as Memory

MUSTAFA, unlike 'Abdallah, is an intellectual deeply imbued with a sense of Kurdish history. Born in the village of 'Askar, he is the author of a book in Kurdish on the Haqqa movement, a twentieth-century school of Sufism deriving from the older Naqshabandi mystical order which has Kurdish roots going back for centuries.[3]

The Haqqa, Mustafa writes, was started in the 1920s in the Zordasht area, which is also where the villages of Guptapa and 'Askar are located. The founder of the movement was Mustafa's great-grandfather, Shaikh 'Abdel-Kareem al-Haj Shaikh Mustafa ibn Ridha al-'Askari, a religious scholar and man of letters who was equally fluent in Arabic, Persian, Turkish, and Kurdish. Shaikh 'Abdel-Kareem was a scourge of the Iraqi religious and political establishment of his time. Mr. Edmunds, the British adviser to the Ministry of the Interior, actually had to pay him a visit in a futile attempt to either convince, bribe, or threaten the Shaikh out of his dissenting ways. 'Abdel-Kareem was something of an Iraqi Kurdish equivalent of Khomeini for the first half of the twentieth century and finally got himself arrested in 1934 and forcibly confined to the city of Kirkuk for six months. He wanted to return to the roots of Islamic law, as opposed to remaining content with their external application in the form of ritual observance. The Haqqa derive their name from al-haq, which means "the Truth" in Arabic. Followers would meet in centers for prayer, converted from people's houses, known as al-tekia. They would sit cross-legged on the ground, rocking their bodies gently back and forth while chanting, "Oh Truth, Oh Truth. We believe in the Truth. We search for the Truth. Our way is the Truth. . . ."

The Shaikh's followers split after his death, as followers are wont to do. But a majority went along with his brother, Mam Ridha (Uncle Ridha), who injected into the original mysticism new nationalist and socialist ideals, including the revolutionary idea (for this milieu) of male-female equality. Ridha's followers went on to participate in the short-lived Kurdish Mahabad Republic of 1946, a milestone event in Kurdish national history which also brought the famous guerrilla leader, Mulla Mustafa Barazani, into the forefront of Iraqi Kurdish politics. They did so by dispatching "traveling brothers," as they were known among the Haqqa, to Kurdish villages to proselytize. After settling down in a new location, these missionaries would become known as "the trusted ones." The Haqqa were often thought of by Kurdish villagers as being atheists because they no longer held to any of the rituals concerning prayer and fasting. Mustafa, who holds them in high regard, disagrees, pointing out that they were believers in God and the Prophet but of a different kind. His book is therefore a journey into the history of the Kurdish national movement from the point of view of the pivotal role of the al-'Askari family in that history.

The name of the family is derived from their ancestral village, 'Askar. Three pivotal figures in modern Iraqi political history were all born here. Mustafa related this tale about one of them, Ja'far al-'Askari, who founded the Iraqi army in 1921:

> My father told me that in 1934 or 1935, Ja'far al-'Askari came to 'Askar and said, "I want to serve you and to serve this village." My father told him, "Allah has been merciful to us, we have no need of anything." But Ja'far insisted, "No, I wish to give something to my village." So my father said, "Fine, build us a school." And Ja'far built the first school for the first grade. It had a long, large room and another small room for the teacher, along with a small patio. This is how 'Askar got its first school.

But 'Askar was also the birthplace of Bakr Sidqi, a cousin of Ja'far's, who led a pogrom against the Assyrians in 1933. For this, Sidqi became an Iraqi national hero. He followed up his victory against defenseless Assyrian villagers from the town of Sumayl by having his too famous cousin assassinated in 1936 in order to lead the Arab world's first military coup. Sidqi then enjoyed the effective rulership of Iraq for nine months before he too was assassinated.

I VISITED the villages of 'Askar and Guptapa in the company of Mustafa and his nephew. Chalaw is lean and fit, in his early twenties, with sharp pointed features and a hawklike nose; he is the spitting image of his handsome father, the Kurdish hero 'Ali al-'Askari, whose portraits adorn Mustafa's house. A huge wallposter of 'Ali recessed into a 4 ft by 6 ft concrete frame is also on the main thoroughfare in Sulaimaniyya where Saddam Husain's once used to be. 'Ali al-'Askari, whose grandfather was Mam Ridha, the leader of the Haqqa movement after Shaikh 'Abdel-Kareem, is the third very important Kurdish personality to be born in the village of 'Askar. But 'Ali was not a mystic like his forefathers. He was a different kind of leader: a guerrilla fighter about whom legends were already being spun when he was killed in 1977 in inter-Kurdish feuding. Chalaw's family then prudently moved the young boy to Sweden, where he lived for many years, only to return to Kurdistan after the negotiations between the Kurds and the Iraqi government began in May 1991.

I traveled to 'Askar in the company of a large group of *peshmergas* in a convoy of Toyota Land Cruisers and what felt to me like enough RPGs, Kalashnikovs, and heavy-duty machine guns to stop a whole Iraqi division. Why so much protection? Chalaw explained the importance of not giving an opportunity for old feuds to run amok. The protection was for him. Somebody might want to start something between the Kurdish political organizations, and they might get the idea that they could do that by assassinating the son of 'Ali al-'Askari. Chalaw travels around with a miniature army to discourage them.

Mustafa pointed out the graveyards that abounded on the hillsides around 'Askar. This was an ancient place with an illustrious history, stretching back to the days when the village had been a focal point on the trade route between Baghdad and Iran. Its famous mosque had trained many renowned mullahs. 'Askar was known to be unusually well developed. In addition to the school that Ja'far built, it had a variety of shops, a full-time resident carpenter, a blacksmith, and various other kinds of artisans. Covering quite a large area, it was a center of agriculture, specializing in growing *shilim,* or darnel grass.

al-'Askar in Arabic means the military, or "men of the army." Never was there a place that appeared to have been so molded in the image of its own name. Or was the name chosen to honor the militant traditions of the place? It hardly matters any longer. For 'Askar no longer exists. Quite literally. You can still see paths, twisting lanes, and the outlines of irregular enclosures that once were rooms where human beings ate, slept, worked, prayed, and played. The devastation is complete: of the two hundred houses that originally stood here, only the foundations and a few retaining walls remain. The Ba'th leave nothing to chance. In the midst of 'Askar's ruins, beside a stream that only three years ago was the center of an important and thriving community, we had an elaborate chicken and rice lunch.

The Role of the Jahsh

MUSTAFA talked about 'Askar and its bombing on May 3, 1988. People had escaped the aerial bombardment in which only conventional weapons were deployed. They had fled, abandoning their homes and everything in them, heading straight for the nearby mountain slopes and woods. I did not come across anyone who had lost a relative in the bombing of 'Askar itself. In Guptapa, on the other hand, some 150 people died in the initial attack, thus proving that in this terrain, chemical weapons are far more suited to Ba'thist purposes.

Not that it made much difference in the end. For the escaping villagers were already surrounded by the Iraqi army, which began occupying strongpoints on May 1, 1988. They took up positions atop the ring of mountains which girdled 'Askar, Guptapa, and a handful of other Kurdish villages nestling in the low ground. Then they dispatched Kurdish *Jahsh* units, headed by what the Iraqi government called its Kurdish "advisers."[4] These units were sent down from the high points to pacify villagers or to round up those who were fleeing, and escort them to huge forts built like medieval fortresses during the Iraq-Iran War to house army units some ten to fifteen thousand soldiers strong.[5] Some villagers slipped through the net and made their way on foot to Iran (as Mustafa and millions of other Kurds were to do yet again in the wake of the failed March 1991 uprising). But on this occasion, most didn't make it. The Ba'th were too efficient.

Mustafa wasn't there on the day of the attack itself, but the following day he slipped into 'Askar and Guptapa with the help of the the very same *Jahsh* units employed by the Iraqi army who had rounded up people from his village and were under strict orders not to let someone like him in. He describes what happened there.

> In truth I could never have reached my village if a group of the *Jahsh* had not helped. They came with me from Sulaimaniyya and brought me here. Army checkpoints were stopping any person from reaching the area. When I arrived, I did not wish to speak with them [the *Jahsh*] because their position is clear. But they came with me. Together, we saw Guptapa: about 150 people were buried beneath the dirt without graves or anything; they were hit by the chemicals and a bit of dirt was thrown on them because of the smell and the bacteria. When they saw this, the *Jahsh* that were with me began to cry, and they cursed themselves.

> It was Ramadan. Emotions reached the point that some of them said, "After this we will not fast nor will we pray, for God has allowed this calamity to fall upon our people, upon our relatives, upon people from our nation." Some began to cry and they helped me carry the bodies. We could not bring them to the village so we placed them in a hole instead and covered them with grass and old clothes that were thrown there. All valuables had already been taken by the *Fursan* and the forces of the Defense of the Nation [names for the *Jahsh* used by the government]. These were not the same people who had attacked the village. But of course they are the same type. The army was in the area and in control, but for a distance of ten kilometers from the village, on both sides, the *Jahsh* were there helping the army to secure the area.

Next to what the Ba'th have done to villages like 'Askar and Guptapa, the role of the *Jahsh* is probably the most emotive, complex, and unresolved issue in Iraqi Kurdistan. The wealthy landowner and tribal chief we encountered earlier (in Chapter 2), who had fought with the regime against his own relatives during the intifada, had very good reasons for what he did. "I took part in the *Anfal* campaign on August 8, 1988," he told Neil Conan. "Twelve thousand Kurdish men were arrested in a military camp in Mosul. All those from eighteen years and above were taken to an unknown destination. One of my close friends told me they had to dig ditches and every one of those twelve thousand was shot. One by one. Shot by a pistol. Whether he died or not, he was buried by throwing dirt on him." Then comes this extraordinary admission, which makes the episode so credible:

One of my friends was taken by the intelligence service. They sent me a message saying that if I guaranteed the loyalty of my friend, he will be released. He was eventually released on bail. As he was being released, on my personal guarantee, he suddenly wanted to ask a question about those twelve thousand Kurds who had been taken. He didn't know they had been killed. He simply knew they had disappeared. But he wanted to have some solid information. The head of the intelligence service handling the paperwork for my friend's release turned to me, smiled, and then said to my friend: "You had better ask this man about their fate. He will tell you." Until now, I have not told this friend of mine what had happened. You see sixty of those missing twelve thousand were his relatives, his brothers, cousins, nephews. . . . I didn't want to break his heart.[6]

During the uprising, the eight parties of the Kurdistan Front granted an amnesty to Kurdish *Jahsh* leaders like this wealthy landowner, and Ba'thist authority in northern Iraq collapsed like a house of cards. The past has not been forgotten, however, and feelings among Kurds on the subject of the *Jahsh* run very high. At one point during the journey to 'Askar, this exchange took place with the driver of our Land Cruiser:

—The *Jahsh* live among the *peshmerga* now; how do you feel about them?

—Miserable.

—I want your true feelings.

—I hate them very much.

—Why do you hate them?

—Because they did the *Anfal* with the Iraqi government.

—How many people were in Saddam's *Jahsh* army?

—Too many.

—Will you ever trust them?

—Not until the day I die. If there was a new *Anfal*, they would take part again. . . .

—Do you think they could possibly still be working for Saddam Husain, or switch sides yet again?

—I think so.

At this point another Kurd sitting next to the speaker snapped out: "He thinks so; I am sure of it."

More Kurdish Memories

A HANDFUL of newly arrived families are back in 'Askar, rebuilding new hovels out of the rubble of old stones. Around the village between the graveyards and beyond, fields have been cleared, marked off by the stones which had to be extracted like teeth from the land. Faint lines of green trail up the hillsides; a few crops are reseeding themselves three years after the Iraqi army visited 'Askar. There is no evidence, however, of all the history that Mustafa is so passionate about. Umbilically tied to the whole formation of modern Iraq—as much as to Kurdistan—the village of 'Askar was erased from the map of Iraq on May 3, 1988, adding another legacy of bitterness to the country's pain. This is the quintessentially Ba'thist attitude to all history: uproot what it is and rewrite it in the shape of what you think it ought to be. They did it to Babylon, converting the foundation traces and stone blocks, which were all that was left of the real thing, into a complex of courtyards and hundreds of rooms that took a thousand Sudanese laborers three years of work, working seven days a week. So why shouldn't they do what they did to 'Askar?

Was there ever such a place as 'Askar? When Mustafa dies, 'Askar will be forgotten by a lot more people.

AFTER lunch, Mustafa took us to Guptapa, a short drive away. The village must have been about two tenths of a square mile in area. Some two thousand people lived here in about three hundred houses. You can walk briskly from one end to the other in ten minutes. Of the three hundred houses originally here, nothing remains, not even the upright foundations and retaining walls I had seen at 'Askar. The explosive experts and bulldozers that followed in the wake of the *Jahsh* and the army were more thorough in Guptapa because they had a lot more to hide.

The telltale casings of at least one chemical bomb did get left behind in the rubble adjacent to the three-foot-wide crater where it had fallen. This kind of bomb doesn't explode with a loud bang, shattering into an infinite number of pieces of flying shrapnel; it makes a sort of popping sound, which allows the two chemicals contained within the tube (separated from one another by an inner casing) to mix. The casing keeps its form, breaking up into large chunks of metal. A big explosion would instantly atomize the chemicals and not allow a reaction to take place. The inner casing is about one sixteenth of an inch thick; the outer is at least one eighth of an inch thick. Twenty-five members of Mustafa and 'Abdullah and Chalaw's family, you will recall, were strewn around the landscape here on May 3, poisoned by chemicals from these kinds of bombs. 'Abdallah saw it all happen and Mustafa came the next day in the company of the *Jahsh* to clear up the mess.

On the day that I visited 'Askar and Guptapa, three and a half years exactly had passed since all this destruction. Mustafa had in the meantime been through a new kind of hell, which he described in a nineteen-page letter to his daughter. Just before saying goodbye, he gave me a copy of this extraordinary letter, written in Kurdish, which told of what Mustafa had experienced and seen during the exodus of nearly 2 million people following the crushing of the March 1991 uprising. It was written from his place of temporary refuge in Iran right after the events that it describes.

The most poignant passages in the letter describe Mustafa's state of mind. He is "shocked," "overwhelmed" by the "horrendous flood that washed everything away." Saddam Husain's helicopter gunships were strafing the outskirts of the city of Sulaimaniyya. "People in the city were screaming and abandoning their homes. Children were singing the national Kurdish anthem. We cannot believe the artillery and helicopters would treat our city like this. All the people headed toward the mountains. . . . The only thought that crossed your mind was fear." Could more have been done to defend Sulaimaniyya? Heavy artillery, he writes, cannot be stopped in its tracks "with stones and broken cars." He feels himself to be living a hallucination: "What happened suddenly to the beautiful spring? Was it only a fantasy? Why the dark clouds and the black rain? Why do we have no dam to block this flood? Is this real or is it illusory? Only hours ago the situation was entirely different."

The letter describes scenes from the forced march through the freezing cold, showers of hail and constant rain which "fell like it was being poured from a *gonda* [a goatskin holder]." A mother sits in a wheelchair being pushed by her son. "This was the third time I saw her on the road." An old man crouches by the roadside with four young children surrounding him who "look like butterflies."

By the third day, people are dying all around Mustafa. "I see one person holding his child in his arms; the child is dead but he doesn't realize it." Nobody stops for anyone else. At one campsite, "there was no place to sit and when they started to pass the bread, thousands of people were fighting over it. It is true what they say: those who are hungry lose their minds."

Mustafa writes on and on, possessed like 'Abdallah by what he has seen, until, finally, the letter grinds to a halt out of sheer exhaustion. "This story does not end. I will keep it for another time. One day it might become a book. I would have to write it, for no one else could. Another time, on my own chair at home, next to my table and between my own books, I will write it. But they are telling me that my chair and table in Sulaimaniyya have been looted."

Chronological time is not a good measure of the chasm that separates the man Mustafa became during the 1988 Iraqi government campaign against 'Askar and Guptapa from the man he is today. "Victory" over Iran was followed by grinding despair, a deep sense of the futility of everything. Such feelings gripped many Kurds between 1989 and 1990. Then came the invasion, occupation, sacking, and annexation of Kuwait, followed by a world war that was left cynically unfinished, not to mention the euphoria of an uprising brutally crushed after a mere three weeks. The shock of such high hopes collapsing in the way Mustafa describes marks a human being. Out of the crucible of this kind of psychological time, new memories are seared into the self, and maybe even a different attitude to the concept of memory itself.

Mustafa's Monument

AFTER returning from Iran in April 1991, Mustafa conceived the idea of a memorial in Guptapa for those who died here on May 3, 1988. Still unfinished, it sits on the very top of a hill, on the site of what used to be a *qal'a,* or castle, according to local folklore. The castle, if it ever existed, has long since disappeared. The memorial overlooks a majestic vista of mountains which snake their way into the horizon as far as the eye can see. In the foreground the mountains frame a lush meandering river valley.

Mustafa's monument is the first thing one sees upon approaching the village. Built of concrete blocks, the most ubiquitous construction material of the Middle East, it looks like the unfinished gable ends of an unroofed house with a pointed arch cut out of each. Mustafa intends to rough-render the bare blockwork of the arches and whitewash the result. The two arches sit on a concrete podium with four steps leading to a flat surface. From here, the arches spring. This exceedingly unremarkable construction sits in an empty oval area framed by a thick, low retaining wall which marks off the site boundaries of the whole memorial from the surrounding landscape. Within the oval to one side is a simple dirt-finished graveyard. The other half is finished in stone pebbles and is intended as a gathering place for weddings and the annual commemoration of the dead of Guptapa.

To establish the graveyard, Mustafa and other family members carried sixty-eight bodies up the hill. It is as though the extraordinary natural beauty of the setting Mustafa had chosen would compensate for how they died. 'Abdallah's children are all here, as is the daughter of Chalaw's cousin. The balance of the 150 or so people who were killed here on May 3, 1988, are still somewhere down below on the other side of the hill under the rubble of Guptapa. Each grave, in the traditional Kurdish way, is an earth mound. Mustafa has established a simple order: each marker is a roughly cut, minimally worked, two-inch-thick slab of stone. "Martyr no. 56" is six-year-old Tishko 'Abdallah 'Abdel-Qadir. "Martyr no. 35" is a four-year-old girl named Diman Hassan. "Martyr no. 32" is fifty-four-year-old Shanam Rashid. And so on. A row of trees is intended to be planted in a straight line down the middle; a flower bed will run around the perimeter inside the thick retaining wall.

Chalaw has his own ideas for how to complete the monument. The two arches, he feels, should be roofed over, and a life-sized sculpture of a Kurdish woman in her national dress erected underneath. Like the French, the Kurds often express their collective national self through the female form. A drawing I saw in the town of Shaqlawa depicted a raven plucking out the right eye of a woman who had her head thrown backwards. It looked like a scene from Hitchcock's film, *The Birds*. The young teenager who drew it explained to me that the raven was the insatiable tyrant whose thirst for Kurdish tears could never be quenched. Kurdishness was represented by a young maiden with long flowing black hair whose face was almost completely concealed by the hovering hulk of black feathers. The heroic idiom of France's Marianne charging into battle holding aloft the tricolor is clearly not appropriate for Iraq today. Maybe that is why Chalaw wants his Marianne to be in the form of a skeleton and to be breastfeeding an infant. Only the breast in the infant's mouth should look life-like and be covered in flesh, he said. Kurdistan, you see, is going to be reborn.

Nothing so disturbs our humanity as the thought of horror and beauty becoming as inextricably bound up with one another as they are in Guptapa. The memorial to what happened here on May 3, 1988, sits atop the very same hill that 'Abdallah, his brother-in-law, and two teacher friends—Diyar and Fayeq—were using as they watched Iraqi planes swoop down and drop chemical bombs onto their village. It overlooks the same magnificent river bend in which 'Abdallah discovered his mother with her mouth biting into the mudbank.

5 / Taimour

"The Heroic Operations of the *Anfal*"

THE Fort of Qoratu was a massive structure of Soviet design in reinforced concrete, typical of many military outposts built throughout northern Iraq in the 1980s during the long and catastrophic war with Iran. It was blown up on September 8, 1991, by the Iraqi army troops who had manned it; this was their final task before withdrawing to a new front line "just over that hill," according to the Kurdish guerrilla commander in charge of our trip. I never saw them. But Taimour, the boy I had come three thousand miles to interview, was brought here in August 1988 when he was twelve years old.[1] Along with his mother, father, three sisters, and every other villager in Qulatcho, and carrying whatever possessions they could manage, the *Jahsh* escorted them the fifteen miles it took to get to this fort.

Amid the rubble there remains a rough maze of corridors and rooms. Inside one room strewn with large chunks of concrete I found graffiti signed by an Iraqi soldier named Yousuf. Alongside his name he had scrawled these lyrics from a popular Arabic love song: "I love you, I wish I could forget you, and forget my soul with you." Next to this someone had left unsigned the lament: "Exercise, exercise, and yet more exercise."[2]

It remains unclear just why the Iraqi troops withdrew from the Fort of Qoratu in the summer of 1991. Surely they had not been pushed out by waves of Iranian ground troops. Nor had the fort been besieged by the Kurdish guerrilla fighters called the *peshmerga* (literally, "those who face death"). It was a heavily armed group of eight *peshmerga*, however, who late in November 1991 escorted me to the fort, situated near the Iraq-Iran border at the southeastern tip of Iraq's Kurdistan region. The *peshmerga* were going to show me evidence of the use the fort had been put to as the war between Iraq and Iran wound down in 1988—evidence of a large-scale Iraqi government campaign, carefully planned and executed, to exterminate a sizable portion of Iraq's Kurdish minority.

I already knew the extermination campaign had a name: *al-Anfal*. From my reading of secret Iraqi government documents seized by the Kurds in March of 1991—when, in the wake of the Gulf war, the *peshmerga* fought their way into all the major Kurdish cities in the north, taking brief control of government buildings and military installations—I also knew the essential tools of the campaign, tools refined in this century by the likes of Hitler and Pol Pot: demolished villages, transfer points, poison gas, firing squads, mass graves. Among the countless official documents seized by the Kurds— Kurdish leaders talk of tons, truckloads—are detailed, mostly hand-written lists of "eliminated villages" whose inhabitants were rounded up and have disappeared. The Kurds have also carefully compiled their own lists of those, mostly but not exclusively men and boys from rural villages, who were taken away and are presumed dead. Two weeks before arriving at the Fort of Qoratu, I'd visited a fort outside the town of Dohuk where, eyewitnesses told me, eight thousand Kurdish men and boys were brought in 1988 and then vanished. It is not possible to say precisely how many Kurdish lives were taken during the period the *Anfal* campaign was waged, but evidence from the highest levels of the regime itself suggests that the number of those killed is not less than 100,000. Kurdish leaders estimate the number is greater than 180,000.

It has long been known that the Kurds who people northern Iraq—today, about 3.5 million people inhabiting an area of 15,000 square miles—have over the years suffered greatly at the hands of various regimes in Baghdad.[3] A bloody pattern was established from very early on, one that continued after Iraq achieved independence from Britain in 1932 and that grew ever more monstrous when the Ba'th Party first came to power.[4] Shoresh Rasoul, a Kurdish activist recently out of Iraq, was five years old when the National Guard of the Ba'th seized thirteen men from his town, Koi Sinjak, in the summer of 1963. They were tied to columns in the town center, after which the residents of the town were brought out to watch the men being executed. The father of Shoresh's friend was one of the thirteen. Whenever Shoresh and his friend passed the columns, his friend would point out the particular bullet-riddled column to which his father had been tied. The columns remained pockmarked until the late 1970s.[5]

Since 1968, the story of Iraq's Kurds has been in large part one of paper concessions from the government (promises of increased representation, agreements to further autonomy), followed by foot-dragging, backsliding, betrayals—and then "resettlement," "Arabization," and "deportations," all of which entailed the constant redrawing of boundaries, and the razing of towns and villages. There are few *peshmerga* who cannot tell you in detail about what Iraqi army troops did to the villagers of Dakan on August 8, 1969; about the scale of the destruction to the towns of Zakho and the air attack on Qala Diza in March 1974 (which led to a flight from the cities that was a precursor to what happened in March 1991); about what happened to the families of the Barazani clan in March 1975, when the Kurdish resistance had its U.S.-funded supplies from Iran cut off after the Shah got the territory he wanted from Baghdad, and he and Saddam Husain initialed the Algiers Agreement; about the chemical attack on the village of Halabja in March 1988 that killed some five thousand Kurdish men, women, and children. Now it is necessary to add to this list the mass killing of noncombatant men and women from Kurdish rural areas between February and September in 1988.

While it is true that promoting one's Kurdish identity in Iraq in any way was, beginning in the early seventies, deemed by the Ba'thist regime to be promoting "separatism," "chauvinism," and "racism"—and thus was a criminally traitorous act—it was understood, even by the Iraqi army and secret police, that one had to be taking action as a Kurd (or have trumped-up charges of such brought against you) before drawing a swift, severe reaction from the government. A Kurd might be arrested for belonging to one of the Kurdish political parties, or for being overheard by an informer to be criticizing Iraqi President Saddam Husain, or for aiding the enemy during the Iran-Iraq War (this was a favorite trumped-up charge).

A Kurd, beginning in the mid-seventies, might also be "resettled" at a moment's notice—at first with compensation, later without—if his village happened to be situated along the Iraq-Iran border. This strip of frontier was gradually thickened, then stretched to include the Turkish frontier. By the mid-eighties, not only villages in border areas but also those in the oil-producing regions in the heart of northern Iraq were being razed, their inhabitants "resettled." With the 1988 *Anfal* campaign, all these precedents came to a climax: simply living in an area designated "prohibited for security reasons" (which now extended to virtually all rural areas in northern Iraq, and included, incidentally, areas inhabited by Assyrian Christians who are not Kurds) became in itself a death sentence.

On the long, rugged drive to the Fort of Qoratu, as we made our way south from the city of Sulaimaniyya in two Toyota Land Rovers, I glimpsed in the weak light of dawn the village of New Halabja, built by the government to resettle what remained of the population of old Halabja, which was leveled after the gassing. This area, and the entire region to the north, was now in Kurdish hands—the "safe haven" created in April 1991 by the joint forces of Great Britain, France, the Netherlands, and the United States, and patrolled from the skies for a while by fighter aircraft flying out of the U.S. base at Incirlik, Turkey. Fighting to put down the uprising against Saddam, the Iraqi army had retaken a number of key cities in early April— using the opportunity to destroy secret police documents, many no doubt *Anfal*-related, that the Kurds had not had time to carry off. Iraqi troops remained in considerable number on the western plain of Iraqi Kurdistan, stretched along a 250-mile demarcation zone, and they continued to control the northern cities of Mosul and Kirkuk. In the weeks before I journeyed to northern Iraq, these troops had begun imposing a tight economic blockade on the Kurdish-controlled region, a blockade that through the harsh winter left the north of Iraq critically short of both food and fuel.

The route chosen kept us along the Iraq-Iran border much of the time. To my left a six-foot-high rampart of earth, built by the Iraqi army during its eight-year war with the Ayatollah Khomeini's forces, blocked my view of the Iranian side for miles at a time. On the Iraqi side were unbroken coils of barbed wire, the hulks of what had been military vehicles, scattered shell casings and craters of various sizes, and rectangular holes crudely chopped out of the sides of hills from which tanks and cannons had once protruded. Bulldozers and mechanical shovels had raked and shaped this land into a lunar landscape of war and desolation. It was a bleak scene, a wasteland of the kind one imagines spread around the trenches of World War I. Only the bodies were missing.

There were no bodies to be found at the Fort of Qoratu either, but it was not hard to imagine what had happened to the thousands of men, women, and children who were brought here from their villages. Did they know what awaited them? Probably not, for in nearly all cases they were persuaded to leave their homes not by Iraqi soldiers but by *Jahsh* units—units comprised of Kurds loyal to Baghdad totaling over a quarter million men. I walked through what remained of the six-foot-wide corridors where these villagers had been led by the *Jahsh* and held like penned animals for days on end. By this point they must have suspected the worst. The ground crunched under my feet: atop the concrete floor lay a thick layer of long-dried human excrement.

Walking around the heavily mined perimeter of the fort—the Iraqi army has planted mines all over northern Iraq; in the town of Penjwin alone, the Swiss Med-Air relief organization estimates there are five hundred mine-related injuries a month, the victims mostly children at play—making my way carefully, I saw on the side facing the Iranian border forty, maybe fifty wagons of the sort Kurdish farmers hook up to the back of their tractors when carting feed or livestock. No doubt it was in these wagons that the Kurdish villagers were carted to the fort. Piles of faded dresses and *sharaweel,* the traditional Kurdish trousers, came tumbling out of these wagons, or lay rotting amid the dirt and clumped yellow grass. Scattered around were plastic soles, all that remained of thousands of pairs of shoes.

And the villagers themselves? In the official documents they are referred to as the "lost ones of the *Anfal.*" They are almost certainly dead—shot and buried, the evidence suggests, in shallow mass graves dug in southwestern Iraq, in the desert near Iraq's border with Saudi Arabia. It was to this desolate corner of the country that villagers brought from forts like that at Qoratu were "transferred," and then executed by firing squads in the very pits that would serve as their graves.

In my walk around the tangled metal and chunky concrete remains of the Fort of Qoratu, less than twenty feet from where I found the graffiti by the Iraqi soldier Yousuf, I found a school notebook, with notes on algebra in Arabic and Kurdish; a beautifully printed explication, in Kurdish, of the Qur'an; and a copy of a novel by the Arab author Miqdad Rahim entitled *There Is Nothing But Love.* A large butterfly was printed on the red front cover. Picking my way about slowly, in a daze, I somehow recalled that I had to have passed by this very spot in the winter of 1965. Then there had been no fort but a village, the village of Qoratu. I was sixteen, with my mother and father on a three-week family trip; we were on our way from Baghdad to visit archeological sites in Iran. Now, on my first trip back to Iraq in more than twenty years, I was undertaking a different kind of archeology, examining the relics, artifacts, and ruins of a monumental campaign of mass murder.

What Is in a Name?

THE most riveting thing about cruelty is the motivation behind it. Everywhere I traveled during the three weeks I spent in northern Iraq last November—in large cities and in the smallest villages—I heard the word *"al-Anfal."* In secret-police documents the reference is always to the "heroic operations of the *Anfal."* In transcripts of Iraqi military communiqués I had read of the "first," "second," and "third" *Anfal* operations, and also, in documents dating from later in 1988, of *Khatimat al-Anfal,* perhaps best translated as "the final *Anfal."* Surreally, the word began to metamorphose after the campaign concluded in 1988. A major Iraqi gas field was named *al-Anfal* in 1989. In Sulaimaniyya I visited a public building that was called, at least until last spring's uprising, *Mujama' al-Anfal,* the Anfal complex. The large outdoor sign identifying it as such was torn down by the Kurds, who took full control of the city in July 1991; but I was shown a small, beautifully carved wooden sign that used to hang in one of the corridors: THE ANFAL POST OFFICE.[6]

Constant invocation of a name, and its usage in different contexts, helps to sanitize its meaning in our consciences, thereby concealing the reasons for having invoked it in the first place. Before the government's campaign of that name, few Kurds or Arabs would have known what *"al-Anfal"* meant. Nonetheless, the first clue to Ba'thi motivation is revealed by this name.

Anfal enters modern Arabic from the eighth *sura* (a chapter or collection of verses) of the Qur'an. The 75-verse revelation, called *Surat al-Anfal,* had come to the Prophet Muhammad in the wake of the first great battle of the new faith at Badr (A.D. 624). A small group of Muslims had routed a much larger force of Meccan unbelievers. The battle was seen as a vindication of the new faith brought about by the direct intervention of God who sent a thousand angels to fight on the Muslim side:

God revealed His will to the angels, saying: "I shall be with you. Give courage to the believers. I shall cast terror into the hearts of the infidels. Strike off their heads, strike off the very tips of their fingers!" That was because they defied God and His apostle. He that defies God and His apostle shall be sternly punished by God. We said to them: "Taste this. The scourge of the Fire awaits the unbelievers."

Did this translate into the idea that 1,364 years later, the boy Taimour is an unbeliever who tasted the scourge of fire from Ba'thist angels? But why? Michel 'Aflaq, the founder of the Ba'th Party, theorized fifty years ago that the Arab revolution of the Ba'th was at bottom a modern reenactment of the Islamic revolution of fourteen centuries ago. It was not for nothing, he argued, that the Qur'an was written in Arabic and revealed to an Arab. Taimour is not an Arab; he is a Kurd who did not speak Arabic when he was taken from his village in the summer of 1988. However, that is not the full story. "They ask you about the spoils, *al-anfal*. Say: *'al-anfal* belong to God and the Apostle. Therefore have fear of God and end your disputes. Obey God and His apostle, if you are true believers.' " *al-Anfal* means the "spoils" of battle. Muhammad's original intent in the Battle of Badr was to attack a caravan led by Abu Sufyan ibn Harb, chief of the Umayyad clan, which was on its way back to Mecca from Syria, richly laden with goods. *Surat al-Anfal* was a Qura'nic revelation designed to define the laws by which booty of this sort should be divided amongst the Muslims, many of whom had had their properties in Mecca confiscated for joining the new religion. Muhammad's purpose was to avoid the disputes and questioning which the whole issue of *ghanima*, booty, was raising among Muslim fighters. Arab tribal traditions to do with *ghazw*, raiding for profit, were being restructured and provided with a new justification:

You seek the chance gain of this world, but God desires for you the world to come. He is mighty and wise. Had there not been a previous sanction from God, you would have been sternly punished for what you had taken. Enjoy therefore the good and lawful things which you have gained in war, and fear God. God is forgiving and merciful.

The Iraqi Ba'th were interpreting the eighth *sura* of the Qur'an to mean that the village Taimour came from, the livestock his family raised, the grain stocks they stored, in fact their every personal possession were lawfully at the absolute disposal of the central government in Baghdad. Qura'nic and post-Qura'nic law on *ghanima* only applied in case of *jihad,* or holy war, and even then it did not provide a conqueror with such license. The Ba'thi use, however, was intended to mean that everything inside the territory covered by the "heroic *Anfal* operations" was religiously permitted—*halal*—to the Iraqi army. Where the lives of the Kurdish men, women, and children from the "conquered" villages also "permitted" to Iraqi soldiers and officers?[7]

I had begun hearing some very strange stories before entering northern Iraq. About Kurdish women, for instance, being sold in a white slave trade that was reaching all the way down to the Gulf. A Kurd I know received a letter in April 1989 from a friend who drove a freight truck between Amman and Baghdad. On one of his trips, his truck broke down near the town of Ramadi. While waiting for it to be fixed, two women approached him, pleading to be taken to Sulaimaniyya. Realizing they were fellow Kurds, he entered into a conversation with them, only to find out that they had been captured during the *Anfal* operations of 1988 and sold by a relatively junior army officer to the shaikh of a local tribe in the Governorate of Anbar. The man had turned down their request and was writing the letter because he was feeling ashamed of himself.[8]

Among the secret police documents I have obtained copies of is a list of people executed between February 1 and August 24, 1989. Five people were executed on March 4; two on March 11; one on March 13; twenty-four on May 30; and so on. Accompanying each name is a case summary. Nothing on the face of it very unusual about that. The list was enclosed with a covering letter, marked "Secret and Confidential," dated August 24, 1989, issued by the office of the president of Iraq. At the top of the page in exquisite Kufic calligraphy (the kind used to give a classical look to Arabic stationery) is printed the phrase: "In the Name of God, the Compassionate, the Merciful." My attention was drawn to Dalshad Muhammad Amin Fattah, a Kurdish writer and literary figure, and the thirty-fifth name down the list. His case summary reads as follows: "The named criminal was a teacher in Shoresh Secondary School for boys in Sulaimaniyya and he taught the Kurdish language in the Latin script, using the chauvinist and separatist ideas which he believed in." Dalshad Fattah had been teaching Kurdish (which is okay) but in the Latin script (which is not okay because he should have used the Arabic script). For this he was shot. But at least he got shot for something. Choosing the name *"Anfal"* eliminates the need even for such reasons.

On the other hand, there can only be as much license in a name as a culture is prepared to accord to it. Names do not acquire meaning on their own. Many people have to become involved. The two women mentioned in the letter quoted above were sold off by an officer to a shaikh who had nothing to do with the army. In the three years since the *Anfal* campaign, these women would have been passed around among a lot of men. Maybe there were middlemen involved. There had to be if Kurdish women were going to reach the twentieth-century harems of exorbitantly wealthy potentates. There is more than gross corruption and criminality involved here; there is the authority of the past being brought to bear on people's lives in the present. This has become very common in twentieth-century Arab nationalist or Islamic politics. Clever Ba'thist ideologues had done their homework when they chose al-*Anfal* as the codename for their 1988 operations in Iraqi Kurdistan.

"May God be my witness that it was God who wanted that which has occurred [the occupation of Kuwait], and not us. I mean our role has been zero," said Saddam Husain, preparing his military commanders in December 1990 for "the mother of all battles." "One of the funny things which you should know, and which I only found out the day before yesterday, is that the symbol of Bush's party is the elephant. 'Hast thou not seen what thy Lord did with the Men of the Elephant?' I mean, when I heard this. . . . ," Saddam's voice slowly fades into silence as if astounded at the wondrous implications of the Qur'anic verse he has just quoted. There follows a fifteen-second silence and one of Iraq's top military commanders takes to mumbling barely audible verses from the Qur'an in the background. "It is the will of God," says another commander loudly. The mumbling in a tone of wonder and amazement goes on.[9] The rest of *sura* 105 of the Qur'an which Saddam did not have to quote because it was so well known to all assembled tells what happened to the Men of the Elephant:

> Did He not make their guile go astray? Loosing upon them birds in flight [*tayran ababeel*], hurling against them stones of baked clay. So it is that he made them like green blades devoured.

In pre-Islamic Arabia, on the day that the Prophet Muhammad was born, Mecca was saved by a miracle from an invasion of Habashis (ancient Ethiopians). Swarms of flying black birds with very tough beaks hurled "stones of baked clay" upon the Habashis, who came riding in on a herd of elephants. George Bush and his army of 500,000 Americans were going to meet the same fate, Saddam was telling his army commanders in December 1990. The sad thing is how well this kind of imagery worked for a majority of Arabs during the Gulf crisis, and how little it is ever actively opposed by the intellectuals who know better.[10] In the Middle East, the past is rarely ever just that. In the shape of the motivation for and legitimation of the present, it hangs like a millstone around everyone's neck.

How Cruelty Escalates

THE Anfal campaign did not come out of the blue. It was the outcome of policies toward the Kurdish people of Iraq dating back to the 1975 Algiers Agreement, and the designation of the first strip of territory from which all signs of human life were henceforth to be "prohibited." In 1976, with Iranian acquiescence, a zone five to ten miles wide all along the Iraq-Iran border was evacuated. Every village inside that zone was destroyed and their inhabitants resettled in new, Iraqi government-designed "housing complexes" on the outskirts of big cities (*mujama'at;* singular, *mujama'*—as they became known even among those Kurds who did not speak Arabic). Compensation, however, was often paid during this phase, and for some families living conditions may actually have improved. Appraisal committees were sometimes set up to establish the compensation value of the confiscated property. The amount paid, Kurds tell me, depended on the political disposition of the families involved. But this was not always applied in immediately obvious ways. For instance, 5,000 Iraqi dinars might be the compensation price for a family with a house and orchard. But if the family was known to sympathize with the Kurdish national movement, the price could rise to 50,000 dinars. The regime was actually trying to bribe these people away from their political allegiances. In the payoffs, each home and family got something, but the head of the tribe got the lion's share (similar tactics were successfully applied to tribal Shi'i leaders in southern Iraq during the Iraq-Iran War). Moreover, the evacuation policies did not affect only those Kurds who had fought against the government or whose sympathies were with the Kurdish opposition; they included the villages of *Jahsh* tribal leaders who had fought with the regime against other Kurds during the 1974–75 rebellion.

Other forms of persuasion employed by the regime included sending respected Kurdish figures to speak on its behalf. The Kurdish minister of social affairs, originally from Qala Diza, was apparently a much-liked man who was sent by the regime to persuade people to leave their villages during the second half of the 1970s. He would tell people: "There'll be fighting if you don't leave, and you'll be hurt. And if you stay behind in your villages, you'll end up ten years behind the times." This particular notable was one of many pro-government Kurds sent to convince people to leave their homes. Religious scholars, *shuyoukh,* and other types of Kurdish leaders were also dispatched on these missions. After the defeat of the 1975 rebellion, Kurds had little choice. But the lengths to which the regime originally went to resettle Kurds, even in these circumstances, is worth noting precisely because of how they were going to change during the 1980s. The persuaders sent by the government would spend several weeks trying to cajole people, and only after they were through would the army come. That is a far cry from what happened to 'Abdallah al-'Askari's village of Guptapa in April 1988. Reliable numbers of people affected in the resettlements and deportations of the 1970s are hard to come by, but in 1978, *al-Thawra,* the official Iraqi government newspaper, admitted that 150,000 people were deported over a two-month period.[11]

The classic case of forced resettlement from this period is that of the Barazani clan from the Babinan area in northern Iraq. The Ba'th did not even try to bribe them off; it chose instead to turn them into an example. The Barazanis were resettled in deplorable, ghettolike conditions in southern Iraq in 1976. There they remained until 1981, when they were relocated to a "new" resettlement camp just outside Arbil called Gushtapa. Out of an original population of 50,000 people, some 20,000 or 30,000 remained. In 1983, Barzan al-Takriti, Iraq's representative at the United Nations (who also sat in at meetings of the UN Human Rights Commission), along with Saddam's half brother, Watban, led a force of *mukhabarat* and special army units to collect several thousand of the camp's menfolk and boys over twelve years of age. These men, an eyewitness told me, were driven southward in a convoy of trucks and last seen on the outskirts of Baghdad. They then officially "disappeared." Several thousand names have been lodged with the United Nations for many years now.

But the few hours I spent in Gushtapa during my November 1991 trip left me feeling that the real tragedy of what had happened here lay in the fate of the living, not the dead. The camp was surrounded by barbed wire in the early stages after the men were taken, and the inhabitants subjected to a daily routine of abuse by the army units surrounding them. Electricity was cut off and all contact with the outside world forbidden. Water had to be carried in in jerry cans, placed on the head in the traditional manner. Soldiers would take pot shots at the cans, one woman recalled, or deliberately spill the contents of the can after she had made the whole journey back and forth. Army and party men took their liberties. Women were raped and forced to serve as concubines. I wanted to interview one such woman. "They would commit suicide rather than talk about these things," I was told by one man. Young babies and children less than nine years old were running around; they could not possibly have had Kurdish fathers. The moral bonds within families, who had anyway lost all their men, were breaking up. Some males who survived the operations (because they were abroad, or in the hills) have taken to refusing to recognize their ties with the inhabitants of Gushtapa. They might stop wearing the distinctive Barazani red headdress, for instance, replacing it with the more innocuous black version. These men are ashamed, and their shame served to ostracize the victims of the Ba'th even further. Gushtapa became a source for prostitutes who plied their trade in the streets of Arbil and even Baghdad. Ba'thist revenge on the proud Barazani clan that has led the Kurdish national liberation movement in Iraq at such a cost was now complete.

As I walked around the camp, and the word spread that we had come to find out what had happened here, women and children began pouring out of their houses. They came with photographs of missing fathers, brothers, uncles, and cousins. At that moment, with the crowds pressing around me, I felt a deep, inexpressible shame that I was born an Iraqi.

The importance of Gushtapa is that it was a dress rehearsal for what was going to be done to much larger numbers of Kurds in the run-up to the *Anfal* campaign of 1988. The growing brutalization of the whole of Iraqi society caused by the Iraq-Iran War can be seen in the evolution of Iraqi government policy toward its Kurdish population during the 1980s. In 1982, the regime began deporting people from areas outside the security strip related to the Algiers Agreement (people had to vacate villages, towns, and even the new "housing complexes" built in the 1970s). If they were compensated at all, the sums were trifling. The government's idea seems to have been to minimize the effect of possible Iranian territorial gains inside Iraq. So, for example, if Iran were to occupy Chwarta after it had been emptied, the political and psychological consequences would not be so great. The new settlements looked like concrete barracks, were often next to army bases, and had no amenities. Kurds were cut off from their whole way of life and did not want to move there. Often, they would slip back to their own villages and start rebuilding them.

The more immediate precedent to the *Anfal,* according to secret police documents captured by Kurdish organizations during the March 1991 intifada, is the elimination of Kurdish villages, which began in earnest in 1986. In one such document dated November 26, 1986, the secret police in Sulaimaniyya, working at the behest of the Ministry of Internal Security in Baghdad, prepared a list of 663 villages "prohibited for security reasons." This was also the idea behind the establishment of a five- to ten-mile security strip along the Iranian border in 1977. The area covered by the prohibition had grown enormously. A cover report to the list explains that electrical services have been cut off to these villages, all livestock removed, and a total ban on all commercial transactions inside and among the villages put in place. Yet, the author of the report noted, this was not quite enough: "Although the economic blockade is being implemented, some necessary foodstuffs are getting through because the roads leading into the villages are not properly secured. Given the nature of the terrain, there is more than one secondary route and these are virtually open." The report recommends that a tighter blockade be created and enforced.

By 1987, it is clear, the government was doing more than tightening blockades. I have studied a ledger seized from a building that once was Sulaimaniyya's Central Security Headquarters. The ledger is legal-size and carefully covered in pink wrapping paper, and on the wrapping paper are printed large, cartoonish white petunias. Covering books like this was the kind of thing we loved to do as schoolchildren in Baghdad as a way of "personalizing" our notebooks. Perhaps the clerk who kept this particular notebook felt similarly; he had also chosen a purple felt-tip pen, and an elaborate calligraphic style, to identify the contents of the notebook on a small square of white paper taped to the cover: "Register of Eliminated Villages."

In all, 399 villages were listed in this notebook. The dates the villages were "eliminated"—all in 1987—were carefully entered alongside each name, and next to each date were map coordinates pinpointing the exact location of each village. All the villages were—had been—situated in four eastern provinces of northern Iraq; it seemed this register was one of a series, each volume devoted to a different geographical area of Kurdistan. None of the villages in the petunia-festooned register had been on the 1986 list I've seen of villages "prohibited for security reasons," but I am convinced—from the evidence as a whole—that these "eliminated" villages had indeed been previously deemed "prohibited." (Cables, files, transcripts, and other papers documenting the *Anfal* campaign have yet to be properly collected and collated, and until such a time they cannot be thoroughly and systematically studied. I first saw some of the documents in London in August 1991. In northern Iraq, each of the eight major groups that make up the Kurdistan Front has its own cache. It will take years simply to sift through all the evidence, provided it can be housed for scholarly study in a suitably academic environment untainted by short-term political considerations. From such a remarkable vantage point, I believe, may someday be written not only a unique history of Iraq but a case study in the workings of a modern police state.)

During my stay in Iraq I could find no one document declaring the beginning of the *Anfal* campaign. But I have in my possession a copy of a decree, signed by Saddam Husain, that established the legal framework for such an operation—and it should prove damning should the top command of the Ba'th ever be brought to trial for crimes against humanity. The decree is dated March 29, 1987; it was issued in the name of the Revolutionary Command Council (RCC), the highest decision-making body of the regime, tightly controlled by Saddam, and it was to take effect immediately. It bestowed upon Saddam's cousin and fellow RCC member 'Ali Hassan al-Majeed—he later became the Iraqi defense minister—total control over northern Iraq, including Iraqi Kurdistan. This control extended to "all civilian, military, and security" institutions, and all laws that might conflict with this control were to be suspended "until further notice."[12]

Using the powers conferred on him by this decree, 'Ali Hasan al-Majeed began eliminating villages, those known for their militancy and especially those that had previously harbored *peshmerga*. The first Kurdish village ever to be attacked with chemical weapons (apart from napalm), was Shaikh Wisan in the Balisan Valley. It was bombed in April 1987, and I saw the rusting telltale chemical gas cannisters when I visited it in November 1991 and talked to the villagers about what had happened. Dr. Ja'far, a Kurdish professional who was working in Military Intelligence at the time in the Republican Hospital of Arbil, was a witness to what happened to the wounded survivors from that particular attack:

> Local people brought them to the Republican Hospital in private cars. The number of casualties was more than 380, old men, women, children, all affected by chemical weapons. They put them in a big ward and the government ordered the doctors not to treat them. They just kept them under supervision and they forbade anyone contact with them. They remained one day in that hospital and the second night they took these people to prison, a big building also in Arbil. They remained there for a few days and afterward they took them to an unknown place. There was a guy who lived close to the prison who says he saw these people taken out at night and buried alive.[13]

A whole slew of increasingly brutal attacks—some using chemical weapons, others conventional explosives—followed later on that year. Kurds fled to the cities and also fled into Iran, but they were not yet being systematically rounded up and transferred to forts for extermination. That came later. This was still a time of experimentation, of testing out various strategies. If the Arab world did not care to know what was being done in its name, some Western diplomats certainly knew, and yet their governments did absolutely nothing to let the rest of the world know. One Western diplomat who visited northern Iraq in the summer of 1987 called the razing of the villages and the relocation of hundreds of thousands of Kurds "a demographic revolution that has taken place under our noses in the past six months."[14] A sense of the role 'Ali Hasan al-Majeed played in Kurdistan in the late 1980s can perhaps best be inferred from the nicknames he acquired among the Kurds. At first he was called " 'Ali Chemical." Later he became even more famous as " 'Ali Anfal."

The name *"al-Anfal"* does not seem to have been applied to any of 'Ali Hasan al-Majeed's operations in northern Iraq before February 1988. I believe that a major decision to escalate the levels of violence against Kurdish villages was made sometime in late 1987 or early 1988. That escalation was given the codename *al-Anfal*. There was nothing secret about the fact that something new was in the works because all through 1988 Iraqis heard over and over again, in all the major government-controlled media, about the "heroic *Anfal* operations." Shoresh Rasoul, who has put more time into studying the *Anfal* campaign than any other person I know, believes the first *Anfal* operation began at 2:00 A.M. on the night of February 22–23, 1988, in the village of Yaakh Simar near Sulaimaniyya. The attacks went on all through the summer of 1988, ending in late August or early September. In the minds of most Iraqis, including former soldiers I spoke with, these *Anfal* operations, which were conducted by the First and Fifth Corps of the Iraqi army accompanied by hundreds of thousands of auxiliary Kurdish *Jahsh* units, were understood to be part of the general war effort against Iran. But in fact a separate, massive campaign was under way—a campaign directed fully at noncombatant Kurds. Some people definitely knew what was going on.

Shortly after the Gulf war, Jamal (a pseudonym), an upper-class Baghdadi professional in his early thirties, and his wife spent an evening with a close friend, Tariq (another pseudonym), and his wife. The two couples quickly got around to talking about the regime. Suddenly, Tariq started talking about something horrendous that his cousin, an officer in state security, had been involved in. The cousin had worked for state security in the northern region for ten years, spending most of his time in Mosul. In confidence, Tariq related how his cousin, 'Aziz, knew of a government order for the killing of 22,000 Kurds. Apparently, because the numbers were so great, the killing had to be done in a special way. When the authorities carried out such killings—'Aziz had said—they put the victims into pits and then covered over the bodies. 'Aziz had himself killed people, although how many and his exact role in this particular operation were not talked about. Tariq also recounted an incident via 'Aziz in which a soldier, his hand shaking, refused to shoot down Kurds, whereupon his commanding officer first threatened him and then asked another soldier to shoot his defiant comrade. The second soldier refused as well. After conferring with headquarters, the commanding officer shot both men himself.[15]

By its end, the 1988 campaign, *al-Anfal,* had resulted in the total destruction of 1,276 villages, according to my analysis of Kurdish sources. This should be compared with less than 12 villages eliminated between 1969 and 1974, a number that escalated to 1,189 in the next five-year period. In total, according to these sources, around 3,500 villages have been destroyed since 1968 (roughly 80 percent of all the rural villages in Iraqi Kurdistan). How can one fully comprehend such numbers? Israel, inside its pre-1967 borders, was built upon the suffering of Palestinians from 369 "eliminated" villages. So, how much collective pain is there when the numbers grow by a factor of 10? I don't know the answer. Indeed, there is no answer to a question like that. Pain, like cruelty, is not relative; it is unquantifiable. Nonetheless, all those Iraqis and Arabs who kept silent while all this was going on have a moral obligation to keep on thinking about what it all means.

The hallmark of the *Anfal* campaign, however, was not the elimination of villages; that had been going on for a very long time now in Iraq, as I have tried to show. The real hallmark of the operation was the bureaucratically organized, routinely administered mass killing of village inhabitants for no other reason than that they happened to live in an area that was now designated as "prohibited for security reasons." This bureaucratic rationale distinguishes the *Anfal* campaign from a war crime like Halabja or the execution of a Kurd as a political opponent of the regime, however that might be defined (for that matter, whether he was really politically active or not is also beside the point). Systematic organized mass murder of this nature has, to the best of my knowledge, never happened before in the modern history of Iraq.

A typical *Anfal* operation is perhaps best described by the regime itself. A letter printed on presidential stationery and marked "Secret and Personal" tells of "2,532 people and 1,869 families" being "captured" during a "heroic *Anfal* operation" and sent to a "camp," the location of which is not disclosed. As to the fate of those captured and imprisoned, I quote here from an audiotape of the proceedings of a meeting of senior army, Ba'th Party, and secret police officers held on January 26, 1989, in Kirkuk, the Kurdish city in northern Iraq. The tape, which I listened to while I was in Iraq, records 'Ali Hasan al-Majeed talking in crude Takriti slang (like Saddam, he is from the town of Takrit) about the Kurds who wound up at forts like that of Qoratu:

[T]aking care of them means burying them with bulldozers. That's what taking care of them means. . . . These people gave themselves up.

Does that mean I am going to leave them alive? Where shall I put these people, so many of them? So I began to distribute them across the provinces. And from there I had bulldozers going backwards and forwards.

How many Kurds were killed, their bodies bulldozed into mass graves? During my three weeks in Kurdistan, everyone, it seemed, had a story about some family member "lost" in the *Anfal*. I had nearly 11,000 names thrust upon me on one list or another. The figure of 182,000 put out by Kurdish leaders is not backed up by lists but is based upon extrapolations made from the number of rural villages destroyed. When I asked Dr. Mahmoud 'Uthman, leader of the Socialist Party of Kurdistan, what he thought the total number of dead or missing might be, he told me of a meeting he had attended late in the spring of 1991, a meeting at which Kurdish leaders and government officials were once again—this time in the wake of the Gulf war and the uprising that immediately followed—negotiating the question of Kurdish autonomy. (A plan was broached and brooded over, but all talk of such autonomy ended in the fall of 1991.) At this meeting, 'Uthman recalled, Kurdish delegates raised the matter of the missing Kurds: perhaps they were still alive in camps in the south somewhere?

'Ali Hasan al-Majeed was at the meeting and, according to 'Uthman, grew upset when the issue of the Kurds rounded up during the *Anfal* campaign was raised. "He became enraged," 'Uthman told me, "slamming shut the file in front of him and leaping up as though to storm out of the room." Then, as if to end all talk of the campaign, al-Majeed shouted: "What is this exaggerated figure of 182,000? It couldn't have been more than 100,000."

The First Encounter with the *Anfal*

I ARRIVED at the Hotel Baghdad in Zakho from the Turkish border around 8:30 P.M. on November 11, 1991. Zakho is a border town in every sense of the word. Allegiances are never what they look like in this town of 125,000 people. Considerable caution had been advised. The rivalry between the Kurdish parties could get bitter, and Ba'thi secret agents among the Kurds lurked around. Shortly after I left, an unknown gunman fired at the car of a former agent-defector, killing all three of his bodyguards. The town had turned into a smuggler's paradise. A Kalashnikov assault rifle, for instance, sold for $150, and a snub-nosed .357 Magnum handgun for $300. Three BBC journalists were killed, and their bodies dumped in a mountain ravine not far from here, earlier in the year. They took the wrong guide to make the crossing into Iraq.

The hotel faced a traffic roundabout, from the center of which rose a concrete umbrella intended to shade the traffic police. Round it ran a slogan: "We want the conscience of every Iraqi to be his watchdog." On the corner, a laundry house sign: *Makwi Gharnata,* lit up the street. The huge stamping irons chugged away, steam billowing all around. Walking down the seedy courtyard, I saw a gigantic red rose painted on a wall. In front of it, a sign read: *Warshat Ahmad al-Faniyya.* Ahmad, who had commissioned the painting, fixes televisions. A blind alley nearby was called *al-Ahrar,* "the alley of the free ones." A poster extolled in verse: "If you ask after me, then this is my way: Freedom for the Kurds and Union for Kurdistan." A sign in the reception area next to my room in the hotel read: "It is the obligation of all guests to place their valuables with the management of the hotel in return for a sealed receipt. However, the management is not responsible for their loss."

For breakfast the next morning I had bread, tea, and *gaymar,* a thick white cream made from water buffalo milk. Shi'ite Arabs from the marshes area south of Iraq make *gaymar.* There was a community on the periphery of the town, I was told, who had been resettled there many years ago as part of the "Arabization" of Kurdistan. I passed by their characteristic mud hut dwellings many times on this journey. Often the villages were abandoned, but not always. Wherever *gaymar* is available for breakfast, you know that a community of displaced Arab villagers still exists nearby. The taxi driver who brought me to the hotel from the border doubled next morning as breakfastmaker and server. He proudly displayed two kinds of bread to go with the *gaymar.* "Saddam's bread," he said, pointing at the brown circular flat loaves, and "Kurdish bread," pointing at a pile of oval-shaped white flour loaves. I ate the Saddam bread.

The original plan was to creep into Zakho unnoticed on the way in and head over the mountain route at the crack of dawn next morning, past 'Amadiyya, straight for the safer environment of Shaqlawa. I had fond memories of riding up the mountains around 'Amadiyya on a mule in the 1960s, and wanted to see the town again. But that was going to be the only stop on the seven-hour trip by Land Rover to Shaqlawa. Things didn't work out that way, and I ended up sleeping in the Hotel Baghdad a second night, because of a man called Subhi Farman whom I met by chance right after my first Iraqi breakfast in twenty-three years.

Subhi is a soft-spoken Kurdish engineer, in his early forties, who used to have a business in Baghdad. Now he does relief work full time from Zakho. But it was what he was doing in his spare time that changed things. For some time Subhi had been noticing women with no menfolk, usually accompanied by children, who had some very bizarre stories to tell. No one took these women seriously. They were strangers to the town and settled in whatever little cranny they could find.

> I met one widow. She had two babies. Both had died. One in the prison in Salamiyya near Mosul and the other in Baharka. I asked her what she wants to do in the future. She said that she wants to work in a humanitarian organization dealing with kids. Like a kindergarten or a hospital for children. Things like that. Because she lost two of her children. She is now alone and she does not believe her husband has been killed. She is waiting for him. She told me that they were in love . . . you know. They got married and she is waiting for him.
>
> KM: Are there many women with stories like that in Zakho?
>
> Yes, yes. So many. Everywhere you can find those people.

The problem, Subhi thought, was that "nobody cared." "No humanitarian organization. No NGOs. Not even the Kurdish parties. Nobody gave any assistance to those people. They have been just swallowed up in the towns. They are living in very miserable places. For example, I met some people who are living in an unfinished building, no windows, no doors. Nothing for heating. And there are children, you know. These are the survivors."

These were leftover people from the *Anfal* operations of 1988. In his spare time, Subhi began to compile their names. He had been working on his list for two months when I met him and had records of five hundred families who had one or more missing members. How many people worked with him on the project? "Well, just me," he said with an embarrassed chuckle. "But later I hired two people to go out into the field. We gathered the information from different parties in the area. Then we sent two people to Zakho area to gather the information and to get photographs from each family and to have the story in detail of what happened to each family in 1988."

How could he afford to hire them, I asked. "We have received some funds from the International Rescue Committee. We have received five hundred dollars." On November 9, four days before we got to Zakho, Subhi started to put the information he had compiled onto properly typed forms, intending to go on in this way until he had used up his grand total of five hundred dollars.

KM: You designed the forms?

Yes, I did. I consulted with my friends about what information would be better to include. I made the form and then I changed it according to what some people advised. You know. Can I have your ideas on it?

Subhi's form was entitled "The Lost Ones of the *Anfal.*" A whole page is devoted to each missing person. Wherever available, a photograph is pinned to the top left-hand corner. The sheet gives the tripartite name, date of birth, income level, marital status, occupation, previous and current address of the family, and the place and date of disappearance. It also lists the number of surviving members in the family from whom the information has been collected and where they are living now, with observations on what these survivors would like to go on and do with their lives. For instance, "The widow is willing to work on a sewing machine. . . ," or, "This family wants a job for their son Tawfeeq, brother of the killed. . . ," and so on.

The following week I was given another list, by a different person, which had 10,666 names on it. But it was nowhere nearly as well organized as Subhi's. All of these names I would later lug back to London. The making of lists is important. But I still don't know what to do with the names I have got. The fact that they are being made means that the *Anfal* is about the present, not the past; it is about memories that are not going to go away. Terrible memories that are going to shape Iraq's future, whether we like it or not.

At the office where Subhi worked, I rifled through the pile of forms he put before me, and picked out a surname at random: the 'Aboush family from the village of Karpit 'Ali. Twenty-one men had disappeared from this village and another eighteen from a village nearby called Karpit Taimour. Ten male members of the 'Aboush family were taken along with everyone else in the village of Karpit 'Ali in August 1988. Since September 1, 1988, the following ten members of the 'Aboush family have not been seen by anyone: Sa'eed 'Aboush, born 1942; Hameed 'Aboush, born 1951; Taggar 'Aboush, born 1952; Rasheed 'Aboush, born 1954; Salim 'Aboush, born 1963; Younis 'Aboush, born 1957; Tahseen 'Aboush, born 1972; Jangir 'Aboush, born 1965; Muslih 'Aboush, born 1974; and Rabah Sa'eed 'Aboush, born 1975.

At this point all previous plans to slip quickly out of Zakho were thrown to the wind. I asked if we could go and meet what remained of the 'Aboush family. The only surviving adult male is a guerrilla fighter named Isma'il. He had been a *peshmerga* for twenty years and escaped to Turkey just before the army arrived. Therefore he had not seen with his own eyes everything that had happened. But Isma'il lived with his mother and the children of his brothers, and they had. This particular group of survivors were living less than ten minutes by car from the office where I was talking to Subhi.

The story as pieced together from the accounts of Isma'il, his mother, and the additional information provided by Subhi, goes like this. On the morning of August 26, 1988, in the wake of a chemical attack on the village of Tuka which had left thirteen people killed the previous day, the 'Aboush family left their village of Karpit. The roads were packed with other fleeing villagers. The army had cut off the roads and surrounded the area. Nobody could give me a good sense of how many villages were surrounded in this particular operation, but there were many. On August 27, two male members of the 'Aboush family made it through army lines across the main road into the northern part of Zakho, escaping eventually to Turkey. Everyone else was cut off and had no choice but to "surrender," along with thousands of other families.

KM: Why do you say "surrendered"; they hadn't been fighting?

The *Anfal* counted everyone, even a child, to be a combatant.

After surrendering, everyone was herded together in a convoy of vehicles which passed through Zakho to a fort built in the 1980s called Nazarkeh, just outside Dohuk. Nazarkeh was under the control of the *mukhabarat* or security police, not the army. Maybe ten thousand families (the estimates vary) were held in Nazarkeh at the end of August 1988. At the fort, some people were released, according to Isma'il, but the majority were held there.

In a stream of consciousness, which jumbled up all chronological sequence, Isma'il's mother put into words what happened to her:

Three brothers said, "We are going to give ourselves up to them." We stayed until we saw the stars and Haji Muhammad said, "I will go and give myself up to them." After that he put things in a tractor and put some of his children in it and we women came to the street. We were separated. So many families were separated. We stayed until the following day in the evening, hungry and thirsty. These kids were with us [she points at the group of young children sitting around her]. This one was newly born. And Rasheed's children were with us. We were in a terrible condition. Like dogs. Some said, "Let's go in the dark." Others said no. Some said, "Let's go this way." Some said, "There are wounded people here." We stood there until night on the street.

There were a lot of young women and old men and women. They took us separately and the young men separately. Young men from seven years on. They were beating them in front of us on the street. They killed men in front of us before taking them to prison. Later they took us somewhere else.

What did they do to people inside Nazarkeh?

Whatever you can imagine, they did. Hitting with bricks, cables, shoes. They brought back some men and I started helping them. But they couldn't move; they were so old and tired. Some came back and some didn't.

Did they beat people in front of you?

Yes, even kids. Both of my sons and anyone who was giving a statement was beaten afterwards.

Did the word "Anfal" get mentioned?

No. We couldn't ask anything because if we asked they would beat us and throw bricks on our back.

Were there any Jahsh with them?

Inside the castle of Nazarkeh, there were no Jahsh. They were all mukhabarat and security forces. The beating was done by men in civilian clothes who wore shirts with short sleeves.

Are some of the children I see here the same ones who were with you inside Nazarkeh at the time? What about that little boy over there?

He was three months old. And this little one and that little one were with us. We didn't know anything when we went there. We didn't know anything. . . . We didn't know! We thought that the world was turning upside down.

A few days after being in Nazarkeh, the security police called out the names of the remaining males. The 'Aboush family was broken up for the last time. Nine of Isma'il's brothers and one nephew, along with eleven other men from his village, were separated out. Between five and eight thousand males were rounded up and driven away together. They were last seen, Isma'il's mother said, at an army checkpoint just outside Mosul.

The womenfolk and children were driven to a large central prison in Mosul called Salamiyya. There they were held for around two weeks. Later they were moved to a resettlement camp called Baharka, which is in the plains area just outside Arbil. In Baharka, each family was allotted 160–220 square yards of land to build upon. There were no buildings at this camp, no water supply, no electricity, no shade, no protective device of any description. All this happened in the peak of the summer heat. Initially, the people of Arbil were not allowed to contact the Baharka detainees or bring them any help from the outside. The camp was surrounded by the army. Things got smuggled in, of course. But later on the army relaxed as the number of people grew. Tents started cropping up and concrete block structures. Children kept on dying every day. In some locations, I was told, there were no more children left under the age of five. There the 'Aboush womenfolk and children stayed for two years, until moving back to Zakho. I asked Isma'il's mother what living in Baharka had been like. "They brought us all and threw us all together. We didn't have anyone and for three days we had nothing. It was like hell."

Karpit 'Ali, the village of the 'Aboush family, was a mere "half an hour away," we were told. So we decided to go there, taking Isma'il with us. We were driven in a Toyota Land Cruiser on what has to be the roughest dirt and stone road I have ever been on. The car leaped up and down like a jackrabbit, heading toward its destination—in fact, two hours away.

Once upon a time there was a village perched up on a hill overlooking a verdant valley. The Khabour River could be seen twisting below, far away in the distance. The sun was about to set, and the sky was shading into dark blue from a rich orange. It was that moment in the late afternoon of a gloriously clear day when every shade of color between two extremes is represented.

But now every built-up structure had been flattened—razed to the ground, metamorphosed into a piece of archeology whose story could only be reconstructed through excavation, and memory. It was impossible to know a village of forty houses had been there unless you were actively searching for it. Sun-bleached pieces of cloth, which once upon a time were brightly colored, lay under the rubble. But you had to look for them and work hard at digging them out. The water source had been concreted up. Agriculture and animal husbandry—the mainstays of the village's economy—could not start up again. The school, the only concrete structure around, had been so perfectly dynamited that its roof had collapsed down flat onto the very floor it once protected. No debris was scattered outside the foundation lines. Isma'il told me that in 1977 he had worked as a day laborer for the municipal authorities of the greater Zakho area building this particular school.

WHAT kind of a mind-set is this that destroys the very things that it once built? Some mysterious force had taken possession of the human imagination so as to engineer the dispatch of thousands of armed men to this beautiful place. They had driven down the same awful excuse for a road as I had. Bumping along in their armored personnel carriers and lorries, transporting bulldozers and carrying guns and dynamite. Why?

When I asked Subhi what the word *"Anfal"* meant for him, he answered lamely at first: "Well, it is just a bad operation."

When is the first time you heard the word *"Anfal"*?

Well, it was in 1988 when they started the so-called *Anfal*. Before 1988 there was nothing called *Anfal*.

When you make these forms and these lists, you are thinking of the *Anfal*. This is what the *Anfal* is. Right?

Yes.

Is the *Anfal* different from what happened in Halabja?

Halabja is not *Anfal*. Halabja is different.

What did the Ba'th say they were doing? Why, from their own point of view, did they take these families from their villages?

To take the fish from the water.

The Second Encounter with the *Anfal*

THE mountain road from Zakho to 'Amadiyya passes through a breathtakingly beautiful landscape. Nothing could quite prepare me for that first sighting of 'Amadiyya from a distance of about twenty-five miles. The day was crisp, cool, sunny and crystal clear. A round city, just as I remembered it, crowned the mountaintop as though it had been fitted into place.

The 'Amadiyya mountain is a symmetrical cone with its top perfectly sheared off in what looks like an awesome feat of ancient engineering comparable to that which gave rise to Herod's great stone platform in Jerusalem on top of which today sits the Haram al-Sharif. The difference is that in 'Amadiyya no one had to construct the round plateau above which the stone walls of the town's buildings rise as slightly more regular continuations of the craggy slopes below; it was nature's gift to Iraq.

Accompanied by Fareeq, one of the two *peshmerga* guards assigned to us in Zakho, I stopped to take a photograph. With his thin, pencil-like mustache, chic Turkish black leather jacket, and modern-style haircut, Fareeq was always totally absorbed and deadly serious about his work. He was twenty-one years old and has been a *peshmerga* since running away from army service on his father's advice in 1987. Whenever I stepped out of the car to take a photo, Fareeq was there, slightly set back and keeping a watchful eye. Fareeq is the perfect soldier, who never considered he was doing me a service as much as he was doing his duty. His cousin—a passive and reserved young man who had a permanently haunted look about him—got captured by the army at some point and passed on to the *mukhabarat*. He remained in their clutches for one month. He was our other *peshmerga,* and his heart was not in the job. Fareeq led the way, looking for land mines even though I had barely wandered a few yards from the main road for a good vantage point.

The drive into town winds slowly up a dazzlingly steep incline. The first building one encounters in 'Amadiyya is a gas station. The station was clogged with cars waiting for their petrol ration. A tanker had just come in and the word had spread. A *peshmerga* in Kurdish folk costume stood stiffly to attention, marking up a wad of papers in his hand as people milled and jostled good-humoredly around him, waiting for their turn to be called, catered to, and crossed off the list. Was this a future bureaucrat of a Kurdish state?

In Zakho I had already begun to understand that the *Anfal* was not a simple operation in which the same thing happened to everyone. There were different patterns across time and space that were applied according to local conditions. Assyrians found in "prohibited areas" were as likely to disappear as Kurds. In the Sindi area, only Kurdish men disappeared. But in the Doski area near Dohuk, in a village called Korvil, thirty-five men, women, and children were shot on the spot by army officers. Why? I have no idea. The officer in charge was reported to have called out: "This is the *Anfal* and you are to be shot." There were two eyewitnesses to this incident whom I wanted to meet. We had been told to locate Kamal at the local headquarters building of the Kurdish Democratic Party in 'Amadiyya. He should have received a cable from Zakho asking him to locate Sayyid Nayif and Sa'eed Chalki, the witnesses, both of whom were residents of 'Amadiyya.

But Kamal had been unsuccessful in locating them; the bottom line was that we would have to hang around 'Amadiyya for a whole day. This was not possible. So I interviewed Kamal instead.

When is the first time you heard the word *"Anfal"*?

In 1988, of course. They said, "We will begin first *Anfal,* second *Anfal,* third *Anfal.* . . .

Did the *Anfal* come to 'Amadiyya?

There was no *Anfal* in 'Amadiyya because the army was already here, stationed in the town.

In the course of my journey, it became more and more evident that big Kurdish cities like Sulaimaniyya, Arbil, and Kirkuk, and large towns like Dohuk, Zakho, and 'Amadiyya, had not been affected by the *Anfal.* This was strictly a rural operation, confined to the villages of the Kurdish countryside. Families collected from the surrounding villages were brought into town in the course of the campaign, Kamal explained, and separated out in precisely the manner described to me by Isma'il 'Aboush's mother.

People divided into three groups. Some of them fled to Iran with their families. Others, they hid themselves in the mountains between rocks and trees. And others they stayed in the villages. Villages like Spindal, Gizeh, Kafnamajeh, and Mijeh. When the soldiers came and saw them, they attacked and captured all of them. They brought them here in 'Amadiyya and separated the men from the women and children. After that, they took them to Salamiyya [Prison] in Mosul. The women stayed fifteen days in Salamiyya and after that they deported them to a big camp in Arbil called Baharka.

Did they separate the men from the women and children in 'Amadiyya?

Here of course.

What happened to the men?

We don't know anything about them.

Which building were they last seen in?

(Kamal pointed to the building right behind him which he had just left to have this conversation.)

No!

Yes, yes. This building. It used to be the teachers' union.

Now it was the headquarters of the 'Amadiyya branch of the Kurdistan Democratic Party. As time went on, I got more and more accustomed to these bizarre juxtapositions, so characteristic of the situation in northern Iraq.

What does the word *"Anfal"* mean to you?

To uproot, to genocide [sic] and to kill everything.

Meeting Taimour

AS FAR AS anyone knows, Taimour 'Abdallah, from the village of Qulatcho, is the only human being to have experienced firsthand the darkest innermost workings of the *Anfal* campaign and lived to tell of it. This much I already knew in London, although I did not really know what the *Anfal* campaign was about, or if the boy's account could be believed; it had been such a wooden and stilted interview. The *Anfal* was at that point just a name for me, one that kept on cropping up in the copies of the secret police documents which I had been given and which maybe had something to do with large numbers of Kurds disappearing in 1988. Many survivors like 'Abdallah al-'Askari had witnessed the attacks on their villages or other rounding-up operations inside northern Iraq. But only one person "disappeared" and then by a miracle "reappeared" to tell us what had happened to him.

Our meeting took place in an abandoned army barracks a half-hour's drive into the mountains that surround Sulaimaniyya. Bombed-out buildings with blackened windows perched on a mountain with unobstructed visibility in every direction. The setting was as remarkable as the base was awful—surrounded by walls, barbed wire, and security checkpoints. Taimour's life since the March uprising had been organized around the fact that he was and still is a prime target for assassination by Saddam's agents. It became obvious the boy had been turned into a symbol, the servant of a cause, a living monument to the suffering of the Kurdish people.[16]

Taimour was very quiet and passive throughout. In the sixteen hours that I spent in his company, he never spoke unless he was spoken to; he always answered politely, but in monosyllables, showing no emotion whatsoever. Was he suppressing everything because of the trauma? Or was he expected to behave like a hero and heroes don't cry? Maybe the set-up of being interviewed in these unfamiliar surroundings by a foreigner was not conducive to the expression of emotion by someone who was after all still a child. He had been dressed up to look like a miniature version of a Kurdish *peshmerga*. Each Kurdish organization has its distinctive sash around the waist, its own favorite tailors and clothing styles.

The privacy that I desperately needed could not be arranged here, so I had to head back with Taimour and a big escort of armed men to Sulaimaniyya. We arrived at a house in the city center, and after the customary hospitalities and endless cups of tea, late in the evening, a private room was arranged and the interview finally started. But the electricity went off all over Sulaimaniyya. It went on and off again for the rest of the evening. Everything that could go wrong did so that day.

As a result, I was nervous and upset. Who could have foreseen so many people hanging around? The idea had simply been to sit down with Taimour and a tape recorder. I had not anticipated such complications.[17] I mention this because the build-up of tension inside me might have affected the interview. I expected too much from him, wanting every little detail of what had happened. Perhaps I came down too hard on the boy.

The interview began with my telling him that I was born in

Baghdad but lived abroad and had come thousands of miles to talk to him. I said that I wanted to hear everything, including the memories he still lived with. "Don't feel that there is any detail which is not worth talking about," I remember saying more than once. I said all this just before the interview began, as though he wanted nothing other than to relive in infinitesimal detail everything that he had gone through. All this must have contributed to frightening the boy. He must have wondered, Who is this man? What does he want of me? What am I going to get out of this? Why should my story be of interest to him? What is he going to get out of it? All through dinner and breakfast the following morning, I saw him stealing glances in my direction. Whenever I turned to smile back, or acknowledge his look, he would turn his face away as though he hadn't been looking in the first place. Taimour had good reason not to trust another human being ever again.

I think the boy did not want to talk to me. Circumstances had thrust him into a nightmarish, cruel world. Maybe he had never even known a real childhood. But he had been told he must speak to this stranger who had come from far away and was useful to his people's cause. He had been fitted up for the occasion and probably given a dress rehearsal or two in what to say or not to say. He didn't want to talk, but he was expected to, and this is a culture where everyone does what is expected of them. Such lessons are drilled into children from very early on.

Taimour began by spitting out his story in one short spurt, adding nothing to what I didn't already know from that first videotape I had seen in August. I had not come all this way to hear a canned speech. Feeling the tension build up in myself, I started all over again, digging for the detail myself with short, pointed, simple questions, no longer relying on the boy. After a while, a rhythm began to be picked up and I felt I was getting somewhere. How did he feel? I don't know. Taimour, I think, was not expecting anything remotely like this. Did his eyes glisten? Once or twice I think he said things he didn't want to say. The thought still preoccupies me. I remember pressing on relentlessly, stopping only because of the damn lights, which kept on going out all over Sulaimaniyya.

What follows is a transcript of the interview, eliminating repetition and that initial spurt along with a few digressions. I have changed the odd word, and the location of small sequences of questions here or there, only for purposes of making what Taimour was saying clearer to the reader:

The day the army took you from the village, do you remember it well?

Yes.

What were you doing?

Before the arrival of the army?

Yes, before the arrival of the army. What were you doing?

The army didn't come to our village.

[Kurdish units employed by the Iraqi army, the *Jahsh,* came to Taimour's village, not the Iraqi army.]

Who did they take?

Everyone. Men, women, and children.

Did any fighting take place?

No.

The *Jahsh* took Taimour and his father, mother, and three sisters, along with everyone else in the village, to the Fort of Qoratu, passing through the village of Melasoura. My line of questioning was intended to find out what a normal day in Taimour's life was like before the *Anfal* came into his life. He either didn't understand me, or he didn't want to answer the question. At this point in the interview we were speaking in Arabic. A bit later on we shifted to Kurdish at his request, via an interpreter, because he said it was easier for him. His answers have been retranslated from his own words, not as screened through the interpreter.

What happened?

The *Jahsh* said they would escort us to [the village of] Kalar, but they lied, and they took us to [the Fort of] Qoratu instead. We stayed there ten days until they sent us to the prison of Topzawa in Kirkuk.

How did they send you there?

By big military cars. The ones called IVA. [IVA is the local acronym for trucks or lorries of East German manufacture, which are widely used in the Iraqi army.]

How many lorries?

A lot.

Ten?

No, no, a lot. Around thirty or forty.

Were there tanks?

No.

How did they take you?

They threw us in the lorries and they took us.

Were there any orders? An officer, for instance, who shouted something, who called the people to come and enter the car? Something like that. Do you remember anything that was said?

No.

They said nothing!

No.

How did you know what to do?

The only thing they said was: "Enter the lorry."

Did they say why you had to enter the lorry?

No.

Didn't they give any reason for what was going on?

No.

All right. They told you, "Come on, get in the lorry." Then what happened?

We got into the lorry.

How? Family by family?

Yes, family by family.

Did they break up families?

No.

How many people were loaded into each lorry?

I don't know.

How many were you in a lorry?

Well, it was full.

Were you seated or standing?

We were sitting.

What happened to the stuff, the furniture, the livestock, and the wagons that you brought with you?

The government took it.

The wagons and clothes I saw in the Fort of Qoratu during my visit there on November 27 are what was left of the personal possessions of Kurdish villagers not confiscated by the army or stolen by individual soldiers. In Qoratu I may even have been walking amidst the personal effects of Taimour's own family.

What did you take to the prison of Topzawa in Kirkuk?

Nothing. Except the clothes I was wearing.

Did you take money?

No, we had no money.

The army took the money?

Yes.

Had you heard of the word *"Anfal"* before? While you were being moved around from one place to the next, did anyone mention the word *"Anfal"*?

No.

You had never heard the word before?

No.

And none of the officers said, "This is an *Anfal* operation?"

No.

How were you feeling on the lorry, as it was taking you and your family away?

I was feeling nothing. What do you expect?

Were you afraid?

Yes.

Did you see fear on your father's face, or your sisters? Were they crying?

Yes.

Your mother?

No.

When you got to your destination, did they keep the family together?

Yes.

What do you remember about the others with you? Do you remember what people were saying?

They were saying nothing. There were women and children crying.

Did you know what was going to happen to you?

No.

Did the other people guess what was going to happen to them?

No.

It was like a big mystery, you had no idea!

No, but when the *Jahsh* came, they had said, "We will make you *Jahsh* as well. We'll take you to Kalar." That's all they said.

So the *Jahsh* lied to you.

Yes.

They lied, because they took him to the Fort of Qoratu instead of to the village of Kalar. The journey to Kalar would not have been unusual for a Kurdish villager to make. Often in the past, the *Jahsh* were used to move villagers from one place to the other. Eventually people would filter back to their original villages. This had been going on for most of the 1980s and the presence of the *Jahsh* would have had a reassuring and a pacifying effect. That is why the Iraqi government was employing them. This time, however, a different operation was being planned. The Fort of Qoratu was a transfer point used for collecting and separating out those Kurds who were going to be killed off. It is difficult to establish to what extent the *Jahsh* were complicitous in the new plans or to what extent they simply thought it was the same old seesaw game between villagers and central government that had become common all through the 1980s.

When you had a chance to be alone without any *Jahsh* or army officers looking at you, what were people saying to each other?

They were saying nothing.

After you left Qoratu, did they say where they were taking you?

Yes, when we got to the lorries, they said, "We will take you to Topzawa, the prison north of Kirkuk."

Were any of the women hurt during the period that they stayed in the Fort of Qoratu?

No, but before we arrived [in Topzawa], they separated out the old women and sent them back to Kalar.

So the old women were not killed?

No.

But your mother and your sisters, they stayed with you?

Yes.

Describe Topzawa for me.

It was very bad.

In what way?

The halls were very hot.

How many were in your hall?

The hall was full.

What was the number of people?

I didn't count them, but it was full.

And what was your food?

Each person's ration for each day was a piece of bread.

How long did you stay in Topzawa?

We stayed a whole month in Topzawa detention center, until they sent us to the place of the shooting.

On that second leg of your journey heading from the Fort of Qoratu to Topzawa, did anything happen that you still remember clearly?

The thing that I remember is that there was no *Jahsh,* just soldiers.

What happened when you reached the prison of Topzawa in Kirkuk?

When we arrived in Topzawa, they put women and children in one hall and the men in another.

In which group did they put you?

I was with my mother and my sisters.

Did you see your father again after being separated?

I saw him one more time in Topzawa and then I didn't see him again.

What was happening when you saw him?

They were taking off his clothes except for the underclothes. They manacled his hands and then they put all the men in lorries and drove them away.

After that you never saw your father again?

No.

Up to when this happened, I want to know if there is any one thing that you remember very strongly, that you remember above everything else, that you will never forget?

Well, I don't know what to say.

What frightened you the most?

I was afraid they were going to shoot us.

Was there one thing that made you especially afraid?

No, I was just afraid of being shot.

What made you think they would shoot you? You didn't know about the *Anfal.* So what made you think they would shoot you?

I was just afraid.

You always expect Iraqi soldiers to shoot at you?

No.

Okay, let us go back to the last time you saw your father. After they separated the men from the women and children, you said they manacled the men?

Yes.

In front of you?

Yes.

Did they manacle the women and children?

No.

What else did they do to your father?

Nothing else.

They didn't beat him?

No.

Did they manacle each man to the other?

Yes, all together.

In one big line?

Yes.

And who was guarding them?

Iraqi soldiers.

Was Topzawa being run by the army or by the *mukhabarat* [party secret police]?

Soldiers and *mukhabarat* were there, but the *mukhabarat* were a little bit away and the soldiers were inside the prison.

The lorries that took your father away were being run and managed by the *mukhabarat,* or the army?

By the army.

Then the army took the men away. Did you see them walking away from you?

Yes.

How many men were with your father, roughly?

There were a lot.

A hundred?

Yes.

Where did they put them?

They put them in IVA lorries.

All the time that they were putting people in IVA lorries, you were watching?

I was standing right in front of the prison door which was closed and there was a hole through which I was looking.

Were there other people looking through the hole?

Yes.

Who?

The women and the families were looking out.

Everyone was crowding round trying to look through the hole?

Yes.

What did you think was going to happen to your father?

We knew they would shoot him.

So at that point did you realize for the first time that they were going to shoot your father?

Yes.

Did you become very afraid at that particular moment?

Yes.

More afraid than you had ever been before?

At that time, yes.

What about the people around you?

There were women. They were also crying.

What were they saying? They must have been shouting something out.

They were shouting and beating themselves.

Did they tear their clothes?

The women? Yes.

Did they pull their hair?

Yes.

Did they throw themselves on the floor?

No.

What about the children?

They were not crying, they were just looking.

Then the lorry drove off with your father. Do you remember seeing it?

Yes, there was a big door [in a compound wall].

How many lorries drove out of the gate, do you remember?

I didn't count them, but there were around twenty maybe, maybe more.

All of the men in the lorries came from your village, from the villages in your area, all of them were from the same batch of people that had originally been taken with you in the beginning?

There were other people also.

New people from different parts?

There were a lot of villagers, they gathered them in this place and they loaded them together. . . .

At this point, the boy's words seemed to trail off and he looked away as though he had lost track of what he was saying. Some of the answers he had given me do not make sense in retrospect. For instance, how could the children have remained calm while their mothers were hysterical with grief and fear? I have the feeling that not all of his answers should be taken at face value. In the interview we had reached the point at which Taimour was reliving his final separation from his father. I should have paused here, or taken a break. Instead, I pressed on. The answers turned mechanical. I was losing the boy. Maybe he was still there with his father, crowded around that hole, reliving that terrible moment.

Are you feeling okay?

Yes.

Now your father was gone. How much longer did you and your mother and sisters and the rest of the women and children stay in Topzawa?

Ten days.

Did they take you away from Topzawa in army lorries like those that had taken your father away?

No, they were white vehicles that were locked.

(This is a puzzling answer for which I have no explanation. Unfortunately, I didn't pursue the line of questioning. Henceforth Taimour and I will both be referring to these vehicles as lorries.)

Did you know who the men in charge were?

No.

How many people were there in each lorry from Topzawa to the place where the shooting happened?

I think it was about one hundred people in each lorry.

Were they all women and children?

Yes.

How many hours was the journey?

From Topzawa, they took us to the Saudi border. They took us about six o'clock in the morning, and we reached the place of the shooting late.

How late?

We arrived at night.

[But there was still light because it was summertime and the sun sets very late in August.]

Did you stop on the way?

No.

Where did you eat lunch?

We had no lunch.

Did they abuse you in any way inside the lorries?

There were no soldiers inside, but it was very hot. There were people dying of thirst. They didn't give us water on the way.

People died inside the lorry?

Three children died.

For how many days did you not have water?

Just that day. When they got us in the lorry, they didn't give us water.

Tell me something about the children who died.

The little boy died of thirst, and a small girl died in our car from thirst and suffocation.

Can you describe her?

Her eyes had gone out of their sockets. And her neck was blue. The girls were not from my village. They were from somewhere else. I don't know where from.

How old were they?

Younger than me.

What did people in the lorry do with these dead children?

We did nothing.

You covered them?

No.

Were they at least pushed to one side of the truck by the older women?

No.

They just lay on the floor?

Yes.

How were you feeling?

There were no feelings. What feelings?

Did Taimour misunderstand me here? Or was he just taken aback at the stupidity of a question whose answer was impossible to formulate in words?

Your mother was with you?

Yes.

Your sisters?

Yes.

What did you think was going to happen to you now?

I was thinking we would be shot.

No one said anything to you about what was going to happen next?

No.

Before, the *Jahsh* lied to you. This time no one even bothered to lie to you?

No, the *Jahsh* who lied to us didn't come to the place of the shooting.

Were the clothes of the officers who accompanied you different from those of the soldiers?

Yes. They were dressed differently.

Khaki?

The soldiers, yes.

What were the officers wearing?

Green berets.

Do you remember how many stars the highest ranking officer in the unit that was in charge of you had?

Two stars.

Since there were no soldiers inside the lorry, why didn't you escape?

The lorry was locked. It had two doors. There was no way to escape.

Metal doors?

Yes.

And the top was metal as well, not canvas?

Yes.

No windows?

Just one small window.

Was it very hot inside?

Yes.

It was August, the hottest month?

It was Ramadan, I don't remember the month.

Okay, now you have reached the place of the shooting. What happened next?

Just before reaching the place of the shooting, they first let us off the lorries and blindfolded us and gave us a sip of water. Then they made us go back inside. When we arrived, they opened the door, and I managed to slip aside my blindfold. I could see this pit in the ground surrounded by soldiers.

Were your hands tied?

No.

When they opened the door of the lorry, what was the first thing you saw?

The first thing I saw was the pits, dug and ready.

Taimour explained to me on a separate occasion that he had pushed the blindfold slightly aside so that he could see without the soldiers realizing it. Hands were obviously needed to clamber off the lorries and into the pits efficiently. The blindfold is a classic technique for isolating victims psychologically from one another, thus reducing the chances of a collective effort to rush the guards and make a run for it. Taimour saw the pits the instant the doors of his lorry were opened. He was still on the elevated platform at this point.

How many pits did you see?

It was night, but around us there were many.

Four or five holes?

No, no, it was more.

More than five, six, seven holes?

Yes, yes.

Describe your pit.

The pit was like a tank dugout. They put us in that kind of a hole.

They pushed you directly off the truck into the pit?

Yes.

How high was it? One meter? Two meters? Could you stand up inside?

It was high.

How high?

Up to the sash of a man.

How many people were put inside?

One pit to every truck.

And how many people were in a truck?

About one hundred people.

Was it just a massive hole?

It was rectangular.

Was it cut very precisely by a machine?

By bulldozers as you would make a pit for a tank.

Taimour's village is near the Iranian border. Tank dugouts litter the landscape around where he grew up. He would be very familiar with them, although he might never have seen a bus in his life. Bulldozers designed to scoop out tank dugouts quickly and efficiently were plentiful and in constant use throughout the eight years of the Iraq-Iran War. These would have been the *shavalat* referred to by 'Ali Hasan al-Majeed which he complained about having to send backward and forward to "bury" people like Taimour in 1988. The cross section through such a dugout would be about one yard deep. The longitudinal section varies in height, with a bund of earth at one end on top of which the soldiers were standing, and a slow incline at the other, on the side where the machine had trundled in and out of to make the hole.

Soldiers were surrounding the whole grave?

Yes.

What kind of guns were they carrying?

Only Kalashnikovs.

And what were they wearing on their heads?

Black on their heads.

They were wearing black!

Yes.

So they were not regular soldiers?

Yes they were.

Have you ever seen soldiers wearing such uniforms before?

No.

Did they have anything on their eyes, like goggles?

No.

Did they have any insignia on their shoulders?

No.

Were the clothes khaki?

No, green.

Green uniforms with black hats, like commandos, or special forces . . .

Yes.

Have you seen special forces before?

No.

And how many men were circling around the grave?

They were all around, but only two soldiers were doing the shooting.

The shooting started after you were all inside the grave?

Yes.

Can you describe it?

The shooting. . . . There were two soldiers, standing here and there [he marks out their locations on the ground, as being at opposing corners of the pit]. We sat in the pit and they fired bullets at us.

Did somebody give instructions?

Yes.

I want to know exactly what he said.

I didn't know any Arabic then. I don't know what he said.

Was it a long speech or a short one?

Just short.

Were the people with you inside the hole saying anything?

Nothing.

Were women crying? Were children crying? What was happening?

It was usual. I was there. What could I think of . . .

You were not expecting to die?

I knew that I was going to be killed.

Was anyone protesting? Did anyone shout out or try to run away, or do something against the soldiers?

No. We had started out early in the morning and when we arrived it
was night; the only thing that people wanted was to come out from the
car. No, nobody did anything.

You just wanted to die and get it over with.

Yes.

I imagine an extraordinary state of collective numbness had
gripped everyone inside the pit. It is reminiscent of the reaction of
Jews being herded into the gas chambers as described in accounts of
the Holocaust. No one protested because they were totally resigned
to the fact that they were going to die. Then the shots started coming from two directions; apparently only two men doing the firing.
A bullet hit Taimour in the left shoulder, a flesh wound. He looked
up and saw that he'd been shot by the soldier standing directly
before him, whom he began running toward.

Did you actually reach the soldier?

Yes.

Did you grab onto him?

I grabbed his hand, then . . .

His hand or his foot?

His hand.

But you were in the pit?

No, I came out and I ran.

You ran out of the pit and grabbed the soldier. That is what happened.

Yes.

Did you say anything to him?

I said nothing. I took his hand. Then the other soldier shouted at the
one I was holding and told him to throw me back in the pit.

Taimour rushed out of the pit in the direction of the incline,
which would have been used by the bulldozer to make the hole. A
ring of soldiers were on that bund, including one of the two doing
the shooting. The other soldier had to have been on the opposite
side, shooting into the hole along the line of the incline. Reaching
the top of the hole by a miracle, Taimour wouldn't have just taken
his executioner's hand; he would have had to grab at it, begging
with his face, and maybe even his voice. There is no evidence,

however, of this extraordinary emotional moment in Taimour's choice of words.

Did you look into the soldier's face?

Yes.

Did you see his eyes?

Yes.

What did you see? What could you read in his eyes, in the expression on his face?

He was about to cry, but the other one shouted at him and told him to throw me back in the pit. He was obliged to throw me back.

He cried!

He was about to cry.

How far away was the officer who shouted?

He was close to him.

The soldier who pushed you back into the hole, was he the one who shot you the second time?

Yes. This soldier shot me again after he received the order from the officer who was standing beside the pit. When he shot me the second time I was wounded here [he points].

A second bullet was fired as he was being pushed into the hole, and entered Taimour's lower back. Both appear to have been light flesh wounds, although by the end of his ordeal the boy would have lost a lot of blood.

The same one who almost cried shot you a second time!

Yes, he was forced to, the other one had told him to shoot.

You fell back into the hole?

Yes.

Were the bullets coming in a continuous stream or just sporadically?

They were stopping and starting shooting again and again.

What was happening to the people around you while the shooting was going on? Did any of them call out, shout, scream, say something that you remember?

People were not shouting.

No one said anything?

No.

No one else ran out of the hole?

No.

No one else tried to rush the soldiers?

No, they were powerless.

And how many men were standing around shooting into the hole?

There were only two who were shooting, and the others were standing.

What were they doing? Watching?

Yes.

Were they dressed differently from the men who were doing the shooting?

Yes.

How so?

The men who stood by were dressed in green, and the others who were doing the shooting were in military uniform.

And who was wearing the black hats?

Those who were watching.

Did there seem to be one boss, one man who was giving the orders? Or more than one?

There were many. One to each pit.

What happened after the shooting stopped?

The soldiers went away and were talking with each other. It was night-time.

They were milling about behind the bund of earth waiting for the bulldozers to come and level out the pit, covering up the crumpled bodies. A few minutes passed like this with Taimour cowering among the bodies, pretending to be dead. Then he says he clambered out and took one last look inside.

I came out of the pit and looked inside. I saw something moving. It was a girl. I said to her, "Get up, let's go," and she said, "I'm afraid of the soldiers, I can't come."

Tell me more about her.

We were sitting in the pit. She was beside me and she had been hit by a bullet in her hand.

She was smaller than you?

She was a very little child.

What was she wearing?

Kurdish clothes.

She got hit in the hand. . . . Did she say anything else?

No.

What about the rest of the people, were they all dead?

They didn't make noises.

When Taimour spoke to the little girl, a few minutes had passed since the end of the shooting. In that last look back into the pit, Taimour saw his mother Sarah, and three sisters, Gaylas, Leyla, and Serwa. He also saw three of his aunts, including Hafsa who didn't have any children, and Ma'souma who had eight. Then, when the soldiers weren't looking, he sprinted off to a nearby empty pit and jumped inside. With a piece of metal, he dug a hole in the sand and curled up in it under the cover of darkness. There he stayed for a while, watching as the bulldozers came and covered up the hole. Vehicles were driving around between the pits. At some point they left and he either fainted or fell asleep. After regaining consciousness, and making sure everyone had gone, Taimour got out of the pit and started walking out into the desert. It was late evening. He remembers coming across two roads, "an old one and a new one," as he put it. He took the new one. After walking for a couple of hours or so, barking dogs came out of the darkness and attacked him. He had stumbled upon a Bedouin tent encampment. A man emerged from the tent and shone a flashlight into his eyes. He took him into the tent. The man's mother, wife, and sister all lived there. They gave the boy food and water, took off his Kurdish clothes, and dressed him up in an Arab *dishdasha*. The family had heard the shooting.

Taimour stayed with this Bedouin family in their tent for three days. They kept him concealed from other families in nearby tents. On the fourth day he was taken to the home of a relative of this family in the town of Samawa. There he was treated clandestinely with medicine and materials brought from the local hospital.

Taimour stayed with this family for about two years, during which he learned to speak Arabic. Today, he speaks Arabic with a southern Shi'ite accent. He grew very close to the people who had saved him and adamantly refused to give me any further information about them.

Eventually, Taimour made it back to Kurdistan. The son of the Samawa family was a soldier and he had a Kurdish friend in the army. This Kurd took down the names of all of Taimour's relatives, and hunted down another one of Taimour's aunts who accompanied the Kurdish soldier to the house of a surviving uncle in the Kalar area. The uncle came to Samawa on a clandestine mission to take the boy back. After a few months, it was felt that Taimour was not even safe with this uncle because maybe the Iraqi authorities had got wind of his escape, and so he was spirited away yet again to the Germiyan area, where he lived with a shepherd until the March 1991 uprising.

AS I LOOK back at the transcript of my interview with Taimour, I realize my questions express no empathy with what he must have been feeling. They were hard, factual, journalistic-type questions, although I was myself at the time in a very emotional state. I must have been distancing myself emotionally somewhat like Taimour himself, who appeared cool, calm, and collected while he talked about the ultimate horror that can be experienced by any human being, much less a twelve-year-old boy.

Toward the end of our interview, Taimour suddenly used the word *"Anfal"* for the first time.

> You used the word *"Anfal."* Previously when I first asked you, you said you had never heard this word used before. When is the first time you heard the word *"Anfal"*?
>
> When I came back from Samawa, I heard it in Kurdistan for the first time.
>
> I see. What do you think *Anfal* is?
>
> *Anfal* means *Kafir* [unbeliever].
>
> Why do you think the Iraqi government called what they did to you *Anfal*?
>
> I don't know.
>
> What do you feel about the Arabs?
>
> Good.
>
> Who did all these terrible things to you?
>
> The Arabs.

So how do you feel about them?

I don't say all Arabs, I just say that. . . .

Did someone tell you to say these things? I want to know how you feel. I don't care what anyone told you to tell me. I want to know how you are feeling inside. Who did this to you, the government or the Arabs?

The government.

If you could choose, what would you want to do in your life now?

I don't know for myself.

Is there something you want out of life very much?

Yes.

What?

To be a known person.

A known person?

Yes.

Known for what?

The *Anfal*.

Do you want to be known more for the *Anfal* or for being a *peshmerga*?

For *Anfal*.

What do you mean "known for *Anfal*"?

I want the world to know what happened to me.

6 ⁄ Remembering Cruelty

UNTIL a short while ago, I thought *"al-Anfal"* was the name of a *sura* in the Qur'an. When Saddam Husain initiated a big military operation in southern Iraq in June 1991, also giving it the codename *"Anfal,"* none of us Iraqi's who were rushing around to get the word out to the media had any idea of the full implication of his choice of term. Refugees fled the regime's vengeance in the wake of the reprisals that followed the failed March 1991 uprising. Whole residential neighborhoods in southern cities were razed. For weeks every Shi'ite male over the age of twelve was liable to be shot and shoveled into mass graves with bulldozers. Any student of religion whom the regime could lay its hands on was killed. People like Abu Haydar who fled all this but who were unable to escape the country took refuge in the marshlands between the Tigris and the Euphrates in southern Iraq. In June, the army began an encirclement, and food, fuel, and medicines were cut off from them. Only in retrospect did I realize that this was a reprise of the terrible Kurdish precedent of 1988.

Human beings will go on debating the nature of truth until the end of time. But there should be no debate over what cruelty is. From now on the term *"al-Anfal"* must forever and for every Arab carry the new meaning that the Iraqi Ba'th gave to it: the officially sanctioned mass murder in 1988 of at least 100,000 noncombatant Kurds.

This new meaning is the beginning of acknowledgment of responsibility for what happened in 1988. There can be no normal future for Iraq without such acknowledgment. The past never just goes away; it has to be confronted before it can be put to rest. A country and a culture that has experienced something like the *Anfal* operations or what all Iraqis experienced during 1991 can never go back to life "as it used to be." Can Taimour go back to being a normal little Kurdish boy again? The memories of what happened in 1988 and 1991 are only two of Saddam Husain's many bitter legacies, which the people of Iraq will have to live with long after he is gone.

Who is responsible for what happened in 1988?

I did not know about the *Anfal* operations until November 1991. Does that mean I am not responsible? The world certainly knew, at least since 1975, that Kurds were being "resettled." Many people knew that hundreds if not thousands of villages were being "eliminated." The *Anfal* is the all-too-logical climax of escalating cruelty that has been going on for years inside Iraq, to the full knowledge of Western governments and Arab intellectuals; the former armed the tyrant, while the latter buttressed him politically. Now cruelty has touched everyone.

Responsibility for the Kurdish dead of the *Anfal* reaches beyond the Ba'thi regime in Baghdad. Does that mean every Iraqi Arab is responsible? On the other hand, so many Kurds might not have perished if other Kurds had not herded them out of their villages to their deaths. Does that mean that the Kurds too are responsible?

Is every Arab responsible? Millions upon millions of words have been written about the destruction of hundreds of Palestinian villages in order to bring about the creation of the Israeli state. And rightly so. Yet many of the very intellectuals who wrote those words chose silence when it came to the elimination of thousands of Kurdish villages by an Arab state. We seem only to know the things that we want to know.

Maybe the Allied governments that destroyed Iraq to force Saddam Husain out of Kuwait are responsible. Many Iraqis remember that back in 1988, Saddam Husain was everyone's friend. George Bush, then Vice President of the United States, personally intervened on behalf of the Ba'thist regime on many occasions, as the United States "tilted" toward Iraq during its war with Iran.[1] They remember those not-so-distant days, they remember how the Gulf war was fought, they see that Saddam Husain was left in power to wreak havoc on his own people, and they ask: Did the President of the United States have intelligence information about the *Anfal,* and did he deliberately ignore that intelligence?[2] One day, I believe we will find mass graves of the sort described by Taimour in the desert west of Samawa close to the Saudi border. It so happens that while the Iraqi uprising in March 1991 was being crushed, Allied forces camped between Samawa and the Iraqi-Saudi border, possibly right on top of those graves, were watching the slaughter. Did someone in the corridors of power in Washington know what they were sitting on?

Remembering the Gulf War

WAR is hell. But not all wars are hell in the same sorts of ways. The way in which the Gulf war was ended by the United States turned out to be far more damaging to the people of Iraq than wartime-related direct casualties. By the summer of 1991, Iraq had been transformed from a modern country, with sophisticated health care, water, and sewage treatment, and electric power systems, into "one of the most impoverished countries in the world." This was the conclusion of the International Study Team, made up of eighty-seven academics and professionals, which visited Iraq in September 1991 to study the impact of the war on the overall health and welfare of civilians.[3] Over one half of the population was still being exposed to fecal contamination in drinking water seven months after the cease-fire. One third of all Iraqi children were malnourished. Food prices had risen by 1,500–2,000 percent while real wages had dropped to less than 7 percent of prewar levels. Waterborne diseases, including typhoid, gastroenteritis, and cholera, were endemic; hepatitis had increased one hundred-fold and meningitis was widespread in southern Iraq. Uncommon and preventable diseases like polio, measles, and tetanus were resurgent everywhere.[4]

In the Gulf war, in spite of more than 120,000 sorties flown over Iraq, there was no widespread destruction and damage to residential areas typical of an indiscriminate bombing campaign. Nor were there the kind of direct civilian casualties one would expect from a bombing campaign of this magnitude (there were between 3,000 and 5,000 civilian deaths).[5] Estimates of the numbers of Iraqi soldiers killed in combat fluctuate between 30,000 and 100,000, with a consensus gradually building that the figures need to be revised downward.[6] Beth Daponte, a demographer who works in the U.S. Census Bureau, estimated 53,000 directly war-related deaths in January and February as compared to 105,000 Iraqis who died as a result of the Iraqi uprising against Saddam Husain and through epidemics and waterborne diseases resulting from wartime damage to the country's infrastructure.[7] She seems to have left out of her calculations the number of deaths among Kurdish and Shi'ite refugees who fled into the mountains after the failed uprising. During this historic exodus of more than 2 million people, Kurds—overwhelmingly children— died at the rate of 450 to 750 a day because of diarrhea, acute respiratory infections, and trauma. In total, probably 25,000 to 30,000 Kurds died.[8] But Iraqi Shi'ites bore the brunt of Saddam Husain's postwar vengeance. No one knows how many tens of thousands of them died.

The high-tech character of the war was such as to terminate Iraq's existence as a modern state for a few months just hours into its start. An entire country was left "brain-dead," as Richard Reid of the United Nations Children's Fund put it. Baghdad, he said, was a city "essentially unmarked, a body with its skin basically intact, with every main bone broken and with its joints and tendons cut."[9] A Harvard Study Team which visited eleven major cities and towns in Iraq from April 27 to May 6, 1991, concluded: "Although the allied bombing may have caused relatively little direct damage to the civilian population, the destruction of the infrastructure has resulted in devastating long-term consequences for health. We normally consider civilian casualties to be only those that are a direct result of injury during war, but this definition needs revision."[10]

The real victims of American technical ingenuity were the children of Iraq. A carefully researched study from the Harvard School of Public Health based on a study population of 16,076 Iraqi children concluded that there was "a greater than threefold increase in infant and child mortality related to the Gulf war, the subsequent civilian uprising and on-going economic sanctions. This increase corresponds to an excess of about 46,897 deaths among Iraqi children below 5 years of age between January and August 1991."[11] Another study focused on the city of Basra, where about 157,000 children live, concludes that out of a study population of 723 children, the majority of whom were between the ages of 0–36 months, 8 percent were medically "wasted" and 24 percent "stunted." Overall, "20% were moderately to severely malnourished."[12] Such studies confirm that the association between the Gulf war and infant mortality and disease was stronger in northern and southern Iraq than it was in the central areas. In other words, proportionately more Kurdish and Shi'ite children died as a direct consequence of the American decision to target the power stations in the country and then wash its hands of Iraq, leaving them unrepaired. For the Middle East as a whole, UN officials estimate that nearly 5 million children risk spending their formative years in deprived circumstances as a result of the Gulf crisis. "We can speak with alarming, grave assurance of a lost generation," said Richard Reid.[13]

The effects of the Gulf war will live on in those children who survived the bombing, the vengeance of the regime, and the ravages of disease and malnutrition. Two psychologists who were part of the International Study Team mentioned previously, and who specialized in the field of childhood traumas, conducted in-depth interviews with 214 Iraqi children of primary-school age. They came to the astounding conclusion that "Iraqi children are the most traumatized children of war ever described." They found levels of anxiety, stress, and pathological behavior unprecedented in their fifteen years of field work in war-torn countries like Mozambique, Uganda, and Sudan. The symptoms described in their report range from "deep depression" to "lack of life." The children were twisted up inside with grief, sadness, and desperate fear. Eighty percent of those interviewed lived in daily fear of losing their families through death or separation; nearly two thirds did not believe they would make it to adulthood. The report concludes: "Even in the worst-affected areas of war-torn Mozambique, children were still playing and behaved like children. The children in Iraq reminded the authors of the descriptions of the 'living dead' from the aftermath of the bombing of Hiroshima."[14]

Early in the fall of 1991, I received a letter from a longstanding family friend, Abu 'Ali (pseudonym), a man of my father's generation whom I looked up to and admired during my adolescence inside Iraq. His letter reenacts the despair that gripped all Iraqis in the months that followed the war. Abu 'Ali had managed to get out of Baghdad with his family and was writing to me from Amman. He had just learned that I was involved in the drafting of a document known as Charter 91, a signature-collecting campaign among Iraqis that builds a connection between human rights and an envisioned political ideal founded on religious and political toleration.[15] The text of the Charter had been published in one of the Arabic dailies available in Jordan, and Abu 'Ali was writing to chide me for being hopelessly idealistic and out of touch with the way things were inside Iraq. His letter sums up, in language better than I know how to invent, the despair and anguish felt by so many Iraqis.

> . . . I don't know if this innocent blue letter paper is going to be able to communicate even a small part of what I feel toward you and the worries for our society which tighten themselves like chains around my heart.

> I think—and please allow me to tell you this—that the ideas of the Charter issue from an ivory tower which has elevated itself so high up into the sky that we who are standing down below can hardly see them or hear where they are coming from. You see, our society today has become like *1984*. There is no one who remembers or who even dares to remember the meaning of words like "freedom," "democracy," "brotherhood," or "humanity." They no longer know what "human rights" are. I mean, what does this have to do with them! Their daily duty today is to clap and shout for Big Brother: "With our soul, with our blood, we will sacrifice ourselves for you, oh Saddam."

> . . . Their only preoccupation is to survive and to live, like sheep. The preservation of their heads seated on top of their shoulders and the filling of their empty stomachs is enough. Or the protection of the little that they now possess from being robbed by the executioners of the party and the police, who are themselves hungry and scurrying about, that too is enough.

> How can you, Kanan, expect such a person to revolt? Yes, it is true, some revolted. But it was for ethnic, regional, or sectarian reasons. Then the ones they revolted against caught up with them. What was the result? Those who were killed from among the revolutionaries were twice the number killed in the Gulf war. Then, their families, possessions, and everything they hold most sacred in the world were treated in the cruelest way imaginable. What happened is beyond words. After this, do you expect a people to rise up when there is a Republican Guard, a *mukhabarat,* and a secret police which has stripped every human value and behaved like savages without a drop of mercy in their hearts for a child, for an elderly man, for a woman, or for a sick human being . . . ?

> After all of this, let me return to Charter 91 and to your call for a "Republic of Tolerance." To whom is it directed? To the Iraqi people? No. Therefore, it must be directed to those intellectuals sitting in their

ivory towers in countries where freedom and peace and security reign. They live in security where there are no secret police watching over them, closing down the ability to think. All these intellectuals have is the hobby of being opponents of the dictatorship in Iraq, and urging the people to revolt. Not one of them has thrown as much as a stone in the face of this regime. People in Iraq kept on hearing the news of this Iraqi opposition abroad, until they grew bored with it. They want action. They want someone who would save them from this unspeakable tyranny. . . .

After all of this, can't you see, Kanan, that the situation in our country today has become hopeless. . . . The whole population of Iraq has given up and has taken to blaming the outside powers (especially the United States) for their condition. They lift their hands to the sky, pleading that God may make America or George Bush or any one of those who speak of humanity and democracy and human rights save them from this pain that they are living through. . . .

In the exemplary light of Abu 'Ali's kind of truth-telling, when they write it up in the history books, what kind of a war will they say this was?

IN JULY 1991, I received a strange telephone call from a television producer who was interested in doing a program on the idea of an American monument to Operation Desert Storm. Somewhere in Washington, it transpired, somebody was thinking of commissioning just such a monument. Maybe the thought had entered the bureaucratic imagination after what Mayor David Dinkins called "the mother of all parades" in New York City on June 10. Nearly 5 million people, the largest crowd for any single event in the city's history, lined the one-mile route from Battery Park to Worth Street. It was a chance for the city to "strut its stuff, despite fiscal crisis and recession, to express gratitude to those who sacrificed and died for the country," wrote *The New York Times* approvingly. Did the writer have in mind the 146 American soldiers who were killed in action, largely by "friendly fire"? Maybe he had in mind what George Bush said on March 1, the day after he called a cease-fire and the first full day of the Iraqi uprising against Saddam Husain: "It's a proud day for Americans and by God, we've licked the Vietnam syndrome once and for all."[16] The question went unasked and unanswered amid the showers of confetti and tickertape which grew so thick, the lead article noted, that "the sky at times grew dim."[17]

Whatever the inspiration for the idea of a monument to the Gulf war, the television producer knew that she was onto a good thing. The idea was to preempt the national debate that was bound to ensue. The dean of the Yale School of Architecture had already been contacted and was willing to organize a design exercise among students which would throw up alternative schemes. A televised discussion of these different hypothetical schemes would serve to highlight the moral issues involved in a way that a Washington committee might not. Maya Lin, who designed the Vietnam War Memorial, was a student at Yale when her entry won the competition for that particular monument in 1981. The program would therefore resonate with all the controversy that her great work produced, at the same time that it took as its point of departure a new generation's attitude to a very different kind of war.

Unfortunately, nothing much came of that telephone call. But the thought behind it poses the question for an American: What is there worth recovering in memory about the Gulf war?

The Vietnam War Memorial works because it eschews patriotism while acknowledging the dead—individually and collectively—as the only worthy reason for having any kind of monument devoted to remembering that particular war. Lin's low-slung tapering black granite wall, inscribed with the names of 58,132 dead Americans, signifies both a nation's shame and its compassion for those it has lost. The reflective surface of the monument evokes contemplation, turning viewers into imaginary participants, implicated in the narrative of a war which is being remembered as a simple list of individual names ordered by the date on which they died. Built into the earth, rather than rising above it in the phallic character of traditional monuments, Lin's memorial has been called a "gash of shame." The sinking black granite wall into which one descends stands in sharp contrast to the white marble obelisk of the Washington Monument. In almost every detail, this object cries out against the glorification of war or the deification of power. Therein lies its eloquence. Now, suppose there had to be a monument to the Gulf war, what ought it to signify?

I think of all those Iraqis like Abu Haydar and Hameed who rose up against the Ba'th regime in March 1991. The President of the United States allowed the great tyrant of Iraq to cut them down with his helicopter gunships. So many of them did not have to die. I think of all those electrical plants which the Army Corps of Engineers could have so quickly put back into temporary working order (the way they did in Kuwait). I think of all those refugees like Mustafa who would not have had to flee into the mountains and swamps. I think of all those children who died unnecessarily of disease and malnutrition. I think of ordinary Iraqis, like Omar, who are routinely subjected to unimaginable cruelties. Last but not least, I think of that letter from Amman, from someone who, like all Iraqis inside the country, has lost what, next to life, is the most precious thing a human being can possess: hope. His truths are the real epitaph of George Bush's unfinished war.

Things didn't have to end like this, and that fact provides the proper moral framework within which a future Maya Lin would need to work, fixing through her art for the sake of American memory this meaning of the 1991 war against Iraq. The Vietnam War and the Gulf war are inextricably connected in the American public conscience. But there are hardly any American dead to memorialize in this war. There are only large numbers of Iraqi dead. If they ever do decide to build a monument to the Gulf war in Washington, its moral underpinning should no longer be a nation's shame, but its lack of compassion.

Remembering the *Anfal*

THE year 1988, the year of the *Anfal,* ought to go down in Arab history books as a special instance of unimaginable cruelty. So special in fact that Saddam Husain himself chose to memorialize it. A "Victory Arch" was unveiled in Baghdad on the first anniversary of the end of Iraq's war with Iran. August 1988 happens also to be the month that *Khatimat al-Anfal,* or the final solution of the Kurdish question in Iraq, was going on. Saddam's idea was for a Ba'thi equivalent of the fifty-four-feet-high Arc de Triomphe at the end of the Champs-Elysées in Paris. The invitation card summoning Western ambassadors and dignatories from all over the world to the opening ceremony described Saddam's monument as "one of the largest works of art in the world." The president rode under his arch that day on a white horse, the Arab symbol of purity and male pride.

The most interesting fact about the monument that people had come to see was that it was conceived by the president of Iraq himself—not as an abstract intention, but as an actual sketch. No one had thought of Saddam Husain as an artist before. The maquette for the monument was worked from plaster casts of the president's own forearms, enlarged to some fifty-four feet in length. These come bursting out of the ground like bronze treetrunks and rise holding a sixty-six-foot-long sword in each fist. The two swords cross to form the apex of the arch at a point roughly 130 feet above ground. Each forearm and fist, with the steel frame onto which it is fixed, weighs 40 tons. Each sword, made of stainless steel, weighs 24 tons. This steel, the invitation card says, was made by melting down the actual weapons of Iraqi "martyrs." War debris in the shape of 5,000 real Iranian helmets, taken from the battlefield, are gathered up in two nets (2,500 helmets per net). These inflated bags get torn asunder at the base, scattering the helmets on the ground around the two points at which the arms emerge from the earth. To look at the helmets in the knowledge that their scratches, dents, and bullet holes are real, that human heads might well have exploded inside them, is as breathtaking as the knowledge that these are not just anybody's arms but replicas of the president's own, down to every last little bump and squiggle.

I have discussed elsewhere the manifold ways in which Saddam's creation so perfectly symbolizes the Ba'thist world that produced it.[18] It is gruesome, but not gruesome in an ordinary kind of way; it is breathtakingly gruesome, uniquely vulgar . . . words failed me then, and they fail me now. The Victory Arch that sits at the center of the city in which I was born and brought up has a quality of awfulness woven into every detail which exceeds that of any other public monument I know, and which is in some final sense incomprehensible.

By contrast, Mustafa al-'Askari's little graveyard memorial to what happened in the village of Guptapa on May 3, 1988, is as ordinary as Saddam Husain's monument is extraordinary.[19] It is ordinary to the point of being uninteresting as a formal object. Two concrete block arches sit on a podium which look like the frame of an unfinished pitch-roofed house. There are no symbolic or visual referents to the extraordinary conditions that gave rise to this creation. There is no impressive "fit" here between physical form and symbolic intention, as there so clearly is in the case of Saddam Husain's Victory Arch. Yet I think it was very important to tell the story of what Mustafa tried to build.

What does it mean to crouch on a hill, as 'Abdallah did on May 3, and watch planes bomb your village with chemical weapons? Then you rush down to the river that you have known your entire life, only to find all your children dead and your mother lying down in the shallow water with her mouth "biting into the mudbank"?

I took you with me on a journey to relive Iraqi pain. I am thinking rationally now; but I couldn't do so back then. Listening to 'Abdallah and Taimour inside Iraq, I felt as though I had reached the point at which the curtain had to come down, bringing everything down with it to a tragic close. Cruelty of this kind is a threat to reason; it defies reflection and analysis.[20] That is why we so often turn our backs on it, not out of lack of empathy, but out of an inability any longer to communicate. Cruelty silences. Maybe that is why the words of cruelty's victims have ended up writing this book for me.

But isn't it here, in the crucible of 'Abdallah's pain and in the moment of my speechlessness, that the meaning of what Mustafa did is born? Isn't it here that civilization itself takes over from barbarism, and maybe even the very idea of "the monumental" begins? Iraqis are great builders of monuments—or so the historians like to tell us. You could even argue that the very notion of "the monumental" was born in ancient Mesopotamia. This is where the first congregation of our species into urban settlements began in ancient cities like Sumer, Babylon, and Eridu. Perhaps this history has left its mark on leaders like Saddam and ordinary Iraqis like Mustafa.

When Mustafa laid out that graveyard and built his arches, he was thinking and acting like that first mythical builder in the world, who must have felt he or she just had to put a mark on this earth of ours—a mark that was not about material things like shelter, work, and subsistence. Architecture, as opposed to building, began from marks like this. Mustafa is like the first architect.

We who are in the business of writing and reading and talking sometimes run the risk of forgetting the deep emotional wellsprings, the elaborations of feeling—whether grotesque or sublime—which lie behind artifacts like Saddam Husain's Victory Arch and Mustafa's memorial. We may despise those feelings or we may admire them. That is beside the point. A monument can work irrespective of whether one likes or dislikes what it stands for.

Confronting the monuments of both Mustafa al-'Askari and Saddam Husain, we are at the very beginning of things, touching life, death, and raw passion at their most vulnerable moments, plumbing for meaning in those dark corners of the human soul where new meanings begin. Monuments in their deepest essence and through their very uselessness are more than aesthetic objects. They are about early memories and how to face up to them, memories that can be so painful as to tear everything asunder, memories that will not be wished away and that end up constituting the very marrow of a community's identity, or lack of it. In spite of its ordinariness—or maybe even because of it—Mustafa's memorial to the dead of Guptapa teaches Iraqis of every ethnic, national, religious, and sectarian group that the real existential question for them is no longer Saddam Husain. It is how to build for themselves a future in conditions where everyone—Arab and Kurd, Shi'i and Sunni—has to confront different varieties of the same legacy of searing pain.

The passage of time does a lot to erase the primal beginnings which so moved Mustafa. Meanings metamorphose. Peeling off accumulated layers of meaning is wonderfully enriching. There is a core, however, underneath all the layers, made up at the very least of a built object and the story of how that object came into the world. We may never get to the bottom of either because they are just too complicated, buried too deep in the mists of time. That is the case with ancient monuments like the Pyramids and the Sphinx. But the search for that core, in spite of all the time that passes, puts the problem in its proper perspective. The paradox of both monuments—that of Saddam Husain and that of Mustafa al-'Askari—each of which commemorates events in 1988, is that hardly any time has passed since their creation. This lack of distance is a measure of how Iraq is teetering today on the precipice of new dangers, ones that no longer emanate from the person or the regime of Saddam Husain.

Saddam Husain's legacy will live on long after he has departed from the scene. If you attack someone for being a Kurd or a Shi'ite, the natural response is to assert that *one is* the very thing one is attacked for being. In Europe such attacks during the interwar years heightened and politicized Jewish self-consciousness, facilitating the creation of the state of Israel in 1948. Then Palestinian identity was asserted as a reaction to Zionism's violent denial of it. The moral of Khalil's story is that Kuwaiti identity, which none of us paid any attention to in the past (including Khalil himself), is here to stay.

So, what will happen tomorrow in Iraq? Kurdish nationalism is stronger and more aggressive today than at any time in the past, fueled by the growing realization of what an Arab state did to the

Kurdish people. Many Kurds may tomorrow choose to split off to form their own state. Sunni-Shi'i hatred is today the most virulent potential source of new violence. These forces are Saddam Husain's legacy to all Iraqis. The question is whether Iraqis have the wisdom to transform that legacy into a force for healing and construction, rather than even more terrible violence.

The essence of a monument lies in its destiny. What, then, are we to make of the fact that Mustafa's memorial isn't even finished and that Saddam Husain's monument was opened in the summer of 1989? According to *Newsweek,* the Victory Arch only just survived the Gulf war when the U.S. Secretary of Defense crossed it off the Pentagon's list of proposed targets in Baghdad.[21] Maybe Richard Cheney did not want to be seen to be launching a war against Iraqi culture. The electricity-generating plants in the country were fair game, but not Saddam Husain's contribution to the visual arts. An apt comment, I think, on the outcome of the Gulf war. But the more interesting question is: Will the Victory Arch survive the wrath of the people of Iraq when the tyrant's day of reckoning finally comes? And will other Mustafas appear?

No one knows the answers to such questions. But we can at least take a stand on the issues involved. We can at least make a judgment. Should Saddam Husain's monument be torn down on the day of his overthrow? Should Mustafa's example be followed by other Iraqis?

The past cannot be excised as easily as a monument can. It leaves traces which have to be confronted. The importance of the year 1988 will grow with time as the full scope of what happened becomes clearer to larger numbers of Iraqis; it is a year that is going to be remembered by different people for different reasons. The Ba'th have lasted longer now than any other regime in Iraq's modern history. What they did and how they ruled should not be forgotten. Like the sword of Damocles, the swords of Saddam Husain's monument will continue to hang over all Iraqis. Even if the tyrant were dead, the people of Iraq are obliged to walk under those swords to exit from his spell. There are memories before which human beings can only stand in awe, speechless. If Saddam Husain's Victory Arch is the last in one generation of Iraqi monuments—those of the 1980s which have already transformed Baghdad—then let us hope that Mustafa's memorial is the first in a new generation of Iraqi monuments, the building of which could commence in earnest on the day of the tyrant's overthrow.

ARE there lessons for Iraqis in Maya Lin's great work of mourning and mastery over memory? An American monument to the Gulf war based in Washington cannot draw upon her work, as we have already said, for the simple reason that virtually no Americans were killed by Iraqis. Yet the war opened up Iraq for the first time, and made it possible for us to know about things like the 100,000 or so dead of the *Anfal* operations and the 3,500 villages like Guptapa.

Let us suppose a new regime were to replace the one that is rotting slowly away in Baghdad. Let us suppose that this new regime was founded on the kind of wisdom that was prepared to acknowledge what was done to the Kurdish people of Iraq. Let us suppose that commissioning a national memorial in central Baghdad was felt to be one small way of making such an acknowledgment. The names of the *Anfal* dead, and the villages from which they came, would of course have to be carefully researched. They would comprise the brief. What might such a monument in downtown Baghdad to the *Anfal* victims of 1988 look like? Where should it be located? From what sources should a new generation of Iraqi artists draw their inspiration?

I relish the completely hypothetical thought that the new monument to the *Anfal* be situated in the immediate vicinity of Saddam Husain's Victory Arch, which should not be torn down, and that it be built in the spirit of Maya Lin's great work in Washington, D.C.

Whither Iraq?

IRAQIS like to think of peace and security as a great white dove which will one day descend upon them. But will it? That is the fundamental question of Iraqi politics today. Nothing else is of equal importance. The Ba'th and Saddam Husain already belong to the past; they are on their way out. But what comes next? No Iraqi should assume that things cannot get worse. I don't say they will; but they can. Everything depends on what Iraqis make out of the terrible force of memory, which tends always to sow dragons' teeth in the shape of the children and survivors of the dead.

The idea for this book started as an oral history of the intifada, an event which could be thought of as a possible dress rehearsal for Iraq's future. It was designed to counteract the shameful pro-Saddam record of Arab intellectuals and public opinion during the Gulf crisis.[1] But I gave up that idea. My sources were patchy. People were still afraid. Others were insufficiently frank. Then, again, maybe I was too close to the material. Above all I came to understand that, from where I stood, at least, the intifada was too complex a phenomenon and too politically charged to be rationally digested at this point in time. A whole population had tasted freedom at the same time as a new summum in human cruelty had been carved out for the historical record. With an iron logic, the rebellion that I fully associated myself with mirrored the tyranny it had so earnestly sought to rid Iraq of. An abyss of human hell opened up—murder, treachery, vengeance-killing, looting, hate, mass murder, wanton desecration—along with acts of the purest self-sacrifice, courage, consideration, and compassion. In the chapter entitled "Abu Haydar," I tried to write of them all, aware of the fact that this first account of what happened in post–Gulf war Iraq is bound to be deficient. One thing, however, the balance sheet of Abu Haydar's intifada and how it was received by other Arabs shows us: a quarter of a century of regionwide political and moral degradation has scarred many, many Arab hearts. Simply writing about all of this was going to burn me.

Individual actions aside, every social group behaved as selfishly as humanly possible. Shi'a rebels in the south killed individually for vengeance in the name of Islam, while the Ba'th killed en masse for survival in the name of Arabism. The educated Sunni middle classes of Baghdad, who could have made a difference, didn't. Worse yet, they sat back and mouthed the new sectarian justifications promul-

gated by the regime or the old nationalist ones promulgated by some of the most prominent journalists and writers of the Arab world. The Kurds never trusted a soul, especially not their Shi'a allies in the south (the feeling was reciprocated). The West gave them a safe haven, and they began negotiating with Saddam, turning their backs on everyone else. Certainly, they never trusted the Iranians. I have yet to meet an Iraqi Kurdish political activist who does not believe that Iranians are congenital liars. Kurdish and Shi'i organizations were forced to work together under Iranian tutelage in the build-up to the Gulf war. Yet, as most Iraqis realize, the involvement of Iran in anything to do with Iraqi affairs is the kiss of death. While most Iraqis accept that Saddam started the eight-year war with Iran, they rightly feel that Khomeini kept it going, forever fueling it with his particular brand of fanaticism. He may have been a pious, ascetic, incorruptible, and God-fearing soul, but he was also an immensely cruel one. A whole generation of young Iranians were sent needlessly to their deaths. His cruelty, like that of Saddam Husain, is all that counts in the end. Both have left deep psychological scars which will take generations to heal.

Earlier, I called the army officer who jumped on top of his tank in Sa'ad Square and tore down the barrier of fear in Iraq a hero. He gave all Iraqis, including myself, the possibility of a future. On March 7, 1991, at Harvard University, the author of Republic of Fear *could go public because of what that man—call him Abu Haydar—started in Basra on February 28. Since then my life, and that of all Iraqis, has completely changed. Iraqis today talk, meet, write, organize, and produce newspapers (more than fifty since the uprising). But Abu Haydar also opened up a Pandora's box, one that had to be opened if Iraq was to have a future. What kind of a future? Seen through the prism of the Iraq-Iran War, the Gulf war, and the intifada of March 1991, the future of Iraq depends on the answer to the underlying question posed in the chapter on Abu Haydar, and maybe even in the whole of Part One of this book: Who is Abu Haydar? For that matter, does Abu Haydar even know who he is?*

The Abu Haydar that I interviewed in a London bed-sit, and around whom I organized Chapter 2, used to be a Ba'thi "until Saddam killed within my family." Saddam began killing within lots of Shi'i families after 1979. This is when the persecution of the 55 percent plus Shi'a majority really began to become a central issue of Iraqi politics. In the late 1970s, commensurate with the growth of

Shi'i self-awareness in the preceding decade (which was of course also suppressed), the Iraqi government began expelling hundreds of thousands of Iraqi Shi'a into Iran on the grounds that they were "of Iranian origin" and disloyal. The rest of the Shi'a were employed in the Iraq-Iran war machine, where they stayed, fought, and died, in ever-growing numbers. Naturally Abu Haydar lost all of his prior illusions in the Pan-Arabist schemes of the Ba'th. He became disillusioned with ideological politics and fought the Iranians for eight long years because he is a professional man and soldiering is what he was trained to do. But Abu Haydar's friends and relations continued to be deported, killed, and driven off to fight senseless wars all around him. Gradually, he learned to hate those who were administering all this pain. He had to turn somewhere for an explanation. There were no new ideas being born inside Ba'thi Iraq. Inevitably it seemed to him that the most basic criteria of group identity and loyalty that he had left—his Islam and his Shi'ism—were the primary object of Saddam Husain's attacks. Further than that he didn't—indeed, he couldn't—go. The strongly Islamic Shi'i character of the intifada in southern Iraq can be explained from such basic considerations.

The problem is that Abu Haydar's political instincts are founded on emotion, not on a broader historical understanding of what the Ba'th are all about as a modern Arab political creation. Contrary to what many Iraqi Shi'a tend to think nowadays, the Ba'th never built a Sunni confessional state in Iraq (one that is institutionally structured along confessional lines like the Lebanese state). Nor did they build one ideologically opposed to Shi'ism as such. The idea that they did is based on the all-too-common mistake of reading present woes back into the past. The irony is that if the Ba'th had built a confessional state in Iraq, things would not be as bad for the Shi'a of Iraq as they are today. Shi'ism would have acquired a measure of protection from the very fact that its distinctiveness from the Sunni or Kurdish or Christian "other" was being recognized in some way, however unjustly. This is how things worked in the Ottoman Empire; it is how things worked in Lebanon. But it is not how things worked in Iraq. The Ba'th have killed more Kurds than anyone else in Iraq. Still, the Ba'th Party cannot be said to be ideologically anti-Kurdish, in the way, for instance, that the Nazis were ingrained anti-Semites. Nothing is more important for Iraq's future than a clearheaded understanding of its past.

The state that the Ba'th built in Iraq is far worse than one built on purely confessional or ethnic criteria. It is worse because it is consistently egalitarian in its hostility to everything that is not itself. The Ba'th demand from all Iraqis absolute conformity with their violence-filled, conspiratorial view of a world permanently at war with itself.[2] Saddam Husain invents and reinvents his enemies from the entire mass of human material that is at his disposal; he thrives on the distrust, suspicion, and conspiratorialism which his regime actively inculcates in everyone; he positively expects to breed hate and a thirst for revenge in Sunni and Shi'i alike. As a consequence civil society, attacked from every direction, has virtually collapsed in Iraq. Every Iraqi—Kurd or Arab, Shi'i or Sunni—was made complicit in the Ba'thist enterprise and turned into a victim at the same time. Every Iraqi carries the marks of that victimhood deep inside him or her. In these conditions, Abu Haydar's desperate recourse to his Islam or his Shi'ism (or for that matter the recourse of other Iraqis to Sunni sectarianism or Kurdish nationalism) is neither an explanation nor a solution to the country's predicament; it is a refuge of last resort, a proof of how complete the social collapse inside Iraq already is.

In the polity that the Ba'th built up in Iraq, the Kurds suffered more than others not because they were Kurds, but because they resisted and fought back hard. Once the Shi'a asserted themselves, they began, like the Kurds, to be attacked as Shi'a. But there are Assyrian, Christian, Turkoman, and Sunni opponents of this regime, all of whom have suffered as much as any individual Shi'i or Kurd. Between the spring of 1987 and February 1988, the Iraqi government destroyed thirty-one Assyrian villages, including twenty-five Assyrian monasteries and churches.[3] The fact that Iraqis are already competing with each other over who has suffered the most is a sign that whether or not Saddam is still around in person, what he represented lives on inside Iraqi hearts. Herein lies the greatest danger of all for the country's future.

Ghosts from all of this brutalization—like Tha'ir the militiaman, who has lived in Iran for the last twelve years of his life, and the Kurdish adviser who fought with Saddam against his own family— these ghosts will keep on returning to haunt Iraq. The Islamic Republic of Iran has already created its own Iraqi Hizbollah, a sister organization to the one in Lebanon, many of whose militants are being infiltrated into the country even as I write. At the same time, the Iranian government is blocking independent Iraqi opposition groups—Islamic and non-Islamic—from access to the beleaguered southern half of the country, not to mention foreign press and international aid workers. God, money, and powerful neighboring states are a potent triumvirate in Middle East politics. But with or without Iran, ignorant, desperate, and gun-toting young men like Tha'ir, living in deplorable refugee conditions, are likely to grow more efficient at the business of being salaried guerrillas fighting under the banner of Islam. When Abu Haydar revolted in March 1991, young Iraqis like Tha'ir joined in his revolt, carrying their victimhood with them in the shape of a ferocious, hate-filled, vengeance-seeking, and profoundly intolerant brand of Islam. Armed with these sentiments, they went on a killing rampage and bungled the intifada, alienating those who might have supported them and those whose support they needed. In the spirit of Um Husain of Basra, I ask: What kind of Islam is this? This is not Islam; this is Ba'thism's mirror image.

All Iraqis are paying the price of the failure of the March 1991 intifada. But the Shi'a this time, rather than the Kurds, are paying more than anyone else. Iraqi Shi'ism thought it knew what suffering is, but never in its modern history has it known suffering like this. In the crushing of the intifada a level of ruthlessness was employed that previously had been reserved only for the Kurds. A brutally naked new kind of sectarian warfare, directed at the mere fact of being a Shi'i, is now a component part of Saddam's legacy. In this, the regime's post–Gulf war weakness was on display, not its strength. Only by whipping up Shi'i-Sunni hatred could the Ba'th have a chance of clinging to power in Fortress Baghdad. The strategy worked not because the Americans didn't support the intifada (which of course they didn't), and certainly not because they actively wanted Saddam to stay on (they would much prefer to have seen him replaced by some other strongman from the army or the Ba'thi inner circle). Nor even did Saddam's strategy of inculcating sectarianism among Iraqis work because he was better armed and better equipped; it worked solely because of a failure of Shi'i political leadership.

The problem is that somebody must speak for all Iraqis, but the Shi'a of Iraq are confused. Abu Haydar is confused. Like so many Arabs, he is beginning to have to think about things more seriously than in the past, yet he still does not know who he is, or even who he wants to be. Is he an Arab? Is he an Iraqi? Is he a Shi'i Muslim, an

*Iraqi Shi'i nationalist, or maybe just a plain old universal Muslim?
And if he is a combination of all these things, which, in his political
view of himself, comes first? Most important of all, where does our
common humanity—in the shape of everyone's equal rights—fit in?*

The answers to these questions are going to determine whether or
not the next generation of Iraqis will even have a future—much less
what kind. Saddam Husain is no longer the main issue of Iraqi
politics; but his legacy is. It will remain the main issue of Iraqi
politics for many years to come. Today, the Shi'a of Iraq are poised
on the edge of the most important question that they have ever
faced in their entire history: *What do they stand for politically? Who
are they?*

Throughout their entire history, Iraq's Shi'a have avoided that
question. They began avoiding it on the day in A.D. 680 that Husain
and his followers died alone on the plain of Kerbala, undefended by
the very people who had asked him to be their governor (something
Khomeini, who was not above a bit of Iranian chauvinism, was
quick to exploit during the Iraq-Iran War).[4] Iraqi Shi'ism has deeply
internalized this tragic moment of its own birth; it thinks of itself as
having been born in a moment of failure, which is annually relived
in the mourning ceremonies known as the ta'ziyya, associated with
that momentous historical event. In this it is distinguished from its
Iranian counterpart, never having ruled itself and knowing only the
language of opposition and rejection. In fact, Iraqi Shi'ism has never
taken the business of government very seriously, and on a personal
level even Shi'ites traditionally shy away from anything to do with
it. They avoid army service or any form of state service or employment. Given half a chance they will opt to become traders, independent professionals, revolutionaries, reformers, mystics, artists; never
statesmen or diplomats. Of the seventeen different Iraqi Islamic opposition groups—most of which are essentially Shi'ite in composition and spirit—none has yet evolved a clear political formula for
government in Iraq. This means that if Abu Haydar does not yet
know whether he is a Muslim or an Arab or an Iraqi, he also does
not yet know who he wants to rule over him—clerics, lay people, or
professional politicians. Then again, in whose name are these un-
knowns going to rule: God's, or the people's, or a combination of
the two? Over what territory? All of these questions remain unanswered among Iraq's Shi'a today, even as the regime in Baghdad
slowly but surely rots away.

Until Khomeini's Islamic revolution opted for a republic in Iran, many Iraqi Islamic activists were still talking about reestablishing the caliphate. Virtually everything that is important to politics has been left wide open inside the Iraqi Islamic movement—a certain recipe for even greater disaster as far as a democratic future is concerned. Today, all Iraqis are thinking about democracy and human rights, but historically the Islamic movement was formed from the 1960s right through the mid-1980s on the idea that democracy was a Western import and foreign to Islam. Most Iraqi Islamic parties have spent the last ten years thinking of themselves as part of a worldwide Islamic movement with Iran as its center. They are deeply unhappy with this today, but they have nothing else to put in its place. With every passing day they see that Iranian power is not being wielded with anything like Iraqi interests at heart. Iraqi Shi'ite refugees and Islamic activists were treated abominably inside Iran from the late 1970s on. Is it any wonder, then, that Abu Haydar is confused?

What gives these issues such burning importance is a central and inescapable new fact of Iraqi politics: only the Shi'a of Iraq are in a position to stop Saddam from snatching victory out of the jaws of his own death in the shape of escalating confessional and ethnic violence in the years to come. By virtue of their numbers, they carry a historic responsibility for that future, greater than that of any other ethnic or sectarian group in Iraq. And important new Arab political talent is emerging from their ranks. Yet no budding Iraqi Shi'a politician has proved himself capable of addressing these questions. The most liberal of them are talking about the desirability of dividing the country into three parts, and complaining at the same time that the Kurds are being paid too much attention by the Western media.[5] Some individual thinkers from inside the Islamic movement are doing interesting work trying to fit Western ideas on democracy into an Islamic discourse.[6] But the majority are weighed down by tradition and completely mixed up on the most elementary questions of politics.

Consider for instance the sentence, "People have rights for no other reason than that they exist as individual human beings." This appears as the first article of Charter 91. Some of the best elements in the Iraqi democratic opposition, liberal Shi'ites who have come out of the Islamic movement, find themselves unable to endorse this trivial foundation stone of any politics based on human rights. In other words, they find themselves unable to extend rights to abso-

lutely everyone, irrespective of any other consideration. Does an apostate have rights? Does the formulation elevate humanism over God as a guiding principle?

The signs are that Iraq's Shi'a are so traumatized by their own tragedy that they are becoming less and less able to think and act like Iraqis. When feelings of this sort supplant all rational thought, as they are doing among many Iraqi Shi'a today, they are bound to spawn intolerance—and with it violence—in the future. All the talk of human rights that is currently fashionable among Iraqis can quickly fall by the wayside; it can easily turn out to be nothing but cheap exploitation of a powerful universal idea solely for purposes of grabbing the West's attention. "You know they [U.S. legislators] like these words [human rights]," one Shi'i activist who runs a human rights organization in the West said to me. The seed of catastrophe for Iraq is present in this kind of dissimulation.

Suppose Abu Haydar decides that his primary loyalties are to an Islamic republic—however packaged in democratic verbiage. The decision will have to confront the fact that Sunni Arabs are today gripped by paroxysms of fear at the mere mention of anything to do with Islam in politics. The up-and-coming new generation of Iraqi Shi'i politicians rightly goes on and on about how the West has exaggerated the "Islamic" Shi'i threat in Iraq—with echoes of the Iranian revolution and Khomeiniism reverberating in the Western mind—but the one thing these same politicians won't talk about is legitimate Sunni Iraqi fears. What is an Iraqi Sunni to think when he sees even the most liberal Iraqi Shi'i intellectuals engaged in rewriting the whole history of modern Iraq in such a way as to "prove" that virtually every modern Sunni politician was secretly a ta'ifi, a closet confessional sectarian? (I have even heard it said that Kamil al-Chadirji, Iraq's great democratic politician, was a ta'ifi. One of the most popular contemporary Shi'i political writers, who worked formerly as a publicist for the Iraqi government, told me in October 1992 that whereas the Shi'a are "the real people" of Iraq, the Sunnis are merely a sect that has been imposed on the country. He added that he has never known a Sunni who was not at heart a ta'ifi. To my mind, this is an inverted version of standard Ba'thist thinking.)

Sunni fears of what the Shi'a of Iraq might do to them if they came to power are much more well founded than the naive assumptions of certain Western leaders and have nothing to do with Islam as such, any more than Shi'i adoption of political Islam has to do with private religious belief. Belief is not what is at stake in the coming struggle between the Shi'i and Sunni communities of Iraq; survival is. After Saddam is gone, when people's lives and those of their loved ones look as if they are on the chopping block, Sunni fears of what the Shi'a might do to them in the name of Islam are going to become the major force of Iraqi politics. The more Iraq's Shi'a assert themselves as Shi'a, the greater will be the tendency of Iraq's Sunni minority to fight to the bitter end before allowing anything that so much as smells of an Islamic republic to be established in Iraq. They see in such a state—whether rightly or wrongly is irrelevant—their own annihilation. In this they will be supported by the Kurds (if they don't already have their own independent state by then). Spurious formulas like "we are all Muslims" are not going to mean anything, just as the PLO's "secular democratic Palestine" never meant anything to Israelis.

The problem is not with Islam as such, any more than it was with Arab unity as a nice idea for sometime in the future. The Iranians, the Algerians, possibly even the Egyptians may one day be able to evolve a democracy out of an Islamic state for the simple reason that people, mercifully, can be flexible even with their most deeply held beliefs. The point is that Iraqi conditions in particular exclude an Islamic option for Iraq. The country is much less homogeneous than those I have mentioned and it has already been devastated by one kind of "politics of faith" (Ba'thism rests ideologically on the idea of iman, blind unquestioning faith in Arabism, which it explicitly took from the Islamic tradition). A stable non-violent new order is not going to be built on another.[7]

Violence and police states always follow whenever the thing that people hold most precious in the world—the innermost core of their belief system—is injected into the center of public life. If the Shi'a of Iraq insist on putting their Shi'ism first in politics, or even if they insist on putting their Islamic identity first, yet another generation is going to go down the drain in Iraq. The warning signs are already upon us.

Let me illustrate with a painful personal experience. When I traveled to northern Iraq in November 1991 to interview the boy-survivor Taimour, and investigate the secret police files captured by the Kurds during the uprising, my motives were met with suspicion from Shi'is resident in the West. "Why aren't you writing about what Saddam has done to your own kind, the Shi'a of Iraq?" many *people complained from among the most enlightened members of the Iraqi opposition. "We are suffering too." I came back from that visit to hear a constant stream of complaints in Europe and the United States that I was abandoning "the Iraqi cause" or "the Shi'a cause" for "the Kurdish cause." "What about us?" asked the Assyrians. "We were victims of the Anfal operations too." Iraqis of all kinds still make that point to me in more or less subtle ways a full year after the BBC film which documented that official campaign of mass murder. The problem of Iraq is that everyone was a victim, and most people, especially the Shi'a majority, only know how to think and behave like victims.*

In private, the word spread among the Sunni Arab Iraqis of London that Kanan Makiya was forging a new alliance between Shi'a mullahs and the Kurdish tribal leaders, in which they figured as the prime target. Moreover, it was totally obvious that he was working hand in glove with the Americans (notwithstanding the fact that the same people also thought that the United States wanted Saddam to stay in power). Finally, when the Iraqi documents captured by the Kurds were transported for safekeeping in the West through the efforts of Human Rights Watch, some Kurdish nationalists objected to Makiya working on them, notwithstanding his efforts to bring the story of the Anfal operations out into the open. For political reasons they wanted an American, not a fellow Iraqi, to tell the world what had happened to them, thus obviating the whole point of the exercise.

This is the wounded human material out of which a new order in Iraq has to be fashioned. The poison of Sunni-Shi'i sectarianism, and of Arab-Kurdish bitterness, either one of which is enough to kill Iraq, are today working together to tear the country apart. The division of the country is already being acted out in people's hearts, before it is played out on the ground at the cost of untold numbers of new Iraqi dead. No Iraqi is immune any longer; everyone has become infected. Virulent strains of nationalism and sectarianism are more prevalent today in Iraq than at any time in the past. They are the driving forces for change even as the best elements in the Iraqi opposition pretend otherwise. Where do we Iraqis go from here?

Let us begin with the fact that everyone acquiesced and compromised with dictatorship (whether willingly or not is irrelevant); that not many are left inside and outside Iraq who have clean hands. Those secret police files transported to the West might show just how many Kurds were in different degrees involved in what was done to other Kurds in 1988. Sunnis and Shi'a were represented everywhere in the Iraqi state, the army, the police, the security services. Omar's story (Chapter 3) is that of an Arab informed upon by a Kurd, and a Sunni interrogated by a Shi'a. Competition over victimhood is a road that can lead only to disaster. Given that the nature of the regime in Baghdad was such as to leave everyone with accounts to be settled, maybe it is better to settle as few of them as human nature, and wise politicians, will permit.[8] A comprehensive general amnesty that is sweeping and far-reaching in scope is the only way to stave off massive bloodletting after the fall of the regime.

The second important acknowledgment is the realization by Iraq's Shi'a—upon whose shoulders the responsibility for Iraq's future principally lies—that Sunni fears are legitimate. These fears have to be politically addressed by Iraq's new generation of leaders as a matter of top priority. Formulas of government are needed that provide iron-clad guarantees against "the tyranny of the majority." Thousands of future Iraqi lives are going to depend on the sincerity with which those assurances are made. The Shi'a have a moral-political responsibility to come up with those formulas. One cannot expect leadership from a minority that is already feeling defensive and under siege with everyone pointing the finger of blame at it. If Iraq dissolves into even more chaos and bloodshed in the post-Saddam era, it will be principally because Shi'i political leadership failed to rise to this historic occasion and to the responsibilities which its own numbers impose upon it.

The third important task that a responsible Iraqi opposition must take upon itself is to embrace federalism as a solution to the Kurdish question within the framework of a unitary Iraqi state. A first step in this direction was taken in the meeting in Salahulddin, northern Iraq, on October 27–31, 1992, when all the different organizations of the Iraqi opposition met under the umbrella of the Iraqi National Congress. I was privileged to be present at that historic meeting and to address the Congress on exactly this topic. Federalism is not a concession which we Arabs grudgingly make to the Kurds; it is the only way to preserve the unity of Iraq. Iraqi Kurdistan lived a very special experience after the end of the Gulf war. Not only is there no going back on that experience, but the future of Iraq must be built on it. A virtual revolution has happened on 20 percent of Iraqi soil since the Gulf war, complete with elections embracing 20 percent of the Iraqi people, and a more or less functioning Kurdish parliament. This was a revolution without grandiose militant slogans and radical rejectionist politics. Either we extend that experience to embrace all Iraq, or we lose it altogether and introduce the logic of partition. Once that terrible logic sets in, it will, I predict, proceed inexorably. Arab will end up killing Arab, Shi'ite will end up killing fellow Shi'ite, and even Kurds will turn on one another. This poor state called Iraq that we inherited with the carving up of the Ottoman Empire may not be much, but, as the carnage which accompanied the dismembering of some states has shown (India in 1947 and Yugoslavia since 1991), it could be a thousand times better than the alternatives.

There is no grievance, no idea, no creed, no religion, no belief, no God worth asserting if it entails taking one more Iraqi life. If, in spite of everything, the Kurds want their own state, then, having failed to convince them that this option might not be in their own best interest, it is incumbent upon all Iraqis to support them to the hilt and to wish them success in their great new adventure of statehood. That particular road is fraught with pitfalls, and I for one certainly hope that the Kurdish people do not choose to go down it. I say this not only for their sake, but because I know their departure is my loss. Unfortunately, the same option is not available to the Shi'is and Sunnis of Iraq. Here is where the real problems of the future lie. These two confessional groups are completely intertwined in Iraq; theirs is an inseparable union if ever there was one. Either they are going to kill one another in droves until one or the other comes out on top, or they are going to find a way of living together; there is no third way.

AS I WENT over and over the events of the intifada and their bloody aftermath, the full realization of the nature of the legacy with which the Ba'th have saddled Iraq began to overwhelm me. I found the cumulative effect of the stories unbearable, deadening to all rationality, a threat even to my own sanity. This second-hand personal experience will be replicated tomorrow inside Iraq on a grand scale, when the full horrors of the past are known even as they are followed by yet more new horrors. Slowly, then, everybody's realization could turn into everybody's numbness. The capacity to have any kind of feeling for another human being could die. Yet Pandora's box had to be opened, and Iraqis like Abu Haydar were brave enough to take the first step. That is the meaning of what happened in March 1991. How much wider is Pandora's box going to be opened in the future? Time and the political wisdom of Iraq's new generation of political leaders will tell. Everything now depends on them. Pessimism about the future of Iraq, as well as the fact that Iraqis now have for the first time the possibility of a future, are both legacies of Abu Haydar's intifada.

"What might have been and what has been," wrote Eliot, "Point to one end, which is always present."[9] Studied truthfully, with no holds barred and no one's feelings spared, the Iraqi intifada of March 1991 is like a lens through which ghosts from the past loom and stark options for the future may be dimly perceived. I am tired of looking through that lens, maybe because I am no longer able or willing to bear so much reality. So I will let Hameed, the nonsectarian young Najafi quoted before in Chapter 2—and with whom I identify—bring this journey through cruelty to a close.

We in Iraq don't have a future. I'm twenty-eight, my life is over. But maybe my children will not suffer as I've suffered. I love my two little children—the boy is two years old and the girl is just seven months. When I feel depressed, I tell the boy, "Maybe when you grow up, you'll fight in a war against Syria, or against Jordan." The only words he knows are "Momma," "Poppa," and "Saddam."

I don't know what I'll do. Maybe I'll go to Jordan to find work there. I have to wear the same clothes every day, because a new shirt now costs 30 dinars. We haven't had meat for a month. We just dream of different meals, but we can't eat them. Most of the money I earn we spend on milk for the baby; that costs 15 dinars a can. We had to sell my wife's jewelry to buy the 10-year-old taxi I'm driving now. When I first bought it, I was driving four to six hours a day; now I'm driving eight to 10 hours a day. It's my dream to give up smoking because it costs two dinars a pack; now I'm smoking more.

I love English plays and poetry. They make me happy. I got interested when I studied English at the British Council in Baghdad. I love *Twelfth Night*: "If music be the food of love, play on!"

I think reading is rebellion. It makes us think and question. But in class, I have to read poems glorifying Saddam, and the students have to memorize them. The compositions they write have to be about topics such as the glory of Saddam Husain. They've killed free thinking. Why should my students be reading? They look at me—110 dinars a month and driving a taxi in the summer—and they think, "I'll be getting out of school and going straight to the army."

My favorite play is *Death of a Salesman,* because a man, Willie Loman, sticks to his dream and sacrifices himself for his children. I like *Waiting for Godot* too; I read it to my mother. Godot represents hope. From where and when it will come, we do not know. But Godot will come. Alone, we cannot do anything. Willie Loman had to sacrifice his life for his children. So we have to stay here, waiting. We are waiting for Godot.[10]

SILENCE

7 ⁄ Who Am I?

Were you [Samir al-Khalil] thinking of visiting your original country, Iraq, carrying your American passport after your American army had installed itself there? You have no right to speak of Iraq and of those who live in it. Iraq and its people are as innocent of you as the wolf is innocent of the blood of Yousuf. You sit in the lap of luxury and in your hand is paper and pencil. This is all that you own. As for feeling and compassion [for Iraq], of that you have none. You should have denounced the attack which sent Iraq back into the twelfth century. Instead, you asked the barbarians to finish what they had started.

Now I don't want to get personal about any of this, but I urge you to look back into yourself and to direct yourself to God, the all-knowing and the all-powerful, especially in these holy days [Ramadhan], asking him for forgiveness for your sins. He is all-forgiving and merciful.
—Commentary in *al-'Arab* newspaper[1]

WHAT is the connection between the passport one holds, the views one expresses, the books one writes, and one's innermost emotional and belief system, which is of course what constitutes one's identity? It so happens I don't have an American passport. Nor have I ever had one. However, after years of working hard at it, I succeeded in freeing myself from the restrictions imposed by that great bane of fourteen years of my adult life, that ball and chain upon my freedom: my Iraqi passport. The day I received the letter granting me British nationality in 1982 was one of the happiest in my life. Although I was fortunate enough to know what freedom was in many ways, on that particular day I tasted it. Now I could travel without restrictions, whether those imposed by the Iraqi state even while I resided abroad, or those imposed by harsh immigration policies and the occasional racist officer at a Western port of entry.[2] Never again would I have to go to an Iraqi embassy, posting friends at the corner of the street to check up on whether or not I came out again. Many Iraqis, Palestinians, Syrians, and Lebanese in forced or voluntary conditions of diaspora and exile will identify with these feelings and with this personal experience.

But there is an unwritten rule among us Arabs that one is not supposed to speak or write about such things, as I am doing now. There is shame attached to changing one's passport; it is perceived to be an act of betrayal of some kind. That is what the author of the passage quoted at the start of this chapter meant when he rubbed in the words, *"your* American passport . . . *your* American army." The same notions of betrayal, it so happens, found their way into the Iraqi legal system long ago. This system explicitly associates nationality with private belief. The law that reformed the legal system in 1977 takes great care to exclude from citizenship "all persons who take a political, economical or intellectual attitude hostile to the Revolution and its Programme."[3] Nor is this an aberration. The law was a distillation of everything the Ba'th had been saying about Arab identity since the 1940s, in Syria, Iraq, and everywhere else the party had a presence. The fact is, I am a traitor, not a citizen, in the eyes of the Republic of Iraq. A bona fide citizen is one who thinks in a certain way, and deviancy is manifest in "bad thoughts" before it is realized in treacherous behavior. The state will not renew my Iraqi passport, and it has other laws which legitimate violence against my person, because of the demonstrable fact—proven by my books— that I think non-Ba'thi thoughts.

In this context, the feelings of shame about changing one's passport are rooted, whether consciously or unconsciously, in similar notions of identity. As these notions enter into open conflict with the exigencies of work, political exile, and even lifestyle preferences, a big lie has to be maintained in the shape of a denial that the change means anything. Many Arabs *enjoy* the very benefits that they will then deny they wanted so desperately as they sought to obtain American or British or French passports. The outcome of such self-deception is that quote from the writer in an Arabic newspaper published out of London who blames me for holding a passport that I don't hold, and who says, in a final ironical twist, that he used to be a great admirer of *Republic of Fear,* until its author was "unmasked" by the political positions he took during the Gulf war.

Who Is an Arab Intellectual?

WHEN Saddam Husain invaded Kuwait on August 2, 1990, the paradigm that had ruled this characteristic Arab discourse on identity was subjected to a most terrible test. Arab nationalist sentiments rooted in the memory of deep historical injustices—the carving up of the Arab world after World War I and the creation of the state of Israel in 1948—came face to face with the ugliness of the regime spearheading Arabism in 1991: Ba'thi Iraq. The whole Arab world was stunned by what Saddam had done. Yet for the first few days after the invasion, a reader restricted to Arabic newspapers would not even have known that Kuwait had been invaded, because the Arabic language press was either engaging in self-censorship or waiting to be told by its financiers what was permissible to write. You had to find out what was going on from the Western media.

Not that this made much of a difference to the vast majority of those who think of themselves as Arab or "pro-Arab" intellectuals. With the exception of the Gulf states and Egypt—which has been living an isolated intellectual life since the Camp David Accords—I am aware of no community of Arab intellectuals, however small, that could make a meaningful political distinction between the interests of the suffering people of Iraq, who had just lost a whole generation in eight years of grueling warfare with Iran, and the tyrant, who was sacrificing them on the altar of yet another adventure.[4] At the same time it became difficult for some Arabs—those most directly affected, overwhelmingly Kuwaitis and Iraqis—to avoid reacting to this latest Middle East crisis on the grounds of what was being done to Kuwait under occupation, and what had been going on inside Iraq during the previous twenty years. A new, self-critical sensibility has begun to enter Arab politics. But like any new thing born into an environment hostile to the idea of self-criticism, it is very, very fragile.[5]

Old habits die hard. They die hardest of all among people who have made it their duty to awaken pride in self and a sense of collective identity by blaming all ills on some "other"—a foreign agency or "alien" culture outside the community one is trying to extol, and often more powerful and dynamic. The painful thing to observe is the unrelenting stridency of the Arab intelligentsia's attempt to blame every ill on the West or Israel. The language gets more unreal, hysterical, and self-flagellating, the less the Arab world is actually able to achieve politically and culturally in modern times.[6]

Consider this all-too-common incident. Ahmad, an upper-middle-class, well-educated young man, was born and brought up in Baghdad. He despises politics, like most educated Iraqis of his generation brought up in Saddam Husain's Iraq. All his friends in the United States, where he recently came to study, were Arabs. Several months after the debacle of the Gulf war, in the course of an evening of partying and fun, Ahmad had a conversation with Mazin, a similarly well-educated Jordanian studying business administration in Chicago. Mazin referred to Saddam as the only "real man" in the Arab world for standing up to the West. Ahmad wanted to know what standing up had accomplished. "Nothing, but he proved to the West that we Arabs are nations to be reckoned with." Nor would Mazin admit that the invasion of Kuwait had been a mistake. Ahmad recalls the conversation:

> He started the war too soon, he should have gotten the bomb first.
>
> So that instead of hundreds of thousands dead, we would have had a few millions?
>
> But then we could have faced Israel.
>
> The only way to face Israel is by shaking hands.
>
> But that is treason!
>
> Treason is killing your own people, dragging them through a bloody long war and then telling them to take Kuwait back.
>
> Well, you are a Kurd, you don't like him anyway.[7]

It is as though someone senses deep down that he is a failure in the present, in the world he knows and has been brought up in, but is goaded into desperate self-assertion, first by the constant reminder of how wonderful and glorious his ancestors were; and second, by the image of apparently omnipotent outsiders, who effortlessly sweep him aside in every real or imagined confrontation. These two factors combine into an ideological apology for his own impotence: his people would be glorious, his state would be all-powerful, but for the 'machinations of the imperialists (or the Great Satan, which amounts to the same thing). What has now happened is that this person's very identity has become constructed in a totally negative way: he is who he is because of who he hates, not because of who he loves or is in solidarity with.[8]

Another way of constructing one's identity, by looking inward self-critically, rather than outward, has not been explored by the Arab intelligentsia as a way of facing up to the crisis of their world after 1967—a world which has been lurching headlong from one catastrophe to another for longer than any of us care to contemplate. A very large number of people have invested much of their lives in constructing and defending this "rejectionist" paradigm, which has now become second nature to a new generation of Arabs like Mazin. Paradoxically, therefore, the greatest threat facing the new self-critical sensibility comes from the very people who ought to be nurturing it: that community of Arab and self-proclaimed "pro-Arab" intellectuals.

What is a "pro-Arab" intellectual? Why is it that we do not hear about "pro-French" or "pro-Latin-American" intellectuals? Because they don't exist. Borges and Márquez think of themselves as writers who come from Argentina and Colombia. One reads them or not largely because of what or how they write, not because of where they come from or the views they hold. Then there are specialists in the work of such writers, who are interested in looking for connections and common preoccupations, but who would never imagine themselves as "pro" or "anti" Latin America. This is not the case with writers from or about the Middle East, who too often project themselves and their work as "Arab," "Palestinian," or "pro-Arab" in the politically charged connotations of those labels. As an old Palestinian friend of mine, who is constantly having to shuttle between conferences, once put it: "I have turned into a professional Palestinian." He was aware of the problem; most Arab and "pro-Arab" writers aren't. The funny thing is that "being a Palestinian" or being a "pro" or even an "anti" Arab spokesperson is an effective strategy for drawing attention to oneself or to one's cause, and it is most effective in the United States.

The very existence of such labels is a sign of how degraded the intellectual climate of debate about the Middle East has become both in the Arab world and in the West. Think of the poisoned atmosphere inside some Middle East Studies departments in universities, especially in the United States, where the Arab-Israeli conflict all too often gets replayed in the pettiest of forms. Semi-professional clubs and informal networks of "pro-Arab" and "pro-Israel" cliques have sprung up even—or especially—in academic life, each of which worships at a particular shrine and has its childish taboos. These islands of boredom in their intellectual predictability create stereotypes far more effectively than the Western media, which at worst simply reiterate them.

Who is an Arab intellectual? This is harder to pin down than one would think because there are no longer any coherent criteria which combine the qualities of being an Arab (and not, say, an Egyptian) with an interacting intellectual community such as one finds in a country like Egypt. "Arab intellectuals, or intellectuals from among the Arabs?" asks Isma'il al-Amin, from the Arabic daily *al-'Arab,* which supported the Iraqi regime through the Gulf crisis. It is a good question, which he answers very poorly: "How can a writer be an Arab intellectual, a carrier of Arabic culture as long as he foot-notes his article, study or book with references that have not the remotest connection to Arabic, neither in language nor in culture nor in thought?"[9]

Behind such a question lies the bigoted assumption, widespread among far more intelligent and westernized Arabs than al-Amin, that there is a hermetically sealed, *uniquely Arab nexus* between how one thinks and who one is, the same nexus that we encountered at the beginning of this chapter. I am not who I think I am; I am *how* I think. Amin believes that even Arabs who write in Arabic may no longer "be" Arabs, because they do not rely solely on Arab sources. His emphasis is not even the classical nationalist one on language as the criterion of identity; it is on "being" an Arab because one behaves or thinks like one, whatever that is supposed to mean.[10]

An Egyptian publishing in Arabic in Egypt is not a "good" Arab intellectual, or the right kind of intellectual, if he sees himself as an Egyptian and if he fits into a circle of publishers, commentators, and readers who are restricted to Egypt. Even his Arabness is suspect if he didn't take the right position during the Gulf war or when Sadat visited Jerusalem. On the other hand, there is no doubt about the Arabness of a professor of Palestinian origin, who teaches in an American university, and who expresses his rejection of the United States in eloquent English, because he "thinks" like an Arab, and because his "cause" is the cause of all Arabs. What if an individual fits in somewhere between these two extremes, as do that motley collection of exiles from all over the Fertile Crescent who live in Paris and London, and write in Arabic for dailies, magazines, and journals appearing simultaneously in the kiosks of capital cities all over the world?

Arabs everywhere have gotten themselves tangled up in knots over these kinds of issues. Iraqis, even those who wish me well, sometimes ask: "Who do you write for?" They want to know whether I write to please a Western audience or whether I write as an Iraqi, "on behalf of the people of Iraq." Many got upset when I visited northern Iraq to document the *Anfal* operations, which took the lives of at least 100,000 noncombatant Kurds. "Aren't you a Shi'ite?" was the implicit question. "Why don't you write about us?" The assumption once again is that one is who one writes for and that one writes only for who one is. A less sophisticated acquaintance of mine, an Iraqi businessman, was actually convinced that I played up the story of what was done to Iraqi Jews in 1969 in *Republic of Fear* only in order to sell more copies of the book. He approved of this marketing tactic on my part because of how much he hated Saddam Husain. Anything I did that would benefit "our cause" was fine with him. His is a more sympathetic way of expressing basically the same way of thinking as those non-Iraqi Arab-Americans who thought of Samir al-Khalil during 1991 as a "self-hating Arab" who wrote critically about the Arab world in order to curry favor with publishers and book reviewers in the West.

In a similar vein, Edward Said has criticized my writing for being "unsympathetic" to Arabs and advancing the thesis that the violence in the Middle East is inscribed in Arab genes. In the same interview on intellectuals and the Gulf war, Said spoke approvingly of a popular source of conspiratorialism in the Arab world, namely, asking of every piece of writing: "who is this person really speaking *for*. As they say in Arabic, *min warrah?*, 'who's behind him?' "[11] The fundamental difference between myself and Said can be boiled down to the fact that whereas I reject the very asking of such questions of any human being, he approves of them.

"I write for myself, like everyone else," is the confusing answer I give to all these critics. So, if Samir al-Khalil happens to prefer to write in English, and if he has lived largely in the West for the last twenty years, and if he called upon the Allied forces to take out the tyrant in the conviction that this was in the best interests of all Iraqis, was he acting as a bona fide Arab given the added complication that the overwhelming majority of Iraqis thought and felt the same way? The irony is that while Said and Arabic newspapers like *al-'Arab* were horrified by the idea of more Allied intervention, even Ba'thist bureaucrats thought the Gulf war was left unfinished:

A group of officials whom I had known as meek and loyal servants of the government were standing around in a circle. "General Shwartzkopf didn't go far enough," said one in a loud voice. "He should have come to Baghdad and finished the job." The others nodded. They didn't seem to care any longer whether anyone heard them.[12]

Always there is an uneasy tension between a clearly inner impulse at work in the act of writing, and the morality of the final result. When I interviewed the Kurdish boy Taimour, he did not want to talk to me (Chapter 5). He had been taught to spew out a canned speech. But I had not come for this. Thinking of myself as a writer, I wanted much more out of him. So, I sat the boy down for two hours and in effect forced him to relive in infinitesimal detail every moment of his trauma. What right had I to do such a thing? Is Taimour better off for it? He has since become a prime target for assassination. Iraqi patriots and Kurds who hate Saddam Husain approve of what I did, seeing in it the necessary subordination of an individual's welfare to the general welfare of all Iraqis. An Arab or Palestinian nationalist, on the other hand, might think that exposing the genocidal campaign of 1988 against the Kurds will be turned by Israel or the West into an attack on all Arabs, and that is bad for the Arabs. Right from the start one's motivations are under suspicion.

I despise both these ways of posing the real human dilemmas involved. The morality of what I did to Taimour is subject to all kinds of important interpretations, the most interesting of which have nothing to do with who I write for, or even who I am. The real and only valid moral questions arise because I write for myself and for no one else. Life would be simpler if I could just turn around and say, "I write on behalf of the Iraqi people, or in order to expose the crimes of Saddam." The fact is, I don't.

The ruling nationalist paradigm of the Arab intelligentsia, severely tested by Saddam Husain's action on August 2, 1990, cannot be understood apart from the gigantic obsession over who is or is not an Arab. Thus far I have illustrated that paradigm using articles from a typical Arabic daily, al-'Arab, not known for the quality of its journalism. But the same obsession is present in one form or another in all the anti-Western rhetoric that comes out of the Arab world. To many Arabs like Mazin, Saddam Husain looked like a saviour, riding in as though from a heroic past in order to uphold "Arab honor" and salve old wounds of frustration and impotence.

However, criticizing the rhetoric of Arab politics, it must be stressed, is not the same as abandoning those who are smarting under the lash of Syrian repression or on the receiving end of constant humiliation and a brutal occupation in the West Bank. I will never forget the experience of sitting in a Palestinian taxi driving from Birzeit to Jerusalem, tailing a Jeepload of jeering Israeli soldiers gesticulating rudely at the six stony-faced Arabs in the taxi. Nor can I forget a scene just outside Jerusalem's Bab al-Khalil, Jaffa Gate, when two Israeli policemen astride jittery horses searched a terrified Arab boy, who cannot have been more than eight or nine years old, by making him turn his school satchel upside down and spill all the contents onto the grass verge. (I witnessed these scenes in October 1990 during a visit to Jerusalem and the West Bank, a visit made possible because I am now a British passport holder.) In that little boy's position, I thought, as I scoured the dirt for my eraser, pencil sharpener, and scattered papers after the soldiers had gone, I too would look upon Saddam Husain as a saviour. Despair and disenfranchisement, when married to constant abuse and humiliation of this sort, will always generate illusory hopes and superstitious beliefs in any people. Nothing I say in this book should be construed as a critique of Arabs whose dignity and very identity as human beings is being assaulted daily by Israeli policies on the West Bank.

The Language of Cruelty

HERE in Part Two, I will be focusing in particular on the views of those cosmopolitan, westernized Arab and "pro"-Arab intellectuals who, more often than not, reside in the West, or who are in a position to write and say what they want. Such people, by virtue of the freedoms they enjoy, are in a position to do something positive for Arabs trapped inside the oppressive countries of the Middle East. Yet in their vast majority they chose, directly or indirectly, either to excuse or to actively go along with the Iraqi dictator's political project. This choice was no momentary lapse; it was a confirmation of the obsessive and deeply unhealthy hold that identity politics has upon Arab intellectuals.

These intellectuals are a very diverse group, sophisticated, and by and large politically aware. My only criterion for including someone in the pantheon of people presented here is that he or she is very accomplished by generally accepted international standards (whether as a scholar, a professional, a poet, or artist of one kind or another). Accepting with Walid Khalidi that in spite of everything, "the Arab world still paradoxically constitutes a single area of psychological, emotional and intellectual resonance transcending state frontiers,"[13] my sole criterion for including someone is that he or she writes from a position of deep empathy with, and sense of belonging to, that world—howsoever defined. Throughout, I am not trying to pillory any individual; I am arguing that a certain way of looking at the world, often entered into with the best of intentions, is *morally bankrupt,* and the principal source of our inability to come to terms with problems that are of our own making. If I write for myself, as I said earlier, I also write from the standpoint of a person who wishes from the bottom of his heart to see this tragic state of affairs reversed.

Consider, for instance, Hisham Djaïet, graduate of the Sorbonne, a knight of France's Legion of Honor and probably Tunisia's best-known intellectual. He is an expert in Islamic history who is also a former critic of Ba'thi practices.[14] But in an interview with *L'Express,* he said that Saddam had "the edge" over the Arab states, which were part of the coalition ranged against him because his newfound Islamic vocabulary "corresponds to a reappropriation of self, to the restoration of a deep identity."[15] The passage from heroicizing to mythologizing to celebrating violence is effortless for Djaïet:

L'Express: Since August 11, 1990, you have presided in Tunisia over the national committee of solidarity that is providing support for Iraq and its leader. Why?

Djaïet: Iraq and Saddam Husain bring hope to the Arab world. For twenty years, the Arab world has been stuck in a frigid, depressing, virtually rotten order: a Saudi-American order whose vision does not go beyond petrodollars. Henceforth a new perspective is opening up, that of unification. And Iraq is its pole and motor.

L'Express: How do you justify the annexation of Kuwait?

Djaïet: I don't have to tell you, as Europeans, that your nations were born out of wars. In annexing Kuwait, Saddam Husain has entered into the dynamics of history. He was trying to make sure of a source of wealth for himself, material means. In addition, he was undertaking the beginning of the unification of the Arab world. Sometimes legitimacy is more important than legality.

L'Express: Even if that were to lead to a generalized conflict?

Djaïet: War has the merit of clarifying things—with respect to your contradictions and with respect to ours. We have everything to gain from this clarification. We have nothing to lose from this war, even if it ended in defeat. Because thanks to Saddam Husain it is taking place on the level of realities—oil, military force, etc, and no longer on the level of symbols.[16]

Like Saddam Husain, Hisham Djaïet is able to convert even the most abject defeat into proof of the indomitable spirit of Arabism. This then produces a definition of what it means to be an Arab, which is itself an affirmation of a prior mythologized assertion of "deep identity." Old myths feed into fresh "theorizing," which rests on matter-of-fact assertions such as this: "Violence creates a new historical positivity that makes one forget old pains and voluntary sacrifices."[17] Djaïet is perfectly happy to see tens of thousands of Arab lives expended in order to repossess historical territory. Is it possible that he has taken to seeing his books as enactments in theory of what Saddam Husain wanted to achieve in practice? To question the factual foundations of this edifice of mythmaking becomes an act of betrayal, indicative only of self-hatred.

The General Secretariat of the Union of Palestinian Lawyers plunged into the same surreal world when it published an advertisement with Saddam's picture in the Jordanian daily, *al-Dustour,* a full week after the war had ended. It read: "Support and Congratulations on Victory to His Excellency the President, Saddam Husain, May God Preserve Him." The advertisement went on to extol the "legendary steadfastness" of the Iraqi leader "in the face of the conspiracy of the evil invaders."[18] A Tunisian literary critic, after describing the destruction of a handful of buildings in Tel Aviv caused by the first Iraqi SCUD missile, wrote, "Oh, this noble destruction is beautiful!"[19] On a more sober note, and before the war had come to an end, the head of Jordan's delegation in the current Middle East Peace talks, Kamil Abu Jaber, predicted that the Iraqi leader was heading toward military defeat. "But he will remain a hero for the next 1,000 years. Schoolchildren will sing songs about him and mothers will call their sons Saddam."[20]

Saddam did not remain a hero for long in the eyes of some. "This is a tragedy. . . . I have been deceived by this man," said Mu'nis Razzaz, a novelist and newspaper columnist in Jordan who came to this realization rather late considering that his father, Munif Razzaz, was a well-known Jordanian Ba'thi who died in an Iraqi prison on the orders of Saddam Husain for supporting a nonexistent "conspiracy" in 1979.[21] During the crisis and just before the Gulf war broke out, Mu'nis Razzaz had declared that since Camp David, the Arab world had seen "too much cowardice. . . . A hero always presents two choices: to win or to lose."[22] Saddam's reputation, it seems, rested on his perceived strength; he turned into a big disappointment only after he lost.

Not everyone mouthed the brutish values of Saddam as uncritically as Djaïet or Abu Jaber. Many intellectuals kept their distance from the Iraqi leader.[23] The more common stance was to support his policies in practice while vehemently protesting one's innocence of his thuggishness at every step along the way. "Even though most Arabs didn't support the invasion of Kuwait, Saddam Husain's fearlessness in standing up to our enemies . . . appeals to the new spirit of the Arab world—a spirit that says we'd rather die on our feet than live grovelling on the ground," wrote the editor of *Jordan Times* and host of Jordanian television's most influential public affairs talk show, Rami Khouri.[24] In Syria, many of the country's most enthusiastic supporters of democracy and liberalization were also the harshest critics of Syria's participation in the Allied coalition.[25] The Lebanese leftist intellectual Fawwaz Trabulsi, long after the war and the uprising had ended and the full scope of the debacle become clear, proudly announced that he had stood by the Iraqi regime without, however, renouncing his opposition to "the repressive relations" that it maintained with its people.[26] Even the Palestinian human rights activist Jonathan Kuttab, a Christian lawyer from East Jerusalem, spoke of Saddam Husain as the bearer of a new "liberation theology." Kuttab thinks Saddam is ruthless and never wants to be ruled by him. Nonetheless, the Iraqi ruler embodies "something revolutionary and wonderful that is expressed in the traditional slogan 'Allahu Akbar,' which I understand as the faith in a great God: Greater than sophisticated airplanes . . . and all the might of the twenty-eight states that attacked Iraq."[27]

But none of these reactions can match that of Kamal Abu Deeb, a professor of Arabic literature at Columbia University, who tapped into the emotional wellsprings of this intellectual mind-set. Abu Deeb is on the editorial board of the innovative theoretical journal *Mawaqif,* and he is the translator into Arabic of Edward Said's *Orientalism,* among many other distinguished literary accomplishments.

After the war had ended, Abu Deeb published a piece of poetic prose entitled *Sarkhah fi Matah (Screaming in a Wasteland)*:

We cannot but be with the nation. . . .

The nation may be a gargantuan tyrant. . . . The nation may be a policeman whose dogs chase us everywhere inside its walls.

The nation may be the cave of our disillusionment, or the slaughter-house of our sweet dreams, or the grave of our freedom and honor. . . . And the nation may be a thousand worse and even more terrible things.

Still, we cannot but be with the nation.[28]

Prison walls are a metaphor for national boundaries. The clear implication is that this prison is Ba'thi Iraq. One is therefore entitled to think the writer has no illusions about the regime of Saddam Husain. Certainly this is what he wants us to think. But why should any Arab want to be aligned with or inside such a terrible place, especially when he has so few prior illusions about it? From the piece, it does not appear that the thought crossed Abu Deeb's mind. Millions of Iraqis—like Abu Haydar, Omar, and Mustafa—were either rebelling against the tyrant or voting with their feet and running away from his prison at the very moment that *an-Naqid,* a London-based Arabic monthly cultural review, was publishing these lines. Presumably in Abu Deeb's eyes, and in the eyes of the editor of this review, their plight and their reasons for rebelling are subordinate to being at one with "the nation."

Abu Deeb's rhetoric is symptomatic of a fundamental cultural malaise. Whose nation is this that "We cannot but be with"? Abu Deeb is a Syrian; he doesn't live in Iraq. Saddam Husain, we all recall, was supposedly leading the Arab nation when he occupied Kuwait and when he lobbed SCUD missiles into Israel. Is this the Arab nation that Abu Deeb has in mind? Probably not, because Abu Deeb doesn't like Saddam Husain. The more plausible explanation is that Abu Deeb's nation is a myth; it is at one and the same time a prison and a fairy tale. Hence Abu Deeb's sense of his own identity is suspended in a void of his own making.

There is a morbid subliminal imperative at work in an article like this. The sentiments it expresses epitomize the anxiety, primal rage, and overt schizophrenia which is the general condition of modern

Arab culture today. In the same breast-beating tradition, during the height of the Gulf crisis the Palestinian poet Samih al-Qasim wrote: "Since the earth is not about to split asunder and swallow me up, let me try then to tear myself apart to swallow up the earth."[29]

These are, I submit, false, self-destructive, and ultimately cruel sentiments. They are false because they are so obviously grounded in a lie, a lie that was being proved to be one at the very moment of writing by the actions of the "prisoners" themselves—the people of Iraq—who, unlike Abu Deeb, were obliged to be in or "with the nation." To paraphrase Milan Kundera, this kind of intellectual mendacity is about gazing "into the mirror of the beautifying lie," and being moved "to tears of gratification at one's own reflection."[30] The fixation upon the sweet lie, to which all real conflicts between people are subordinated, is the most depressing thing about the Arab intelligentsia's reaction to the Gulf crisis.

Even more important, it is very dangerous. Dangerous because it takes place at the expense of life as it is really lived, and finally at the expense of the real lives of people. It is as if Khalil, Abu Haydar, Omar, Mustafa, Taimour, and all the flesh-and-blood individuals that I have quoted in Part One of this book do not exist, or have been turned into a theoretical abstraction. That is the source of the cruelty of this language. Like Nizar Qabbani's poetry, Abu Deeb's mythmaking and Samih al-Qasim's self-flagellation operate at a gigantic distance from the actual feelings of Iraqis and Kuwaitis as they experience the world which these men of letters are writing about. There were horrors unfolding all around, and there was a rhetoric about those horrors; the two were separated by an unbridgeable chasm. This is a cruel rhetoric, one that does not take as its point of departure the sufferings of the people who have to live inside the prison walls. On the contrary, it subordinates their pain to the importance of leaving the walls of this combined prison and fairyland guarded and intact.

But the most heartbreaking reaction of all to the Gulf crisis came from people who made a vocation of human rights. Moncef Marzouki, president of the Tunisian Human Rights League, the largest such organization in the Arab world, focuses on the lies and distortions of those "soldiers of psychological war," the Western media, "which we envied and admired." Their talk of the decimation of the Iraqi air force by the Allies is, he says, "today the laughingstock of all." He thinks the Iraqi army put up a brave fight, which the Arab world would be able to use to heighten its awareness of Western limitations. The "determination, the defiance and insolence" of the Iraqi soldier was a classic instance of "the human being confronting the machine."

> [T]he brutal crushing of Iraq . . . will not change a thing. One can dare and challenge technology. If the latter has suddenly ceased to impress, what is to be said about the values?
>
> In the Gulf war, it is not only Western information and technology which have failed, but above all the credibility of the famous values of the West. The dogma [of human rights], because that is what it is, is sinking all along the southern shores of the Mediterranean. . . . Paradoxically, only insofar as we Arab democrats succeed in uncoupling and disassociating the democratic project and the values of human rights from Western centrism will we be able to salvage something from the rising tide of all "isms."[31]

Marzouki is telling it straight from the heart; he writes as though he is on the verge of packing it all in and giving up on his profession. After taking the usual ritual distance from Saddam Husain, he proceeds to heap one paragraph of abuse after the other on top of the Kuwaitis whose city had just been sacked and whose oil fields were just about to be set on fire. The "rights" of countries and of peoples were at issue in all of this, no matter which way one looked at the crisis. Do Kuwaitis not have rights just because Marzouki despises them? Clearly something very complicated is going on in the mind of a man who has committed his life to defending civic freedoms, and yet is still unable to react in a way that is consistent with that commitment. "Sometimes legitimacy is more important than legality," Djaïet said. The same chilling sensibility is at work in Marzouki's notion of "Arab democracy." In the course of a demonstration expressing solidarity with the arch tyrant of modern Arab politics, he called on Iraq to make use of its chemical weapons.[32]

Accepting Arab Frailty

THESE ways of talking, of thinking, of setting political priorities, have ruled the Middle East for a very long time now. After the creation of the state of Israel in 1948, they began sweeping through the entire ideological spectrum. In the Mashriq, Arab liberals became an extinct species; communism withered, bent, and finally broke under the onslaught of nationalism, long before the collapse of the Soviet system. Islamic militancy, on the other hand, had no problem with the language in the first place; the idea of a rapacious West descending on the Muslim world is as old as the Crusades. Neither Arab nationalism nor Islamic political activism has yet developed even the most primitive conception of political "rights," whose most elementary underpinning is the absolute isolation of all matters of belief from entitlement and obligation in public life. Wherever one looks, it seems, the principle of "human rights" in politics is on the run in the Arab-Muslim world. That is why the idea of an "American Crusader plan" for the region was so all-pervasive in the rhetoric that accompanied the crisis in the Gulf.[33]

In its latest Gulf crisis incarnation, Arab nationalism creates an even more dangerous conundrum of identity than before—one that is wildly at variance with the actual condition of Arabs, especially the intellectuals among them. That condition is factually one of fragmentation and atomization, regardless of whether one is struggling to survive under siege in Birzeit University, writing for the Arab newspaper conglomerates of London and Paris, preaching from the rostrums of Western universities, or in exile from one of the many regimes that have choked off all civility in the Arab world.

In 1979, the year he fled Saddam Husain's Iraq, the Iraqi poet Fawzi Kareem wrote:

> Each sail not counted as yours, oh policeman of the border,
> Sailing not in useless search for The Meaning
> But fleeing from all those black meanings,
> Know that it is mine.[34]

A poem like this overturns Djaïet's obsession with Arabness and Abu Deeb's self-flagellating anxiety over who he is, because it rests on the poet's celebration of his difference and his individuality. Kareem has accepted his condition as one of "fragmentedness." He has done so with a degree of grace—why (God forbid!), he has even been able to make something of it. His poem is a humble act of acknowledgment and self-renewal at the same time. In the absence of such acceptance of the multiple, frail, non-ideological nature of the human condition, a continuing and increasingly morbid hatred of the West and Israel is going to remain the focus onto which increasingly degraded notions of "Arabness" or "Islamic identity" are pinned. This is what is so deeply and personally frightening about the current predicament of the Arab world. In the end, it doesn't matter what local coloring that hatred takes (anti-imperialism, Arab nationalism, Palestinian nationalism, religious fundamentalism). The important point is that today all these ideologies are being boiled down into pure unadulterated hate.

Half a century ago, Michel 'Aflaq, the founding "Duce" of the Ba'th Party, had captured the essence of what Kareem was running away from: "nationalism is love before anything else."[35] 'Aflaq's "Republic of Love" has since been realized in the shape of Saddam Husain's Iraq. Think of Kareem as one of the many Iraqis who have become desperate to escape the suffocating embrace of so much love, and you can see how a new Arab sensibility is born, one whose logic is a repudiation of the old paradigm that welded my identity into *how I think,* not into *who I think I am.*

But it was the Syrian-born poet Adonis, that innovator in the forms of the Arabic language, who first began constructing the scaffolding of new literary forms around which a new quality of Arabness could be built. Adonis is one of the most distinguished writers in the Arabic language today. In his writings of the 1960s, he explored the complex terrain between culture and politics. He has delved into the history of ideas, East and West, and he has plumbed psychological and emotional depths that many Arab intellectuals have avoided. In 1986, he gave up on Beirut to live in Paris, with a sense—as he put it—that "something in the Arab world has died."[36] His voice greatly influenced poets like Kareem. This extract from a 1982 poem, for instance, was written inside war-torn Beirut:

> My era tells me bluntly:
> You do not belong.
> I answer bluntly:
> I do not belong,
> I try to understand you.
> Now I am a shadow
> Lost in the forest
> Of a skull.[37]

The realization that one has turned into a "shadow" that no longer "belongs" in a world ruled by violence is the beginning of wisdom. The first act of reclamation is to move from the knowledge that something has gone wrong toward a new kind of Arab humility, one that is founded on an acceptance of human frailty.

Throughout the Gulf crisis Adonis chose to remain silent, thereby expressing an anguish that he clearly felt to be in the culture itself at this crucial juncture. He is one of the few who sensed that no one had anything new to say, which troubled him greatly.

However, goaded and taunted by the editor of the cultural page in the Arabic daily *al-Quds al-'Arabi,* on March 11, 1991, he broke his silence in the aftermath of the Gulf war with an article entitled "The Prayer and the Sword: Or Savage Democracy." The article begins with the assertion that the Gulf crisis and the war it gave birth to have created a new, deteriorating "western rhetoric" about the Arab world. This rhetoric should make us all pause to rethink the nature of the relationship between the Arabs and the West. The example that Adonis singled out to illustrate his point is an article by Hans Magnus Enzensberger. This was a bold attempt to reexamine the much-bandied-about comparison between Saddam Husain and Hitler. Enszensberger's point was that both men had in common an urge to self-destruction and a complete inability to distinguish between their own individual fatality and that of the collectivity of all Iraqis or all Germans.[38]

Adonis considered this line of thinking from a German writer and a leading leftist democratic intellectual, who played a prominent role in Germany's 1968 student movement, to be "exaggerated to the point of mystification." Saddam Husain of course is a nasty, unpleasant dictator. But the idea of comparing him to Hitler was going too far. The implicit assumption of Adonis's argument was that "your" Hitler certainly was the incarnation of all evil, but "our" Saddam Husain is a run-of-the-mill despot. Moreover, Saddam's brutishness was, Adonis asserted, a fact known to all Arabs.

When all things are equally nasty, then nothing is really nasty at all and one is simply unable to make distinctions any longer. Making distinctions, however, is the very stuff of a creative engagement with the world.

I remember a feeling of sadness sweeping over me as I read Adonis's article, for I too had read Enzensberger's commentary. And although I had certain reservations—his view of Iraq was too "German"—my impressions were exactly the opposite of Adonis's. The point of Enzensberger's article, a point which Adonis had completely failed to see, was the humbling one of integrating the phenomenon of Saddam Husain into *his own country's* experience of political evil. To read Enzensberger and to accept in the core of one's being the reality of Iraq's experience under the Ba'th, was to understand the commonality of the human condition, and to refuse its glib division into East and West, or north and south, or Arab and anti-Arab. Adonis had failed this test. The failure, it became clear, had nothing to do with personal integrity and knowledge of classical texts or modern thought, areas in which Adonis is greatly cultured. He had failed to see what Enzensberger really meant because he was emotionally unprepared to see it. Emotional blocks like this are the greatest obstacle to the emergence of a healthy sense of identity, one that fully embraces the "other."

Many Arabs realize that something has gone terribly wrong. Djaïet speaks of a "frigid, depressing, virtually rotten" Arab order; Abu Deeb writes of prisons; and Adonis, who is in a different league entirely, chose silence. Unfortunately, it is not enough to realize that something is amiss, for the realization may lead to conclusions such as "war has the merit of clarifying things." That frightening banality was still being defended by many Arabs long after some horrible realities ought to have been thoroughly clarified. Djaïet and Abu Deeb's politics of despair is saturated in violence, hatred, and bitterness. These give rise to despairing conclusions like "we have nothing to lose in this war," and they lead to dismissal of even the figleaf of a shared morality with Kurds or Jews or Sunnis or Shiʿis.[39] The result is always more Arab and Muslim dead.

The nationalism of too many cosmopolitan "anti-imperialist" Arab intellectuals today speaks only to base sentiments associated with that rising pile of bodies. In the current historical conjuncture—not always or for all time—it is incapable of rising above them because it is so deeply hostile to accepting a notion of individual human rights in politics not based on double standards. This kind of nationalism did not come out of the blue. It is a historically formed amalgam of sentiments and traditions traceable to the historical role of the Arabs in the creation and spread of Islam. Like Islam, Arab nationalism is not going to go away. It is a component part of culture, not an explicit political ideology. It "reflects less a collective will freely consented to than a 'culture of consensus' with theological connotations that condition the collective Arab unconscious."[40]

When Shaikh Asʿad al-Tamimi, the leader of the Islamic Jihad movement in Jordan (and a strong supporter of Iran during the Iraq-Iran War), called Saddam Husain's "return" to Islam "a high point in the Islamic awakening" of the 1980s, he is meeting people like Djaïet, Abu Deeb, Kuttab, and Khouri on the same cultural-historical ground.[41] The fact that westernized cosmopolitans might be embarrassed by the Shaikh's admiration for Khomeini, and his desire to have the caliphate of the eighth century restored under Saddam, is irrelevant. For culture is the terrain on which Shaikh As'ad and nationalist intellectuals met during the 1990–91 Gulf crisis, just as stereotyping is the terrain on which they meet with Nizar Qabbani in spite of the latter's honorable personal position toward Kuwaiti suffering during the crisis. Nationalism has always derived great strength from the existence of such a common ground with Islam, or with a pre-Islamic Arab Bedouin tradition like *hija'*. That is why it has lasted for so long and can renew itself time after time. Culture is also the area in which these sentiments and traditions will have to be interrogated and reshaped in the future in order to become consistent with a less cruel view of the Arab condition—one that is founded on the idea of inviolable individual political rights.

The sentiments underlying cultural nationalism should never be mistaken for Pan-Arabism alone (whether Nasserism, or Ba'thism, or any other kind of Arab nationalism). In fact, the political forms it takes are very malleable. Yesterday, they revolved around Sati'a al-Husri, Michel 'Aflaq, or Jamal 'Abdel-Nasser and the romantic ideal of *umma 'arabiyya wahida,* one Arab nation. In the wake of the Iranian revolution, the same sentiments that created Ba'thism turned into Islamic revivalism and the sudden rediscovery of political Islam by one formerly secular intellectual after another (the Egyptian ex-Marxists Muhammad 'Amara and 'Adil Husain, for instance). During the Gulf crisis, cultural nationalist feeling revolved around hating the West and taking pride in Saddam's personification of Arab-Muslim strength. Tomorrow, they are likely to turn into rabid hatred of the "wrong kind" of fellow Arab.

This world of attitudes, emotional responses, and cultural images does not need a well-constructed political ideology to make itself felt in speech and intellectual discourse. An "issue" is all that it takes to bring that formless emotional amalgam bursting out into the open. On August 2, 1990, Kuwait became that issue. In less than two weeks, "linkage" fused Kuwait onto the Palestinian question. The most ominous sentence in the Djaïet interview—"legitimacy is more important than legality"—was a sentiment shared by every Arab who couldn't see what all the fuss over Kuwait was about, but could only see the unfolding of yet another grand Western design against the Arab world.

8 ' New Nationalist Myths

THE GULF CRISIS was, in the words of the Egyptian rationalist thinker Fouad Zakariyya, a "crisis of 'exposure.' "[1] It flushed the historically formed chimera of nationalist identity out into the open. Until Saddam Husain made his move in August 1990, much of the force of this amalgam of tradition, history, and religion appeared to have dissipated into the festering resentments and factionalized politics of anti-Western extremist groups. Appearances were deceptive because different volatile elements had not yet coalesced into anything with a coherent shape. The combination of the Iraqi leader's action and the reaction of President George Bush had the effect of crystalizing these undercurrents into an extraordinary emotional eruption. Differences between nationalists, Islamicists, Marxists, and democrats dissolved in the face of the commonly perceived threat from the West. Irrespective of what these different intellectuals might have thought about Saddam Husain's invasion if the West had not become involved, the far more significant point is that none of them would have got as worked up about Kuwait as they in fact did *because* the United States and Western Europe did become involved.

Saddam flushed a discourse out into the open which, it must be emphasized again, *is not* the invention of the ordinary Palestinian in the Occupied Territories who suffers daily humiliation by the Israeli army. Nor is it the invention of the average Iraqi whose whole psychology has been deformed through fear; nor was it invented by those Kuwaitis who had to live through seven months of a horrible occupation. In fact, this discourse—whether its authors are aware of its effect or not—is indifferent to and irresponsible toward the real problems of Palestinians under occupation, just as it was indifferent and explicitly cruel to people like Khalil, Abu Haydar, Omar, Mustafa, and Taimour.

This discourse is invented and reinvented by people such as Kamal Abu Deeb, Mahmoud Darwish, Hisham Djaïet, Edward Said, Rami Khouri, Muhammad 'Abid al-Jabiri, George Tarabishi, 'Abdel-Rahman Munif, and many of the most talented and famous writers and artists of the Arab world.[2] It is invented by people who are attached to universities inside and outside the Arab world, others who are journalists or who write for newspapers published in London that appear the next day on the streets of Riadh, Beirut, Algiers, Paris, and Washington. Saddam Husain flushed us all out into the open. He did this by forcing everyone to adopt a political position on what he had done. In so doing, the whole apparatus of evasion and hiding behind sophisticated veneers—which we all employ to get on with daily life—was laid bare. Arab was revealed to fellow Arab in all of his or her nakedness, and this in a culture fixated upon shame, which abhors nudity.

In the face of what became a nationalist deluge, and in the light of what we know about the regime in Iraq, I can only describe this eruption as a collective hysterical outburst that represents the deepest feelings of most established Arab intellectuals. This is particularly true of those whose political views were formed by the crushing defeat of Arab armies in the 1967 war.

The irony is that many of these writers and opinionmakers came to intellectual maturity by reacting against an earlier rhetoric in culture and politics, a rhetoric which was discredited by the defeat of 1967 and associated with leaders such as Jamal 'Abdel-Nasser, Ahmad Shuqairi, and Michel 'Aflaq. Yet, their ways of describing the world have collapsed into the very paradigm which they think they have left behind. This is especially true of the Palestinian intelligentsia, in particular those outside the Occupied Territories (in part because it is the most dispossessed and in part because of the demise of Beirut, the cultural heart of modernity in the Mashriq). "Palestinian support for Iraqi President Saddam Husain's invasion of Kuwait on August, 1990 . . . is much more nuanced, ambiguous, and equivocal than it has been portrayed," argued Rashid Khalidi of Chicago University.[3] But the spectacle of what used to be called "the vanguard" of the Arab revolution rallying enthusiastically behind the most barbarous dictatorship the modern Arab world has known is something which has to be faced squarely: it cannot be wished away with faint-hearted apologies.

The anti-imperialist rhetoric during the Gulf crisis was a constellation of separate interlocking assertions. No two adherents of this discourse ever had to consult with one another or to agree on the relative weight to be given to each assertion. Nonetheless, the sum of these positions forms a uniform view of the world, and, most importantly, identical ways of ordering political priorities. The language is by no means simply a Pan-Arab view of the world; it is *a modern nationalist discourse,* which is culturally Arabo-Muslim in its foundations, but which can be espoused by Arab Christians as well, and Arab Shi'is as well as Sunnis. Arabs of every description partake in it, irrespective of how much time they have spent in the West, whether or not they speak Arabic, and including even those who emphasize completely different political ambitions (a Palestinian state, a Greater Syrian sovereign entity, a Lebanon free of Syrian domination, or a new Arab Muslim empire).

This discourse has added a set of new myths to the Arab nationalist lexicon developed since 1967:

1. THE CRISIS AS AN AMERICAN CREATION

Samir Amin, the Egyptian leftist economist, believes that the decision to destroy Iraq's military potential was "taken by Washington and Tel-Aviv around May 1990," and "we know *almost* certainly now that [the invasion of Kuwait] was a trap set by Washington."[4] Muhammad Hallaj, a former vice-president of Birzeit University currently based in Washington, D.C., thinks that "there is evidence to suggest that the campaign to discipline Iraq began on the day its war with Iran ended on 8 August 1988."[5] Neither Amin nor Hallaj tells us what their sources are. We are asked to accept their claims on faith. Edward Said, University Professor at Columbia University, did not fall into the trap of choosing dates. He wrote that Saddam Husain was *"almost* invited into Kuwait."[6]

In the absence of any supporting evidence, words like "almost" and phrases like "there is evidence to suggest that" evoke the smell of great conspiracies while making a disingenuous claim to innocence. A moment's reflection should be enough to convince us that Saddam Husain did not ask anyone's permission when he invaded on August 2. For one thing, he is too paranoid for that. But these gentlemen's hearts do not allow them to say what their heads would quickly tell them is true. Hence the caveats and the qualifiers, which are sometimes all that it takes to be irresponsible.

The high-ranking Tunisian civil servant Mustafa al-Fayyali ratchets up the stakes one more notch with the fantastic assertion that "it will become clear with definite evidence [which he admits does not yet exist] that the roots [of the Gulf war] go back to the beginning of the 1980s, and that the planning to explode those roots was born in the wake of the Camp David agreement. We would not be exaggerating if we were to say that Iraq in particular was being targeted back then."[7] We are being asked to accept the notion that the United States gave military aid to Iraq during the Iraq-Iran War (with a view to helping it win that conflict) and simultaneously plotted to destroy the beast that it had created.[8]

These are not arguments; they are undocumented assertions, resting on a conspiratorial view of politics and motivated by an emotional antipathy to the West, an antipathy that sustains itself at the expense of a critique of the Iraqi regime. Unfortunately, providing dates and suggesting that leaders were "invited" to invade countries implies actors and conscious volition. The arguments' power of conviction rests on facts, not grand conspiracy theories or complicated schemas of how imperialism operates in the world; it also rests on the assumption that the Iraqi leader is either a puppet or very stupid, or that the United States is infinitely more omnipotent than he is stupid. Hidden here runs the thread of consistent denigration of the independent powers of initiative of leaders like Saddam. A politically active Iraqi living in the shadow of the Ba'th who underestimated his regime in this fashion would end up dead.

The moral thrust of such opposition to American policy during the Gulf crisis is in striking contrast to articles like Christopher Hitchens's "Why We Are Stuck in the Sand." The article builds a case that U.S. Ambassador April Glaspie, in her famous July 25, 1990, meeting with Saddam, "signalled" that the United States had no objection to an Iraqi redrawing of the borders of the Gulf. Hitchens's complete lack of illusion about the Ba'thist regime is forged into the very structure of his argument, in striking contrast to the previous examples I have quoted. (Whereas Hitchens traces the whole history of Iraqi persecution and American betrayal of the Kurds, for instance, Edward Said casts doubt on whether or not the Iraqi regime ever gassed its own Kurdish citizens. Moreover, he chose to cast this doubt at the very moment that Iraqis were rising up against their regime and were threatened with being gassed yet again.)[9] Thus, in the case of Hitchens, the beginning of the whole Gulf affair is judged against a factual question: What exactly happened during the Glaspie-Saddam meeting?

I think Hitchens got it wrong, however, putting more weight on both Glaspie's and Saddam's words than they can bear. In these diplomatic situations, part of the game of "nods" and "tilts" which Hitchens is unraveling is that ambassadors say what the other side likes to hear, and presidents of Saddam's ilk "hear" what they want to hear. Hitchens's argument rests on the premise that "Glaspie is speaking under instructions," and therefore that the State Department knew of Saddam's intention to invade Kuwait before the meeting. If so, surely the rules of the game themselves suggest that there are less messy ways of "tilting" and "signalling" permission to Saddam than by Glaspie saying, "I think you know well that we as a people have our experience with the colonialists."[10]

A principled opposition to the Gulf war does not require: (a) denying that the Iraqi regime gassed its own citizens; (b) inventing dates to prove that the United States not only started the fighting on the ground (which it did) but that it sent Iraq into Kuwait (which it didn't); or (c) generally imputing a reasonableness to the Iraqi invasion of Kuwait which it never possessed.[11] Why did so many Arab intellectuals bother to make assertions for which there is no evidence? Something other than estimation or underestimation of leaders is involved, something called transfer of responsibility. Responsibility was being transferred by Arab intellectuals away from where it so obviously lay, namely, with the Ba'thi state of Iraq, onto the United States. In this exercise, those anti-war activists who acted out of an emotionally understandable but nonetheless knee-jerk opposition to anything the American state chose to do unwittingly played into the hands of the worst kind of despotism.[12] Were the motives of those who did the transferring "objective," or were they exculpatory? Whose "interests" were served by the transfer? Obviously, whether these intellectuals intended it or not, the interests served were those of the perpetrator of the originating act of aggression.

2. SADDAM AS VICTIM

The stakes get raised when someone like Fawwaz Trabulsi coins the idea that "even as a victim," Saddam "agreed to play the role of criminal." What does Trabulsi mean here? In a 1991 article, he goes on: "Iraq had just emerged from its war against Iran with the kind of military potential that could alter the regional balance of forces with regard to the two local pillars of imperial domination: Israel and the oil regimes of the Gulf. It became imperative to . . . destroy its military and economic capability. The Iraqi leader reacted by invading Kuwait."[13] In other words, Saddam chose to commit political suicide, thus satisfying the deepest desires of U.S. imperialism. Here denial of the Arab capacity for independent action is carried to absurdity.

Every shred of a growing body of evidence suggests just the opposite: that until the last minute, the United States built Saddam Husain up because it wanted him as a strategic ally in the region to counter Iran. There was no American intention to cut the Iraqi dictator down to size until *after* he took everyone by surprise by entering Kuwait. On the other hand, Trabulsi is more reasonable than some; at least he imparted a *moment* of real choice and independent initiative to Saddam, however reactive, and at least he considers the invasion of Kuwait to have been a mistake. Hisham Ahmad, an assistant professor of political science at the University of North Dakota, will have none of that. Before August 2, the United States was determined to deny Iraq "its sense of dignity and to thwart its thriving nationalism." His point is that Iraq would have been victimized regardless of whether or not a dispute with Kuwait had crystalized.[14]

The view that Iraq was going to be smashed by the West anyway because it was becoming too powerful gets played out in different scenarios, the most common one being that the United States, true to form, creates an Arab patsy called Saddam Husain whom it builds up as a bulwark against Iran (or for other strategic imperial reasons). Then, after deciding that the local dictator must go—and the reasoning behind this is always fuzzy in the minds of the myth's upholders—it demonizes its own creation, transforming him "into a worldwide metaphysical threat."[15] Certainly it served U.S. and Allied interest to fantastically exaggerate the military capabilities of the Iraqi regime. But in the absence of any discussion of the dire threat Saddam Husain represented to the region—to other Arabs in particular—the point turns into its opposite: everybody is always a victim whenever anyone has something to do with the United States.

Moving on to the poets, consider what Lebanon's Unsi al-Haj wrote: "Of course the invasion of Kuwait was a mistake." And of course, "Iraqi rule is not dear to the hearts of democrats and freedom lovers. . . . Of course, of course." Then he heaps scorn on himself for asking silly questions about justice. "Our questions here are nothing other than proof of our naivety, proof of the silliness of our innocence in this American age which despises the truth and the weak and hates those with greater traditions and deeper roots in history than itself. How stupid of us to ask and to feel pain, instead of to kill." However, only Americans kill employing "treacherous force, not any kind of force. We [Arabs] are satisfied with killing in the imagination. We are satisfied to curse, and then to die."[16] Victimhood is such a soothing balm.

Unsi al-Haj worked as an editor of the cultural pages of the Lebanese daily *al-Nahar*. He is French-educated, from the kind of Lebanese Christian background that did so much to modernize Arab thinking in the late nineteenth century, but which turned away from the discourse of Arab nationalism after World War II. He is, by his own admission, at home with Baudelaire, Edgar Allan Poe, the Surrealist movement, Breton, Novalis, Eluard, Walt Whitman, Charlie Chaplin, and Henry Miller. In the same breast-beating article, al-Haj, while listing all the Western "greats" who have influenced him, lays the blame for the Lebanese civil war on the Machiavellian politics of the United States, "which sold us in the marketplace of deals," and was "extremely successful in making Lebanon follow in the train of the poverty-stricken, hungry and destroyed countries, after it had been, in spite of its many problems, the flower of the Arabs and of the East."[17] The Lebanese, it seems, had nothing to do with what happened to their country.

Such words tell us more about the pathology of a culture than they do about the momentous event which evoked them. The same pathology was at work in the story of Marwan Arandas, a hardworking student at the University of Jordan who belonged to no Palestinian organization. After careful planning, and while the Gulf war was in full swing, Marwan set off on a suicide mission across the Jordan River to shoot as many Israelis as he could. He and two of his friends succeeded in killing nobody, but were themselves killed. "At least he did something," a fellow student said at his commemoration ceremony, held in a packed hall in Amman.[18]

Unfortunately, the language to which al-Haj reverted has developed a strong foothold in the culture. Victimhood has been turned into something like a new Arab art form, without anyone seeming to realize that it is the greatest killer of solidarity with others that could possibly be invented (carried to yet further extremes, it destroys the very possibility of legitimate government, replacing suspicion with trust in everything political).

A key factor in the generalization of this language throughout the culture has been the hallowed status of Palestinian dispossession in 1948, which has become for Arab politics what the Holocaust is for Israeli politics: mirror images of one another and of a syndrome in which oppressed and oppressor emulate one another in a seemingly inescapable spiral of escalating distrust. The respective historical tragedies of both Israeli Jews and Palestinian Arabs have become unquestionable articles of faith, deeply constitutive of identity. The same forces are at work today among the Kurds and Shi'a of Iraq as they were among all the communities of Lebanon during the civil war. But identity must go beyond memory if it is not to be forever mired in the past, turning into a pathological view of the world which has no room for other people's suffering. If Iraq disintegrates as a unified political entity after Saddam Husain is gone, it will be because lack of empathy has become the new Arab political norm.

3. SADDAM AS BISMARCK

During the crisis, popular opinion in Jordan, the Occupied Territories, and in the Maghrib saw in Saddam Husain a Saladin-like saviour.[19] "Archaeology flies to the aid of liberation," as Jacques Berque said when it was Jamal 'Abdel-Nasser's turn to be the incarnation of redemption.[20] But it was left to George Tarabishi, the translator of the works of Freud and Trotsky into Arabic, and the author of some twenty influential books, to construct an interpretation of the Iraqi tyrant as an Arab Bismarck. Janus has a two-sided face: from the one he looks out at the world as a "victim," and from the other he is its "iron-fisted" strongman.

Having reminded his readers of the history of German unification under the "Bismarckian grip," Tarabishi goes on: "What happened in the Gulf [on August 2] was not a choice between autocratic unity and democratic fragmentation; it was a choice between unity or fragmentation each of which carries the stamp of autocracy. No one doubts that unity through democracy is a thousand times better than unity through autocracy. But isn't an autocratic unity better at least one small amount than autocratic fragmentation? . . . What happened in the Gulf, therefore, whatever the motives of the regional actor [Iraq], was a national act."[21]

The notion of Arabism being invoked here is associated with the desire to be "superior to," or "on top of," or "bigger than" someone else. In the case of the Moroccan philosopher Muhammad 'Abid al-Jabiri, or the Tunisian historian Hisham Djaïet, both of whom refuse any critique of Ba'thism, it is an outrightly amoral Arabism.[22] The same applies to the thinking of Elias Khouri, the Lebanese novelist best known for his book *The Little Mountain*. He justified Saddam Husain's action with the remarkable idea that Kuwait, before Saddam Husain invaded it, was as "occupied" as Palestine, because its rulers invested their wealth outside the Arab world and "executed" the policies of the great powers.[23] "Arab strength," or ascendancy, resides in bringing Kuwait, which has been "occupied" by the Sabah family presumably, back to the Arab fold. During the Gulf crisis, raw power considerations like these came first in the minds of many intellectuals, and they judged everything around them accordingly; that is the meaning of the symbolism of Saladin or the Bismarck analogy. The underlying principle is that the sovereignty of the part (be that part a state like Kuwait, a national grouping like the Kurds, or a solitary Iraqi individual), *is subordinate to* the sovereignty of the whole (be that whole Saddam Husain's Iraq, or an imaginary Arab union of the future). The prior claim of the part (say, the whole of Kuwait, or an individual Iraqi) in the shape of its *right* to be left alone (not annexed, or allowed to think one's own thoughts) is denied. Politics is reduced to extending outside the "artificial" boundaries of Iraq into the whole Arab world (beginning with Kuwait) the very principles that are already the norm inside. There is no longer any criterion whereby such intellectuals can even keep their distance from the killing of Iraqis who were opposed to their own regime; hence the anger at the West during the Gulf war was complemented by a silence that was expressive of a complete lack of compassion for Iraqis being cut down by Saddam Husain in the wake of their failed intifada.

In an interview on the lessons of the Gulf war, the Egyptian writer Fouad Zakariyya said that he had not come across a single Arab intellectual living in the West who was not "sympathetic with Saddam Husain." He then told of a conversation with one of these intellectuals, "who kept on praising Saddam and what he had done to the West. This was before the war. After half an hour of listening to him, I said, 'You say Saddam stood steadfast in face of the West, that he taught the West a lesson, and that he is an exemplary Third World leader. . . . But, what is the issue that Saddam is standing up for?' He couldn't answer me. The problem is not that he couldn't answer, the problem is that it became clear that he had never asked himself the question before. This is the great catastrophe. . . . The only thing that impresses him about Saddam is the fact that he is fighting. This is the same sentiment you find among teenagers when they hear about a gangster who stood up all alone with his submachine gun against a force of 200 policemen. They are impressed even though he is a gangster."[24]

Tarabishi, al-Jabiri, and Djaïet are not like the intellectuals described by Zakariyya because hatred of the West is not the driving force of their concerns. If the West had gone along with Saddam Husain's annexation, they might actually have become as pro-West as they turned out to be anti-West. Unlike Arabs who had serious misgivings about what Saddam Husain did, but couldn't see the forest from the trees *because* the United States was involved, their support for Saddam Husain's action on August 2 is grounded in a devaluation of human rights as a political criterion in Arab affairs. Such intellectuals (none of whom are Ba'this) are ideologues in that they will support anything so long as it feeds into the project of Arab unity. They will even support "their" Bismarck's "blood and iron," and his acquisition of chemical and nuclear weapons, in spite of the fact that his iron is being used to shed Arab blood.

4. "ARAB" STRENGTH AND SADDAM'S ARMY

The Bismarckian analogy—the "intellectual" version of the Saladin imagery so beloved by Saddam himself—rests on far more dangerous foundations than the mere rejection of the principle of human rights in politics. I am referring to the perception that Saddam Husain's military might was in some sense a source of strength for all Arabs, a view held by the overwhelming majority of Arab intellectuals before, during, and after the Gulf War—both inside and outside the Arab world.

From the numerous examples one could use to illustrate the point, I will choose the one that I found to be most offensive because of the high caliber of some of the people associated with it. During the so-called Second Arab National Conference, held on May 27–29, 1991, in Amman, a 7,000-word "Statement to the Nation" was issued, riddled with the usual clichés of Arab politics concerning world Zionist conspiracies and "the Arabs are the carriers of the message of Islam to the whole world," along with new assertions such as "this conference cannot but be optismistic as it reviews our great long history. . . ." In the shadow of all those Iraqi dead, and all those burning Kuwaiti oil wells, such triumphalism was grotesque.[25]

But let us not linger here. Instead, consider the emphasis given in the statement to "the destruction of the military force of Iraq . . . and the imposition of unbalanced restrictions on the growth of an Arab military capability" by the West (leaving out all references to "prior intent and careful calculation" by the United States).[26] The conference noted something it calls "a distortion in the military balance in the Arab region," designed to "realize and secure an Israeli military superiority over Arab forces." Did the non-performance of the Iraqi army during the Gulf war in spite of its grossly inflated size (7–10 percent of the gross population) not show that there was also a "distortion" going on inside Iraq *because of that very army,* a distortion that was arguably even greater than that which would ensue through its destruction? In the most ominous passage of all, the statement notes that industrial advance "is a necessity to face the coming dangers, and here special mention should be made of the need to quickly take advantage of non-traditional Iraqi weapons, which Iraq is obliged to destroy [according to UN resolutions]. These should be transferred to other Arab countries in order to take advantage of what Iraqi military industries achieved before the Gulf war and using this to modernize other Arab forces."[27]

These gentlemen, it seems, want to deal in nuclear bombs, biological warfare research, and chemical weapons. The mentality is the same as that of Moncef Marzouki—the president of the Tunisian Human Rights League who, the reader will recall, demanded that Iraq use its chemical weapons.[28] The underlying idea of all such declarations is that Saddam Husain's million-strong army—along with his SCUD missiles, nuclear bomb potential, and his other weapons of mass destruction—all this somehow represents a real strength that belongs to all Arabs in their struggle against "the Zionist enemy." With this strength, the collectivity of all Arabs is expected to exact concessions from Israel on the Palestinian question.

The fact that this army was responsible for uprooting parliamentary political life inside Iraq in 1958 in the first place is ignored. The fact that over the last ten years Saddam Husain's army has hurled an entire generation of Iraqis to their deaths in ruinous wars is put aside. And the fact that this is an army that has only ever been effective against other Iraqis, especially the Kurds, this too is put aside.

This false idea of strength, this idea that somehow you can build strength in the shape of weapons and forgo the hard task of finding it in the creative productive potential of your own society, has been at the center of Arab politics for a very long time now. It has been there at the very least since 1967, when it was tested and found wanting. In 1990, this idea found its perfect exponent in the military machine of Saddam Husain. However, Saddam Husain is no Jamal 'Abdel-Nasser, who was at least genuinely popular. The refusal to give up on this underlying tribal-nationalist idea of strength has brought nothing but misery and violence to the Middle East.

The principal organizer of the May 1991 conference, Khayr al-Din Haseeb, was also the moving spirit behind an earlier conference on "The Crisis of Democracy in the Arab Homeland." A 900-page volume of the proceedings was published in 1984 under the same title. Over one hundred Arab thinkers, academicians, and liberal policymakers met over five days to debate the subject and to discuss practical obstacles to the realization of democracy in the Arab world (along with case studies for different Arab countries).

The symposium was held in Cyprus because it had been banned in every Arab country approached by the convenors. This should have imparted a great deal of excitement to the proceedings. Indeed, one or two contributions did convey a critique of contemporary Arab practices. But on the whole these were couched in very abstruse theoretical language, language which was unlikely to offend any dictator. Not a single participant described concrete abuses in his own country. Far too many were preoccupied with finding confirmation or "equivalences" for modern democratic ideas in "the Arab-Islamic heritage." All were agreed on the objective of Arab unity, although some took issue with the demagogic way in which this issue had been put in the past. Nothing was said about the completely different moral outlooks which Arab citizens had to acquire on individual or state sovereignty, personal privacy, toleration, self-determination, or the status of non-Arab minorities; these necessarily follow from the adoption of a truly different notion of freedom from the one that has dominated Arab discourse in the whole modern period.

The introduction to the proceedings stressed that a central "objective reason" for placing increased attention on the question of democracy in the first place was "the grave failure of Arab regimes to confront Israeli aggression." But the rallying call which was used so many times in the past precisely to snuff out individual freedom, or the freedom to be separate and different, was always "Everything for the battle" against Israel. These deadly old formulas on the Arab-Israeli question are always a litmus test of real interest in democracy.

Whenever the "crisis of democracy" in the Arab world gets wedded to "the struggle against Israel," one knows in advance that nothing is going to change for the better in Arab politics. A fondness for weapons of mass destruction and leaders like Saddam Husain is invariably the outcome.

A different view of strength and democracy did emerge from the dark depths of the Iraqi experience in the aftermath of the Gulf war. Charter 91 is a signature-collecting campaign signed thus far by several hundred Iraqi writers, artists, and men and women from every walk of life. Along with recommending the abolition of conscription and the setting of a legal upper limit of 2 percent of Iraqi national income for military expenditure, the Charter has this to say on war:

> Real strength is always internal—in the creative, cultural, and wealth-producing capabilities of a people. It is found in civil society, not in the army or in the state. Armies often threaten democracy; the larger they grow, the more they weaken civil society. This is what happened in Iraq. Therefore . . . a new Iraqi constitution should . . . have as its first article the following: "Aspiring sincerely to an international peace based on justice and order, the Iraqi people forever renounce war as a sovereign right of the nation and the threat or use of force as a means of settling international disputes. The right of belligerency of the Iraqi state will not be recognized."[29]

5. "LINKAGE"

On August 12, 1990, Iraq floated a so-called peace plan based on the idea of "linkage," or the simultaneous withdrawals of Iraq from Kuwait, Israel from the Occupied Territories, and Syria from the Lebanon. On the surface, this plan looked to the overwhelming majority of Arab intellectuals like a reasonable way of defusing the Gulf crisis. Even the most critical of Arab thinkers felt that in one form or another (for instance, incorporating the idea of sequential withdrawals of Israel from the West Bank after Iraq's from Kuwait), it was a creative approach to the tangled conflicts of the Middle East. Ibrahim Abu-Lughod, professor of political science at Northwestern University in Illinois, and member of the Palestine National Council, wrote up the standard justification. Coming from a Palestinian with longstanding experience of Arab betrayal of Palestinian aspirations, it was very unsettling to find Abu-Lughod writing that Iraq addressed "linkage in terms of the principles and norms of international relations and law," while the Bush administration "ridiculed" Iraq's "commitment" to the Palestinians. Just in case hardened cynics like myself might have developed the suspicion that there was opportunism in Saddam Husain's "peace plan," Abu-Lughod assures us that "the reverse is true." The truth, according to Abu-Lughod, has to do with "Iraq's historic support for the Palestinians," and its converse, the " 'real' intentions of the U.S." What were those intentions? To "cripple any potential Arab power that could be used to advance Arab welfare."[30]

Muhammad Hallaj, director of the Palestine Research and Educational Center in Washington, D.C., went further. Not only did the regime of Saddam Husain "advance Arab welfare," not only did it have "an undeniable commitment" to the Palestinian cause, but Iraq's very rise as a military power was "motivated by *an Arab need* to create an Arab military deterrent to Israel. . . . Iraq . . . is the only Arab participant in the 1948 Arab-Israeli war that never signed a permanent armistice agreement with Israel. Thus, for the Palestinians, Iraq's linkage between the Gulf crisis and the Palestine question is not just a cover for local ambitions."[31]

In the heat of the Gulf crisis, words like these swirled around in public meetings and in articles in the press. This relentless wallowing in illusion filled me with anger. I kept on asking myself, what on earth had gone wrong? Had the readers of books and editors of famous journals absolutely no sense of their own history? What Arab regime had ever done anything for the Palestinian cause, much less the most brutal and morally reprehensible of the lot?

What would have happened, I thought to myself, if the Palestinians themselves had been the first to reject the idea of "linkage" proposed by Iraq? They would then have created *their own* concept of linkage, one which had the great benefit of not being bound up with the expansionist ambitions of a criminal state. A comprehensive repudiation of actual Iraqi ambitions by Palestinian intellectuals would have challenged the rest of the world to repudiate Israeli occupation of Arab land by *example,* not by vacuous moral exhortation. The stature of Palestinians in the Middle East peace talks would be much higher than it is. Instead, one Palestinian intellectual after another told the world that since others had double standards, they were going to deal in them as well. This they proceeded to do with great professionalism. The moral high ground, present in the justice of their case, and which is the only real strength that the Palestinians have ever had going for them, was thus handed to Saddam Husain on a platter.

The sharp rise in Saddam Husain's popularity among Palestinians predates "linkage." It began with his famous April 2, 1990, speech about launching a "fire that would eat up half of Israel." Saddam was referring metaphorically to his 2,000-mile missile developed in 1989, known as Tammuz I, or *hijarat ababeel*. The Iraqi press during this period was constantly dropping hints that Iraq would retaliate with chemical weapons if Israel made a conventional attack on Iraq (like the 1981 attack on Iraqi nuclear installations). In fact, throughout the Arab world—including Saudi Arabia and Kuwait—there was tremendous enthusiasm for what was perceived to be an Arab military leap forward spearheaded by the Iraqi president.

By October 1990, in East Jerusalem an "apocalyptic" feeling was in the air, according to a Palestinian school principal. "As if really huge things are happening all around us and we are just tools."[32] Two American helicopters had just disappeared over the Arabian desert. "Immediately all over our neighborhood, everybody said this is a sign from Heaven." He went on to describe how Palestinians returning to their homes from Saudi Arabia reported seeing the descendants of the flying birds mentioned in *sura* 105 of the Qur'an, *tayran ababeel*, gathering once again over the holy mosque of Mecca. The Qur'an relates how these birds by a miracle saved Mecca from certain destruction at the hands of the Habashi hordes by hurling at them "stones of baked clay."[33] Saddam Husain had this imagery in mind when he called his new missile *hijarat ababeel*, or "flying stones." Something big was in the works, ordinary Palestinians thought, and George Bush was going to get his comeuppance for having dared to take on the Arab world's new Saladin. Finally, during the Gulf war, when Saddam began throwing his "flying stones" at Israel in the shape of militarily ineffective missiles, Israelis scurried about looking for shelter while Palestinians waited for the air-raid sirens to rush up onto the rooftops to clap, play music, and cheer the missiles on, even though the missile was as likely to fall on an Arab as it was on a Jew.

In a "Letter from the West Bank," Amal Abulabbd (pseudonym), a Western-educated Palestinian woman whose family fled into exile in 1948, passed on these revealing entries from her diary of the war:

Tuesday [sic], *11th February:* At 1:27 a.m. Shams woke me up. . . . Shams . . . was woken up by the sound of sirens from outside and by the sounds of jubilation—whistling, *zagharit* [ululation]. Some may feel this is unacceptable behavior. However, if looked at within the proper context it is not. It wasn't an indication of wishing individual Israelis hurt—rather it was wishing them to feel in some tiny measure the massive pain and suffering they have been inflicting on Palestinians and Lebanese during the past 45 years or so. It was happiness that at last an Arab leader had managed to "attack" Israel when we have become used to being attacked.

Saturday, 23rd February: . . . The air siren alarm was sounded shortly before seven and you should have heard the cheers, whistles and "alahu akbar! [God is great!]" that resonated as the missile passed over the town.

Sunday, 24th February: . . . People in the West Bank believe the Iraqi army can hold out for at least six months and longer if they manage to get spare parts.

Tuesday, 26th February: I can't begin to describe the feelings of utter dejection that engulfed me at 3:30 a.m. when I heard that Iraq was withdrawing from Kuwait and was requesting a cease-fire and that the Allied Forces' response was heavier bombing of Baghdad and the retreating Iraqi forces.[34]

A mood of complete unreality permeated by superstition, with swings of wild euphoria and despair, gripped Palestinians of all social classes throughout the Gulf crisis. "After the Iraqi ruler made his assurances of having supernatural forces on his side," said Najib Abu Rakiya, a Palestinian-Israeli high school teacher, "reports of miracles began to proliferate. Peasants heard hens which recited verses from the Qur'an. The face of Saddam Husain was widely reported to have been seen on the surface of the moon. All over Israel, the Muslims began to obsessively explore mystical and fanatical religious literature. . . . Prophecies brought many to the verge of madness."[35]

The worst culprits, however, were not simple Palestinian peasants or people like Amal Abulabbd, who were at least honest about their feelings; they were those secular, cosmopolitan intellectuals operating out of academic and research institutions in the West who dressed up their support for the Iraqi action in "anti-imperialist" and theoretical finery. With the exception of Walid Khalidi of Harvard University, I cannot think of a single prominent Palestinian in the United States—among the many who now reside there—who did not, at least publicly, succumb to the worst kind of nationalist mythomania (in private conversation, some Palestinians clearly had no illusions about the Iraqi leader; however, they also felt that making those criticisms public during the Gulf crisis was an act of national betrayal). Saddam Husain invaded Kuwait, and "experts" in Arab politics were immediately convinced that with his "Arab" strength crumbs of comfort were going to be tossed in their direction in the shape of Israeli concessions. This is what the struggle against Israel amounted to in the minds of intellectuals. One didn't know whether to laugh or cry.

Inside Israel, however, at least one Palestinian did not fall for the nonsense swilling around him. The seventy-year-old writer Emile Habibi, born in Haifa, publicly denounced "linkage" the moment the idea was advanced by Saddam Husain. He did so on the grounds that "the only linkage that Palestinians would come out with is the one that ties their cause to the fate of the Iraqi leadership."[36] He went on to hold the Palestinian political leadership and the entire Arab intelligentsia responsible for inculcating illusions about Saddam Husain among ordinary Palestinians.[37]

Habibi's long experience as a political activist inside Palestine-Israel, starting with the Palestinian rebellion of 1936–39, had taught him to be deeply cynical of any attempt by the Arab regimes to champion the Palestinian cause: "Every time Israel was put in a corner, isolated, and on the verge of making concessions, along came what we in the Palestinian lexicon call *al-faraj al-'Arabi,* 'the Arab salvation.' " Habibi supported the UN partition resolution of November 29, 1947, a position that was labeled "treacherous" at the time and could have cost him his life. Nor did he think that the Arab armies went to war in 1948 in order to create a Palestinian state. "The opposite is true: the Arab armies came in order to prevent the establishment of another state in Palestine. And ever since then the Arab regimes, together with the British and the Americans, have exploited the Palestinian question for their own conspiracies, for waging their inter-Arab wars."[38] In 1991, *al-faraj al-'Arabi* came in the shape of a "Saddamesque fantasy," or as Habibi put it more poetically, "the dark-skinned knight on his white horse."[39]

Habibi never fell for the more sophisticated variations on this kind of mythmaking. He has always seen through the lies and deceptions of the Arab regimes over the Palestinian question. But he doesn't just say that he can see through them—which everyone, of course, claims to be able to do—he actually takes up a political position accordingly, however isolating that may turn out to be. Habibi saw that *any* Palestinian acceptance of *any* version of Saddam Husain's plan of "linkage" instantly detracted from the democratic thrust of Palestinian nationalism.[40] Unlike Abu-Lughod and Hallaj, Habibi clearly felt that no genuine Palestinian democrat should ever agree to pay that kind of a price just because he or she was desperate to have a state. Habibi spoke out, even when it was dangerous for him to do so, arguing that Saddam's proposed cure for Palestinian desperation was far worse than the condition itself.

The stakes in this polarization between someone like Habibi and the rest of the Palestinian intelligentsia are very high, and go to the core of Palestinian politics. They correspond to the growing divisions between Palestinians inside Israel and the Occupied Territories, politically represented by such impressive new political personalities as Hanan 'Ashrawi and Faisal al-Husaini, against those who are outside and still loosely gathered around the PLO and Yasser Arafat. In this division, a fundamental choice between two concepts of freedom is being played out.

Bizarre as it may seem, the Iraqi annexation of Kuwait was genuinely seen by the Ba'thi state, and by the majority of Arab intellectuals, as an extension of the total amount of freedom available to the Arab people. The anti-imperialist rhetoric of both Pan-Arabism and Palestinian nationalism revolves around the idea of "freedom from" either imperialism or Zionism, as the case may be, toward unity of an artificially fragmented whole (the Arab world) or a yet-to-be-created state (a future Palestine in the Occupied Territories, for instance). Freedom lovers everywhere should support the annexation of Kuwait—a "national act," in Tarabishi's mind—for this reason. From such a perspective, the nature of Saddam's regime, and what was being done in Kuwait, is entirely secondary. Even when such intellectuals abhor the regime in private—as I am sure someone like Abu-Lughod does—adhering to this notion of nationalism explains why they will so steadfastly champion it in public.[41]

The underlying assumption of the nationalists was that the annexation of Kuwait was "legitimate," or "understandable," "historically speaking," even if it was illegal (or in spite of Saddam's tyranny). "Linkage" to them meant that if Kuwait had to be given up—separated from Iraq—in the name of a legalism, or a formality like "international law," which was so obviously being imposed on the Arabs by Western manipulation of the United Nations, then the

Arabs ought to be compensated with something. Why not a piece of Palestine? It is as though nearly 200 million Arabs had nothing else to hold them up in the world except two props: Saddam Husain and the PLO. If the United States, and the Allied coalition, were absolutely insistent on knocking down one of these precious props (Saddam Husain), then the very least they ought to do was to stiffen up the other (the PLO). "Linkage" derived its moral force among Palestinians from this kind of thinking; and to reject Saddam Husain's "peace plan," based on linkage, looked as though one was indulging in double standards in relation to the whole issue of Israeli withdrawal from Occupied Arab lands.

This nationalist equation has a terrible reverse logic. Suppose the West were willing to let Iraq have Kuwait. Why shouldn't it demand "compensation" in the form of permanent Israeli annexation of the West Bank? This follows from the logic of linkage as set out by Abu-Lughod and Hallaj. The only reason this thought didn't cross the minds of these authors is that they don't think Saddam Husain is perfidious enough to strike such a deal with the West.

The democratic alternative upheld by Habibi runs counter to this nationalism. Deep down in the emotional heart of things where all political positions begin, a genuine democrat would instinctively understand that Kuwaitis and Palestinians, being under occupation, were both victims of gross injustice. Therefore, the "natural" linkage was between their fates, not with that of the Iraqi leadership. Empathizing with Kuwaitis under occupation is automatically an affirmation of the democratic content of the Palestinian struggle, a struggle that is based on the idea that rights, *all rights, not just your own,* should never ever be made subject to any higher principle (like Arab unity or Israeli "security"). The logic of the pro-Saddam position is that Palestinian rights are conditional on the Iraqi leadership achieving at least some of its objectives. The logic of a democratic position is just the reverse: *Palestinian rights begin with Saddam Husain's defeat and the restoration of Kuwaiti rights.* The more ignominious his defeat, and the more complete the restoration of that which has been usurped, the greater is the eventual Palestinian democratic gain.

The democratic thrust of Palestinian nationalism never originated in the abstract desire to "liberate" Arab lands; it originated concretely *in the desire to have rights* which are today being denied inside the exclusively Jewish state because of the simple fact that one is an

Arab. The Palestinian right to be left alone, to be treated the same as everyone else, to be rid of the brutalities of an army of occupation, all these are legitimate democratic demands placed on the Israeli state, which is today denying them. This denial does to Palestinians (albeit with nothing like the same severity) what the Iraqi state has been doing to all Iraqis for nearly a quarter of a century. In other words, the Palestinian moral claim upon the conscience of the world originates in the very thing that Saddam Husain wants to take away from more and more Arabs by annexing Kuwait.

6. THE "ARAB SOLUTION"

In January 1991, when the Gulf war broke out, I was in Cairo attending the annual Arabic language book fair. A key event, which everyone was waiting for, was the address of Muhammad Hasanain Haikal, former confidant of Jamal 'Abdel-Nasser and editor of the Egyptian newspaper *al-Ahram*. The hall was packed to overflowing. We were all waiting to hear what Haikal, who on September 12 had written that "only an Arab solution can meet the psychology of the Arab mind," was going to say.[42]

Haikal began telling us stories about his experiences with his friend, "Jamal." I remember a story about Qaddafi vividly. The Libyan monarchy had just been overthrown and this unknown upstart was calling for immediate union with Nasser, his idol. The Egyptian president, having no idea what the new Libyan leader was like, dispatched his trusty lieutenant Haikal for an exploratory meeting. Haikal returned to be met by Nasser at the airport. "So tell me, what's the guy like?" Nasser asked impatiently at the first opportunity. "You don't want to know," Haikal answered. But Nasser did want to know. Haikal replied: "He is a catastrophe!"

We all roared with laughter. Haikal continued with his views on the position of every state on the Gulf crisis. But he left out Egypt. He talked about what each political leader had done right and what he had done wrong. Again, he made everyone collapse in laughter. It was a sunny, cool Sunday afternoon on January 13, two days before the expiry of the UN deadline for Iraqi withdrawal from Kuwait. Hell was about to descend on the people of Iraq. The audience got a bit impatient: "You left out Egypt, tell us what you think of the Egyptian position." Haikal grinned, enjoying himself immensely. "I will tell you only that I don't understand Egypt's position," he teased. "We could have played a leading role, but we didn't." The audience shouted back good-humoredly: "What should we have done?" Haikal was now really getting into the swing of things: "I have my views on that but I prefer to remain silent." The crowd roared back in unison: "Tell us! Tell us!"

More jokes and more laughter. By the end, he was so witty, we were almost falling off our seats. Haikal knows that he is so important, so special; he understands Arab politics so much better than anyone else—after all, he was Nasser's closest confidant. His views, therefore, carry an electric charge. Anyway, that is what he thinks. He tightrope-walked us around the Arab world for three hours, and back into the hall where we were packed like sardines. Haikal enacted in front of a thousand people the charade that an Arab solution in the first two months of the crisis would have involved. In the end he said nothing, just as the Arab League would have done nothing. That is Haikal. That is also the "Arab solution" at this historical juncture. No one understood this better than Saddam Husain. In fact, he was banking on it when he invaded Kuwait.

During the Gulf crisis, Noam Chomsky, like Muhammad Hasanain Haikal, argued that there was an alternative to war, namely, negotiations and diplomatic settlement. "But the United States has shot down every hint that there might be a diplomatic track ever since the beginning . . . Proposals of this nature have been floated repeatedly by Iraq and proposed by Jordan, the PLO, France and others who are trying to find a way out of this catastrophe."[43] The major features of the settlement Chomsky had in mind involved some form of guaranteed access for Iraq to the Gulf, "which everybody agrees is not an unreasonable request." But Iraq, which Chomsky himself on another occasion called "perhaps the most violent and repressive state in the world," showed its reasonableness by invading, sacking, and annexing an incomparably weaker and less aggressive neighbor.[44] Why was Chomsky choosing to draw attention to Saddam Husain's reasonableness at a time like this? Another feature of a negotiated settlement, according to Chomsky, would be deciding about the Iraqi claim on the Rumaila oil field, "95% of which is inside Iraq, 5% inside Kuwait, over what is an unsettled and disputed border. . . . Harder map conflicts than that have been negotiated." I have no idea where Chomsky got his percentages, but with the deck stacked in this way, Kuwait might as well stop being so unreasonable and just give Iraq what it wanted as there is nothing left to talk about. Chomsky also came down in support of a "plebiscite or other expression of popular will inside Kuwait"[45] as part of a settlement. But he omitted to recommend the same for Iraq. Why?

The very peculiar thing about the Chomskyan scheme of things is the assumption that if you allow yourself to think that there is a moral principle at stake in Saddam's takeover of Kuwait, "then you've got an argument, a plausible argument that you shouldn't pursue a diplomatic option and that we just have to go to war."[46] Hence the burning desire to dig up all this Iraqi "reasonableness" and fish around for a settlement, which could only have been achieved by conceding an enormous moral and political victory to none other than the "most violent and repressive state in the world." Hence also the need to stress the hypocrisy and cynical posturing of the United States and the constant references to Panama, Grenada, El Salvador, and Vietnam. Like the "Arab solution," Chomsky's position reveals a complete unwillingness or inability to think through the specifics of the situation from the point of view of the people who are living it on the ground and *the consequences for them* of Saddam Husain getting away with something that could be palmed off as a victory.

The assumption that moral principles were not primarily at stake in the invasion of Kuwait forecloses from someone like Chomsky the only reasonable grounds for opposing the Gulf war. This was the view that even though important moral principles were at stake, they had to be compromised, because of the terrible consequences in human terms of acting upon them. That is a perfectly legitimate, even an excellent argument for being opposed to the Gulf war, one which would have set Chomsky apart from someone like Muhammad Haikal. But it was not the one that he, along with many other American and European anti-war activists, adopted.

7. ARAB OIL AS THE DRIVING FORCE OF WAR

As far as one can tell from reading the proceedings, every participant in a March 1991 conference held in North Africa to evaluate the impact of the Gulf crisis on the future of the Arab world agreed with the economist 'Abdel-Jaleel al-Badawi that "it is elementary that Arab oil was the principal axis of the Gulf war."[47] By this al-Badawi meant that "when Iraq demanded a reevaluation of the price of oil, she was striking at the founding mechanisms of the world economy and threatening a commodity that was both a lifeline and a source of great profits most of which were being transferred to the north. . . .

For this reason Saddam became the man who had to be toppled just as Mossadeq was before him in Iran and Allende in Chile and Qaddafi in Libya.''[48]

I do not question the fact that a steady supply of oil coming from the Middle East is of strategic importance to the West. But in the imagination of someone like al-Badawi, for instance, the fiction still persists that economic relations between Iraq and the West are governed by exploitation which works inexorably to the advantage of the advanced capitalist countries. Saddam Husain, therefore, is less a brute than he is an Arab Robin Hood who was valiantly attempting to redress that economic imbalance in favor of the Arabs before the West struck him down (just as he was ostensibly going to correct the geographical incongruence of wealth and population inside the Arab world in favor of the poor and penniless).

Leaving al-Badawi's mistakes aside—there is no oil in Chile—the first question that comes to mind is that surely the "oil factor" was far more significant to the party that invaded Kuwait, namely, Iraq, than it was to the West. If he had gotten away with it, Saddam would have doubled his income (even before he raised prices) with an imperceptible increase in costs. That would have made Iraq a more powerful regional power than it already was. This, it is fair to assume, is what intellectuals like al-Badawi and Samir Amin want. The economics of such dreams of grandeur in the Iraqi experience of the 1980s were neatly summed up by the Iraqi banker, Ahmad Chalabi:

In 1980 Iraq had $30 billion dollars in cash, $35 billion in civilian commodities and at least $11 billion in weapons. By 1989 Iraq had a foreign debt in excess of $100 billion and virtually no cash reserves. In the same period Iraq received more than $119 billion in new oil revenues. If one selects the relevant items and adds the figures, one can see that Iraq spent the staggering sum of $295 billion between 1980 and 1989. What was this money spent on? Mainly defending the Eastern flank of the Arab world against the Persian enemy. What does that mean? It means that this money was spent on bringing death and destruction . . . . What is the cost of the replacement value of the infrastructure, productive facilities, capital equipment, housing, remittances of foreign workers bought in to replace Iraqis busily defending that flank and the lost opportunities to the country in that period? How does $200 billion sound? Conservative.[49]

Chalabi concluded that approximately $495 billion would have been thrown away in order to bring Iraq back to where it had started in 1980 when it launched its first foreign war adventure. These are mind-boggling numbers. What makes them possible? Oil income. Yet at no point throughout his post-1968 political career has Saddam Husain ever had to challenge the West in order to get his hands on such sums (the way the Iranian leader Mossadeq had to do in the 1950s). Arabs, after all, own their oil today, and they get a far better price for it than is justified by the actual cost of its production. In fact, the price of oil in the world today bears no relation to that cost; it is like a gigantic rent, exacted on all consumers of oil, many of whom are in the Third World.

If the past is anything to go by, the West would not have had anything to fear from Saddam Husain's new oil-pricing policy had he got away with his second foreign war adventure in Kuwait. It was after all the West's great ally and pillar of support, the Shah of Iran, who took advantage of the 1973 October war to set in motion the greatest price increases ever seen in this sector, increases which upset the whole relation between the First and the Third Worlds (the Shah of Iran, it will be recalled, ousted Iranian Prime Minister Mossadeq in a CIA-sponsored coup in 1953). A country like Iraq stands in the front line of those who benefited from the 1973 quadrupling of the price of oil. Those increases, over the years, are the source of the wasted $495 billion estimated by Chalabi.

Iraq and Iran were able to slog it out for eight long years, casting into oblivion a whole generation of young Iraqi and Iranian men, only because of the enormous scale of this rentier income. No other two "normal" economies—in which state income depended on social taxation and therefore a certain measure of real wealth-producing ability in the shape of internally produced new goods and services—could possibly have fought such a senseless war for so long.

While the fighting was going on, naturally the Western "imperialists" were only too happy to sell guns to the combatants. As the mountain of Iranian and Iraqi bodies grew, Western arms companies and dealers made huge profits. No one is trying to deny that. But someone had to want to buy the guns and fight the bloody war in the first place in order for so many Arabs and Iranians to die. The Iraq-Iran War floated on the price of a barrel of oil not because anyone forced the Ba'thist regime in Iraq, or the Islamic Republic of

Iran, to head down this particular road, but because the blood lust of both Saddam and Khomeini went completely unchecked by, among others, Arab and Muslim intellectuals, like al-Badawi, who participated in the nationalist hysteria over Saddam Husain during the Gulf crisis.

The past, however, is not always something to go by. That is one reason why so much of the world, led by the United States, acted to force Saddam Husain out of Kuwait. The United States and the Western European states are aging powers, conservative and bureaucratic in their decision making. They are interested in "stability" and fixed relationships, more than they are in fiery democratic principles. They stick to countries like Saudi Arabia and Israel just because they are there; they represent the status quo. Following the same logic, they stuck by Saddam Husain all through the 1980s. But when the Iraqi leader proved himself to be as unpredictable as he was nasty, the Western powers suddenly woke up to the fact that it would only be a matter of time before he did it again, and again, and again. No government acted in the Gulf crisis because of a deep-seated concern with the Kuwaiti right to self-determination or because of Saddam Husain's human rights record; they were concerned about things like falling Arab "dominoes" which could, in the long run, disrupt the steady supply of oil to their economies.

Granted the unpredictability of Saddam Husain, and the strategic importance of all that oil, I still think it is doubtful that the United States would have done anything about Kuwait if left entirely to its own resources. Liberating Kuwait was a very expensive business indeed (costing around $70 billion, according to White House March 1991 estimates, of which the United States was going to pay $15 billion).[50] Iraq was no Grenada, nor was Saddam sitting on America's doorstep, like Noriega in Panama. Could the United States, with a budget deficit that rose from $220 billion in 1990 to an estimated $348.50 billion in 1991, and with a national debt of $3.5 trillion, three and a half times the size it was just ten years ago, have footed the bill for expelling Iraq?[51] Not without plunging the United States into a far more serious recession than the one that has already gripped it. The American economy no longer has the resources to engage in big foreign adventures; according to some analysts it has long been in severe decline by world standards, and that decline is still going strong.[52] Someone else had to want to bankroll the Gulf war effort, and to provide the U.S. army with the necessary logistical support for the high-tech, low-casualty, and very costly war which was the only kind it knew how to fight. Japan and Germany, reluctantly and after a lot of arm-twisting, came up with $3 billion for the military effort.[53] That left the lion's share of $52 billion, which was contributed enthusiastically and willingly by other Arab countries. Using its vast oil income, Saudi Arabia in particular put up most of the money, buying the services of the world's largest army, just as it buys virtually everything else that it consumes (with the exception of religion). From this rather different perspective on the Gulf war, it is possible to agree with al-Badawi that Arab oil was indeed its "principal axis."

8. CULTURAL IMPERIALISM

Edward Said was one of the first major Arab intellectuals to respond publicly to the new situation created by Saddam Husain. His response seems to have been instinctual—a "gut" reaction to the crisis which, not surprisingly, was consistent with a world view that has been developed in his many very popular books. Writing in *The Independent* (London) ten days after the invasion of Kuwait, Said had nothing to say about Saddam Husain. The focus of the article instead was on Western culpability: "Is it too much to connect the stark political and military polarization [building up in the Gulf] with the cultural abyss that exists between the Arabs and the West?"[54]

"Culpable for what," I wrote in response at the time. "This is not the nationalization of the Suez canal; this is the forcible annexation of one Arab state by another. This is Saddam Husain, not Jamal 'Abdel-Nasser. Would Edward Said have this maker and creature of the Ba'thi republic become kingpin of all Arab politics? Does he seriously think that the Palestinians will then be able to negotiate with Israel from a position of strength (not their own strength of course, but Saddam Husain's)?"[55] Said's article went on to emphasize the "overwhelmingly non-Kuwaiti" population of Kuwait, and the apparently significant fact that "with few exceptions governments in the area have had little historical legitimacy; that they have derived their status from colonialism, force or sheer buying power."[56]

But "history" is precisely what leaders like Saddam Husain use to justify the terrible things that they do. At the same time, "historical legitimacy" (or the lack thereof) is a justification for the demolition of the entire modern Arab state order. For Kuwait, in this respect, is no different than Jordan, than Syria, than Lebanon, than Iraq itself. Why couldn't Saddam Husain's men find a single Kuwaiti to join his puppet government for the few days that he kept up that particular pretense? Because they weren't there. It seems that the passage of time, the growth of state machineries, the issuing of passports, the fact that a few generations have been brought up inside an entity called Kuwait (however artificial, historically speaking) does have some meaning after all. Politics, not history, is what was at stake in the actions of the Iraqi army in Kuwait.

Said's main subject in that first response to the Gulf crisis, how-ever, is culture, not history. The eruption of the Gulf crisis, he was arguing, revealed deep-rooted Western prejudices against Arab cul-ture, which arise out of the history of their relations. Said was not alone in emphasizing this. One Arab intellectual after the other said similar things. The Lebanese novelist Elias Khouri saw the Gulf crisis as the "end phase of an imperialist project which goes back to the collapse of Mohamed 'Ali's attempt [to unify the Arab world]." He could see "indications of a new crusades" looming over the horizon rooted in an orientalist "complex toward the East" which still ruled Western psychology.[57] George Tarabishi wrote of "a civilizational crisis," which fits into "an organized campaign of cultural invasion of the Arab world."[58] Al-Tahir Labeeb, professor of sociology at the University of Tunis, talked in all seriousness about a new phenome-non called "Bushism" which, no longer content with securing American economic and political interests, wanted to force upon the world a "universal totalitarian character" by projecting itself as the arbitrator between good and evil "on the universal level."[59] Fawwaz Trabulsi, a Lebanese secular leftist, wrote of the Arab masses "who have not forgotten that their main enemy is the United States," with its "aggressive culture" and "colossal contempt shown to their religious and cultural identity—Islam."[60] The subtitle of a book of articles on the Gulf war, by a collection of the most famous names in Arabic letters, was: "From Cultural Invasion to the Gulf War."[61]

'Abdel-Rahman Munif, one of the most gifted novelists writing in the Arabic language today, was a contributor to this volume. Writing a full month after the end of the Gulf war, while the upris-ing against the regime in Baghdad was being brutally crushed, he chose to reflect back upon the Crusades and ask why the West was so intent on "resuming its wars in this region." The answer, Munif thinks, is the West's desire "to eliminate the region's history, civilizations, cultures, and religions." What is most remarkable is the degree of fantasy that is brought to bear on the facts. Thus, speaking of Jewad Salim's monument to the 1958 revolution which sits in a square in central Baghdad, Munif writes that "it is *probable* that this monument has been blown up, or that only its base is standing. The same goes for historic monuments thousands of years old."[62] Nothing of the sort happened to this monument or to any historic monument in Iraq as a consequence of the Allied bombing. However, the tanks of the Republican Guard, which were not mentioned in Munif's article, did as we have seen target and seriously damage historic and religious shrines while they were busy pulverizing whole residential districts in Basra, Najaf, and Kerbala.

The image of Arab culture being swamped by the West goes to the emotional heart of the nationalist paradigm (as it does to the Islamic paradigm in the shape of a fear of alien "Western values"). The distorted prism through which modern Arab nationalist politics looks out at the world is well illustrated in Said's August 12 article. The "cultural abyss that exists between the Arabs and the West" is illustrated by a stream of Arabic book titles, all of which supposedly got short shrift in the West because of an inbuilt Western racism toward the Arabs. Certainly, racism toward Arabs exists in the West (as racism exists everywhere else in the world). And Western imperial history has conditioned the forms that this racism takes. But surely it is painfully self-evident that Western culture today (though not all throughout its history) is immeasurably more tolerant of cultural, religious, and ethnic differences than Arab culture. Said, however, is not interested in the Arab world as it really is; he is only interested in blaming the West for the mess created by Saddam Husain. His way of doing so in this particular article in *The Independent* is to paint an idyllic picture of an Arab literary renaissance pulsing with new books and exciting new ideas, all of which are being deliberately shunted aside by racist Western publishers, editors, and book reviewers. This depiction of the state of Arabic culture is simply untrue.

Consider the state of the Arabic book. A 1989 issue of the Arabic weekly *Shadha* devoted a considerable amount of space to "The Reality of the Arabic Book and Its Crisis." The magazine interviewed many Arabic language publishers and booksellers, to find out the causes of the profound decline in quality, numbers, and availability of Arabic language books—a decline all agreed had reached serious proportions. Riadh El-Rayyes, the same Arabic language publisher who issued the book with the subtitle "From Cultural Invasion to the Gulf War," spoke of the proportionately low numbers of readers among Arabs by comparison with the West; Mai Ghoussoub, a director of al-Saqi Books, drew attention to the dearth of new titles, and the low and declining cultural level of the average Arab reader; Hisham Mu'awiyya, owner of Ibn Sina Arabic Bookshop in Paris, thought the problem began at childhood. Everyone, including the writer of the article himself, agreed that they were dealing with deep-rooted problems originating in Arab culture itself (and not in its relation to Western culture).

In an important article in the Arabic daily *al-Hayat,* Andre Gaspard, a director of the al-Saqi publishing house, surveyed at length the daunting problems he faced as an Arab publisher in the West. (Incidentally, all these publishers and bookshops outside the Arab world are a phenomenon of the 1980s, created by Beirut's suicide. Europe has replaced Beirut as a haven for quality books in Arabic and on the Middle East.)[63] Gaspard lists problems of state censorship and control of all distribution networks, an inability to reach the Arabic reader directly, rampant piracy, the phenomenon of the illiterate publisher (still predominant), the absence of the notion of copyright, royalties, or any ethical standards in the production of Arabic books, the imperative of sacrificing quality in order to get anything published on the part of both the writer and the publisher, the corruption endemic in the book distribution system, the declining quality of the average book, and so on and so forth. A bleaker picture could not have been painted.

But reading Said or Tarabishi or Munif or any one of a number of other prominent Arab intellectuals, one has no idea that any of this is going on, no idea that on a day-to-day basis these are the formidable obstacles faced by Arabs who are in the business of making their own culture. Instead, we are led to believe that all problems (from the politics of the Gulf crisis to Arab culture) stem from the West's policy of "monolithic reductionism where the Arabs and Islam are concerned."[64]

Inverting Said's rhetorical question in his article in *The Independent,* about the connection between the military build-up in the Gulf and "the cultural abyss that exists between the Arabs and the West," I am moved to conclude with one of my own: Is it too much to connect the stark political and military polarization created by Saddam Husain with the cultural abyss that exists today *inside* the Arab world itself? The Gulf crisis did not reveal Western prejudice against the Arab world as much as it did a deep-rooted crisis within Arab-Islamic culture at this critical juncture in its history.

WALID KHALIDI has written of "the failure of the Arab political order, as it has evolved since the end of World War II both in the Mashriq and Maghrib, to approximate in any of its constituent sovereign states to minimal levels of genuine power sharing or accountability in government, much less to self-governing parliamentary institutions operating within democratic forms and constraints."[65] The responsibility for that failure can no longer be placed on the West or Israel, as Arab intellectuals are so fond of doing. It cannot even be placed only, or primarily, on the shoulders of the rulers of the Arab world. Men like Saddam Husain, Hafiz Assad, King Fahd, and Yasser Arafat do not know how to behave differently. They are indigenous creations of modern Arab political culture, which until now has failed to produce anything better. The deeper problem lies not in their psychology, but in the distorting lens through which they have been viewed by the real source of failure in the culture— modern Arab intellectuals.

I have, in effect, been arguing that *the language of human rights* and *the language of Arab nationalism, or political Islam,* have become totally irreconcilable. This is not to say that no benign forms of nationalism exist or that Islam is in some way inherently resistant to coexistence with a politics founded on human rights. Islam is no different from any other world religion in its potential for adapting to a politics of human rights, and Arab nationalism could be as flexible or "reinterpretable" as any other ideology.

The problem is that neither nationalism nor political Islam in their current incarnations are intellectually equipped to bring about a fresh cultural start in the politics of the region. Their greatest failure, as I see it, is that they have failed to evolve a genuinely convincing language of rights in politics. Both have become fossilized, backward-looking and steeped in a romanticism of "struggle" which is conducive to violence. This language is today compacted against a wall of self-inflicted Arab suffering and pain. A new start can only begin from the brutal hard facts of that pain. It must begin with an Arab groundswell of revulsion at cruelty in the Arab home and cruelty on the Arab street, a groundswell which views someone like Saddam Husain as the principle of cruelty incarnate, not as the principle of Arab strength.

Covering up for the Iraqi regime's cruelty during the Gulf crisis was not just a "small mistake" of a misguided handful of people; it was a deep-rooted failure that must be acknowledged as such if we are to have a new beginning. If the cycles of violence, bloodshed, hopelessness, and despair are to be brought to an end, then Arabs must look inward—not outward to the West—and begin to realize that they are overwhelmingly responsible for the deplorable state of their world. More specifically, no political thought is worth thinking in the future that does not have the Khalils, Abu Haydars, Omars, Mustafas, and Taimours of this world at the center of its concern.

9 ˈ Landscapes of Cruelty and Silence

THE STORIES of Khalil, Abu Haydar, Omar, Mustafa, and Taimour might be seen by some as singular aberrations, outside the course of modern Arab history. One sympathizes with the plight of the victims, but there is nothing in any of the stories that has a general bearing on the rest of the Arab world. It is possible, therefore, to say, "We didn't know." Or even, "We couldn't possibly have known." Iraq was after all such a closed state. Some Arab friends, who agree that terrible things happened in Iraq, succumb to the explanation of an Iraqi national pathology, a unique vulnerability that the country is presumed always to have had to absolute or authoritarian rule. The rest of the Arab world, in their view, thus cannot be held responsible for what happened in Iraq.

This position is untenable for a variety of reasons. To begin with, since the late 1960s, cruelty has become rampant in all those countries of the Mashriq that experienced wars, civil wars, occupations, collective punishments, armed guerrilla organizations, terrorist attacks, intifadas, mass deportations, and expanding state bureaucracies for whom the principle of torture is the norm. This is not to deny the uniqueness of the Iraqi experience, and certainly my intent is not to remove the emotional burden of that uniqueness. On the contrary, only a cross-country comparison allows us to understand exactly what is singular about what happened in Iraq. By the same token, such a comparison would allow us to understand what is, for instance, specific to Lebanese, Palestinian, or Syrian cruelty.

Violence has been spreading within individual Arab countries to embroil larger and larger numbers of people. What's more, it has crossed over from one country to the next. Not only religious minorities and ethnic groups but also entire religious majorities (Shi'ites in Iraq and Sunnis in Syria) today feel more threatened than ever before and are responding in kind. Palestinian nationalism was forged and hammered into the prickly and defensive thing that we see today in the crucible of its denial by Zionism. The more it was attacked, the more powerful and politically regressive it grew. These are perfectly natural, all-too-human responses to denial of identity through aggression. Unfortunately, however, they are also breeding grounds for nationalist, religious, and ethnic fanaticism accompanied by a weakening of state ties of loyalty and allegiance. The unity of Iraq today, like Lebanon yesterday, is threatened by these forces. The spiraling logic of violence in the Middle East in recent years is therefore both cause and effect of the increasing inability of individuals and political groups to establish an identity for themselves that is not exclusively reactive and hostile to others in its origins.

But does that imply there is an Arab uniqueness, or a "national" Arab pathology where violence and cruelty are concerned? This idea makes even less sense than the one of an Iraqi proclivity toward violence; there is after all so much less homogeneity of experience inside the whole Arab world than there is inside the boundaries of Iraq. The most interesting thing about Iraqi institutionalized violence as compared to, say, Lebanese anarchy, is how different the one is from the other, not how similar. The most interesting thing about it is the various forms that it takes, the rhythms to which it is subject, the forces which make it recede, escalate, or erupt with frenzy on the public stage at any given moment. In the Middle East, violence has tended to be ideologized and to fill public space. Such an observation is not a comment on how much more violent or cruel the Arab world is by contrast with some other part of the world. Clearly, there is violence everywhere one looks in the world. The purpose of a comparison is always what is at stake. My purpose here centers on the question: Is cruelty on a rising curve within the Arab world, considered as a regional unit?

The first problem in answering this question is one of adequate documentation. Reports published by organizations like Amnesty International and Human Rights Watch document the rising curve of human rights violations in the Middle East. But these are partial in scope and totally inadequate as descriptions of the overall scale of what happens daily. More importantly, the reports are not being prepared by Arab organizations, which are in a position to get much more in-depth information. Thus they are easily brushed aside by nationalist, anti-imperialist, and Muslim intellectuals, or even by Arab community organizations in the West, and used instead as evidence of how much the outside world likes to pick on them.[1]

Cruelty can appear to be growing when in fact we are only becoming more aware of it. Something like that is happening in Iraq now. Daily we are acquiring new information about past atrocities. Difficult as it may be, we must not let that new information overwhelm our judgment of what is happening today in Iraq and what might happen tomorrow. Cruelty, for instance, is increasingly appearing as a theme in new Arabic literature (more often than not in fiction written by Arab women, particularly Lebanese women).[2] The fact that we know more about cruelties that happened in the past, and that a handful of women writers in particular are becoming vocal about it, is all to the good. On the negative side of the balance sheet, however, the question has to be asked: Would it have been possible for the Iraqi state to kill as many Kurds as it did all through the 1980s if a deep-rooted climate of insensitivity had not developed throughout the Mashriq? Why is there still no definitive study of the Lebanese civil war written in Arabic? And why is there not one of the Syrian 1982 massacre in Hama in which anywhere between 10,000 and 40,000 people may have been killed?[3]

An intelligentsia internalizes the state of its world, whether explicitly or subliminally; its language is invariably being shaped by it, either through acknowledgment or through denial. Decreasing revulsion at cruelty is, in the long run, as dangerous as cruelty itself. If the dominant Arab intellectual currents had had their way in 1990–91, the Arab world would today almost certainly be faced with a much stronger Saddam Husain who, having digested Kuwait, would be preparing to attack another Arab country. Why is it that during the Gulf crisis hardly any Arab intellectuals enquired into the consequences for other Arabs of the Iraqi Ba'th getting away with swallowing up Kuwait? The nightmarish cruelties that became the norm inside Iraq would have been exported yet again. How many more people like Khalil, Abu Haydar, Omar, Mustafa, and Taimour would have been living under occupation, humiliated, tortured, gassed, and killed? Scapegoating the West and disregarding cruelty are in this regard two aspects of the same language of denial and unwillingness to face up to the consequences of one's own words.

I cannot "prove" that cruelty is increasing inside the Mashriq. However, I think that it has become too "normal" and accepted by

Arab intellectuals, especially those who reside in the West and are most removed from it; hence this book. What follows is a brief journey through forgotten landscapes of cruelty and silence in the Arab world. One day they will have to be properly confronted. This journey is not a substitute for coming to grips with the phenomenon of rising cruelty in the Middle East. It is merely a sketch painted in large sweeping brushstrokes. One may argue that it is not a good idea to paint such pictures, regardless of whether or not they are true. On the other hand, cruelty thrives in the dark. To make it go away one needs to shine on it the brightest possible light.

Cruelty and the Arab Woman

THERE ARE two faces to cruelty: a public and a private one. Even when the physical act of cruelty is undertaken publicly—for instance, if it is inflicted by the machinery of a state or by a crowd on the rampage—it is preceded by a web of private moral assumptions which make the particular violation possible. From this point of view, a study of cruelty in the Arab world must begin with its most ubiquitous target: the Arab woman.

'Aziz Salih Ahmad is the name on an index card measuring 3 × 6 inches which first came into my possession in the form of a fax in the summer of 1991. It was hard to read, being the fax of a fax of a photocopy following probably in the wake of many other photocopies. The chain originated in the Central Security Headquarters Building of Sulaimaniyya. Ahmad was (and for all I know may still be) a policeman, an employee of the General Security Organization of Iraq. A facsimile of the entries on the card (with the handwritten entries shown in italics), is given below:

Secret Contracts	Type no. (2) General Security

General Index Card

Curriculum Vitae

File number 43,304

Tripartite Name: *'Aziz Salih Ahmad*
Date of Birth: [left blank]
Profession: *Fighter in the Popular Army*
Activity: *Violation of Women's Honor*

Mr 'Aziz Salih Ahmad is a civil servant paid a salary to rape Iraqi women.[4]

The barbarism of a state that employs people as rapists and what goes on in the mind of a man like 'Aziz Ahmad are important questions. For the moment, however, I am concerned with what a document like this tells us about how widespread the practice of rape must have become in order for such paperwork to be routinely generated. When the prisons of the *mukhabarat* and the army were stormed during the March 1991 uprising, scores of women with children born to them in prison were released from the quarters that housed them inside the prison compound.[5] Every major prison seems to have had its own specially equipped rape room (replete in one case with soft-porn pictures stuck on the wall opposite the surface being used). In occupied Kuwait, a rape center located in Shuwaykh, I have been told, was painted olive green and had "Liberate Palestine" written on the walls in blood.[6] The children born to these rape victims have ended up in the Dar al-Tufula orphanage on the outskirts of Kuwait City, while special counseling for rape victims—women and men—is being provided in the al-Ragei Clinic, newly established by Dr. Rahman al-'Asfour for this specific purpose.[7]

From the stories I heard while inside Iraq, and that have been leaking out since the Gulf war wherever there are Iraqi refugees, there is simply no doubt that "official" rape was rampant in Iraq, maybe even out of control, lacking any sort of checks.[8] How is it that the state could get away with something as ugly and bestial as this? The answer unfortunately does not reside solely in Saddam Husain's nastiness, which is what all Iraqis—including myself—would like to believe; it resides in a marriage between his kind of evil and one of the most hallowed assumptions of Arab cultural identity, the secret of which is captured in the phrase "violation of women's honor." 'Aziz Ahmad's employers are "violating" something that they officially describe as "honor."

The honor of a family is perceived in Arab-Islamic culture to be located in the bodies of the women of that family, in their virginity first and foremost, but also in the clothes that women wear, in the modesty with which they deport themselves. The veil acquires its importance in the culture precisely because it acts symbolically to protect this honor from public view, and hence ostensibly to enhance it. This was the reasoning behind Khomeini's edict on the veil in the first year of Iran's Islamic revolution. When 'Aziz Salih Ahmad rips off an Arab or a Kurdish woman's "veil," and violates her sexually, he has in fact penetrated to the inner sanctum of an entire family's honor. He is not being paid to satisfy his own lust or even to attack his victims because they are individual human beings (to extract information from them, for instance). He is being paid to dishonor an entire family name. Mr. 'Aziz Salih Ahmad's victims do not even possess the dignity of having been raped because they are sentient beings, with private thoughts, feelings, and beliefs of their own. They are merely instruments in the realization of someone else's dignity and "honor."

Feelings of shame—as opposed to guilt—are traditionally associated with violations of honor. "If guilt is about behavior that has harmed others," writes the psychologist Robert Karen, "shame is about not being good enough."[9] Typically, shame is a feeling "akin to being caught out in the open and desperately wanting to hide." The core of one's identity is suddenly at stake, but not necessarily because of anything that one has done. Whereas guilt is a self-reflexive judgment to do with perceived moral failure, shame is about conformity, acceptability, and other people's judgment of your character. "To be ashamed is to expect rejection, not so much because of what one has done as because of what one is." This kind of a debilitating feeling in the victim's next of kin is what the employers of Mr. 'Aziz Salih Ahmad are banking on. Therefore, the seeds of such a seemingly unimaginable idea as employing civil servants as rapists are first planted here: in the organization of traditional society around such codes of honor and shame.[10]

"To break someone's eye," is an old Bedouin expression, which was turned into state policy in Iraq through the employment of a rapist like 'Aziz Salih Ahmad. The people of Takrit were famous under the Ottomans for the way they would "break the eye" of any non-Takriti governor who might be imposed on them by central government. The newly appointed governor, along with his wife and children, would be invited for a welcoming feast in the house of a local notable. On the way back, the party would be ambushed by a group of armed masked men. The governor would be forced to watch his wife being gang-raped, after which the men would whip off their masks, show the governor their faces, and disappear into the night, killing no one. Such a governor could not ever again preside over the affairs of Takrit. By the late 1970s, the most famous "aristocratic" Baghdadi families were having their eyes "broken" by the new upstart Ba'thi rulers, even though these families had long ceased to wield political influence or even economic power in the country. Young women from such families were kidnapped off the streets on their way to and from some of the famous clubs of Baghdad. They would disappear for a few weeks, and then reappear. Everybody would know what had happened to them, but no one would dare (or want) to say anything about it. (This happened to both Sunni and Shi'i families. If anything, the famous urban Sunni families, who built modern Iraq and were not from Takrit, were especially targeted.)[11] Finally, one should remember in this context the fiendish thing that was done by the Iraqi army in the Gushtapa resettlement camp just south of Arbil after the "disappearance" of thousands of Barazani males in 1982. The abuse that was heaped on the women of Gushtapa by the army surrounding them, over a period of ten years, had as its prime target that great symbol of Kurdish national honor, the Barazani name.[12]

Political cruelty often begins at home. One route to such cruelty passes through shame, which current research is increasingly identifying as "an important element in aggression."[13] Amal Musairati is a sixteen-year-old Palestinian girl from Ramleh who was beaten to a pulp by her brother in the winter of 1991 because he was filled with shame by the fact that his sister was having a relationship with a man. Her mangled body was dumped outside Kibbutz Gan Shmuel to make it look as though she had been killed by a Jew. Sara Abu Ghanam, from a well-known Ramleh family, dared to fall in love with a "black" Arab who was considered not good enough for the "family honor." She eloped with him, was captured by the Israeli police and handed back to her family. They quickly married her off to her cousin, 'Abid Abu Ghanam. Her body was found in a deep well in a citrus grove near Rishon Lezion, a suburb of Tel Aviv. The murderer was her new husband.[14] All over the Mashriq and around the Mediterranean (north and south) there are women like Amal and Sara, who are being beaten, brutalized, and not infrequently murdered in order to preserve the "honor" of their families. So important is this honor that sometimes mothers and grandmothers become active participants; they egg on the menfolk to murder their own daughters. May, a young Palestinian woman who is with the *al-Fanar* (Lighthouse) Arab women's organization, which demonstrated outside the Ramleh police station, and which has devoted itself to bringing this violence out into the open, has been beaten many times herself: "My grandmother was murdered because of the honor of the family fifty years ago, and from the day I was born my mother told me my end would be like my grandmother's."[15]

Other captured Iraqi police documents gradually coming to light show how the same honor and shame traditions that led to the "private" murders of Amal and Sara were put into "public" service by Saddam's Iraq, which many Arab intellectuals actually supported during the Gulf crisis as a way of redeeming Arab "honor" in the struggle against Israel. For instance, one document currently being held by the Iraqi Communist Party in the town of Shaqlawa shows that the Baghdad police used to place a videocamera in a ladies' tailoring shop frequented by wealthy women. A particular woman, named in the document, was filmed in the act of undressing to try on a new suit of clothes. The film was used to blackmail her into working as an informer for the police (I was told by a young woman just out of Baghdad that she has assumed for years that such cameras exist in public toilets, which she and her friends therefore never use).[16] In this particular case, the woman accepted working for the police. Why? Who was she more afraid of, her husband, or the Iraqi secret police? Clearly the husband, otherwise the police would not go to the trouble of taping her in the act of changing her clothes. Such husbands are, therefore—wittingly or not—as complicit as the Iraqi secret police in the victimization of the women of Iraq.

Another document I saw in Sulaimaniyya tells of a nurse in the employment of the secret police. She was the handler of a whole network of "virgin" women, all of whom had been blackmailed into working for the police and provided with the reassurance that their hymens would be sewn back up again by this nurse to restore their virginity. Clearly, the fear of being discovered by their own families loomed large enough to force them to cooperate with the police (incidentally, the Israeli army and police are known to employ the same fears of Palestinian women prisoners during interrogation without going to the same lengths as the Iraqi police).[17] The Iraqi writer 'Isam al-Khafaji reported a similar story following his visit to northern Iraq in 1991:

> Kifah is a barely literate young woman from al-Mishkhab, a town south of Baghdad. As a *mu'tamana* [a low-grade ranking in the Ba'th Party] she was instructed to pose as a nurse and go to Kurdistan after the defeat of

the March uprising. Her assignment was to gain the confidence of those who controlled the region, and then invite other agents to join her under the guise of health workers. Kifah had been told the US was the only armed presence in Kurdistan. When she found herself amidst a flood of armed Kurds, she panicked and simply surrendered. . . . Kifah told me how she had been recruited. In 1988, newly married, she was stopped by four *Amn* [secret police] officers in a car who told her to go with them to answer questions about her husband. She was taken instead to an orchard, where she was forced to drink alcohol and was raped by the four men. This was all videotaped. The agents threatened to send the video to her husband, who would most likely kill her. Kifah felt she had no choice but to work for the Security Directorate. She began her career by "recruiting" three friends through the same practice—pretending to take each of them to a house to visit a friend. Instead, *Amn* officers would be waiting.[18]

When I was in northern Iraq, I heard that several rings of women agents like Kifah had been captured by the Kurds and were being held in the Zakho area. Before I could get to interview them, they were shot.

Traditional codes of honor and shame provided the appropriate conditions within which a policy of official rape could work effectively as a means of controlling Arab or Kurdish society. But, taken by themselves, these conditions do not explain the breadth and depth of the phenomenon of sexual abuse in modern Iraq. The widespread use of rape accompanied the particular way in which Iraq became modernized under the Ba'th; it is part of a wholesale breakdown in social mores, among which are countervailing traditions that had protected women in the past (to a limited extent and as part of their presupposed inferiority to men). Traditions such as a strong tribal structure probably continue to serve as a partial deterrent on sexual abuse in socially more conservative societies like Saudi Arabia and Jordan.[19] One problem with taking this argument too far, however, is that no reliable information exists about what is actually happening to women in a place like Saudi Arabia because the same countervailing traditions cast a pall of silence over the subject. Is there more, less, or roughly the same amount of sexual abuse of children, for example, in Saudi Arabia as there is in Ba'thi Iraq? No one really knows.

On the other hand, important differences do exist. A social worker employed in the women's section of Jordan's Juweideh

Prison told me that a section of the prison is called *ghurfat al-zina,* the adultery room. Police roaming the streets of Amman apparently have the powers to detain unmarried young Jordanian women in the company of men unrelated to them. The couple are taken to a medical officer and the girl's virginity tested. If she is not a virgin, the police immediately inform both families. The families then negotiate the feasibility of marriage. Should the man refuse to marry the woman he was with, thus rescuing her family's honor, both are charged. The sentences are light, and within two months the man is released. But the women are compelled to stay on beyond the period of their sentences. My informant told me that for the period she worked there, roughly half of the women in the adultery room in Juweideh Prison had no sentences to serve and some of them had been there up to five years. Why were they kept on? Because they needed protection from their own families. The Jordanian police was unwilling to take responsibility for a girl being shot or stabbed to death on the prison steps on the day of her release (an actual incident). Eventually, the police start hunting for husbands who will marry the women in their custody. Old men from distant villages who are looking for a fresh lease on life are candidates. Otherwise the girls are married off to young men who turn out to be pimps hunting for prostitutes.[20]

Clearly, the same honor and shame system is at work in "conservative" Jordan as in "radical" Iraq, the difference being the relationship between state and society in the two cases. The Jordanian state is both complicit in the honor and shame system and valiantly attempting to mediate its worst manifestations; it is situated therefore somewhere in between the Palestinian case (of no state intervention) and the Iraqi extreme (of employing official rapists). What is much less clear is how much women get out of these differences.

The revolutionary Ba'th differ from the ruling monarchy in Saudi Arabia in that they have torn to shreds the inherited traditional social fabric, giving rise to a twisted new kind of Iraqi modernity that is neither traditional nor modern (in the sense of being based on new values of individuality and community such as became the norm in the West with the Enlightenment). How does sexual abuse under the Iraqi Ba'th compare with what is going on today in the Islamic Republic of Iran? Again, we just don't know. On the other hand, one can conclude that a country like Iraq has been left with the worst of everything; its society is suspended in a void, no longer having any real traditions (Islamic or otherwise) from which it can draw at least temporary comfort. This conclusion has enormous political implications for the shape of things to come in the post-Saddam era.[21]

Rape as an act of conquest and subjugation of whole societies, involving deliberate national humiliation as a means of suppression and social control, has often accompanied warfare and social breakdown. It seems, for instance, to have become widespread among some paramilitary organizations in former Yugoslavia in the summer of 1992.[22] A half a century earlier, in the so-called Rape of Nanking, a defenseless Chinese city occupied by the Japanese army in 1937, it is estimated that 20,000 cases of rape occurred during the first month of occupation.[23] For nine months in 1971, after the declaration of independence from Pakistan by Bangladesh and the entry of Pakistani troops to quell the rebellion, it is reliably estimated that between 200,000 to 400,000 Bengali women, 80 percent of whom were Muslim, were raped by Pakistani soldiers:

> As the full dimensions of the horror became known, those who looked for rational, military explanations returned again and again to the puzzle of why the mass rapes had taken place. "And a campaign of terror includes rape?" Aubrey Menen prodded a Bengali politician. He got a reflective answer. "What do soldiers talk about in barracks? Women and sex," the politician mused. "Put a gun in their hands and tell them to go out and frighten the wits out of a population and what will be the first thing that leaps to their mind?" . . . The rapes were so systematic and pervasive that they had to be conscious Army policy, "planned by the West Pakistanis in a deliberate effort to create a new race" or to dilute Bengali nationalism.

> Theory and conjecture abounded, all of it based on the erroneous assumption that the massive rape of Bangladesh had been a crime without precedent in modern history.

> But the mass rape of Bangladesh had not been unique. The number of rapes per capita . . . had been no greater than the incidence of rape . . . in the city of Nanking in 1937, no greater than the per capita incidence of rape in Belgium and France as the German Army marched unchecked during the first three months of World War I, no greater than the violation of women in every village in Soviet Russia in World War II.[24]

Nonetheless, there is something unique about "official" Iraqi rape. Here the state was getting away with waging war on its own population, not only through chemical warfare on Kurdish villages, but by unleashing rapists on women of every ethnic and religious group in the country. But rape is not only what was done to Iraqi women; it is in a sense what was done to Kuwait, and it is the perfect metaphor for what was done to the whole of Iraqi civil society by its own state. I think of rape as the generic form of the whole Ba'thi modus operandi in politics.

In due course, will we find out that violations against women increased in the course of the modernization of other Arab and Muslim countries (where the same honor and shame codes prevail in spite of modernization)? The Gulf war took the lid off the rot in Iraq; that is the only reason we know so much about what has been going on since the 1970s. If I have been using Palestinian examples, it is only because an Israeli-Arab women's organization, *al-Fanar,* is able to be active inside Israel collecting the information and publicizing it in the Hebrew press. Israel is more open than any other country in the Mashriq. That openness was also behind the public furor that arose over the publication of the booklet *Women for Women Political Prisoners—Jerusalem* in December 1989. An organization of Israeli women has documented cases of sexual abuse of Palestinian women by the Israeli police (strip searches in public, constant sexual innuendo, threat of rape, use of photographs of Palestinian women being fondled by Israeli security officers as means of pressuring confessions, etc.).[25] Does the existence of this information, and its absence for Saudi Arabia and Jordan, suggest that the situation in these particular Arab countries is better? The exact opposite is more probably the case. The problem is, we still don't know just how bad things are in these countries because the same formidable wall of silence is erected over the abuse of women here as exists in Iraq. That silence is after all what created "official" rape inside Iraq.

But back to our "official" rapist. What kind of a man is 'Aziz Salih Ahmad? Anger, deep and terrible, holds together the twisted life of the common rapist. One study of a group of American rapists has established that as many as 80 percent were abused children.[26] These men grew up with feelings of martyrdom, self-pity, and distrust, and characteristically lacked all compassion for other people.[27] Why do such men rape? They rape in a tragically misguided attempt to regain a measure of control over their broken lives. The Iraq-Iran War, the Lebanese civil war, the 1982 Hama massacre, and all forms of nationalist and religious fanaticism, have created many such twisted men in the Middle East.[28] In Khan Yunis, a town in the Gaza Strip, a man who had just recently discovered his Islamic roots locked up his four sisters, whom he was convinced were whores. He then set the room on fire while he sat outside reading passages from the Qur'an to himself.[29] It is probable this man was mentally unstable. But why did his deranged behavior find this particular way of expressing itself? That is the social and political question at stake here.

'Aziz Salih Ahmad, by contrast, is a civil servant; in all likelihood he is not deranged. He could be a mundane, banal, and completely unexceptional man, like his counterparts in other government offices. Dr. Haritos-Fatouras, who has spent fifteen years researching the minds of torturers who served in the Greek dictatorship of 1967–74, is firmly convinced that "good" torturers have to be fashioned and trained into their job by the workings of a whole state system. Obedience to authority, not sadistic impulses, are what those selecting potential torturers look out for.[30] In the organized rape of forty young Muslim women of the town of Tuzla in Bosnia-Herzegovina in the summer of 1992, Serbian forces told their victims they were acting under strict orders. One of the rapists admitted to his victim that he was "ashamed to be a Serb." Nonetheless, he and his comrades went about their mission, fortifying their resolve by taking special pills.[31] Likewise, could it be that the "official" Iraqi rapist 'Aziz Salih Ahmad is duly fortified by the state, only to go home after a tiring day's work to a wife and children, just like the rest of us? That is the most terrifying thought of all, far worse than imagining him to be deranged. In all probability 'Aziz Salih Ahmad is no different from hundreds of thousands of young Arab men all over the Arab world. According to Haritos-Fatouras, he could be anybody. For that matter, who says he is an Arab? A Kurdish friend of mine tells me the name is Kurdish.[32] I don't know for sure. Nonetheless, the deranged man in Khan Yunis who thought he was being a good Muslim even as he burned his four sisters alive shares something with 'Aziz Salih Ahmad, however ordinary a man he might be. Both are sick creations of modern Arab politics and society, who see themselves as avenging past humiliations even as they torture or rape or abuse Arab and Kurdish women.

Nor are the women themselves immune from the cycle of violence. According to Lea Tsemel, an Israeli lawyer who has dedicated her life to fighting for Palestinian rights, one of the ways that Palestinian women used to try to escape from the circle of oppression in the family was to commit some offense in the name of the Intifada, thereby gaining back the social acceptance that they had lost as a result of asserting their own personality. For instance, "There was the case of a woman who was forced to marry against her will. She became pregnant and ran away. The father brought her back by force to the house of her husband. Then she tried to throw a fire bottle on a bus, while inside the bus. This was a way to put an end to an intolerable situation. Maybe she wanted to die herself. This was a heroic way to escape from an oppressive family, a way which might bring the woman social immunity."[33]

In a recent Israeli documentary entitled *Behind the Veil of Occupation,* directed by David Benshitrit, a young Palestinian woman from the Shati' refugee camp who was arrested by Israeli Security for being an activist in the resistance gives an extraordinary account of what happened to her in prison. She was put in a cell "completely naked," she says, with a large man, who was told in Arabic by the security officers at the door of the cell that he was free to do with her whatever he wanted. The man is a fellow Palestinian whose role inside the prison is unspecified. She then starts to have an argument with this man in which she tells him: "If you want to take my virginity, go ahead. It will not take my honor, the honor of Palestine, with it." The film ends leaving open the question of whether or not the man placed in the cell finally assaulted her.

Apart from confirming the apparently widespread use of the Arab honor system by the Israeli security forces in forcing confessions from Arab women detainees (as previously mentioned), the story is important and doubly tragic because it also shows the association in the victim's mind of the "honor" of Palestine with her own virginity. The traditional system remains intact, except that the locus of honor has been shifted for the activist victim from her family, upward to the whole of Palestine and the struggle for self-determination. This "revolutionary" usage, in more or less refined language, was very common among Arab intellectuals who supported the Iraqi regime during the Gulf crisis. In one of those refreshing but rare exceptions that give hope, the Palestinian poet Salman Masalha vigorously denounced the idea of "lost Arab honor" during the Gulf crisis in an article with that title. The essence of his argument is that Arabs need to subordinate the idea of their honor to that of their freedom, a freedom "which means not just my own freedom, but, much more decisively, freedom of the other."[34]

When other Arab countries are opened up as Iraq has been and the Arab press becomes as open as its Israeli counterpart, or when Arab intellectuals are willing to come to terms with the complicated motives behind such practices and to denounce them instead of praising them as heroic acts of struggle against the "Zionist" enemy or imperialism, we just might find out that the worst cruelties of the modern Arab world were invented by the most "revolutionary," "progressive," "rejectionist," and "anti-imperialist" men and regimes. As Mai Ghoussoub, a Lebanese feminist, put it: "It has been all too easy to conflate the imperialist and the infidel, and to mobilize the masses to avenge the humiliations inflicted by Western civilization on Islamic identity. . . . In this setting of 'internal' conformism for purposes of 'external' confrontation, there is no better symbol of cultural continuity in the Islamic world than the veiling of the woman, refuge par excellence of traditional values. . . . The rigidity of the stature of women in the Arab family has been and continues to be the innermost asylum of Arabo-Muslim identity."[35]

Whenever that identity felt itself threatened, it turned womanhood into its last bastion. Womanhood thus becomes the site of the greatest cruelties and the greatest silence. That is what the avalanche of stories coming out of Iraq concerning women is all about. Even children get a generally better deal out of life than Arab women. There is a traditional (private) side to this cruelty and a modern (public) one. No doubt the two are connected. But they are also conceptually separate, and must be examined as such. Traditional cruelty toward women always originated in their powerlessness and diminished status in the culture. "When a girl is born in an Arab home, it is a disaster," says Tamam Faheela, a thirty-year-old Palestinian nurse from Acre. "The discrimination starts from the moment the girl baby is born. The message she is impregnated with is that her body is a sin. The prohibitions start in childhood. It is forbidden to play with the boys, forbidden to wear shorts or sit comfortably. She must be modest and quiet so as not to arouse anyone sexually. It is a terrible fear."[36] Women's bodies are deemed simultaneously the font from which all honor derives and a source of *fitna,* or public sedition. That is why Arab tradition feels so threatened by female independence. Women's powerlessness is therefore the original source of all cruelty directed at them.

Modern cruelty, on the other hand, begins when women like Amal and Sara assert themselves, as they are doing now all over the Arab world, by making choices which threaten traditional society:

they elope, refuse to obey their fathers, insist upon choosing their husbands, marry for love, join political organizations, do community work, and so on. A licensed breed of rapists like 'Aziz Salih Ahmad never existed in Iraq before the Ba'th created them. The rape of such active women by men like 'Aziz Salih Ahmad—a deformed and twisted but quintessentially *contemporary* Arab man—is an added new cruelty, which takes place on the grounds of an unwritten silent contract between traditional male-dominated Arab culture and "modern" public life, whose most cruel epitome is the Ba'thist state of Iraq.

Ever since General Zia al-Haq promulgated Pakistan's new Islamic penal code in 1979, known as the Hudood Ordinances, the same phenomenon of political rape could be observed rising in that country. It is estimated that 80 percent of Pakistani women taken into police custody on charges of *zina* (extramarital sex with consent) are sexually assaulted while in custody.[37] One wonders if the same phenomenon may not be happening in the Islamic Republic of Iran. In India, in 1986, a *Times of India* newspaper editorial noted a dramatic increase in custodial rape.[38] Moreover, in spite of official concern at the highest levels of the Indian government, women community organizers and human rights workers appeared to be the prime targets for rape.[39] If this is how bad the situation is in countries like India and Pakistan, which enjoy a relatively large measure of legal protection and political freedom, what on earth must the situation be like in the Arab world where only despotisms and archaic monarchies rule? Only when that terrible contract between tradition and modernity is broken inside Arab society itself, pioneered by brave Arab women like those who founded the *al-Fanar* organization, will this kind of cruelty start to diminish.[40]

Much of what is specific to cruelty in the modern Arab world is traceable to violence against women. This arises from the importance that the male-female divide has in the culture. My hypothesis is that growing cruelty toward Arab women has accompanied the modernization of the Arab world. If true, this is a very disturbing conclusion in its general implications for the future. I have argued the hypothesis in these pages on the basis of the limited evidence at my disposal, not proven it "beyond reasonable doubt." How many 'Aziz Salih Ahmads were there in the employ of the Iraqi government? Ten? One hundred? It hardly matters because 'Aziz Salih Ahmad is one of those extraordinary exceptions that sheds light on the norm. His kind of cruelty in the Arab world is the thin end of the wedge into every other kind.

Political Cruelty

THE transition from cruelty in the home to public cruelty in the street or by the state is always and everywhere effortless. I shall begin with the wantonness and scale of the cruelty inflicted by the modern state machineries of surveillance and repression that came into existence all over the Arab world during the 1970s and 1980s. Torture is practiced routinely and in ever more sophisticated ways in all of them. In Syria, for instance, a detention center in Damascus has been turned into a "research center" for the development of new torture techniques.[41] Amnesty International has recorded thirty-five different methods of torture carried out in specially equipped chambers. The main targets of torture in 1990–91 were the members of Islamic organizations, or opponents of Hafiz Assad's Gulf war policy. Wading through the morass of detail is always numbing where cruelty is concerned. A person runs the danger of turning bitter, of being sickened to the point of wanting to withdraw from the way the world is. Sometimes, however, a single extraordinary image can bring it all back into vivid focus.

That is what happened to me when I spoke to Sa'eed, a Syrian engineer in his early thirties, shortly after he had paid a visit to his hometown, Hama. In February 1982, Hama was turned into an object lesson in cruelty designed to leave an indelible impression on all Syrians. Anywhere between 10,000 and 40,000 people from the city were killed by the Syrian army over a two-week period, in the course of crushing what the Syrian government claimed was a revolt inspired by the Muslim Brotherhood organization. Very apprehensive and filled with foreboding, after having spent ten years abroad, Sa'eed returned to the city of his ancestry. The place had in the meantime shrunk to about half its former population of 250,000, with the bulk of those who fled ending up like him in the Gulf states, Saudi Arabia, Europe, or America. An archetypal image of how cruelty lives on, long after all the blood and gore has been covered up, was seared into my mind by what Sa'eed said.[42]

> Reality hit me when I went there. Before this visit, I was encased in a shell of fear. The kind of fear that says you don't open your mouth, you

don't take photos, you don't do anything, you don't even look at the destruction, because if you stand there staring, they might arrest you. People in Hama were basically paralyzed, in a state of shock. Their first priority was: "Don't do anything because anything could happen. We just want to get over it." It's like somebody getting cut and the first thing they worry about is how to stop the bleeding.

The reaction from the people of Damascus had been total denial. Some even went to the extent of saying that Hamawis [people from Hama] were the instigators. Several intellectuals in Damascus said they deserved it because they were the Muslim Brotherhood and if they got into power the whole country would go backwards. Sort of like Algeria [and the 1992 elections]. I think the Muslim Brotherhood label was used a lot by such people to justify what the government was doing. Even if there were Muslim Brotherhood members there, they couldn't have been organized to that extent. I know a lot of people in Hama who were killed during the massacre and they were not being organized by anyone. It is as if other Syrians were totally remote from what happened to the people of Hama. The fact that they hadn't experienced the pain themselves made them remote. This fear, or sense of denial, is an easy way out of things. They then don't have to feel responsible for what happened.

Hama had its own character. The people were notorious for being conservative, stubborn and proud. They were always very closely knit and took great pride in their city. We had neighborhoods which knew how to make fun of each other, but in a nice way. Basically there were two parts to the city: the Christian quarter with a very beautiful church, and the Muslim quarter which is where I came from.

When I returned to Syria after all those years, I traveled around taking slides. I felt that each slide was like a little piece of frozen memory which was liable to extinction. Each slide was an addition to my memories. So I traveled around everywhere. I spent some time in Damascus. I went further south. I visited some old cities in the north. And I spent one full day in Hama.

My first shock was the people. People more than buildings because you see I was expecting to see physical destruction. The people were living dead, like ghosts. These are the same people who were full of life, very happy, very emotional as I remembered them before 1982. One second they would get mad at you, and the next they would hug and kiss you. But now they were dragging themselves along on the streets. Children were not running anymore, their faces emotionless; their eyes had no depth—no soul to them.

The next shock was the buildings. I told you I had mixed feelings about going back to Hama. I had survived for ten years through memories, through holding onto certain images. As a matter of fact whenever I sit down to sketch anything, I sketch Hama itself: its waterwheels, the streets, those beautiful old buildings that I have such strong memories of. So I was afraid of going back. I was not sure that I would be in control of those feelings. At the same time I wanted to go. I felt I had to face up to it. So I went for one whole day.

Hama is in a valley. There is a hill, you used to have to go up the hill and down again into the city itself. But now the highway has been changed so that you go around the hill and don't see the city all at once spread out before you. The first thing that you see is a huge statue of Assad at the entrance to the city. I recall he was standing with his hands open, like in a welcoming gesture. I drove on past lots of new stone and white-colored buildings, all built after the massacre. The old parts of the town were not being taken care of like before. Cracks here and falling bricks there. People didn't identify with their town anymore. I think they just wanted to wipe out the old memories by building new buildings.

I drove into the Keylania quarter, which used to be the most beautiful part of the town with lots of trees. I realized at once that the river Orontes which runs through the town was not flowing anymore. The water wheels were not turning. They used to be green and now they are just a rotting yellow color standing in a dried-up river with stagnant patches of water in it. I thought to myself, What can I take a picture of? I took some anyway, but when I developed the film later everything turned out overexposed. I tell you, Hama has become a ghost city.

I arrived at the bridge which crosses over into Keylania. I stopped, got out of the car, and looked over across the river. There was nothing. I looked again because I was getting confused over my location and started seeing double images: one which was coming out from my inner eye, my memories, and the other of something else, new, that was out there. There was total conflict between the two sets of images. My first reaction was to turn my back on where Keylania ought to have been and shut my eyes. But I eventually turned back again and opened them. I was looking at a bald hill; this was Keylania. There used to be from the very spot where I was now standing a magnificent panorama of beautiful old, closely packed homes, with domes and underground passages and vaults which led to a Casbahlike complex of shops and houses. The people had run into this quarter when the army's attack on the city had started. Keylania was then surrounded by tanks and artillery and pounded into oblivion. Now they had tidied it all up into this earth mound, a bald hill out of which there rose a tower built over the bones of all those dead people which are still there in the foundations. The tower is a brand-new Meridien Hotel.

MOVING on in these landscapes of cruelty and silence, we come to Saudi Arabia, which stopped flogging, amputating, and beheading people in public for a ten-month period during the Gulf crisis. But that was not because of a newfound concern for human rights. The Saudis did not want hundreds of thousands of Americans to get too direct an exposure to their own interpretation of the Islamic tradition in punishment. After the Americans were gone, however, in an effort to make up for lost time, sixteen people were beheaded in "Chop Square" in Riadh over a three-week period in June 1991. "Even Saudi liberals, who would like greater democracy and more freedom for women," wrote Martin Amis of the Associated Press, "said they supported the harsh Islamic punishments."[43] These "liberals" said that such cruel forms of punishment were prescribed by the Qur'an and could not be disputed, no matter how openhearted one's views on other subjects. Nonetheless, they felt it necessary to speak on the subject only under conditions of anonymity. Saudi Arabia had after all expelled some 750,000 harmless law-abiding Yemeni nationals over a six-week period in September and October of 1990, for no other reason than that the Yemeni government had abstained in the vote taken in the Arab League to send troops to defend Saudi Arabia.[44] Many of these people had lived in Saudi Arabia all their lives. Yet their meager savings were confiscated at the border, and Amnesty International claims that large numbers were arrested and tortured by Saudi security forces.[45]

Kuwaitis, incidentally, did far worse to Palestinians. Before expelling the 300,000-strong Palestinian community from Kuwait—most of whom had never known Palestine or any other country—hundreds if not thousands were hunted down after liberation, arbitrarily arrested, and if they did not "disappear," it was because they had been gunned down in public or brutally tortured and killed.[46] It is as though the Kuwaitis were intent on doing to the Palestinians what the Iraqi regime had done to them.

The country the Yemeni workers expelled from Saudi Arabia were thrown into was no better than the one they had just been thrown out of. In the eyes of forward-looking intellectuals, South Yemen has been a model of "progressive" Marxist nationalism set in a peninsula of excruciating backwardness. More was done here to establish health care and education, and to provide women with the necessary conditions for work, than in any other Arab state. Nonetheless, on the morning of January 13, 1986, while tea was being served to the fifteen members of the ruling Politburo, a gangland-style massacre by President 'Ali Nasser of all his rivals began. One of the guards holding the leader's Samsonite attaché case whipped out his Skorpion machine pistol, and began raking the minister of defense up and down his back with bullets. Two weeks of street fighting ensued, which included roundups, mass killings, and thirteen thousand dead people whose bloated bodies were left lying in streets.

Explaining why the fighting was so fierce, a Southern Yemeni said: "They executed so many people, not just the politicians, that everybody felt, 'Either I must stand up and fight or I'm a dead man.' "[47] More frightening than the incident itself—which is but a drop in the ocean compared to what has been going on in the more "sophisticated" countries of the Fertile Crescent—is the fact that most Arabs have forgotten about it if they ever knew about it in the first place. Thirteen thousand people died in two weeks less than six years ago in a very "progressive" country, and everyone is in agreement that no great issues of principle were at stake. Was this about reverting to tribalism? But in tribal warfare there were rules of conduct regarding violence which held the ancient system of raiding for profit in some sort of balance. The point about what happened in places like Yemen in 1986, Lebanon during its civil war, and Iraq during the March 1991 intifada is that there were no longer *any* rules. Politics and society simply broke down completely. Anarchy ruled.

ACCOMPANYING the spread of institutionalized cruelty in countries like Iraq, Syria, and Saudi Arabia are qualitative changes in the forms of violence. The tendency invariably is toward more cruel forms, not less. Early on in the Lebanese civil war, for instance, the car bomb was discovered to be an effective weapon of mass terror in Beirut. But then it got upgraded into a device known as the double car bomb. This works by attracting a crowd through an initial, relatively mild explosion, which is then followed by the real thing.[48] Three thousand six hundred and forty-one car bombs exploded during the Lebanese civil war, killing 4,386 people and wounding 6,784.[49] The official casualty toll for all fifteen years of that war is 144,240 killed, 197,506 wounded, and 17,415 still missing. For some inexplicable reason these figures include the thousands of Lebanese Shi'ites and Palestinians who died fighting each other, but they do not include the thousands of Palestinians in refugee camps who died fighting one another. Nor do they include Palestinian civilians butchered in 1982 by Christian militiamen under the watchful eye of the Israeli army. More conservative estimates put the number of dead in fifteen years of the Lebanese civil war at 120,000 people, and the number of wounded at 300,000. In other words, 4.5 percent of Lebanon's 1975 population was killed and a further 11.5 percent physically scarred by the experience.[50]

One must not leave out all the unquantifiable psychological damage, or the cultural disintegration represented by the fact that between 800,000 and 900,000 of the most enterprising individuals have emigrated from what used to be, culturally speaking, the most exciting country of the Middle East. Where did these people go? To the West, of course, where else? You can see all the new Lebanese- and Palestinian-owned shops along Broadway and on the Upper West Side of New York City, none of which were there ten or fifteen years ago. These émigrés left a crucial piece of geography from the point of view of the history of Arab-West relations. The Lebanon they were forced to put behind them is today stagnating in every sense of the word.

No form of violence was left unexplored or untested on civilians during the Lebanese civil war. In fact, some new ones were added to the world's cluttered lexicon (the madcap suicide bomber, the anonymous urban sniper, the random kidnap-for-ransom, the "let's kill everyone in the family" way of settling an argument). The best accounts we have of "the events," as the Lebanese like to call them (a popular euphemism that goes one up on Ireland's "troubles" in reaffirming the inability of the Lebanese to acknowledge the catastrophe) are the work of first-class Western journalists like Robert Fisk, and of Lebanese women (to the best of my knowledge, a definitive account of the underlying cultural-political dynamic of that war has still not been written in Arabic, or by an Arab male). The cruelties of the civil war are indelibly captured in this haunting scene taken from the end of Jean Said's moving book, *Beirut Fragments: A War Memoir:*

> Several years ago, in one of the recurring attempts to restore law and order, an example was required to put fear into the hearts of ordinary criminals who were increasingly active in the anarchic conditions. . . . They took a man and tried and condemned him for murder. He was carried, screaming and kicking, to the gallows in the public garden. . . . There was no question of his guilt. He had confessed to the murder of his landlady and her son. He had, indeed, not only killed them, but mutilated them as well. . . . He was deranged, the police said. . . .
>
> He was carried, tied, and manacled, and the black hood was forced over his bucking head. It took five or six men to hold him down and place his neck in the noose. He screamed and kicked and struggled, and had to be held until the last twitch of his poor broken body . . . as the dawn light filtered through the palm trees in the garden.
>
> The pictures were all over the newspapers . . . this spectacle of justice being done. There was hardly a murmur of protest: He wasn't much worth protesting over. He was the very dregs of a humanity as mutilated as his victims' bodies. In the middle of a cruel war . . . one pitiful, deranged man had been chosen to expiate all the crimes, and had been dragged to an ignominious death in a public garden at dawn, and this was perceived as Justice.
>
> And it was a kind of justice, in a world without justice, that Justice should be thus represented.[51]

FROM Syria, to the Arabian peninsula, to Lebanon, and next to the Palestinian intifada, which began with such high hopes in December 1987. How many Palestinians were killed by other Palestinians during the intifada for being "collaborators"? Twenty-one months into the intifada, the Israeli Ministry of Defense released statistics claiming that of about 1,800 incidents involving Palestinians in the Occupied Territories between June and September 1989, almost 60 percent were attacks directed at fellow Palestinians, which resulted in seventy deaths. These were often very brutal killings, which included mutilating bodies and torturing victims before executing them, the kind of detail that provides grist to the mill of the Israeli propaganda machine. These seventy deaths over a four-month period should be compared, the Israelis claim, with twenty

Palestinians killed by other Palestinians over the preceding eighteen-month period.[52] In other words, as the political horizons of the intifada dimmed, it began eating itself up. This is an all-too-common phenomenon, which we have seen before in South Africa (the "necklacing" of so-called collaborators) and in Northern Ireland (shooting people's kneecaps, a tactic of the IRA).

Are these reports coming out of the Israeli Ministry of Defense true? And if so, why was inter-Palestinian violence not denounced by the hundreds of Palestinian intellectuals stationed all over the West just as vigorously as "necklacing" was denounced by Nelson Mandela and other black South African leaders?[53] In a long article on the subject, Joost Hiltermann, who has worked with the Palestinian human rights organization *al-Haq,* did not deny the facts published by Israel's Ministry of Defense. On the contrary, he updates the number killed from December 1987 to May 16, 1990, to 207 people.[54] However, he does not criticize these murders; instead, he chooses to justify them: "What has dropped out of the narrative [in the media coverage of these killings] is the Palestinian definition of collaborators as those who work for the enemy against their own people, and have therefore forfeited their right to membership in the Palestinian community." The author may not be aware of it, but this is a classic Ba'thist definition of "treason," which was used to deny hundreds of thousands of Iraqis of both their citizenship and their lives. Hiltermann accuses the Western news media of "extracting the issue of retribution from its historical and political context," and instead characterizing it "in the Orientalist syntax of 'intercommunal strife' among 'Arabs.' "[55] Hiltermann puts "intercommunal strife" and "Arabs" in quotation marks. Why? Does he think there is something "Orientalist" about these words? Does putting murder into a "historical" context justify it? What kind of human rights is this?

Significantly, there are new Palestinian voices coming out of the Occupied Territories that will no longer go along with such double standards practiced by "pro-Arab" intellectuals in the West. Dr. Haydar 'Abdel-Shafi, chief Palestinian negotiator in the Middle East process, denounced, in the East Jerusalem daily *al-Quds,* the very killings that Hiltermann had been justifying.[56] He wrote of the need for a reevaluation of the four-and-a-half-year-old Palestinian intifada, saying that it was necessary for Palestinians themselves to come to terms with the fact that it had become characterized by random violence. Bassam Eid, a Palestinian journalist working for the same East Jerusalem daily, decided to investigate the killing of a pregnant mother of four who was found hanging from a tree in a graveyard, accused by Palestinian youths of collaboration with the Israeli military authorities. His findings clearly showed that she had not been a collaborator and Eid took the extremely grave step of calling her murderer a "vile terrorist." The day his story appeared, he received an anonymous call demanding a correction. Eid refused. The caller wanted an explanation and Eid agreed to meet him personally, an act of extraordinary personal courage under the circumstances. Eventually Eid spent a total of five hours with fifty Palestinian youths who assailed him for what he had written and who praised the killer (whom they refused to identify) as "one of us."[57] Like the *al-Fanar* organization, and the emergence of a different, more humane leadership among Palestinians who live within the pre-1967 borders of Israel or in the Occupied Territories (evident in personalities like Hanan 'Ashrawi and Faisal al-Husaini), 'Abdel-Shafi's article and Bassam Eid's example are instances of the tentative emergence of a new self-critical Palestinian sensibility in politics.

FINALLY, to end with Iraq, which for me personally is where it all begins. Whole volumes have yet to be written on cruelty here, and on the silence of Arab and "anti-imperialist" intellectuals toward that cruelty. For the time being, I will note how uninteresting were the deaths of between 500,000 and 1 million Iraqis and Iranians in that war to the very same people who talked only about the hypocrisy of the West during the Gulf war. "The American government claims that it is a protector of human rights . . . but in its savage war in the Gulf it defended a minority of kings and princes while bringing about the killing and expulsion of millions of poor people. . . . Where are human rights in the cities of Basra, Kirkuk, Kerbala and others which have experienced total destruction," wrote the Washington-based Palestinian researcher Dr. Hatim al-Husaini, mourning "the Arab and Islamic peoples who have paid the greatest price of all for the American Gulf war."[58] The Iraqi poet Sa'di Yousuf, who was born in Basra, does not feel the same way.

> I say: The fifty thousands of Basrans were not killed by the
> Americans except through the beast who, in one minute, had

> strangled thousands in a Kurdish village named Halabja.
> Full circle came the great rupture.
> The Abbasid caliph's brother, Al-Muwaffaq, once led the
> army to Basra, to slaughter the rebellious black slaves, the
> Zanj, and to keep a street in the city named after him to this
> day. But the beast who aimed the artillery of his T72 tanks at
> the houses of the city, and at the chests of its children—the
> descendants of that rare color in the civilization of the Arabs
> —did not leave a single street that might, one day, be towered
> with an obelisk from which our martyr's names,
> the children of Basra, would stare at us.[59]

Basra was affected more than any other Iraqi city by the American air campaign, and yet its prize poet, Sa'di Yousuf, chose to write about what "the beast" of Halabja did to it. On the other hand, it was destroyed several times over during the Iraq-Iran War, about which Dr. Husaini had nothing to say. The "Great Satan" which in Husaini's lexicon is called "the Western monopoly companies" was not doing the destroying back then, and that was all that mattered to him. Husaini is angry at the policy of the United States toward the Middle East. Rightly so. But does he really care about human rights in Basra, not to mention Kerbala which, incidentally, was left virtually intact by the Allied forces throughout February 1991? It was left intact for Saddam Husain to destroy in March. The corpses of those Iraqis killed by the Iraqi Republican Guard in the wake of the March uprising had still not rotted away even as he was writing.

While Iraqi and Iranian dead were accumulating in eight years of fighting, some of the most famous names in Arabic letters, along with thousands of more mundane intellectuals, visited Baghdad, receiving prizes and attending poetry carnivals (famous names like Nizar Qabbani, Mahmoud Darwish, 'Abdel-Wahhab al-Bayati, Ghada al-Samman, Su'ad al-Sabah, Karees Madhi, Tawfeeq Yousuf 'Awwad). Many simply attended the cultural jamborees being financed by Iraq as tourists who were having their expenses paid. There was nothing objectionable about that. But others allowed themselves to be used to provide political support for the policies of the regime. Around the time that gold medallions were being handed out in Baghdad, thousands of Kurdish villages were being wiped out by the Iraqi government in a zone which starts some 70 miles from where the splendiferous literary festivals of Saddam Husain were held. Between 1986 and 1988, just under 2,000 villages were destroyed. In 1988 (as we have seen in Chapter 5), at least 100,000 noncombatant Kurds were routinely murdered in an organized government campaign called *"al-Anfal,"* which bears all the hallmarks of genocide, by the very regime that people like Dr. Husaini supported during the Gulf crisis because they thought it was going to help them liberate Palestine. Did these intellectuals know what was going on in Iraqi Kurdistan? If they didn't know all the gruesome details, they ought to have expected the worst.

In an article entitled "Mahmoud Darwish and the Dead-End Road," the Iraqi-Arab writer Amin al-'Issa (who escaped from Iraq during the massive anti-Communist campaign that immediately preceded the launching of all-out war against Iran) addressed his hero Darwish, the most famous name in Palestinian letters, with the anguish of one stabbed in the back:

> Terror has penetrated today into every little corner of the country, and if silence is no longer possible, then acquiescing to it is betrayal. Have the killers turned into patriots? How can you allow yourself to repeat the tunes of the Ba'thists regarding those patriots who were forced to leave their country? You know the facts well. This regime began its war against them before it began its war against Iran. Is fascism a matter of interpretation? Iraqi patriots carried their country in their hearts and in the glances of their eyes. With their blood they continue painting a brighter future for it.[60]

Why is the Iraqi writer al-'Issa so upset at the great Palestinian poet, Darwish? Because in 1986, a full five years before the Gulf war, Darwish was Saddam Husain's keynote speaker at a major conference of Arab writers held in Baghdad and attended by thousands of Arab literati. In his speech Darwish spoke of "the crime of silence" and the "treachery of silence." But he was not talking about the silence of Arab intellectuals toward what was being done to the people of Iraq—Kurds and Arabs alike—by their own regime. He was criticizing Iraqis like al-'Issa for remaining in exile during a time of war against the Persian enemy and for "pointing their daggers towards the liver of Iraq and to the soul of Palestine at one and the same time." At the end of his speech, given in front of an assembly of the high command of the Ba'th Party, the poet concluded by heaping praise and thanks upon the "moon of Baghdad [Saddam

Husain?]" and the great land of Iraq, "which guards the Eastern gate of Arab hope, and which has brought heroism down into the present from the realm of mythology."[61] This sad story acquires its full meaning in light of the realization that Mahmoud Darwish knew exactly what he was doing when he chose to eulogize Saddam Husain's regime. The same Darwish, twenty-three years earlier, during the first Ba'thi experience with state power in Iraq in 1963, wrote these bitter lines about what was then being done by the Ba'th to Iraqi Kurds:

> In the land of Kurdistan,
> Where terror and fire keep vigil,
> Where now you say,
> "Long live Arabism!"
> Pass by the land of Kurdistan.
> Pass by, Oh Arabism.[62]

10 ⁄ Defining Silence

HUMAN life was not always held in such low regard in the Arab world. Until the 1967 war, Arab sensitivity to human rights abuses was not worse than that of any other people in the developing world. That is not to imply that it was adequate, simply that it was in keeping with other parts of Asia or Latin America. Since 1975, and the beginning of the Lebanese civil war, the Arab world east of Egypt has become an exceptionally nasty place. The forerunners for Lebanon were the glorification of violence, armed struggle, and ideas of revolution, all born decades earlier in Iraq and Syria. The result is that Arab human rights sensibilities today lag behind other parts of the developing world like India and Latin America. Powerful despotisms and populist lawlessness are accompanied by an intelligentsia with no liberal or "rights-centered" critique of either. Meanwhile, wealth on an unprecedented scale has been flowing into the Middle East, even as Arabs themselves have been running away from the region in ever-growing numbers. They run away not because there are no economic opportunities, but because cruelty has everywhere become the rule.

This cruelty is a highly specific phenomenon of the 1970s and 1980s, with no general implications for "the Arabs" or "Islam." The critical moment in the change from a set of political and intellectual preoccupations typical of much of the Third World to the current extraordinary brutality of the Mashriq was, paradoxically, one of the most intellectually innovative interludes in modern Arab politics. I am thinking of the 1967–75 interregnum between the Six Day War and the outbreak of the Lebanese civil war.

For a few short years after 1967 a handful of intellectuals like Sadiq Jalal al-'Azm and Adonis, along with journals like *Mawaqif,* subjected everything around them to searching criticism. The titles of 'Azm's books alone tell the story: *A Critique of Religious Thought, Self-Criticism After the Defeat, A Critique of the Thought of the Palestinian Resistance.* The importance of these books is not that they were "correct" in some timeless sense. There is no such thing in culture. Nor did they "accept" Israeli or Western meddling in the affairs of the region; they were still "rejectionist" works, in the Arab political lexicon. Their importance lies in the fact that they looked inwardly, into Arab and Muslim political-cultural defects, without seeking outsiders to blame. A current was emerging in Arab thought that did not swing between triumphalism and breast-beating, the twin poles of contemporary Arab discourse. Many passages from these writings retain a striking relevance:

> Merely to use the expression, *al-nakba,* the catastrophe, with reference to the June [1967] war and its outcome carries to a certain degree an apologetic logic along with a running away from responsibility. For one upon whom a catastrophe has befallen cannot be held responsible for it. Or, if he was responsible, then that responsibility is very partial in relation to the enormity and magnitude of the event. For this reason we [Arabs] have become used to attributing catastrophes to fate, time and nature, in other words, to factors over which we have no control.[1]

The most important and long-lasting legacy of the 1967–75 period was the emergence of the Palestinian Resistance movement. During those crucially important (and still inadequately studied) years, Arab political discourse went through cycles of euphoria, renewal, and reaching out for new ideas, followed by hopelessness, despair, and the beginnings of retrenchment into tradition. But the 1967 war was a test, which, in the end, even the inwardly reflective, secular stance of al-'Azm and Adonis failed. Israel was still there, stronger than ever, still an unfathomable entity in Arab eyes. *Self-Criticism After the Defeat* did not go far enough; it remained trapped inside the limitations of underlying assumptions like: What is wrong with us such that *they* succeeded in defeating *us* so overwhelmingly? How can *we* change so that we can do to *them* what they did to us the next time around?

The ground was now left clear for radical ideologies of every description: Ba'thism, vulgar Marxism, Islamic political activism, Arab socialism, and militant local nationalisms (Palestinian, Lebanese, Greater Syrian, etc.). None of these ideologies—for all their important other differences—is capable of evolving a view of the world centered on a conception of human rights or the inviolability of the human person as the central principle of a modern vision of Arabness. Moreover, in spite of the great multiplicity of post-1967 voices, in the end it turned out everyone had only "anti-imperialism" and "anti-Zionism" in common. You could always get quite far in Arab politics by blaming everything on the West or on Israel. There used to be mitigating ideas in the post-independence Arab political experience which complicated this simplemindedness. It is important to remember that there were liberals and democrats in the Arab world in the 1940s and 1950s. Tragically, 1967 blew what was left of their ideas away. As cruelty spread, feeding on itself all through the 1980s, every kind of variety in Arab politics was choked off. Sickly thought-killing resentment was all that remained. It is as though we had regressed since al-'Azm wrote *Self-Criticism After the Defeat*.[2]

The anti-Western rhetoric of the Arab intelligentsia during the 1990–91 Gulf crisis is a fossilized restatement of the same evasion of responsibility that al-'Azm was criticizing in the wake of the 1967 war. The rhetoric had grown cynical and bitter with age, losing the only things it had going for it: hope in a new and better order, and the fervor of belief that one was capable of changing. A quarter of a century has passed since June 1967, and a new generation of much more sophisticated Arab writers and thinkers today edit journals and occupy chairs in famous universities throughout the Western world. On the surface they are so different from the Ahmad Shuqairis and Muhammad Hasanain Haikals of a previous generation. They argue about modernism and tradition, about democracy and Islam, about representations and counterrepresentations of East and West. They write in English, French, and Arabic, publishing simultaneously all over the world. But when it comes to cruelty in their own backyard, committed by "their own" people, the strange thing is they are more infantile than their predecessors. Ever-increasing denial of ever-growing cruelty has created a completely untenable gap between the way these intellectuals talk and the way their world really is. When Saddam Husain invaded Kuwait, all these people fell headlong into that gap—a gap which is in the final analysis one of their own making.

MY GENERATION, which includes many of the intellectuals I have been quoting in this book, was formed politically in the crucible of the 1967 war. Edward Said, for instance, although born in Jerusalem, became acutely conscious of his Palestinian-Arab identity after the defeat of Nasser's armies and the emergence of Palestinian hope. We all went through broadly similar kinds of experiences, whether we were living in Beirut, in London, or in New York. I started off in politics as a young activist supporter of the same Palestinian organization as both Said and al-'Azm. As I worked virtually full time in support of the Palestinian movement, I became aware of myself as an Arab for the very first time. Even as the Ba'th were legitimizing their power in Iraq on the grounds of the ideology of Pan-Arabism, I was being attracted to their old idea of an "Arab revolution." But it was not Michel 'Aflaq's formulation of the 1940s that was attracting me; it was a new version articulated by Palestinian intellectuals and fired by the example of the rising Palestinian movement. My sense of myself as an Iraqi, which was never something I had been anxious about, receded into the background. Nor was I changing in isolation from everyone else. Wherever you looked, identities were being re-imagined, wrapped up in bright new ideas which had come shooting out of the darkness like lightning bolts.

The onset of the Lebanese civil war tested this instant mental universe of young Arabs against reality, where it really counted. In this test, the halo of the Palestinian organizations lost its aura completely. In Lebanon these organizations exercised power and, consequently, stopped being just "resistance" organizations. It now became clear that they had become as corrupt and as nasty in their practices as all the others around them. Palestinian organizations ran their protection and taxation rackets just like everyone else. They looted and sniped and kidnapped and muscled in on ordinary Lebanese and on helpless Palestinian civilians. They invented ingenious new ways of killing and hurting other Arabs, just like everyone else. What difference was there, to the ordinary Lebanese, between a Palestinian "mafioso" and his counterpart from the Murabitoun or the Phalange? The very ground had been taken away from under their feet by gangs of thugs. What difference did it make whether the ones who were doing the taking belonged to this gang or that? In Lebanon, it all boiled down to killing over little bits of other people's turf. Everyone sold their soul to "their" little mafia for a piece of protection. So it happened that stagnation, hopelessness, cynicism, and despair took over where grand revealed truths once used to beckon.

With the onset of the Lebanese civil war, the intellectual renovation that had started in 1967 ground virtually to a complete halt. Nowhere was the stagnation as noticeable as among the Palestinian intelligentsia. Understandably, this intelligentsia was completely preoccupied with defining its newly discovered "Palestinianness" vis-à-vis an Israel that was itself being corrupted by the experience of occupation (of territories and people captured in 1967). Israeli politicians had in the meantime picked up a nasty trick or two from their Arab counterparts: deny that any such thing as a Palestinian existed, and call occupied territories "Judea and Samaria." In the Mashriq, all through the 1980s, everyone made the worst choices, Palestinian intellectuals included. Wedded as they were to the leadership of the very same organizations that had behaved so abominably in Lebanon, they did not even attempt to claim the moral high ground that was opening up for them all through the 1970s and 1980s. At a time when South Africa was producing a Nelson Mandela, Czechoslovakia a Václav Havel, and Poland a Lech Walesa, Palestinian intellectuals stuck to "their" Yasser Arafat. In such choices, the failings of an entire generation are summed up. Are such a gifted people as the Palestinians—with the largest, most cosmopolitan, and best-educated intelligentsia in the Arab world— unable to improve on Yasser Arafat as their leader in all these years of organized political activity?

The mere act of putting such questions down on paper frightens me. I have no answers. All I can do is point to the glaring collective failure of an intelligentsia to evolve a language of rights and democracy to supplement the language of nationalism. It is as though the two were perceived by Arabs to be theoretically as irreconcilable as they have practically proven to be nonexistent in the Mashriq. Words like "freedom," "democracy," "justice," "human dignity," and "human rights" have lost all meaning in the hands of the same intellectuals who go on and on about Western "hypocrisy." They no longer believe in the very things that they so vociferously denounce the West for not believing in.

Those lost old meanings need to be reconquered and reappropriated. But not in the form of "alternative" definitions, nor in the shape of simply stating that "we are all" against the nastiness of the Ba'th. These are just not good enough. All too often, the language of denial and rejection is an excuse for inaction; even worse, it can become a justification for cruelty. That is what it proved to be in that "crisis of exposure" which began on the day Saddam Husain invaded Kuwait. Only new ways of thinking, founded on the deepest kind of unreasoning revulsion against the cruelty and intolerance that has been perpetrated by Arabs against their fellow Arabs, or against Kurds and other national minorities of the Middle East, can carry conviction and hope to the longsuffering peoples of this part of the world. A new self-critical discourse is needed, one that is rooted in a thoroughgoing insistence upon the inviolable sanctity of human life and the subordination of everything else to this criterion. To the extent that Palestinian intellectuals rightly expect all Arabs to join hands in fighting against their oppression, they must start to understand that they have morally failed all Arabs in this respect more than anyone else.

At a time when large chunks of the rest of the world (Eastern Europe, Latin America, China, South Africa) were beginning to discover human rights/democracy and struggling with home-grown tyrannies and Stalinist bureaucracies, the best and most gifted Palestinians were writing learned books that rested on statements such as:

> . . . all academic knowledge about India and Egypt is somehow tinged and impressed with, violated by, the gross political fact [of imperialism] . . . *that is what I am saying* in this study of Orientalism. . . .

> It is therefore correct that every European, in what he could say about the Orient, was consequently a racist, an imperialist, and almost totally ethnocentric.[3]

Orientalism as an intellectual project influenced a whole generation of young Arab scholars, and it shaped the discipline of modern Middle East studies in the 1980s. The original book was never intended as a critique of contemporary Arab politics, yet it fed into a deeply rooted populist politics of resentment against the West. The distortions it analyzed came from the eighteenth and nineteenth centuries, but these were marshaled by young Arab and "pro-Arab" scholars into an intellectual-political agenda that was out of kilter with the real needs of Arabs who were living in a world characterized by rapidly escalating cruelty, not ever-increasing imperial domination. The trajectory from Said's *Orientalism* to his *Covering Islam:*

How the Media and the Experts Determine How We See the Rest of the World is premised on the morally wrong idea that the West is to be blamed in the here-and-now for its long nefarious history of association with the Middle East. Thus it unwittingly deflected from the real problems of the Middle East at the same time as it contributed more bitterness to the armory of young impressionable Arabs when there was already far too much of that around.[4]

As cruelty grew, there was less and less objective reason for that bitterness by comparison with any other period in the long and thorny history of the Arabs and the West. There is an aging, declining West out there, not a crusading, imperial one. American foreign policy had been decisively defeated in Vietnam, routed by Khomeini in Iran, and seemed to have been made by buffoons in the Lebanon (when a lone suicide bomber dispatched more than two hundred Marines in one blow). Israel had been forced out of Egypt. Iran was "lost" to the West for a whole historical period. Arab financial power was without precedent. In these conditions, the most interesting intellectual question to reflect upon was no longer how omniscient and omnipotent American power was in the world, but how *ineffectual* it had become when it did do something (which was rare) in the face of the intractability of the problems of the politically independent countries of Middle East. The classic instance of this, ironically, is the Gulf war—a war financed by Arab states to resolve an inter-Arab conflict. If, from an Iraqi point of view, this war was left unfinished, that was not for lack of American initiative. Iraq was destroyed and Saddam Husain remained in power not because the West wanted him to stay on, but because the Allied forces were terrified of inheriting the responsibilities that necessarily accompanied finishing the job.

The argument implicit in the agenda of Arab and "pro-Arab" intellectuals based in the West was that *only the West* could do something about a regional problem like the Arab-Israeli conflict because that problem was "historically" of its own making. "We Palestinians are not responsible," the thinking goes, "because we are always and only history's victims." The Israeli invasion of southern Lebanon and the murder of some twenty thousand innocent Lebanese and Palestinian civilians by indiscriminate shelling was seen by the Palestinian-Arab and "pro-Arab" intelligentsia as *caused by* American policies in the first place, just like Saddam Husain's invasion of Kuwait. Not until after the Gulf war could you talk to Israelis or fight for your rights inside Israel; you had to address yourself constantly to Americans. The very notion of waging a fight for "rights" addressed directly to Israeli public opinion (where the evidence suggests it might have found support) was deemed compromising. Why is it that Nelson Mandela can talk to Pik Botha, but a Palestinian intellectual cannot talk to his Israeli counterparts, the best of whom would fall over themselves at the opportunity? Instead of directly grasping at this central core of the problem, Palestinian intellectuals during the 1980s indulged in one doomed war after the other directed at the "biases" of the U.S. government or American media networks. In fact, the one Palestinian who espoused a radical redirection of political priorities lived inside Israel-Palestine, and was well and truly ostracized by those of his peers who did not.[5]

Like the poem of Nizar Qabbani, "Abu Jahl Buys Fleet Street," *Orientalism* operates through a populist ethos of Arab prejudice built up over a very long time; it does nothing to reshape Arab stereotypes of the West, even though its author is probably the most perfectly situated Arab to do so. The book makes Arabs feel contented with the way they are, instead of making them rethink fundamental assumptions which so clearly haven't worked. Maybe that was never the book's original intention. But books have a life of their own which is independent of the intentions of those who write them. I am addressing myself to the young Arab readers of *Orientalism,* who remain to this day its biggest fans. They desperately need to unlearn ideas such as that "every European" in what he or she has to say about their world is or was a "racist." The very adoption of the book in academic institutions of learning in the West—at a time when empires had long since collapsed (Britain and France) or were in a state of terminal decline (the United States)—suggests the irrelevance of its guiding thesis to modern Western scholarship on the Middle East. The ironical fact is that the book was given the attention it received in the "almost totally ethnocentric" West largely because its author was a Palestinian, just as *Republic of Fear* was taken seriously only after Saddam Husain had invaded Kuwait, and because its author was an Iraqi. It is time we faced up to such home truths.

Orientalism was intended as a cultural-political project modeled after Noam Chomsky's work on the connections between the Vietnam War and notions of objective scholarship.[6] Ironically, the only reference in it to the modern Middle East is in the opening sentence of the Introduction: "On a visit to Beirut during the terrible civil war of 1975–1976 a French journalist wrote regretfully of the gutted downtown area that 'it had once seemed to belong to . . . the Orient of Chateaubriand and Nerval.' He was right about the place of course, especially so far as a European was concerned. The Orient was almost a European invention. . . . "[7] From then on, the real world of Arabs disappears in a book that shaped how young Arabs thought about that world. The final irony, however, is that most Lebanese do in fact miss seeing the Orient of Chateaubriand and Nerval, at least as much as the French journalist who was being quoted.

Four years before Adonis gave up in despair and disgust on the "gutted downtown areas" and "civil wars" of Beirut to go and live in Paris, he wrote these lines:

> The killing has changed the city's shape—This rock
> Is bone
> This smoke people breathing.[8]

Lines like these ring with truth. As does Adonis's remark in 1986 that "Something in the Arab world has died."[9] Walid Khalidi said something similar when he wrote about "the absence since the mid-seventies of a moral center of gravity in the Arab world."[10] Refracting these comments through the prism of the Gulf war and the landscape of cruelty sketched out in the previous chapter, we need to go much further today. There has been an implosion, a moral collapse in the Arab world—not just a drift or a loss of centeredness. The consequences of this collapse are going to remain with us for generations to come, no matter what happens in Iraq or Lebanon, and irrespective of whether or not the holy grail of an Arab-Israeli settlement is finally grasped.

"Da' illi beena, minna wa feena" (The disease that is in us, is from us and inside us), sang 'Aziz 'Ali, the Tom Lehrer of Iraqi pop singers in the 1940s and 1950s. 'Aziz 'Ali is the kind of Arab intellectual who no longer holds sway inside or outside the Mashriq today. If by a fluke someone like him does emerge, he is marginalized and not treated very seriously by the intellectuals themselves. Throughout this book I have tried to draw attention to such rare exceptions to the thundering herd approach to politics so characteristic of Arab intellectual life in recent years. The writer Emile Habibi, the news-

paper editor Lutfi Mash'our, and the poet Salman Masalha, for in-stance, are among the tiny handful of Palestinians I have already mentioned who voiced *in public* positions on the Gulf crisis which Iraqis opposed to the regime in Baghdad can respect, regardless of whether or not one agrees with every nuance. As it so happens, all three are Israeli-Arabs in whose personal experience honesty and reality meet in a way that they don't with most of those Arab intel-lectuals that I have been criticizing. I emphasize the "public" nature of the positions that these Palestinian exceptions took, because in private many Palestinians took excellent positions. But they felt in-timidated and ruled by that other ever so destructive dictum of Arab cultural nationalism: never wash your dirty laundry in public, and especially not where a westerner can see you.

In 1939, on Baghdad Radio, 'Aziz 'Ali had this to say about our Arab malady:

Ya nas musiba musibatna,	(Oh people, how calamitous are our calamities)
Nihchi, tufdhahna qathiyatna,	(We speak up, only to get exposed by our affairs)
Niskut, tuktulna 'illatna,	(We shut up, only to be killed off by our maladies)
Bas wayn nwali wujhatna,	(Where are we to hide our faces)
Dalina ya diktoor.	(Show us the way, oh doctor)[11]

'Aziz 'Ali's formal education did not go beyond secondary school, yet he was fully literate in Arabic, Kurdish, English, Russian, and German. He was a civil servant and, in his spare time—as a pop singer and songwriter—he was a scathingly biting critic of govern-ment and the backwardness of his fellow Arabs. He made good fun out of superstition, often holding the individual Iraqi responsible for his condition. Yet he spent years in jail for his activities against the British-influenced pre-1958 monarchy. 'Aziz 'Ali had counterparts like 'Ali al-Wardi in the field of academic sociology, and Kamil al-Chadirji, Iraq's great democratic politician. In private, 'Aziz 'Ali used to tell this joke of why he "retired" and stopped writing songs: "In the old days they would stick me in jail for a few days, slap me around a bit, and then give me five dinars and tell me to go home. Afterwards, they slapped me around a bit more, kept me in a bit longer, and stopped giving me the five dinars. But still they let me go home. These people today, you know, they don't seem to know how to take a joke."

The inability to handle criticism or to take a joke stems from an unwillingness to look into oneself, to be a little bit ashamed before the awesome mess that the Arab world finds itself in. The machinery of state, wherever it is located in the world, lacks a sense of humor; we all grow up expecting that. The specific malaise of the Arab world in our time, however—by contrast with 'Aziz 'Ali's time—lies principally in its intelligentsia, not in its regimes. "When we consider the responsibility of intellectuals," Chomsky wrote in a classic 1966 essay, "our basic concern must be their role in the creation and analysis of ideology."[12] Responsibility grows, he rightly argued, by virtue of the very privileges that intellectuals enjoy: the leisure, the facilities, the training, and the access to information. Yet, often, those very Arab intellectuals who studied in the West turn out to be the worst offenders; they are, therefore, the most responsible. They churn out intelligent nationalist ideology inimical to a genuine concern for the human rights of others far better than the Saddam Husains of this world. Everyone expects propaganda to issue from Ba'thi spokespersons. But the intellectuals I have been quoting—by virtue of the positions that they occupy—are deemed to be rational and responsible interpreters of the Arab world both to Westerners and to the Arabs themselves, who unfortunately will still look up to an Egyptian teaching at the University of London more than they will to someone teaching at 'Ain Shams University in Cairo.

Paradoxically, the most dissembling of modern Arab and "pro-Arab" writers are also those in a position both to know the truth about their world and to influence a younger generation of Arabs to adopt a healthier way of looking at it. Why did things turn out this way? The phenomenon does not arise from individual inadequacies of these intellectuals—or worse still, from some inscrutable quality of the Arab mind (a racist way of looking at things). Nor does it arise from deep within the historical wellsprings of the Arab or Islamic tradition. It arises from the inner logic of the governing ideological paradigm—cultural nationalism—which includes in its totalizing embrace Marxists, nationalists, Islamicists, and even some who have ostensibly made of human rights a vocation.

It arises from the particular way that identity has been forged by people who have suddenly come to the realization that they desperately need to have one. In that search, they have felt it necessary to put aside everything which is complex and individual, and therefore richly laced with life, in favor of the colorless language of "victim-hood," which can only provide a false sense of collective reassur-ance. Under the circumstances of diaspora, exile, fragmentation, and atomization, the double tragedy is that this genre of nationalist mythmaking is not even a language culled from the actual experi-ence of living in a community. That is the secret of its stridency and intolerance. Those who are the most incessantly preoccupied with who they are are often the most confused on the question. They have good reason to be in the case of the countries of the Mashriq after 1967. Lebanese, Iraqis, Palestinians, and others all saw their notions of identity either break down completely or get reassembled hastily out of bits and pieces plucked from here and there. The outcome is a shriveled-up view of everything that one has in com-mon with the rest of the world.

In Iraq, the Ba'th established the most stable polity in the modern history of the country. They did so on the basis of an intransigent insistence on the artificiality of Iraq's own borders, thus undoing the decades that had gone into the formation of a new awareness of something called Iraq. The consequences of this can be seen in the political movements that have arisen as a reaction to Ba'thi despo-tism; they are either "Kurdish" or "Shi'ite," or "Muslim" or "Arab." None of these labels are going to solve the problems of Iraqis, Arabs, or Kurds, Shi'ites or Sunnis. Who is going to speak for *all* Iraqis after Saddam Husain is gone? Do we have to start each time from scratch?

In Lebanon, the generation that rallied in their hundreds of thou-sands to the Palestinian cause after 1967 did so by rejecting the idea of Lebanon that had been created by their fathers and grandfathers. Then those who had known the golden years of the 1960s emi-grated, because life became unbearable. Today, Lebanon is popu-lated by a generation that does not even have a memory of a united country. The youth grew up in a divided city run by gangs of thugs. They have experienced fifteen years of civil war and have been forced by circumstances and the exigencies of survival to think of themselves as "Muslims," "Christians," "Maronites," or "Shi'ites"—less and less as Lebanese. The young generation, which should today be entering the workforce, has therefore been cut off twice from the one that originally founded the country as one entity. There is no continuity between the generations, an indispensable prerequisite for the formation of a sense of identity.

The irony is that the post-1967 "anti-imperialist" discourse which failed so abysmally in 1990–91 itself arose as a reaction to the preceding Arab nationalist rhetoric in politics and culture (that of Muhammad Hasanin Haikal, Jamal 'Abdel-Nasser, and Ahmad Shuqairi). With the benefit of hindsight, the two today look frighteningly similar. What happened to my generation, the generation of Arab intellectuals brought up on the *naksa,* the Arab defeat in the Six Day War? Maybe we didn't take the critique of the Arab world far enough between 1967 and 1975. Or maybe the problem was that we went a little bit too far, breaking more taboos than society could bear; I really don't know. The fact that we spoke so many different languages at the time—Marxism, Nasserism, Ba'thism, Palestinian nationalism, as well as Arabic, English, and French—didn't matter, as things turned out. For, like intersecting circles, these ways of describing the world kept on meeting on the same bit of common ground. When the boundaries of the circles began to rot and crumble away, all that remained was "we are Arabs" or "we are Muslims," and "there is Israel," and "this is the Palestinian cause." That's about it, and, if one stops to think about it, it is not much. Certainly, it is not enough. In the end, these turned out not to be different languages at all; they turned out to be a poverty of ideas, a vacuum of language. In the end, Lebanon was lost, Iraq waded through eight years of carnage, Kuwait was invaded, sacked, and annexed, and the Palestinian organizations supported the arch tyrant of modern Arab politics to the hilt. The most cosmopolitan of Arab intellects became, for a moment, the intellectual mainstay of precisely the kind of regime they claim to reject. The intellectuals who generate the ideas—not that unsavory collection of tyrannies, monarchies, and autocracies that wield the guns—are therefore the ones whom the next generation of young Arabs must hold accountable for the moral collapse of their world.

SILENCE is not born out of fear; it is born out of the poverty of thought. Our vacuum turned out to be a spiritual vacuum, but one that could never be filled by religious belief alone. Silence is what Salman Rushdie, in *Midnight's Children,* called the "hole in my heart." The politics of silence is that bizarre state of affairs that allowed a Lebanese leftist (Trabulsi), a Jordanian newspaper editor (Khouri), a Tunisian historian (Djaïet), a Syrian literary critic (Abu Deeb), and a Palestinian human rights activist (Kuttab), all to meet under one umbrella in defense of "the rights" of a tyrant that not one of them would ever dream of living under. The fact that such a meeting place not only exists but has become so vast, holding in one terrifying embrace so many different and well-educated Arabs, is the principal obstacle to the emergence of a less violent or more tolerant politics in this part of the world.

The Gulf crisis revealed Arab silence to mean first and foremost a loss of empathy with the other, a retreat from the public realm into the comforting but suffocating embrace of smaller and smaller units of identity like tribe, religion, sect, and family allegiances. Silence is a synonym for the death of compassion in the Arab world; it is the politics of not washing your dirty laundry in public while gruesome cruelties and whole worlds of morbidity unfold all around you. Silence is choosing, ostrichlike, not to know what Arab is doing to fellow Arab, all in the name of a knee-jerk anti-westernism which has turned into a disease. Health "is infinite and expansive in mode," reaching out "to be filled with the fullness of the world," writes Oliver Sacks. If so, then Arab silence is like a sickness, "finite and reductive in mode."[13] Silence is the language of a narcissistic inwardness, endeavoring always to reduce the world to reflections of oneself. Silence in the Arab world is silence over cruelty.

In the end, the contention of this book is very simple: the politics of keeping silent over escalating cruelties inside the Arab world, cruelties inflicted for the most part by one Arab on another, is principally responsible for an Arab moral collapse which has today reached epidemic proportions. Leaders like Saddam Husain thrive on the silence of the Arab intelligentsia toward cruelty. They are also *created by that silence.* Intellectuals created the discourse of silence. Silence is a way of talking, of writing; above all, it is a way of thinking that obfuscates and covers up for the cruelty that should today be a central preoccupation of those people who make talking, writing, and thinking their business. Breaking with this silence is the moral obligation of every Arab, in particular the "intellectuals" among us. Nothing else is of comparable importance—not even the "struggle against Israel." For all of us who love and identify with this corner of the world, it isn't easy or nice to say such things. That doesn't make them any the less true.

I did not attempt to grapple with the very complicated question of how we got into such a terrible state. That kind of a project needs distance and takes years. Meanwhile, the dead are still accumulating in the Arab world; the stench of their bodies is overwhelming; I no longer have the stomach for "scholarship" on such questions. This book was never about scholarship in the first place. Maybe it isn't possible for the proper distance to be obtained by anyone today. It is enough to know that things didn't have to turn out this way, and it is enough to know that we still hold in our own hands the key to reversing silence. The first step out of the morass is the ruthless and radical one of uprooting, from deep within our own sensibilities, the intellectual and moral authority that blaming someone else still carries today among us Arabs. If I have bent that stick as far as I know how in the opposite direction, it is because I firmly believe that only upon its demise can a healthy, multi-dimensional, and pluralist meaning to Arabness be born.

The second step is to "put cruelty first." This wonderfully simple aphorism has the great quality of being deeply anti-ideological in its disregard for the idea of sin, whether in its religious form (transgression of divine rules), or in its modern form of "historical blame." The two forms are interlinked and go to the roots of the modern Arab malaise. One can only inflict physical pain on a living creature, an individual being weaker than oneself. As Judith Shklar points out, when this activity is judged as "the supreme evil,"

> it is judged so in and of itself, and not because it signifies a denial of God or any other higher norm. It is a judgement made from within the world in which cruelty occurs as part of our normal private life and our daily public practices. By putting it unconditionally first, and with nothing above us to excuse or to forgive acts of cruelty, one closes off any appeal to any order other than that of actuality. To hate cruelty with utmost intensity is perfectly compatible with . . . religiosity [and all ideologies], but to put it first . . . is a purely human verdict upon human conduct.[14]

Change for the better will only come in the Arab world when a new generation of young Arabs become incensed at the unacceptably cruel state of their world; they need to become so revolted as to lose every vestige of shame, speaking out without caring who is listening, or to what nefarious use some people will inevitably put their words. It is a terrible and an exciting time to be a young Arab. Pan-Arabism as a political creed is dead for now, but "Arabness" is in greater flux than at any time since the end of the first centuries of Islam. If the principal task of this book was not scholarship, then it was the simpler one of identifying a malaise and trying to find new ways of describing it. History and scholarship can wait for better days, which I am certain will come. But when?

Notes

Introduction

1. Samir al-Khalil, "Drowning in the Gulf of Lies," *The Independent*, August 25, 1990, p. 28.
2. For an obituary of Faraq Fouda, see Adel Darwish *The Independent*, June 10, 1992.
3. The book is entitled *Al-Madaris al-Yahudiyya wa al-Iraniyya fi al-'Iraq* (Baghdad, 1984); in English, *Jewish and Iranian Schools in Iraq*. Fadhil al-Barak's book is discussed in the first chapter of *Republic of Fear*.
4. As reported by Iraqis from Baghdad, and later circulated in October 1992 by a reputable London journal that does not permit references to be made to itself.
5. A pirated Iranian edition of surprisingly high quality has even appeared under the title *Jumboori Wahshat,* trans. Ahmad Tadayun (Tehran; Tarhno, 1992). I am indebted to my friend Houshang Chehabi for obtaining a copy for me and translating extracts. In the translator's introduction, the reader is cautioned that whereas I have a lot of interesting things to say about Iraq, due to the sophistication of the average Iranian reader it has not been felt necessary to comment on my obvious ignorance on all matters to do with the Islamic Republic of Iran. So, for instance, wherever I draw a parallel between the cruelty of Saddam and the cruelty of Khomeini during the Iraq-Iran War, although my idea is translated faithfully and in full, the word "Imam" is inserted in square brackets before every appearance of Khomeini's name. A sad comment on the state of publishing in the Arab world is that the care taken in the translation of this Iranian edition, and the quality of the book's production, far exceed those of all three Arabic editions.
6. See Habibi's article in the London Arabic daily, *Al-Ouds al-Arabi,* March 20, 1991.
7. Samir al-Khalil, *The New York Times,* March 27, 1991.
8. See Chapter 6, Remembering Cruelty, note 1.
9. The film was a BBC *Everyman* documentary, directed by Gwynne Roberts, which aired for the first time in the United Kingdom on January 12, 1991. It was shown in the United States on "Frontline" in March 31, 1991, under the title *Saddam's Killing Fields*.
10. *Al-Ouds al-Arabi,* part one, "How Did the Book *'Republic of Fear'* Become a Legend?" was published on February 5, 1992. The quote marks around the title of the book are in the original. Part two, "Out of Despair Comes Mental Pandemonium," was pub-

lished on February 6, 1991, and its title, Hadidi acknowledges, is borrowed from a critique of my political positions in March 1991 written by Alexander Cockburn in the *New Statesman and Society*.

11. See Said's interview with Barbara Harlow entitled "The Intellectuals and the War," *MERIP Reports*, no. 171 (July–August 1991), pp. 16 and 18.

12. I am indebted to Latif Rashid for first passing on to me these copies of Iraqi secret police files dealing with the *Anfal* campaign. Barham Saleh gave me other documents which also proved very important to establishing what had happened to Taimour. Shoresh Rasoul translated Taimour's words for me from the Kurdish. It so happened that Shoresh was the driving force behind the preparation of a list of 7,558 Kurds who were believed to have disappeared during the 1988 *Anfal* campaign. He did the work clandestinely inside Iraq at great personal risk. Before Saddam Husain invaded Kuwait, the list was spirited out and passed on to Amnesty International. Shoresh eventually settled in London and told his story in person to Amnesty. His account must have sounded fantastic, even by the cruel standards of the Ba'th, because he left a January 1991 meeting with Amnesty feeling that no one believed him. It is as though the enormity of the crime militated against those who make it their business to know such things believing that it could have happened. By an extraordinary coincidence Shawrish remembered that the name of Taimour 'Abd Allah, born in 1978 in the village of Qulatcho, was on that original list of disappeared persons. Moreover, I had an official register of "eliminated villages" and Qulatcho was on that register. The boy was a victim of something much bigger than even he was aware. Miraculously, he had slipped through the net of the 1988 Ba'thi campaign of mass murder code-named *"Anfal."*

13. Primo Levi, *The Drowned and the Saved* (New York: Vintage Books, 1989), p. 12.

1. Khalil

1. In Arabic: *ya layta ummi lam talidni li'ara 'adhab hadha al-zaman*.
2. Khalil was interviewed by me in London in the summer of 1991.
3. *The Sunday Telegraph*, March 3, 1991, p. 17.
4. The story of the uprising in Iraq, or *intifada*, as it is known among Iraqis, which began in the southern city of Basra on the day that the Gulf war ended, February 28, 1991, is told in Chapter 2. I will refer to this uprising henceforth as the intifada.
5. The quotations come from three outstanding reports: the dossier "Highway to Hell," published by the *New Statesman and Society*, June 21, 1991; Julie Flint, "The Real Face of War," *The Observer*, March 3, 1991; and Michael Kelly, "Carnage on a Forgotten Road," *The Guardian*, April 11, 1991.
6. Kelly, "Carnage on a Forgotten Road."
7. Robert Fisk, "Horror, Destruction and Shame Along Saddam's Road to Ruin," *The Independent*, March 2, 1991.
8. Quoted in an article entitled "Burnt Bodies Litter Highway . . . ", *The Guardian*, March 2, 1991.
9. The phrase *"al-'Iraqiyya al-majida"* was first coined during the Iraq-Iran War to exalt the childbearing Iraqi woman who willingly gives up her children to die for Iraq. An Iraqi cynic, observing the flood of financially desperate unmarried Iraqi women going to Amman, Jordan, in the wake of the Gulf war to make some money in prostitution, retorted: *"al-'Iraqiyya al-majida saret ib-dinar lil-Urduni"* (The glorious Iraqi woman goes for a dinar to the Jordanian). "The Iraqi government eventually dealt with the problem by passing a law banning all women from traveling outside the country alone.

During the Gulf crisis, "lost Arab honor" was deemed to be at stake by many Arabs and was used as a justification for supporting the Iraqi regime. Like Saddam Husain's *"al-'Iraqiyya al-majida,"* it derives from the traditional honor and shame system, whose cruel workings as far as Arab women are concerned are discussed in Chapter 9, Landscapes of Cruelty and Silence.

10. Some of the best reporting on this was done by Robert Fisk, who certainly cannot be considered "soft" on the Allied forces. "In the immediate days that followed the liberation of Kuwait, many journalists, including myself, were struck by the very wicked and evil behavior of the Iraqi military hierarchy in Kuwait itself. The looting was on an extraordinary scale. The killings and the torture were real. They had shot children in front of their parents. They had used drills to crucify people. This sounds like typical war propaganda. I didn't believe it all until I got there and saw bodies in the mortuary with drill holes through their hands and legs, and through their eyes." Quoted in *New Statesman and Society,* June 21, 1991, p. 27. See also his article, "Something Evil Has Visited Kuwait City," *The Independent,* February 28, 1991.

11. Yitzhak Ben-Ner, *Ta'to'on* (Tel Aviv: Tsad HaTefer, 1989), pp. 80–81. I am grateful to Emmanuel and Aliza Farjoun and Lamees Khouri for tracking down this novel and translating extracts.

12. Moncef Marzouki's article ran during the war under the title "L'Occident fourvoye," *Le Monde,* February 6, 1991.

13. From Kevin Dwyer's excellent book on the human rights debate in the Middle East, *Arab Voices* (Berkeley: University of California Press, 1991), pp. 166–67.

14. 'Abdel-Rahman Munif, "Ay 'Aalam Sayakoun? Al-Muthaqafoun al-'Arab wa al-Nidham al-Duwali al-Jadeed" (Which World Shall It Be? Arab Intellectuals and the New World Order) published in *'Awdat al-Isti'mar: Min al-Ghazw al-Thaqafi ila Harb al-Khaleej (The Return of Colonialism: From Cultural Invasion to the Gulf War),* by various authors (London: Riadh El-Rayyes Books, 1991), p. 40.

15. Nor was this prejudice restricted to Arabs. Some anti-war activists in the United States indulged in it. See, for instance, the disgraceful cartoon in *Z Magazine* (June 1991), p. 17. A grotesquely fat, evil-looking Kuwaiti leaning against his Mercedes-Benz with oil wells in the background (and a veiled wife and daughter inside the car), next to a scrawny, dumb-looking Kurd, dressed in tatters, with his wife and daughter bringing up the rear. Whatever the author's intention, the cartoon is insulting to Kuwaiti and Kurd alike.

16. I have used the translation by the Iraqi writer Khalid Kishtainy in his book, *Arab Political Humour* (London: Quartet Books, 1985), p. 59.

17. Hazim Saghiyeh, a writer and friend, commented on this argument by observing that a crucial intermediary sociological link is needed in analyzing the phenomenon, one that locates the groundswell of "hatred" expressed by so many Arabs toward Kuwaitis during the Gulf crisis—and *hija'*—in the historical-sociological phenomenon of *'asabiyya,* or tribal solidarity, which gets greatly intensified in moments of crisis or weakness. *'Asabiyya* was brilliantly integrated into an analysis of the rise and fall of Arab empires centuries ago by the great Arab historian ibn Khaldun. In a personal letter, Saghiyeh added these observations to the argument developed in this chapter: *"Hija'* originally, before al-Mutannabi and even before Islam, was born with the intensification of al-*'asabiyyat* (competing tribal solidarities). It tended to gather momentum with the weakening of 'unity' created by Islam (the poets Firazdaq and al-Akhtal in the Umayyad period are a case in point). Moreover, I think, the *'asabiyya* expressed toward Kuwaitis was a combined phenomenon, coming as it did in a time of vast wealth differentials created by oil money. It is, therefore, the *'asabiyya* of some groups toward others in the shadow of a culture that places inordinate emphasis on origin and

tribe. So what if one were to add jealousy to this explosive combination? *Hija'* in the Arab world today sips from these murky waters."

18. For this assessment of Qabbani, see Salma Khadra Jayyusi, *Trends and Movements in Modern Arab Poetry* (Leiden: E.J. Brill, 1977), vol. 2, p. 664.

19. Nizar Qabbani, *'Abu Jahl Yashtari Fleet Street,* from the Arabic literary monthly published in London, *an-Naqid,* no. 10 (April 1989), p. 10.

20. From the poem, *"Limadha Aktubu?"* (Why Do I Write?) from Nizar Qabbani, *Qasa'id Maghdhoub 'Alayha* (al-Quds; Wakalat Abu 'Arafah, 1987), p. 14.

21. For another instance of this, see Nizar Qabbani's article in *al-Hayat,* July 11, 1992. On this occasion the poet wants to point out how scorned all Arabs have become in the "New World Order." But the image that pops into his mind to describe Western racism is more interesting than anything he has to say on the subject itself. "The last thing that the Arabs expected, after spending themselves silly during the Gulf war, was to become toward the end of their life Sri Lankans. Maybe they dreamed of becoming Americans, or Britons, or to be French or Swedes or Danes . . . or at the lowest end of the scale, Cypriots." Instead, the First World insists on treating them as Sri Lankans who are, in the poet's view, the lowest of the low because they "sweep streets," "clean plates," and waste their time "raising children." Halfway through the article, the poet comments on how "the smell of a person has become a reason for deporting him, or imprisoning him, or trying him," in a country like France, for instance. Qabbani is being sarcastic, of course, but he goes on to press home the point, by observing that whereas "half of all Europeans sleep with their dogs in one room, and eat with them off of the same plate," the Islamic religion is founded on the idea of the "cleanliness of the body and of the spirit." A nice rebuttal, steeped in low-key irony, is provided by the Saudi writer Ghazi Gossaibi in *al-Hayat,* July 13, 1992.

22. See, for example, the superb article by the black American scholar Henry Louis Gates, "Black Demagogues and Pseudo-Scholars," *The New York Times,* July 20, 1992.

23. Nizar Qabbani, *an-Naqid,* no. 33 (March 1991), pp. 6–7. Qabbani's use of *al-watan* is a tricky notion to render in English. In classical usage, *watan* carried the sense of the English word "home," and was associated with family memories and place of birth. In the nineteenth century it went on to take the meaning of the French *patrie,* or the German Fatherland, or country very broadly defined. The allusion always is to a place to which one is attached in a very sentimental way and not for religious reasons. That place may be Egypt or Syria but it can also be the whole Arab homeland, *al-watan al-'Arabi.* From the context it is clear that Qabbani is referring to this latter "homeland," which I have chosen to render as "nation" throughout this book. (The same usage is applied to those writers and analysts whose views on the Gulf crisis are discussed in Part Two.)

24. Nizar Qabbani, *an-Naqid,* no. 35 (May 1991), pp. 4–7.

25. *Alef-Ba,* no. 814, June 2, 1984. In the same issue, equally obsequious letters are printed from Su'ad al-Sabah, a member of the Kuwaiti ruling family and an advocate of "progressive" left-wing nationalist causes; 'Abdel-Wahhab al-Bayati, an Iraqi poet and another household name in Arabic letters, like Qabbani; and Roger Garaudy, the French leftist writer and Middle East specialist.

26. I interviewed Hanan (pseudonym) in the United States in October 1992.

2. Abu Haydar

1. Khalil gave me this police officer's diary but for obvious reasons I do not feel at liberty to give the man's name. It is interesting to note that he records being told by the

minister of interior, on August 2, 1990, in a special meeting of all the police officers being dispatched to Kuwait, that "you are going to go to the Governorate of Kuwait, which is a governorate like all the other governorates of Iraq." In other words, the Ba'thist intention all along was to annex Kuwait, and this was not a hasty on-the-spot move by Saddam taken after the crisis had developed. On the Ba'thi policy to transfer the Marsh Arabs into government settlements modeled after those into which hundreds of thousands of Kurds were moved throughout the 1980s, see Patrick Cockburn's article, "Tide Turns Against the Marsh Arabs of Iraq," *The Independent,* May 7, 1992.

2. Quoted in John Simpson, *From the House of War* (London: Arrow Books, 1991), p. 357.
3. Habeeb (pseudonym) was interviewed in the summer of 1991 in Europe by an assistant of mine who prefers not to be identified. The interview was written up from notes after the meeting.
4. Taken from chronology of the uprising prepared by the al-Khoei Foundation, based in London. According to this chronology, the events in Sa'ad Square started at 4:30 A.M. on February 28 (i.e., before the cease-fire formally came into effect). According to other accounts, it started in the early hours of the morning of March 1, 1991.
5. Quoted in Patrick Bishop's report in the *Daily Telegraph,* March 2, 1991.
6. I am indebted to Zuhair Hamadi for having introduced me to Kadhum al-Raysan, whom I interviewed in Vienna on June 18, 1992.
7. The deportation of Shi'ite Iraqis into Iran began in 1971. The first to be deported seem to have been people who still held Iranian passports, even though their fathers and forefathers were born in Iraq and had lived and worked there under the aegis of the Ottoman Empire. Tens of thousands of people (possibly up to 80,000), including in particular large numbers of Fayli Kurds (Shi'i Kurds), were deported in this first wave. The following neighborhoods in Baghdad were targeted: Qanbar 'Ali, al-Qishla, Bab al-Shaikh, Gahwat Shakr, al-Khulani, Aqd al-Akrad. Then the campaign slowed down to a trickle, and might even have stopped altogether. On April 6, 1980, the deportations suddenly started up again, but on a much more massive scale. Five to six thousand people daily were being trucked to the Iranian border and dumped there. Now all Iraqi passport holders who were classified in their nationality papers as being "of Iranian origin" were included. Hundreds of thousands of Iraqis who fit this classification had been deported in this way by the early 1980s. (Figures range from 200,000 to 400,000.) The Iranian government used to issue statistics but stopped after a while. The official Iranian count is said to have reached 165,000.) Many thousands of others fled before the authorities could round them up. It is estimated that 2 million Iraqis have Iraqi nationality papers with the designation "of Iranian origin." I am indebted to Dhia Kashi for providing me with details of the deportation campaign, which remains unfortunately very poorly studied.
8. The *Anfal* is the codename for a 1988 Iraqi government campaign targeting the rural areas of Iraqi Kurdistan. The full story of the campaign is told in Chapter 5, Taimour.
9. Fatma (pseudonym) was interviewed by me in London in the summer of 1991.
10. My meetings with Abu Haydar (pseudonym) were made possible by Ghanim Jewad, who tirelessly hunted down sources of information on the intifada for me. For Ghanim Jewad's trust in me, without which this chapter could not have been written, I am deeply grateful. Abu Haydar was interviewed in London in the summer of 1991.
11. Other common chants, which I have been able to cull from various sources, were *"Allahu Akbar"* (God is Great) and *"Ya Husain!"* (Oh Husain! Husain is the son of 'Ali, and a Shi'i symbol of martyrdom)." Slogans written on the walls included: *la za'im illa Hakim* (There is no leader except Hakim—i.e., Muhammad Baqir al-Hakim,

the leader of the Supreme Islamic Assembly based in Iran); *Thawra Islamiyya; la shar-qiyya, wa la gharbiyya* (Islamic revolution, neither East, nor West). During the intifada, Saddam was often called *"taghiya,"* a Qur'anic word for "despot" or "tyrant" made popular by Khomeini during the Iranian revolution in relation to the Shah. It carries the idea of despotism rooted in overweening pride and disregard for God's law.

12. The Iraqi government shifted army and party units out of their quarters and into school buildings because the Allied forces were not targeting them. That is why this school in Najaf was the scene of such a fierce battle. The story and quote is from five hours of taped conversation between a group of Najafi rebels who are carefully reconstructing the events of the intifada in an Iranian city. The conversation was recorded very shortly after the events with the purpose of documenting what happened. I was given three tapes, all unquestionably authentic, by a Shi'ite Iraqi who prefers not to be identified. Henceforth this source will be referred to as the Iran Tapes.

13. The quote is from the Iran Tapes.

14. For more on 'Aziz 'Ali, see Chapter 10, Defining Silence.

15. From the Iran Tapes. Ridha al-Fahham is another popular poet who was captured and tried in Najaf, although I do not know his fate.

16. See his excellent article, "Reports Lift Veil on Shi'ite Uprising in Iraq," *The Wall Street Journal,* December 31, 1991.

17. The expression used by the rebels is *y'alino 'an tawbatihi,* which carries explicitly the idea of a return to God. This is what one of the rebels said: "An instruction was issued by the *sayyid* . . . that the one who gives up his arms and declares repentance should not be killed. And so the people started to come. As God is my witness, one of these people was a lieutenant who was brought by his wife and child. She also brought one of his cousins who was also a Ba'thi. He handed in his arms and then signed an agreement [*sajjala ta'hud*] which said that he was now with the revolution. Of course, such a man remained under a guaranty [*yabqa tahta al-kafala*] from others"—from the Iran Tapes. This is of course the Ba'thist vocabulary of crime and punishment, down to the finest little detail, like imposing on other members of the family a guaranty of good behavior of the victim in question. I cannot confirm whether or not the *sayyid* named by the rebel actually issued such instructions.

18. These stories and others are in the Iran Tapes.

19. Fatma (pseudonym)—see note 9.

20. From the Iran Tapes.

21. This *sayyid* from Najaf, interviewed by me in the summer of 1991, went on to play a leading role in the intifada. I constructed this monologue from my notes written immediately following our meeting.

22. Spitting on dead bodies, or on people about to be killed, is widely practiced by the Baghdad regime starting with the seventeen Iraqis strung up in public in January 1969—among them thirteen Iraqi Jews—and ending with the latest episode involving forty-two merchants killed on July 25, 1992. The Ba'th forced people to walk by and spit on them. The interview with Hameed (pseudonym) was conducted in Iraq in the summer of 1991 by Tony Horwitz, author of *Baghdad Without A Map,* to whom I am deeply indebted for allowing me use of his notes. Hameed says that "some people produced a small newspaper, about three to four pages, that contained the latest news from the intifada and inspiring passages from the Qur'an." I have heard about this newspaper from more than one source but have unfortunately been unable to obtain a copy.

23. The date on the *fatwa* is 18th of Sha'ban, 1411 of the Muslim calendar, which corresponds to March 5, 1991.

24. The Iran Tapes.

25. The untranslatable colloquial Iraqi expression used by Habeeb for what Saddam sounded like on the radio is *maakil qazoq*.
26. The reference is to Muhammad Baqir al-Hakim, the Tehran-based political leader of the Supreme Assembly of the Islamic Revolution in Iraq (also referred to as the Supreme Islamic Assembly). The Assembly, which played an important role during the intifada, was formed in 1982 and has always been based in Tehran. The organization describes the Islamic Republic of Iran as "the foundation (and the prime mover) of the World Islamic Revolution." For a while it acted as an umbrella organization, grouping many different Islamic groups, but in recent years it has become associated solely with the person of al-Hakim. See Joyce N. Wiley, *The Islamic Movement of Iraqi Shi'as* (London: Lynne Rienner Publishers, 1992), p. 60.
27. The interview with Hameed (pseudonym) was conducted in the summer of 1991 by Tony Horwitz. See note 22.
28. I conducted this interview in London in August 1991 with a high-ranking commander in the Kurdistan Front who prefers to remain anonymous.
29. Hadi (pseudonym), a young Kurdish militant from Khabat, participated in the incident and described what happened to Nabaz Kamal, who interviewed him for this book in September 1991 in Vienna. For more on these housing complexes, known as *mujama-'at sakaniyya,* see Chapter 5, Taimour.
30. The memorandum must have been prepared about the time that the leaflets threatening chemical attacks on cities in the south were dropped from helicopters. Many refugees from the south claim to have seen such leaflets, and have described a virtually identical document to the one captured in Dohuk for the cities of Najaf, Kerbala, Basra, 'Amara, and Nasiriyya. Item 7 of what seems to have been standard instructions issued to security offices all over Iraq refers to a "technical department," which "should give support by using techniques under instructions and supervision of the department officer and deputy officer, [name]." This euphemism refers to the use of chemical weapons on civilian demonstrators. All quotes are from a copy of the document in my possession.
31. Sarwar was interviewed for this book by Nabaz Kamal in Austria, September 1991.
32. In an extraordinary propaganda move, the People's Mujahideen sent a crude video to members of the Congress of the United States which alleges that Iranian Revolutionary Guards, disguised as Kurds, had attacked northern Iraqi cities, including Sulaimaniyya. The Mujahideen claim in the video that they defeated this Iranian attack and show the corpses of the very Iraqi Kurds they killed in defense of the regime of Saddam Husain. On this, and on the origins of the intifada in northern Iraq, see the report entitled *Civil War in Iraq,* by Peter Galbraith, written for the Committee on Foreign Relations, United States Senate, May 1991.
33. The interview with the Kurdish adviser was conducted in northern Iraq by Neil Conan of National Public Radio in May 1991. I am very grateful to him for providing me with a full transcript of his tapes. In order to protect the identity of the interviewee, I have removed all names.
34. Hana' (pseudonym) is a young Arab woman from Baghdad who lived with her Kurdish husband in Sulaimaniyya. She was interviewed for this book by Nabaz Kamal in the summer of 1991 in a camp for Iraqi refugees in Europe. In Baghdad, Saddam's portraits were defiled at night. A resident of al-A'dhamiyya told me she woke up one morning to find a small hole in the place where Saddam's mouth used to be and a carefully placed shoe sticking out of it (a visual way of saying: "Saddam *maakil qazoq'*").
35. I have taken Mas'oud Barazani's words from the transcript of the film *A Dream Betrayed,* directed by Gwynne Roberts and first shown on British television, Channel 4, in April 1991.

36. This incident was witnessed by Hadi (pseudonym), a young Kurdish militant, from the government-built "housing complex" at Khabat near Raniyah. Hadi was interviewed for this book by Nabaz Kamal in September 1991 in Vienna. A similar story was told to Geraldine Brooks during her visit to northern Iraq. " 'I saw them catch one of the torturers,' my dinner host whispered later. 'They had him in the street, a mob around him. When I pushed my way through, they were just about to cut off his ear.' My host had begged them to stop. The man with the knife looked up at him furious. 'Did you have a son disappear? No? Then you have nothing to say here.' " *The Wall Street Journal,* April 20, 1992.

37. This letter was written by Basil (pseudonym), a resident of Baghdad, to his brother Omar (pseudonym), who is currently in the United States. Basil had fled with his family to Sulaimaniyya to hide from the Allied bombing. There he witnessed the scenes described in the letter, before fleeing yet again, only this time from retribution by the Republican Guard. This letter was sent from Iran, where Basil and his family ended up for a short while. I have seen a videotape filmed in the Central Security Headquarters Building shortly after the events described by Basil. The bodies described by Basil had still not been removed and the Kurdish colleague who showed me the film claimed that a count had been made of the number of people killed during the forty-eight-hour battle which exceeded nine hundred people. Following the harrowing events in Sulaimaniyya, Basil went through another kind of hell trying to get his family safely out of reach of the wrath of the Republican Guard. The story of Omar, Basil's brother, forms the next chapter of this book.

38. See Simpson, *From the House of War,* p. 359. My interviews with ordinary citizens of Basra confirm Simpson's account.

39. In other words, apostasy in political Islam is exactly the same idea as treason in the Ba'thist mind-set. Treason, called *khiyana,* however, is against Arabism, not Islam, and absolute loyalty is owed to the Ba'th Party, the only rightful agent for the promotion of Arabism. In his writings of the 1940s, this connection with Islam was explicitly made by Michel 'Aflaq, all of which emphasizes the dire need for a new liberal thinking among Muslim thinkers in order to "reinterpret" or revise such cruel doctrines.

40. Um Husain was interviewed in London by me shortly after her arrival from Iraq. She spent the period of the war in Nasiriyya and Basra, and had an extremely negative view of the intifada in spite of the fact that she had suffered at the hands of the Republican Guard after they regained control.

41. Taped interview with Um Husain of Basra by KM.

42. Saman was interviewed for this book by Nabaz Kamal in the summer of 1991 in a camp for Iraqi refugees in Europe.

43. Nine museums in all were ransacked and burned in the north and south of Iraq during the intifada. Some four thousand objects are estimated to be missing. A part of the Iraq Museum's collection based in Baghdad had been moved to Kirkuk to make way for the splendid collection of Islamic objects stolen by the Iraqi government from Kuwait during the occupation. Ironically, whereas these got returned to their rightful owners (in October 1991), the Iraq Museum collection stored in Kirkuk was thoroughly looted during the Kurdish uprising. By accident, some objects were later discovered in their crates by the side of the road. The rest—figurines, cylinder seals, statues, inscribed tablets from Sumerian, Babylonian, Assyrian, and medieval Islamic times—have started to show up on the international art market, offered by Iranian dealers to collectors and museums in London and New York. See the article by the Iraqi archaelogist Selma al-Radi, in *The Nation,* May 11, 1992, pp. 624–25.

44. *Husainiyyas* are typically modest Shi'i places for prayer and meeting, often founded by wealthy private benefactors.

45. Taped interview with Fatma (pseudonym) from Samawa by KM.

46. The hidden Imam, like all Imams, is a descendant of the Prophet. For more on this Shi'i messianic idea, see Bernard Lewis's article, "The Shi'a," *New York Review of Books*, August 15, 1985.

47. My source for this extraordinary story is one of the Najafi rebels in the Iran Tapes.

48. I am referring to the semi-official biography entitled *Saddam Husain: The Man, the Cause and the Future* (London: Third World Centre, 1981), written by the Lebanese journalist, author, and expert on the Middle East, Fouad Matar.

49. The two-page handwritten undated testimony was dictated inside Iran, probably to a clerk working for the Supreme Islamic Assembly. I am indebted to Haydar Hamoodi for collecting this and other material from Iran for the purposes of this book.

50. See Liz Thurgood's report in *The Guardian*, July 23, 1991.

51. See Julie Flint, *The Observer*, March 10, 1991, p. 14, and the report in *The Independent* on Sunday, March 17, 1991, p. 16. See also BBC Summary of World Broadcasts, April 4, 1991, The Middle East.

52. The names of Najafi families killed by Iraqi ballistic missile attacks are taken from *Mass Killings During and After the March 1991 Uprising in Iraq* (London: Organisation of Human Rights in Iraq, 1991), p. 10 (referred to henceforth as *Mass Killings*). The quote from Saddam Husain is from a speech on April 2, 1990, about Iraq's new secret weapons. See also my Chapter 8, New Nationalist Myths.

53. Voice of Rebellious Iraq 1957 GMT 26 March 1991, reported by the BBC. See Summary of World Broadcasts, March 28, 1991, The Middle East.

54. *Endless Torment: The 1991 Uprising in Iraq and Its Aftermath* (New York: Middle East Watch, 1992), p. 52 (referred to henceforth as *Endless Torment*).

55. At the insistence of the Iraqi government, the Ayatollah was buried before dawn the following day with only six people permitted to attend the funeral. No displays of public mourning were allowed. Two obituaries that summarize the Ayatollah's life and works are Michael Wood's in *Dialogue*, a newsletter published by the Public Affairs Committee for Shia Muslims (September 1992), p. 8, and Chibli Mallat's in *The Independent*, August 10, 1992.

56. *Mass Killings*, p. 5.

57. Bob Drogin, "Iraq: Saddam Hussein 'Offers Soldiers Bounty for Killing Babies'— Shi'ites Face Retribution," *The Guardian*, March 29, 1991.

58. *Endless Torment*, p. 51. See also *Ahdath Adhar 1991 Kama Yarwiha Shuhoud 'Ayan (The Events of March 1991, As Seen by Eyewitnesses)*, produced by the Documentation Centre for Human Rights in Iraq, Tehran, 1991, p. 17 (henceforth referred to as *Ahdath Adhar*). This excellent document, produced under difficult conditions by Iraqis in Iran, is based on large numbers of eyewitness reports taken shortly after the uprising. I am indebted to Haydar Hamoodi for obtaining it.

59. *Mass Killings*, p. 11.

60. See *Ahdath Adhar*, p. 15, for what happened along the Hindiyya road. The same document gives instances of families being strafed fleeing the Governorate of 'Amara, pp. 21–22. See also *Endless Torment*, p. 51; Drogin, "Iraq: Saddam Hussein"; and *Mass Killings*, pp. 16 and 18.

61. Drogin, "Iraq: Saddam Hussein."

62. Um Husain was interviewed in London by KM shortly after her arrival from Iraq.

63. See *Endless Torment*, p. 51; Julie Flint, "Iraq: Saddam Declares War on Shias as More Kurds Come Down from Mountains," *The Observer*, April 28, 1991; and *Mass Killings*, p. 6. The names of twelve hospitals in southern Iraq attacked in the way described in this paragraph are given in *Ahdath Adhar*, pp. 67–68.

64. *Mass Killings*, p. 7.

65. See *Mass Killings*, pp. 9, 6, 11. For the concrete-block method of execution, see *Ahdath Adhar*, p. 42. See also pp. 16–17 for reports of burying people alive, running them down with armored vehicles, and throwing them off helicopters and planes.

66. Nora Boustani, "A Trail of Death in Iraq," *The Washington Post*, March 26, 1991.

67. *Mass Killings*, pp. 21 and 23.

68. *Ahdath Adhar*, p. 37.

69. Reported by Reuters on April 8, 1991, and the chronology of the revolt prepared by the al-Khori Foundation, based in London.

70. *Endless Torment*, p. 52.

71. Simpson, *From the House of War*, p. 6.

72. See *The Guardian*, Saturday, March 9, 1991, p. 7; Kim Fletcher's report in the *Sunday Telegraph*, March 24, 1991, p. 19; and Flint, *The Observer*, April 28, 1991.

73. A partial list of clerics killed or disappeared from the Bahr al-'Uloum family includes the *Saadeh* (plural of *Sayyid*) 'Ala' al-Din; 'Ali al-Sayyid; Mustafa al-Sayyid; Amin al-Sayyid; Muhammad Husain al-Sayyid 'Musa; Muhammad Safa Musa; Muhammad Ibrahim al-Shirazi and Sayyid Baqir (his son); 'Ammar al-Sayyid 'Aboud; and Sayyid Ja'far Bahr al-'Uloum. See *Mass Killings*, p. 23; *Ahdath Adhar*, pp. 51–56; and Flint, *The Observer*, April 28, 1991.

74. The most comprehensive account of physical destruction is in *Ahdath Athar:* pp. 44–46 identify ten mosques and *husainiyyas,* and eleven seminaries and libraries, destroyed in Najaf. Kerbala suffered far worse damage, with 117 *husainiyyas,* mosques, religious schools, and important religious sites completely destroyed by the regime, all of which are identified by name and location on pp. 57–63. Lists of destroyed mosques have also been made available to me through the Organisation of Human Rights in Iraq based in London. See also Liz Thurgood, "Iraq: President Saddam Initiates Drive on Shi'ite Holy Cities," *The Guardian*, July 23, 1991; and Kathy Evans on the leveling of the graveyards in Kerbala, "Nooses Dangle in the Breeze at Shia Shrine," *The Observer*, May 26, 1991.

75. *Mass Killings*, p. 19.

76. Liz Thurgood reported that government plans in the summer of 1991 were to demolish the ancient walls of the Shrine of 'Ali and replace it with chain-link fencing. A new fence would make the shrines easier for the government to control and harder to turn into fortresses—*The Guardian*, July 23, 1991.

77. The quote is from Ayatollah Khoei's grandson and spokesman, as given in Patrick Cockburn's article, "Islamic Treasures Stolen," *The Independent*, January 10, 1992, p. 12. See also Patrick Cockburn, "Iraq's Ancient Treasures Are the Hidden Casualties of War," *The Independent*, July 15, 1991, p. 12.

78. The series began on April 3, 1991. I have been able to obtain copies of the first four articles from which these quotes were taken.

79. See, for instance, Shibley Telhami's Op-Ed piece entitled "Stay Out of Iraq's Civil War," *The New York Times*, April 5, 1991, p. 25. Telhami is a professor of international relations and Middle East politics at Cornell University and he acted as an adviser to the U.S. Mission to the United Nations during the Gulf crisis. His position was by his own admission not based on principle. In an interview with Ted Koppel on ABC News Nightline, on April 2, 1991, Professor Telhami said: "I'm not a defender of the U.S. administration. I, for example, think that the U.S. could and should right now stop what's taking place in Kuwait against third-party nationals." In other words, U.S. intervention against Kuwaitis to help Palestinians is acceptable and necessary. But intervention to stop tens of thousands of civilian Iraqis from being slaughtered by Saddam Husain is not.

80. Extracts are from a full transcript of his talk delivered in London on October 20, 1991,

during a conference organized by *Rabitat Ahl al-Bayt,* an international Islamic organization.

3. Omar

1. There are sixteen divisions in Iraqi Military Intelligence *(al-Istikhbarat al-'Askariyya),* each responsible for a different kind of crime. The sixteenth division is the most secret and powerful among them, with powers that allow it to arrest virtually anyone at the highest levels of government. This appears to have been the division responsible for Omar's arrest.
2. Extracts appear in Chapter 2, Abu Haydar.
3. Omar is a quintessentially Sunni name, just as Abu Haydar is a Shi'i one. The implications of this choice of names on my part are as deliberate as the stories about Omar and Abu Haydar are true.
4. In pre-1958 Iraq, the "River Force" were army patrol boats which were stationed in the marshes region of southern Iraq in order to keep the Shi'ite tribes under control. They represented the closest thing that landlocked Iraq had to a navy.
5. During the Gulf war, units of the Iraqi army known as *al-Quwwat al-Khasa,* the special forces, controlled death squads whose job it was to terrorize Iraqi soldiers at the front so that they would not run away. The members of these squads, according to a captured Iraqi soldier, had to be from the Ba'th Party and "change their names so that they can never be identified. If a man is Muhammad they call him Husain. They have no emotion. They show no mercy." Reported in Robert Fisk's article, "Caught Between Bombs and the Death Squads," *The Independent,* March 1, 1991.
6. Madinat al-Thawra, known officially as Madinat Saddam, is a poor Shi'ite suburb of Baghdad formed during the 1950s and 1960s through rural-urban migrations from the south. It is famous for its political militancy; some 1 million people live there today.
7. *'Arak* is the Iraqi national alcoholic drink, made from dates. Omar had finished a bottle of it with his friend earlier in the evening.
8. In Arabic: *Inta mudhad lil-hizb wa mudhad lil-thawra.*
9. The expression used virtually all the time is: *Inta haqid,* which means being full of hate and spite.
10. In colloquial Arabic: *ib salati, ib muqadesati, illa akhalikum tihchoon.*
11. The colloquial Iraqi expression for the standard weapon wielded by all guards in Omar's prison is *sawndah* or *kaybul.* The weapon is a black plastic-coated electrical cable, about one inch in diameter and three feet long. Colloquial prison slang has developed the expression, *"mat jawah al-kaybulat"* (He died under the cables).

4. Mustafa

1. The attack on Guptapa took place during an Iraqi 1988 campaign which lasted for about eight months, code-named *"al-Anfal."* It was designed to eliminate rural life in vast tracts of land designated by the government as "prohibited for security reasons." Its workings, as far as I was able to determine them from my visit to northern Iraq in November 1991, form the subject of Chapter 5. The *Anfal* campaign took place over four stages, each targeting a different area. Guptapa was attacked during the "second *Anfal* campaign," as it was officially referred to by the Iraqi government.
2. The interview is given in full at the end of Chapter 5.
3. The Naqshabandi "way," as it is called in Arabic, originated in Tadjikistan in Central

Asia, and spread to India, Iran, and Kurdistan. But it received a boost in Iraqi Kurdistan through the proselytizing activities of Mawlana Khalid al-Naqshabandi, who was born in the town of Qara Dagh in 1779, just miles south of the Iraqi city of Sulaimaniyya.

4. See Chapter 2, for the role of one of these Kurdish advisers during the March 1991 intifada.

5. I visited the forts of Dohuk and Qoratu in November 1991. A description of Fort Qoratu appears at the beginning of Chapter 5.

6. This interview was conducted in northern Iraq. See Chapter 2, note 33.

5. Taimour

1. See the Introduction, and note 12, p. 330, for how I found out about Taimour.

2. In Arabic, the lyric reads: *"ahwak, wa atmana law ansak, wa ansa roohi wayak."* Followed by *"al-tadreeb, al-tadreeb, thumma al-tadreeb."*

3. The Kurds are an ancient Indo-European and largely Sunni Muslim people, who today number more than 20 million. They are spread mostly across a mountainous arc encompassing southeastern Turkey, northwestern Iran, northeastern Syria, and Azerbaijan, as well as northeastern Iraq. The Kurds' language and traditions are distinct from those of the Turks, Persians, and Arabs who control the countries within whose borders the Kurds largely reside; in Iraq, they comprise the largest non-Arab minority group, making up about 15–20 percent of the population.

4. With the break-up of the Ottoman Empire at the end of World War I, the Kurds were promised, in the Treaty of Sèvres (1920), a "scheme of local autonomy" in northern Iraq. But that clause of the treaty was never ratified and was completely eliminated from the Treaty of Lausanne, which established the boundaries of modern Turkey, Syria, and Iraq in 1923. By then, armed Iraqi Kurdish tribes were already in open rebellion in the north against the British mandate government of King Faisal I in Baghdad. With its eye on the region's rich agricultural lands and two large oil fields, Baghdad was not about to let northern Iraq assert its Kurdish identity. In December 1925, the British government convinced the League of Nations to rule against Kurdish statehood. Baghdad, on its own, had already said as much; in 1924, the mandate government brutally put down the Kurdish rebellion.

5. Related by Shoresh Rasoul in a conversation with Ayad Rahim in London, February 1992.

6. The first Ba'thi use of the word *"Anfal"* that I have been able to trace is in Iraqi military communiqués beginning at the end of February 1988, which refer to something called the "first *Anfal* operation." The "second *Anfal* operation" was led by someone called Major-General Ayad Khalil Zaki, according to communiqué no. 3109, broadcast on Baghdad Radio on April 2, 1988. It talked of "traitors" in the Qara Dagh area who were being firmly dealt with. These military campaigns go on being trumpeted about on Baghdad Radio all through the summer, until finally everything culminates in something called *Khatimat al-Anfal,* the Final Anfal, which began in earnest in August 1988.

7. In Persian, the word *"Anfal"* is also used to mean "booty," but it has developed as well the meaning of "gift," *bakhshish.* For the same word to carry both of these seemingly contradictory meanings makes sense by reference to its origins. Booty that has been divinely legitimated is not stolen; it is a gift from God to those who have done the taking and to the Muslim community at large. In the Battle of Badr, the bulk went to the Muslim warriors. Of the remainder, verse 41 in *Surat al-Anfal* of the Qur'an says: "Know that one fifth of your spoils shall belong to God, the Apostle, the Apostle's kinsfolk, the orphans, the needy, and those that travel the road." Increasingly, in the

new vocabulary that begins to emerge in the post-1979 Islamic Republic of Iran, the meaning of *anfal* metamorphoses into public property pure and simple. The progression is from booty to gift to public property. Today, when Iranian clerics use *anfal*, it refers to land, resources, forests, rivers, and even mountains. Something similar is happening to the word in Iraq when it is used, for instance, as the name of a post office.

8. Jim Muir reported similar stories of children and women being "auctioned off to rich Kuwaitis and Saudis as wives," which he heard in northern Iraq. Apparently Kurdish soldiers serving in the Iraqi army during its occupation of Kuwait "recognized female relatives who had been sold into marriage there." See his article, "Behind the Grim Kurdish Flight," *The Christian Science Monitor*, April 18, 1991, p. 1. As far as I have been able to establish, Muir, in this article, is the first journalist to mention the word *"Anfal"* as the Iraqi government's codename for a massive campaign of repression.

9. I have a tape recording of Saddam speaking to his military commanders from which I have translated this extract. The full transcript was published in *al-Hayat*, the Arabic daily published in London.

10. See also Chapter 8, New Nationalist Myths.

11. Quoted in the comprehensive and excellent study by Martin van Bruinessen, "The Kurds Between Iran and Iraq," *Middle East Report* (July–August 1986), p. 27.

12. Kurdish sources claim that an official directive exists, from 'Ali Hasan al-Majeed's Office for the Organization of the North, which speaks of eliminating all life found in those areas that have been officially designated "prohibited" for administrative or security reasons. Specifically, I am told, the directive states that persons found inside such areas "shall be killed." The directive—addressed to all branches of the party, the different security services, Military Intelligence, and the First Army Corps (based in Kirkuk) and the Fifth Army Corps (based in Arbil)—would have set the policy for the *Anfal* operations and had to have been issued shortly after the March 29, 1987, decree by the RCC. I have, however, been unable to obtain or see a copy of this alleged directive.

13. Dr. Ja'far was interviewed by Gwynne Roberts in my presence in Arbil in November 1991. Shortly after the attack on Shaikh Wisan, Dr Ja'far defected from the Iraqi army and made his way to London.

14. See Allan Cowell's report, "Iraqis Are Facing a Growing War from Within," *The New York Times*, September 22, 1987, p. 6. As the title of the article indicates, the official Western perception was the one handed to them by their Iraqi allies (in those not so far gone days) that Iraq was responding to Kurdish guerrilla resistance. In my opinion, the evidence does not support this. The people exterminated were overwhelmingly non-combatants. See also Patrick Tyler's report, "Kurdish Guerrillas Pose Growing Threat to Iraq," in *The Washington Post*, February 19, 1988, p. A15, which drew attention to the widespread human rights abuses associated with "razing hundreds of villages and forcibly resettling thousands of Kurds."

15. The interview with Jamal (pseudonym) was conducted by Ayad Rahim in London, in February 1992.

16. After my interview, the interviews of the human rights organizations that followed, the Special Envoy of the United Nations (Max von der Stoel), and countless journalists all through the winter of 1992, it appears Taimour had served his purpose. The boy has since apparently been abandoned to fend for himself with a male relative but without *peshmerga* protection. That at least is what a journalist found out when he returned to Kurdistan during the Kurdish elections and tried, unsuccessfully, to see the boy and learn how he was getting on.

17. The whole interview was filmed by Gwynne Roberts, with whom I was traveling. A clip from it was shown on the BBC *Everyman* film, *The Road to Hell*.

6 . Remembering Cruelty

1. See the "Why We Are Stuck in the Sand" by Christopher Hitchens in *Harper's Magazine*, vol. 282, no. 1688 (January 1991). See also the definitive special report entitled "Iraqgate: How the Bush Administration Helped Saddam Hussein Buy His Weapons of War and Why American Taxpayers Got Stuck with the Bill," *U.S. News & World Report,* May 18, 1992.

2. This question was asked by Kenneth Roth, deputy director of Human Rights Watch, in his letter to *The New York Times,* July 13, 1992, p. A14.

3. See Executive Summary, *Health and Welfare in Iraq After the Gulf Crisis: An In-Depth Assessment,* by the International Study Team (Cambridge), October 1991, p. 3.

4. Ibid., pp. 4–5, 12–13, and 21. The situation has gotten steadily worse in the south of the country in the months following the publication of the report, although it will have improved in the center, where power was restored by salvaging parts, and in the north, which has since become a "liberated" zone and is open to outside help.

5. *Newsweek,* January 20, 1992, estimated 2,500–3,000 civilian deaths during the air war. Until February 11, 1991, official Iraqi government figures put the figures at 650 dead and 750 wounded. On that day these figures were revised upward by the religious affairs minister, who spoke of "thousands" of civilian casualities. See *The New York Times,* February 12, 1991. The highest early estimates spoke of 5,000–15,000 deaths. See the *British Medical Journal* 1991; 303: 303–06.

6. *U.S. News & World Report* claimed in its issue of January 20, 1992, that on the eve of war, "Iraq may have had as few as 300,000 soldiers in the Kuwait theater, less than half the 632,000 claimed by General Schwartzkopf or the 540,000 estimated by the Pentagon. . . . Similarly Iraqi casualties were probably far lower than the 100,000 estimated by the Defense Intelligence Agency. In fact, as few as 8,000 Iraqi soldiers may have been killed in the Kuwait theatre of operations during the 43 days of combat."

7. Daponte was fired after releasing her estimates. The ensuing publicity forced her employers to come up with new figures. These further tipped the balance in favor of the argument that the real casualties of this war came after it ended and not while it was being fought. After the American Civil Liberties Union took action, however, she was reinstated in April 1992, whereupon she promptly accused the U.S. Census Bureau of trying "to suppress and delay the release of information that is embarrassing to the current administration." See *The Washington Post,* March 6, 1992, p. A6, and the *Boston Globe,* April 14, 1991.

8. *Journal of American Medicine,* vol. 266, no. 5, August 7, 1991, p. 639. See also the *British Medical Journal,* 1991; 303: 303–06.

9. Quoted by Murray Kempton in *New York Newsday,* March 3, 1991. See also the report issued by UN Headquarters in New York, "WHO/UNICEF Special Mission to Iraq," February 1991.

10. Published in *The New England Journal of Medicine,* September 26, 1991, p. 980. "Starvation and high infant mortality in Iraq are now well documented," wrote the prestigious British medical journal *The Lancet,* in its November 9, 1991, issue (vol. 338, p. 1180). "None of us will be able to say in the future, 'We did not know.' "

11. "Effect of the Gulf War on Infant and Child Mortality in Iraq," Center for Population Studies, Harvard School of Public Health. This excellent report which at present remains unpublished, was written by Sarah Zaidi and is based on a representative sample of Iraqi households.

12. I am quoting the draft of an as-yet-unpublished paper entitled "Child Nutrition and Armed Conflicts in Iraq," kindly supplied to me by the author, Walid al-Douri, and based on data collected and analyzed by Najib A. Armijo-Husein, Wafaie Fawzi, and G.Herrera-Acena—all from the Harvard School of Public Health.

13. Reported in *The Guardian,* March 28, 1991.

14. From "The Impact of the Gulf War on Children in Iraq: Child Psychology Study," by Drs. Atle Dyregrov and Magne Raundalen, dated September 28, 1991. See also Executive Summary, *Health and Welfare in Iraq After the Gulf Crisis: An In-Depth Assessment,* pp. 24–25.

15. Charter 91 is a campaign organized around a 1,400-word document which calls, among other things, for a moratorium on capital punishment, the abolition of conscription, and a 2 percent of GNP constitutional upper limit on military expenditure. Just under four hundred expatriate and exiled Iraqis of all ethnic and religious denominations, from various walks of life and vastly different political affiliations, had put their names to Charter 91 as of November 1992. A copy of the Charter in four languages (Arabic, Kurdish, Assyrian, and English), along with the list of signatories, has been published by Charter 91, P.O. Box 2724, London W2 4XS.

16. Quoted in *The Washington Post,* March 2, 1991, p. A13.

17. *The New York Times,* June 11, 1991.

18. See Samir al-Khalil, *The Monument: Art, Vulgarity and Responsibility in Iraq* (London: André Deutsch, 1991).

19. See Chapter 4.

20. "Putting cruelty *first* is . . . a matter very different from mere humaneness. To hate cruelty more than any other evil involves a radical rejection of both religious and political conventions. It dooms one to a life of skepticism, indecision, disgust, and often misanthropy. Putting cruelty first has, therefore, been tried only rarely, and is not often discussed. It is too deep a threat to reason for most philosophers to contemplate it at all." Judith Shklar, *Ordinary Vices* (Cambridge, Mass.: Harvard University Press, 1984), p. 8.

21. *Newsweek,* March 18, 1991. I am indebted to my friend Lawrence Weschler for drawing my attention to this item and its significance. Our conversations on the subject of Maya Lin's Vietnam War Memorial, monumentality in general, and the Gulf war provided me with the stimulus to write this chapter in the way that I have.

Whither Iraq?

1. Most non-Iraqi Arab intellectuals comprehended what was going on in Iraq in March 1991 along the lines of Jordan's foreign minister, and the head of its delegation in the Middle East Peace talks, Kamil Abu Jaber, who blurted out in an interview: "Israeli agents are all over north and south Iraq, for God's sake," and "Iranian agents are all over . . . under the guise of helping Iraq." If Abu Jaber was unwise enough to say things like this in public, thousands of others thought them in private. They thought this way because, as we shall see, it so nicely dovetailed with everything else they had been saying during the Gulf crisis. Abu Jaber is quoted from an interview he made with John Blake for the BBC Everyman film *The Devil We Know,* broadcast in the U.K. in the summer of 1991. I am indebted to John Blake for the transcript from which this quote was taken.

2. Ba'thi reliance on Takritis in the upper echelons of power is not enough to make the state they built confessional. The character of a state is a matter of its "legal" structure and the ideological agenda it serves. While Pan-Arabism has an affinity to the Sunni

tradition in Islam, there is, once again, nothing in the ideology of Pan-Arabism to exclude the Shi'a, which is why so many of them became Pan-Arabists in the 1960s and 1970s. From both the ideological and structural points of view, therefore, there is nothing "Sunni" about the Ba'thi state headed by Saddam Husain. The problem is in the nature of Ba'thism itself, and in all those members of the Iraqi opposition who insist on thinking of the Ba'thi state as Sunni, or confessional, and who by so doing are themselves fanning the flames of future confessionalism which could tear up Iraq.

3. This particular group of destroyed villages, churches, and monasteries was carefully described in a memorandum dated April 18, 1988, circulated to the United Nations and Amnesty International by the Assyrian Democratic Movement. For a report on the persecution of Iraqi Christians, see "Kurdistan's Other Victims," *Newsweek,* June 17, 1991, p. 33.

4. Iranian propaganda at the start of the Iraq-Iran War talked of "back-stabbing Arabs," a reference to the "betrayal" of Husain by the people of Iraq in A.D. 680. See Amir Taheri's article in the *International Herald Tribune,* October 10, 1980.

5. This complaint is not only morally grotesque, it is without foundation. I have studied a compilation of virtually every article that appeared in the Western press on things Kurdish between 1986 and 1989 put together by the Kurdish Relief Association in Palo Alto, California, under the title *Kurdistan On Fire.* Until 1988, the number of articles dealing with Kurdish suffering is very few, largely to do with the Iraq-Iran War, and never once is there a suggestion of genocide or mass murder. In 1988, the Kurdish problem—largely because of the March gas attack on Halabja that killed five thousand people—attracted the attention of the foreign press. The word "genocide" was first mentioned on April 3, 1988, in the *San Jose Mercury News.* In 1988, one or two reporters started comparing the Kurdish problem to the Jewish Holocaust. The articles mentioned the deportation of Kurdish villagers to the south of Iraq, but their destination was not known, nor was their fate. During September 1988 more articles were written about Kurdistan than at any other time. By the beginning of October, the number of the articles had once again dropped dramatically. I do not praise or criticize anyone for this; it is so obviously the way of the world.

6. See, for instance, the article by Muhammad 'Abdel-Jabbar, *"Al-Dimuqratiyya Majmu'at Aliyyat li-Tandhim al-Hayat al-Siyasiyya,"* in *al-Bilad,* no. 90, pp. 48–50.

7. See "The Formation of the Iraqi Ba'th," Chapter 6 of *Republic of Fear,* for the idea of *iman* in Ba'thist doctrine of the 1940s.

8. I found such wisdom in the Kurdish leader Mas'oud Barazani when I interviewed him in northern Iraq in October 1991. Few family names in Iraq have as much claim to suffering as the Barazani name. Yet it was clear that the extent of the moral collapse inside Iraq, the loss of trust among Iraqis, as he put it, had a greater claim on his thinking: "The pain is so deep between us and the government, and even between some Iraqi groups, that it is very difficult to cure it. But if we adopt the path of forgiveness, and try to open a new page, we will be living for the next generation. For our children there must be forgiveness, otherwise we are going to dive into a sea of blood." I left that meeting feeling that all Iraqis could not do better than have someone like this preside over the reconstruction of a post-Saddam Iraq.

9. T. S. Eliot, "Burnt Norton," *Four Quartets* (New York: Harcourt Brace Jovanovich, 1988), p. 14.

10. Hameed has read Beckett and is referring to his Godot. But could it be that in the back of his mind he is also thinking of the hidden twelfth Imam of Shi'ism, *al-Mahdi al-muntadhar* (the awaited Mahdi, or guide to the straight and clear path)? According to Shi'i doctrine, the twelfth Imam did not die; he disappeared, and his reappearance will mark the dawning of a just age. My point is that maybe Hameed awaits his Godot as

the Shi'a of Iraq await their Mahdi. Real hope for the future begins with such cross-cultural transfusions, especially when entered into with Hameed's kind of open-mindedness.

7. Who Am I?

1. Usama Wathiq, *"Ba'da an inqasha'at al-ghimama"* (After the Blindfold Was Lifted) *al-'Arab*, the London-based Arabic daily, April 22, 1991.
2. Being born in Baghdad, however, is still a restriction, regardless of what passport one holds. In December 1991, returning from my trip to northern Iraq via Turkey, I was refused entry to the United States at Logan Airport and sent packing back to London. The immigration officer couldn't handle the fact that I was born in Baghdad, had two entry stamps to Turkey with no country in between, and was carrying a suitcaseful of Arabic newspapers and documents. Fortunately, with the help of the Center for Middle East Studies at Harvard University and Kenneth Roth of Human Rights Watch, I did not have to wait months in London to clear the whole thing up.
3. See "The Reform Law of 1977," discussed in chapter 4 of *Republic of Fear*. See also the historical roots of these laws in Ba'thist ideology from the 1940s in chapter 6.
4. I can think of individual exceptions to this rule like Hisham Milhem, the correspondent of *al-Safir* in the United States, whom Iraqis regard with affection; Hazim Saghiyeh, a correspondent in *al-Hayat* who wrote about the Kurds when no other Arab would; Wadhah Sharara, a professor of political science at the University of Lebanon, who never lost sight of how central to the crisis the repulsive character of the Iraqi regime was; Salah Zeghidi, the Tunisian sociologist and former director of the General Union of Tunisian Workers; Walid Khalidi of Harvard University; Lutfi Mash'our, the editor of *A-Sinnara*, an Arabic weekly for Israeli Arabs published in Haifa; Salman Masalha, the Israeli-Arab poet; and the Palestinian writer and satirist Emile Habibi. No doubt there were others whom I have missed.
5. Describing the scene in the Maghrib, Salah Zeghidi wrote that the Maghribin intelligentsia "seem to have at last achieved that 'junction with the masses' that some of them—the most 'engagé'—have been hoping for. . . . In Tunisia . . . most of the intellectuals identified themselves totally with Saddam Husain's policies. Many of them became run-of-the-mill militants, throwing themselves enthusiastically and often passionately into demonstrations in favor of Saddam's Iraq, without taking any distance." From "De la maturité de la pensée à la dérive politique: Lettre Ouverte à Hichem Djaït," in *Les Cahiers de l'Orient* (June 1991), p. 32. I am indebted to Professor Avram Udovich for drawing my attention to this important article.
6. "The true motivations underlying the groundswell of emotion provoked by the Gulf War deserve to be studied carefully, but one can be sure that 'rejection of the West,' the central theme of the 'integrist' school of thought for the last few years, especially in Tunisia and Algeria, and visceral hatred of the Gulf Arabs, seen as the ultimate nouveau riches, arrogant in their presumption, played a major role. Maghribin intellectuals lost themselves totally in the white heat of public opinion, which they fed . . . rationality, discernment, objective distance, and critical sense disappeared as if by magic." Ibid., pp. 32–33.
7. A true incident in an unpublished short story by Ahmad Titinchi (pseudonym), called "The Bistro."
8. The nationalism of Wathiq's commentary in *al-'Arab* with which I opened this chapter is of this ilk. Samir al-Khalil is not entitled to the quality of "Arabness" because he fails to blame the real devils: the United States and Israel.

9. *al-'Arab,* June 24, 1991.
10. Sati'a al-Husri, the great Arab nationalist thinker of the interwar years, emphasized language as the basis of his theory of nationalism.
11. Edward Said, "The Intellectuals and the War," *MERIP Reports,* no. 171 (July–August 1991), p. 16. See Introduction. To be called a self-hater, which I have been subjected to on several occasions, is a logical derivative of Said's way of characterizing other people's ideas. A discussion of the issues raised by Said's interview written by Afsaneh Najmabadi, entitled "Said's War on the Intellectuals," and followed by Said's response, was published in *MERIP Reports,* no. 173 (November–December 1991), p. 2.
12. From John Simpson's account, in *From the House of War,* p. 10.
13. Walid Khalidi, *The Gulf Crisis: Origins and Consequences* (Washington, D.C.: Institute for Palestine Studies, 1991), p. 4.
14. "Ba'thism presents the Arab nation as a given which must be made concrete in history and translated into a political reality. The Arab nation is not a fact. It does not exist now any more than it has ever existed. . . . The Ba'th have failed to gain a large audience among the Arab masses. It has had no effect on the intelligentsia who are most open and aware of worldwide trends in thought. . . . [I]ntellectuals cannot, without betraying themselves, subscribe to a purely nationalist ideology that is fatally poor and contains the seeds of fascism." Hisham Djaïet as quoted in Salah Zeghidi's "De la maturité de la penseé . . . ", pp. 40–41.
15. Hisham Djaïet in an interview by *L'Express,* February 7, 1991. Among Djaïet's many books is *La Personnalité et le Devenir Arabo-islamique (Identity and the Arab-Islamic Future).*
16. *L'Express,* February 7, 1991.
17. Quoted in Salah Zeghidi's "De la maturité de la pensée . . . ", p. 40.
18. *al-Dustour,* March 7, 1991.
19. Ahmad Hadhek Elorf writing in the Tunisian journal *al-Chaab,* in which he has a weekly column. Quoted in Zeghidi's "De la maturité de la pensée . . . ", p. 34.
20. Quoted in the *Financial Times,* February 27, 1991.
21. The quote from Mu'nis Razzaz is from the Associated Press in Amman, as quoted in the *Boston Globe,* February 27, 1991.
22. See *Newsweek,* January 7, 1991, p. 22.
23. The Lebanese writer and translator of Freud's works into Arabic, George Tarabishi, is an example. I take up his reasoning on the Gulf crisis in the next chapter.
24. Rami G. Khouri, "The Bitter Fruits of War," reprinted in *The Gulf Reader: History, Documents, Opinions,* edited by Micah L. Sifry and Christopher Cerf (New York: Random House, 1991), p. 403 (henceforth referred to as *The Gulf Reader*).
25. See the report by Judith Miller, "Syria's Game: Put On a Western Face," in *The New York Times Magazine,* January 26, 1992, p. 19.
26. Fawwaz Trabulsi, "Harvest of War," *MERIP Reports* (July–August 1991), p. 32.
27. Quoted in an article by Danny Rubinstein in *Ha'aretz,* March 4, 1991. I have used the translation by Israel Shahak from his collections from the Hebrew press.
28. Published in London in the Arabic literary monthly *an-Naqud,* no. 33 (March 1991), pp. 4–5. The Arabic *matah* has no exact English equivalent. It combines the meanings of pride and haughtiness with being led astray, distractedness, and lost wanderings in a wayless desolate land. The title therefore captures perfectly the sense of anger and deep anxiety so characteristic of Arab rejectionism and which we saw earlier in the poetry of Nizar Qabbani (Chapter 1).
29. Samih al-Qasim, *"Nahnu al-Aan Wathiqa Tarikhiyya"* (We Are Now a Historical Document), published in *an-Naqid,* no. 30 (December 1990), p. 5. By "We," al-Qasim means "We Arabs."

30. Milan Kundera, *The Art of the Novel* (New York: Grove Press, 1988), p. 135.

31. Moncef Marzouki's article ran during the war under the title "L'Occident fourvoye," *Le Monde,* February 6, 1991. It starts: "Seen from the southern shores of the Mediterranean, the Gulf war is shaping up as a prelude to the divorce between the West and the Arab world. . . . " In the article Marzouki thanks M. Chevènement, on the left wing of the French Socialist Party, who used to be defense minister for Mitterand and who is famous for selling weapons to Iraq on a vast scale throughout the 1980s. Why? Because Chevènement resigned from his post as defense minister in support of Iraq. For more on Marzouki's organization, the Tunisian Human Rights League, see Chapter 1.

32. As reported by Salah Zeghidi in his article, "De la maturité de la pensée . . . ", in *Les Cahiers de l'Orient,* p. 35.

33. See, for instance, the article by the Sudanese writer Dr. Hasan Maki Muhammad Ahmad, which appeared in the London-based Arabic daily, *al-Quds al-'Arabi,* on May 2, 1991. The article develops the argument that "the West is the greater loser" of "the mother of all battles," because "no matter what the immediate consequences of the war by way of destruction and despair, the final consequences will benefit the project of an Islamic revival." That is of course a cruder version of the position of Djaïet. But references to the Crusades was by no means restricted to Muslim writers. See, for instance, the article "We Have No Choice But to Fight America," by the philosopher Hasan 'Asfour, *al-Quds al-'Arabi,* September 18–19, 1990.

34. From his collection entitled *'Atharat al-Ta'ir* (Beirut: Al-Mu'asasa al-'Arabiyya, 1985), p. 7.

35. This is the title of an article by Michel 'Aflaq, which first appeared in *Fi Sabil al-Ba'th* (Beirut: Dar al-Tali'a, 1959), pp. 29–30.

36. Part of a conversation with Fouad Ajami reported in Ajami's article, "The Tragedy of Arab Culture," *The New Republic,* April 6, 1987.

37. The extract is from "The Diary of Beirut Under Siege, 1982," a poem by Adonis about Beirut, published in a bilingual anthology of Arabic poetry entitled *Victims of a Map* (London: Saqi Books, 1984), p. 135. The translation is by Abdullah al-Udhari.

38. Originally published in *Der Spiegel,* Enzensberger's article appeared in English in the *Los Angeles Times,* February 14, 1991, Part B, p. 7.

39. According to Salah Zeghidi, when thirty-six Tunisian intellectuals published a declaration in August 1990 denouncing both the annexation of Kuwait by Iraq and American aggressive moves in the Gulf, they were labeled "supporters of foreigners," "a French fifth column," and "agents of imperialism and Zionism." *Les Cahiers de l'Orient* (June 1991), p. 34.

40. The words of 'Abdel-Rahman Hafidi in *Liberation,* March 2, 1991, as quoted in *Les Cahiers de l'Orient* (June 1991), p. 34.

41. From the report by Tony Walker, "Moslem Militants Want Saddam as Caliph," *Financial Times,* January 10, 1991.

8 . N e w   N a t i o n a l i s t   M y t h s

1. Fouad Zakariyya, *Al-Thaqafa al-'Arabiyya wa Azmat al-Khaleej* (London: Kuwait Research Company, 1991), p. 3.

2. References to the views of these thinkers are cited throughout this book.

3. Rashid Khalidi, "The Palestinians and the Gulf Crisis," in *The Gulf Reader,* p. 423.

4. Samir Amin, "The Real Stakes in the Gulf War," *Monthly Review* (July–August 1991), p. 15. Italics added.

5. See *Arab Studies Quarterly* (henceforth referred to as ASQ), vol. 13, nos. 1 and 2 (Winter–Spring 1991), p. 5. Italics added.

6. Edward Said, "On Linkage, Language, and Identity," in *The Gulf Reader,* p. 439. Italics added.

7. From the proceedings of a March 1991 conference attended by one Lebanese, one Iraqi, and thirteen North African academics in the social sciences. Published as *Harb al-Khaleej wa Mustaqbel al-'Arab: Hiwar wa Mawaqif* (Tunis: Dar Saras, 1991; henceforth referred to as *Harb al-Khaleej),* p. 93. Italics added. For the same view with yet a third set of dates, see the paper by Fath-Allah Wal'ilo, a professor in economics at the University of Muhammad the Fifth in Rabat, p. 50.

8. The United States certainly did support Saddam Husain to the hilt up until the invasion of Kuwait. No doubt this support encouraged the Iraqi leader to go ahead with his plans. But why should it be the reason why he wanted to invade Kuwait in the first place? The extent of U.S. support of Iraq up to August 2, 1990, is set out in the definitive special report entitled "Iraqgate: How the Bush Administration Helped Saddam Hussein Buy His Weapons of War and Why American Taxpayers Got Stuck with the Bill," *U.S. News & World Report,* May 18, 1992.

9. In an article published on March 7, 1991, while the Iraqi counteroffensive against the uprising that broke out on February 28 was in full swing, Edward Said wrote: "The claim that Iraq gassed its own citizens has often been repeated. At best, this is uncertain. There is at least one War College report, done while Iraq was a US ally, which claims that the gassings of the Kurds in Halabja was done by Iran. Few people mention such reports in the media today." *London Review of Books,* March 7, 1991, p. 7. Since when has Said been a fan of American War College reports? It is commendable to drag such a completely discredited document out of the woodwork for the purpose of showing the history of U.S. hypocrisy as far as Iraq is concerned. But Edward Said chooses to believe that it in fact casts doubt on the completely incontrovertible fact—known for years—that Iraq began gassing Kurdish villages with an attack on the Kurdish village of Shaikh Wisan in April 1987. In those days, the regime was still testing out its new toys; extensive and systematic gassing covered in all the international press took place all through 1988.

10. Like Hitchens, I think it is advisable to reason on the basis of assuming nefarious intentions to all states and governments. But from the evidence that he provides us with, it is unreasonable to conclude that what Glaspie "really" meant was that "one large problem with the anomalous borders of the Gulf is the fact that they were drawn to an obsolete British colonial diagram." See Hitchens, "Why Are We Stuck in the Sand," *Harper's* Magazine (January 1991). A different account of this meeting is given by John Simpson, in *From the House of War,* pp. 101–05. Simpson cogently argues that at the time of the meeting, Saddam himself "had no clear idea in his own mind what he would do" (p. 102).

11. On (c), see also my critique of Noam Chomsky later in this chapter.

12. During a trip to northern Iraq in November 1991, a Kurdish intellectual gave me a copy of the Ba'thist equivalent of *Time* Magazine. In it was an article hailing "The American Thinker Noam Chomsky" as one who "has exposed the anti-democratic practices of the West." Ignoring everything Chomsky has said about the nastiness of the Ba'th in the past, the article emphasizes the "chasm between rhetoric and reality" which Chomsky has opened up in the ranks of Western liberals. With Arab intellectuals in mind, not Western liberals, that is, ironically, a good statement of the task I have set myself in this book. *Alef-Ba,* no. 1208, November 20, 1991, p. 6.

13. Fawwaz Trabulsi, *MERIP Reports* (July–August 1991), p. 30.

14. *ASQ,* pp. 14 and 20.

15. Edward Said, in *The Gulf Reader*, p. 439.
16. Taken from an essay/poem entitled *"Khawatir Tahta Da's al-Khayl"* (Thoughts Under the Hooves of Horses), published in *'Awdat al-Isti'mar: Min al-Ghazw al-Thaqafi ila Harb al-Khaleej*, by various authors (London: Riadh El-Rayyes Books, 1991), pp. 172–73.
17. Ibid., p. 172.
18. The story is told in detail by Phil Reeves, "Harsh Logic of Koran and the Kalashnikov," *The Independent*, February 12, 1991.
19. See the survey of Arab opinion by David Hirst, "Humiliation of 'Saladin' Dawns on His Supporters," *The Guardian*, February 27, 1991.
20. Jacques Berque, *Arab Rebirth: Pain and Ecstasy* (London: Saqi Books, 1983), p. 49. In the year 1970, Bergue notes, Saladin inspired fifty new literary titles.
21. George Tarabishi, *"Jarimat al-Gharb al-Muzdawajah"* (The Double Crime of the West), published in *'Awdat al-Isti'mar*, pp. 162–63. The same comparison with Bismarck crossed Muhammad Sid-Ahmad's mind. "It is no secret to any Arab that Saddam Husain's regime is one of the most repressive in the world. . . . [But] why should Saddam not do for the Arab nation what Bismarck did for Germany?" *MERIP Reports* (January–February 1991), p. 17.
22. In a series of five articles published in the Arabic daily *al-Quds al-'Arabi*, Muhammad 'Abid al-Jabiri, author of the highly influential study *Takween al-'Aql al-'Arabi (Formation of the Arab Mind)*, supported and argued for the political project of the Iraqi Ba'th. In one article devoted to the topic "Who Is Saddam Husain? The Experience of the Past and the Horizons of the Future," he presents the Iraqi leader as a visionary leader with a "national project for liberation, modernization and unity, including the achievement of self-determination of the Palestinian people." Never once does he even mention the human rights record of the Iraqi regime. The articles appeared on January 31, 1991; February 2–3, 1991; February 5, 1991; February 9–10, 1991; and March 3, 1991.
23. Elias Khouri, "Al-Haqiqa wa al-Wahm (Reality and Illusion)," *al-Safir*, September 1, 1990, p. 10.
24. The interview was conducted by Hazim Saghiyeh and appeared in *al-Hayat*, April 4, 1991.
25. The conference elected Khayr al-Din Haseeb, director of the Arab Research Center [Center for Arab Unity Studies] and a former governor of the Central Bank of Iraq, as its general secretary, along with a secretariat of twenty-five people with a broad geographical spread to implement the work (two Iraqis, one Jordanian, three Palestinians, three Lebanese, one Syrian, one Yemeni, ten North Africans, and four persons from the Gulf states). Among the more important signatories are Hisham Sharabi, a professor at Georgetown university, and the Moroccan philosopher Muhammad 'Abid al-Jabiri. All quotations are from a mimeographed version of the fifteen-page statement put out by the conference.
26. Why, for instance, should a critical thinker like Hisham Sharabi wax so indignant at what the Allied forces did to Saddam's Republican Guard? In an article written long after the Republican Guard had brutally crushed the March rebellion, killing far more innocent Iraqi citizens than the Americans ever killed soldiers of the Republican Guard, he chose to focus solely on their losses as proof of American criminality in the Gulf war. See "The American Crime and the Initiative of Mr. Baker," *al-Quds al-'Arabi*, April 29, 1991.
27. "Statement to the Nation," mimeo, p. 4.
28. According to Salah Zeghidi in his article "De la maturité de la pensée . . . ", in *Les Cahiers de l'Orient* (June 1991), p. 35.

29. From Charter 91, article 5. See also Chapter 6 and note 15.

30. Ibrahim Abu-Lughod, "The Politics of Linkage," in *Beyond the Storm: A Gulf Crisis Reader,* edited by P. Bennis and M. Moushabeck (New York: Olive Branch Press, 1991), pp. 184, 188–89.

31. Muhammad Hallaj, "Taking Sides: Palestinians and the Gulf Crisis," *Journal of Palestine Studies,* vol. XX, no, 3 (Spring 1991), p. 45. Italics added.

32. Quoted in *Hadashot,* October 10, 1990.

33. Saddam Husain used this Qur'anic imagery often. See Chapter 5.

34. From *The Women's Review of Books,* vol. VIII, nos. 10–11, (July 1991), pp. 11–12.

35. Quoted by Yizhar Be'er in *Ha'aretz,* March 22, 1991. I have used the translations kindly provided by Israel Shahak in his Report no. 67, entitled "Palestinians in Israel Debate Democracy in a Self-Critical Mood."

36. See Habibi's important interview with Huda al-Husaini in the Arabic daily *Asharq Al-Awsat,* May 3, 1991.

37. In a talk given at the Kufa Gallery in London on May 17, 1991, Habibi criticized the mass of Arab intellectuals for their inability to fill the "vacuum" that was created by the Gulf crisis. Why, he asked in a later article, did this happen? "I see 'the sin' lies in the neglect by creative Arab intellects, with a handful of marginal exceptions, to take up the role for which they primarily exist, namely, protection of the conscience of their people from corruption." *al-Quds, al-'Arabi,* May 22, 1991.

38. See his interview with Y. Elgazi in *Ha'aretz,* May 30, 1991.

39. See his article in *al-Quds al-'Arabi,* March 20, 1991.

40. The democratic content of Palestinian nationalism is, of course, lacking entirely in the Pan-Arabism of someone like Hishan Djaïet or Muhammad 'Abid al-Jabiri.

41. I developed this same argument in relation to the Iraqi action against Kuwait at greater length in an article that appeared in *New Statesman and Society,* August 31, 1990.

42. Muhammad Hasanain Haikal, "Out with the Americans, In with a New Arab Order," *The Times,* September 12, 1990. For some inexplicable reason, Haikal broke an initial six-week silence on the Gulf crisis by publishing his first opinion in the London *Times*.

43. Noam Chomsky, *On U.S. Gulf Policy,* Harvard University, Cambridge, Mass., November 19, 1990 (Open Magazine Pamphlet Series, Westfield, N.J., 1991), p. 2.

44. Noam Chomsky, *The New World Order,* Bates College, January 30, 1991 (Open Magazine Pamphlet Series, Westfield, N.J., 1991), p. 5.

45. Chomsky, *On U.S. Gulf Policy,* p. 2.

46. Ibid., p. 11. Later in the pamphlet Chomsky argues that the United States is always against diplomacy and negotiation, because its policies are unpopular in the Third World and it would lose out completely if it gave up its constant recourse to force and violence. This dogmatic assertion is belied by the experience of the Iraqi uprising in March 1991, when both Arab and Kurdish rebels called for Allied and U.S. help to overthrow the Ba'thist regime.

47. *Harb al-Khaleej,* p. 29.

48. Ibid., p. 34. The same reasoning is present in Samir Amin's previously cited article, "The Real Stakes . . . ", *Monthly Review* (July–August 1991), pp. 16–19.

49. From an unpublished mimeo by Ahmad Chalabi, entitled "Money and Power in Iraq," February 20, 1990, p. 7.

50. Figures from Donna Smith, "U.S. Analysts Worry About the Cost of Bush's New Order," *Reuters,* March 18, 1991.

51. Figures from Mark Sommer, "What the U.S. Can't Afford," *Christian Science Monitor,* August 6, 1991, p. 18.

52. See for instance the article by Edward Luttwak, "Is America on the Way Down?" in *Commentary* (March 1992), pp. 15–21.

53. Figures from James Risen, "Bush Won't Hike Taxes to Fund War," *Los Angeles Times*, January 22, 1991, Business section, p. 1.

54. Edward Said, "Tragically, A Closed Book to the West," *The Independent*, August 12, 1990. On the eve of the Gulf war, Said criticized the Iraqi action in strong words. See his article, "Empire of Sand," in the *Weekend Guardian*, January 12–13, 1991. While this article adds a critique of the contemporary Arab order to Said's world view, which is to be welcomed, no conclusions are drawn. The underlying priorities, in my view, remained the same, as evidenced by Said's opposition to the principle of Allied intervention on behalf of the Iraqi intifada against Saddam Husain.

55. Samir al-Khalil, "Drowning in the Gulf of Lies," *The Independent*, August 25, 1991.

56. Said, "Tragically, A Closed Book . . . ", *The Independent*, August 12, 1990.

57. Elias Khouri, "Al-Dir'aal-Amriki! (The American Shield!)," in *al-Safir*, August 18, 1990, p. 10.

58. Tarabishi, *'Awdat al-Isti'mar*, pp. 159 and 164. Italics in the original.

59. *Harb al-Khaleej*, p. 112.

60. Trabulsi, "Harvest of War," *MERIP Reports* (July–August 1991), p. 32.

61. The full title is *'Awdat al-Isti'mar: Min al-Ghazw al-Thaqafi ila Harb al-Khaleej (The Return of Colonialism: From Cultural Invasion to the Gulf War)*, by various authors, including Kamal Abu Deeb, Samih al-Qasim, Muhammad Baradah, and Unsi al-Haj (London: Riadh El-Rayyes Books, 1991).

62. See his article, "The War Against a Civilization," which appeared in *The Guardian*, April 1, 1991 (italics added). An amended and expanded form of the article appears in *'Awdat al-Isti'mar*, pp. 33–44.

63. See the long interview with Gaspard in *al-Hayat*, May 30, 1989, entitled "They Are Killing the [Arabic] Book."

64. Said, "Tragically, A Closed Book . . . ", *The Independent*, August 12, 1990.

65. Khalidi, *The Gulf Crisis: Origins and Consequences*, p. 2.

9. Landscapes of Cruelty and Silence

1. Sometimes, even when such reports are prepared by Arabs, they are ignored. During its 1991 national convention, the American-Arab Anti-Discrimination Committee (ADC), which claims that it is a "non-partisan service organization committed to defending the rights . . . of Arab-Americans," blocked the efforts of the Washington-based Iraqi human rights organization Concerned Citizens for the Defense of Human Rights in Iraq to have a table to disperse its literature. (At the same convention, a 92-page dense collection of 30 speeches, statements, interviews, letters, and messages by Iraqi government officials entitled *Iraq Speaks*—more than half of which are from Saddam Husain—was available for sale. The purpose of the collection, according to its editor, Fred Moore, is to "present the Iraqi point of view." Adorning the cover of the book is a green map combining Kuwait and Iraq with the border erased between them, and a "fact sheet" inside explains that the population of Iraq is "20 million (including the 19th governorate)." The ADC was founded in 1980 "in response to stereotyping, defamation and discrimination directed at Americans of Arab origin" (quotes are from the 1991 ADC *Activity Report*). Nonetheless it rarely deals with human rights abuses inside Iraq or in the Arab world generally. The ADC deals instead with Israeli human rights violations and Arab-Americans' civil rights. In a conversation on this particular subject on May 11, 1992, between Albert Mokhiber, president of the ADC, and Iraqi-American journalist Ayad Rahim, Mokhiber said that all the regimes in the Arab world violate human rights, and if the ADC were going to speak about

these violations, where would it stop? Were they supposed to have twenty-two panels at each convention? It would go on forever. I bring this incident up because the ADC is the largest Arab-American organization in the United States, representing some twenty thousand Arab-Americans, and its views are broadly representative.

2. One thinks, for instance, of the work of Lebanese women writers like Hanan al-Shaikh, Andree Chedid, and Etel Adnan. Male writers are by and large still stuck in a "rejectionist" nationalist and anti-imperialist rut. For more on this distinction, see the study by Evelyn Accad, *Sexuality and War: Literary Masks of the Middle East* (New York: New York University Press, 1990).

3. The only Arabic book on Hama that I know of is entitled *Hama: Ma'sat al-'Asr alleti faqet Sabra wa Shatila* (Cairo: Dar al-I'tisam, n.d.). It has no author's name on it and is probably the collective effort of the Muslim Brotherhood. The best account of what happened is in Thomas Friedman, *From Beirut to Jerusalem* (New York: Farrar, Straus & Giroux, 1989), chapter 4, Hama Rules. The upper figure of 40,000 dead circulated among Syrians from Hama. Amnesty International published a report speculating that the number killed ranged from 10,000 to 25,000. No one really knows.

4. Since receiving the fax, I have checked and rechecked the authenticity of this index card. Although I never got to see the original, which was captured by Kurds during the March 1991 uprising, I have seen a videotape with the original clearly in it taken at the time the offices were being ransacked. There wasn't enough time for anyone to forge the document. From this and other testimony by Kurds and Western journalists who were present at the time, I have no doubt that the document is authentic.

5. This is according to testimony given by Ahmad Bamarni on September 26, 1991, in Paris at the proceedings of an "Indict Saddam" tribunal, organized by Iraqis to explore whether or not charges of war crimes and crimes against humanity can be brought against the Ba'thist leadership in Baghdad. At this same tribunal Dr. Hisham al-Hasan, a medical practitioner in the United Kingdom, in a deeply moving testimony, said that several of his Iraqi women patients were raped by the security services in Iraq during the 1980s. See also the collection of eyewitness reports entitled *Ahdath Adhar 1991 Kama Yarwiha Shuhoud 'Ayan* (Tehran: Al-Markaz al-Watha'iqi li-Huqouq al-Insan fil-'Iraq, 1991), p. 33.

6. I am indebted to Hilary Mann for this information. She visited the rape room shortly after the liberation of Kuwait City. I have also obtained a videotape showing the rape room of the Central Security Headquarters Building in Sulaimaniyya shortly after the uprising, with heaps of discarded and rotting women's clothing piled up against a nearby wall.

7. See the article by Andrew Hogg, reporting from Kuwait City, entitled "Saddam's War Legacy: Babies Without a Past," *The Sunday Times,* January 26, 1992. After visiting the orphanage, Hogg writes: "The nursery, decorated with cartoon figures and colorful mobiles, hardly looks like a home for the children whom Kuwait would rather forget. But it is an uncomfortable fact that most of the babies here are living reminders of the Iraqi invasion, born to Kuwaiti women raped by Saddam Husain's soldiers. Estimates vary, but during the seven-month occupation more than 500 Kuwaiti women are believed to have been raped, some repeatedly." The babies in Dar al-Tufula are those born to women who did not have the advantage of a discreet abortion or any support from an understanding family. They face a life of shame.

8. See for instance the testimony of Um Hasan al-Bayati, a Turkoman lady who witnessed a variety of forms of sexual abuse while in detention. Her testimony was given during hearings into Iraqi human rights abuses held in Tehran on May 23, 1992, and reported in *Sawt al-Kuwait,* June 13, 1992. See also Jim Muir's report, "Behind the Grim Kurdish Flight," *Christian Science Monitor,* April 18, 1991, p. 1, in which he writes: "Many

sources say that with stubborn political prisoners, it was common practice for female relatives to be brought in and raped in front of them to extract confessions." Women have been "disappearing" in Iraq in mysterious circumstances since the late 1970s when the repression really began to take a hold. A little-known London-based organization called the International Committee for the Release of Detained and Disappeared Women in Iraq (BM Box 9308, London WC1N 3XX) did sterling work in the 1980s collecting information, providing lists, and publicizing the plight of these women in the West.

9. Robert Karen, "Shame," the cover article in *The Atlantic*, vol. 269, no. 2 (February 1992), p. 47. Subsequent quotes in this paragraph are from this thirty-page study.

10. I am indebted to conversations with Mai Ghoussoub over the years for the ideas being developed here, although of course she is in no way responsible for what has been written. See in particular her seminal book, *Al-Mar'a al-'Arabiyya wa Dhukouriyyat al-Asala* (London: Dar al-Saqi, 1991). An earlier version of the same argument appeared in her article, "Feminism—or the Eternal Masculine—in the Arab World," *New Left Review*, no. 161.

11. I am indebted to Faleh 'Abdel-Jabbar for telling me about this Takriti custom, which dates back to Ottoman times, and about the bizarre compulsion that seems to have developed in Ba'thi ruling circles from the late 1970s onward to "get at" the well-known aristocratic families of Iraq.

12. See Chapter 5 for a full account.

13. See Karen, "Shame," *The Atlantic*, p. 40.

14. The stories of Amal Musairati and Sara Abu Ghanam, along with others, are written up in an article entitled "Guaranty for Murder," by Matti Regev in *Kol Ha'ir*, November 8, 1991. Regev wrote earlier on this subject in 1988, when he revealed an uncharacteristic tolerance on the part of the Israeli authorities toward Arab murderers of Arab women for "honor crimes." I am indebted to Israel Shahak's reports for the English translation of this article. See Shahak's collection of articles on the subject of "family honor" crimes, much of the information for which comes from the courageous activities of the *al-Fanar* Palestinian women's organization, which focuses on the issue. See also his excellent Report no. 83, "The Beginnings of Palestinian Feminism," dated August 23, 1991. On November 4, 1991, *al-Fanar* organized a demonstration outside the police station of the town of Ramleh which had handed Amal Musairati back to her murderers. The Palestinian demonstrators accused the Israeli authorities of bending to, and complicity with, "backward traditions." See *al-Fanar*'s Arabic newsletter published in Haifa, Israel, dated December 1991, p. 2.

15. Quoted by Regev in *Kol Ha'ir*, November 8, 1991.

16. I was told about this particular document by Abu 'Ali (pseudonym) in Shaqlawa (northern Iraq) in November 1991. Abu 'Ali was in charge of organizing and classifying some 8,000 documents which were captured by the Iraqi Communist Party in March 1991. I did not get to see the original myself. A senior Kurdish writer, poet, and political activist can confirm from lists captured by the Kurdish organizations that during the 1980s, "making videos with secret cameras became a real industry" in Iraq. He cited specific cases of sexually explicit videos circulated by the regime itself with a view to humiliating particular Kurdish personalities, who, often, were already heavily compromised because of their collaboration. See the interview by Annelie van Ammelrooy and Isma'il Zayer in the Dutch human rights journal, *Mensen Rechten* Magazine (May 1992). Middle East Watch is also in possession of Iraqi police documents which illustrate the use of threats to expose sexual infidelity as a tool to recruit police informants.

17. See the report by Teresa Thornhill, *Making Women Talk: The Interrogation of Palestinian*

Women Detainees by the Israeli General Security Services (London: Lawyers for Palestinian Human Rights, 1992), which shows through case studies how the Israeli Security has "developed certain techniques specifically for women. These include sexual harassment, [and] manipulation of the Arab notion of 'female honor' " (p. 17). See also note 25, below.

18. From 'Isam al-Khafaji, "State Terror and the Degradation of Politics in Iraq," *MERIP Reports* (May–June 1992), p. 16.

19. I am indebted to Mai Ghoussoub for pointing out to me the importance of thinking through this distinction between a country like Saudi Arabia and Iraq.

20. My informant, who wishes to keep her identity concealed, was interviewed in London in the summer of 1992.

21. The use of Islam in the politics of some elements of the Iraqi opposition is justified by the need to return to "roots" and "tradition" after all the upheavals of the Ba'thi years. One point that such justifications always ignore is that these roots no longer exist. It does not matter how many people shouted Islamic slogans during the March 1991 uprising because the same crowds that shouted, *"Allahu Akbar!"* (God is Great), were tearing everything down around them. Nihilism in the name of Islam is also a Ba'thist inheritance which has as little to do with traditional Islam as does the employment of a civil servant "to violate women's honor." There can be no such thing as a return to "real" Islam in Iraq because Iraqis have already been thoroughly and irreversibly "modernized" (in the bad sense of the term, not the good). There can only be *the use of Islam* as a modern political ideology to replace Ba'thist ideology with equally pernicious results (and to the long-term detriment of Islam itself). Iraqis today desperately need to put aside all forms of ideological thinking in politics, including Islamic forms.

22. See the report by Roy Gutman based on interviews with twenty victims in *New York Newsday,* August 23, 1992, p. 7 and 39.

23. This is the figure officially arrived at after exhaustive presentation of evidence by the International Military Tribunals held in Tokyo in 1946. From Susan Brownmiller's classic study of the subject, *Against Our Will: Men, Women and Rape* (New York: Bantam Books, 1980), p. 58.

24. Ibid., pp. 86–87.

25. A summary of these cases, in addition to a brief comment on the reponses to the December 1989 booklet, is provided in *Women for Women Political Prisoners—Jerusalem* (Jerusalem, semi-annual report, January–June 1990); see pp. 12–13 for cases of sexual abuse.

26. The 1982 study was done in Oregon. See "The Mind of the Rapist," *Newsweek,* July 23, 1990, p. 46.

27. "One of the most consistent elements in rape of all kinds is the absence of empathy; attackers are able to persuade themselves that the victim wanted or deserved to be raped." Ibid., p. 50.

28. The interviews with Iraqi women which form the raw material of Sana' al-Khayat's book *Honor and Shame* (London: Saqi Books, 1990) were conducted during the Iraq-Iran War. The violence in personal and interpersonal (but non-political) relations present in their depiction of family and sexual relations is an outcome of many years under the Ba'th regime. Similar interviews conducted in the 1950s or 1960s, before violence had become so institutionalized, would not, I suspect, have produced the same results.

29. See Regev, *Kol Ha'ir,* November 8, 1991.

30. See the article by Emma Daly, based on a conversation with Dr. Haritos-Fatouras, entitled "The Ordinary People Who Are Capable of Evil," in *The Independent,* August 10, 1992.

31. From an extended report of the incident by Roy Gutman in *New York Newsday*, August 23, 1992, pp. 7 and 39.

32. Ahmad Titinchi, the author of the short story I quoted in Chapter 7.

33. Quoted by Regev in *Kol Ha'ir*, November 8, 1991.

34. Salman Masalha, "On Arab Honor Lost," *Ha'aretz*, March 27, 1991. The quote is taken from a translation by Israel Shahak included in his Report no. 67, entitled "The Palestinians in Israel Debate Democracy in a Self-Critical Mood."

35. Mai Ghoussoub, *Al-Mar'a al-'Arabiyya*, pp. 9–10.

36. Quoted in an article, "With All Due Respect to My Family, I Want to Live," by Amy Ginsberg, in *Hadashot*, November 12, 1991. This article is included in the Shahak collection cited in note 14.

37. This figure is taken from an article by the lawyer Asma Jahangir, "The Many Faces of Rape," in the Pakistani publication *The Herald Annual* (January 1992), p. 52. The *Herald* devoted eighteen pages to different articles on "The Politics of Rape" in Pakistan, following two notorious cases of settling political scores through rape which involved women from opposite ends of the social spectrum. I am indebted to Sarah Zaidi for bringing this material to my attention. The gravity of the situation in Pakistan, and the way in which the Hudoud laws clearly conflict with basic principles of human rights, are set out in a 153-page report by Human Rights Watch entitled *Double Jeopardy: Police Abuse of Women in Pakistan* (New York, 1992).

38. *Times of India* is quoted in *Women in the Front Line*, an Amnesty International Report, March 1991, p. 19, as saying: "Custodial rapes seem to be occurring so frequently that 'cop molests woman' has become an almost daily fare for newspaper readers. Considering that as many as 97% of rape cases are either cancelled or sent back as 'untraced' by the police according to its own admission, the difficulties in dealing with custodial rape cannot be underestimated."

39. See "Against Their Will," in *Focus*, an Amnesty International publication, February 1992, p. 4.

40. *al-Fanar* (The Lighthouse) was founded in the spring of 1991, according to one of its members, Suzanne Nasser, interviewed by Ayad Rahim in May 1992. Its foundation was sparked by the case of a twenty-year-old Palestinian from the Galilee village of Iksal whose father had been raping her since she was fifteen. Finally, she became pregnant and was found burned to death in a car. The Israeli police let the father off the hook and Palestinian women began gathering a petition calling for him to be tried. Today, the women of *al-Fanar* lecture in Arab villages and at high schools on the issue of honor and shame in Arab-Muslim society. When the Muslim cleric Shaikh Muhammad Husain Ghadir said in an interview on radio that "family honor must be guarded," and if a woman "shames her family, something must be done to her, even killing her," the women of *al-Fanar* demanded from the Attorney General of Israel that the Shaikh be charged for incitement to murder. See also Ginsberg in *Hadashot*, November 12, 1991.

41. "Statement of Amnesty International on Human Rights in Syria," Washington, D.C., April 24, 1991.

42. See note 3 for other sources on the Hama story apart from this interview with Sa'eed conducted in the United States in the spring of 1992. Sa'eed is, of course, a pseudonym.

43. See the report by Martin Amis of the Associated Press published in the *Nashua [New Hampshire] Telegraph* on June 14, 1991. See also the *Boston Sunday Globe*, June 9, 1991.

44. See the report by Judith Miller, *The New York Times*, October 30, 1990.

45. See the report of Amnesty International as quoted in *The Times* (London), November 2, 1990.

46. See the report by Middle East Watch, "A Victory Turned Sour," September 1991; and Amnesty International News Release on Torture and Killings in Kuwait, dated April 18, 1991.

47. I have drawn all details from three reports by John Kifner in *The New York Times,* on January 22, January 30, and February 9, 1986.

48. The double car bomb is, incidentally, in the same tradition as the Israeli practice in Lebanon of bombing the same spot in a Palestinian refugee camp twice in quick succession.

49. Figures published in *al-Nahar,* March 6, 1992. The first official casualty figures of the Lebanese civil war, as confirmed by the Information Office of the Beirut Police Department, appeared in this issue of *al-Nahar.* Unless indicated otherwise, I have relied on this as my source.

50. These figures are from Salim Nasr's paper, "Lebanon: New Social Realities and Issues of Reconstruction," reprinted in *Precis,* a publication of the MIT Center for International Studies, vol. 3, no. 1 (Winter 1991–92), p. 13.

51. Jean Said Makdisi, *Beirut Fragments: A War Memoir* (New York: Persea Books, 1990), pp. 243–44.

52. All statistics are from an article entitled "The Intifada Turns Against Itself," in *The Economist,* September 16, 1989, p. 41.

53. One Palestinian who broke in public with the wall of silence over these murders was the writer Emile Habibi. See his articles in *al-Quds al-'Arabi,* March 20 and May 22, 1991.

54. Joost Hiltermann, *The Nation,* September 10, 1990. Habibi, incidentally, refers to three hundred deaths of so-called collaborators in his stinging critique of Palestinian extremism in *al-Quds al-'Arabi,* March 20, 1991.

55. *The Nation,* September 10, 1990. The title of the article is "The Enemy Inside the Intifadha."

56. As reported in the *Boston Globe,* May 30, 1992.

57. Eid left the meeting in despair, saying in a follow-up interview that he might be next in line. See the account in the *Boston Globe,* June 20, 1992.

58. From his article in *al-Quds al-'Arabi,* April 9, 1991.

59. The poem, entitled *"Madinat al-Qarn al-Auwal"* (City of the First Century), was written on March 7, 1991, while the Iraqi uprising against the Ba'th regime, which began in Basra, was being crushed. It is reprinted in Arabic and in an English translation by the Palestinian writer Anton Shammas, in *Mediterraneans: A Quarterly Review,* double issue nos. 2 and 3, pp. 78–81.

60. Amin al-'Issa wrote his article under the pseudonym M. Yahya. Entitled *"Mahmoud Darwish wa al-Tareeq al-Masdoud* (Mahmood Darwish and the Dead-End Road)," it was published in *'Iraq al-Ghad,* March 26, 1987.

61. All quotes are from the full text of Mahmoud Darwish's comments, which was published in the Paris-based Arabic weekly *al-Tali'a al-'Arabiyya,* no. 151, March 31, 1986, pp. 38–39.

62. Darwish's poem, entitled "Kurdistan," is quoted in al-'Issa's article, cited in note 60.

10 . Defining Silence

1. Sadiq Jalal al-'Azm, *Al-Naqd al-Dhati Ba'da al-Hazima* (Acre: Dar al-Jaleel, 1969), p. 20.

2. An exception is Wadhah Sharara, a professor of political science at the University of Lebanon, who wrote an excellent article in the immediate aftermath of the invasion of

Kuwait which reverberates with the themes of 'Azm's early work. See his "Self-Criticism in the Course of the Defeat," published in *al-Hayat* on August 25, 1991. Sharara took on board the corpus of nationalist and populist rhetoric even as it was swilling all around him in Beirut; under the circumstances, that was a brave thing to do.

3. Edward Said, *Orientalism* (New York: Random House, 1979). The quotes are from the Introduction, p. 11 (italics in the original), defining what the book is going to be about; and from Orientalism Now (p. 204), defining what Said thinks of as "latent" Orientalism, present, as he says, in "every" European.

4. For criticisms of the work by Arabs, see Sadiq Jalal al-'Azm's "Al-Istishraq wa al-Istishraq M'akousan," published in the Arabic magazine *al-Hayat al-Jadida,* no. 2 (January–February 1981). This appeared in English under the title "Orientalism and Orientalism in Reverse," in *Khamsin,* no. 8 (Ithaca Press, London, 1981).

5. Witness the furor caused by Emile Habibi's acceptance of Israel's most distinguished literary prize in May 1992. Habibi was denounced by one prominent Arab intellectual after the other (for instance: Mahmoud Darwish, 'Abdel-Rahman Munif, Samih al-Qasim, George Tarabishi, 'Aziz Azmah, Jaber 'Asfour, Hisham Sharabi, and many, many others). For short comments by these and others on why they opposed his accepting the prize, see *al-Hayat,* March 24, 1992. Habibi was also criticized by the Palestinian Union of Writers and Journalists. It should be noted that Habibi was supported, however, by that new generation of Palestinian leaders from inside Israel and the Occupied Territories, people like Hanan 'Ashrawi and Faisal al-Husaini. In defence of Habibi's action, see the excellent critique by Hazim Saghiyeh, "The Question of Emile Habibi," *al-Hayat,* March 30, 1992.

6. See *Orientalism,* p. 11.

7. Ibid., p. 1.

8. From Adonis's 1982 poem about Beirut, published in the bilingual anthology of Arabic poetry entitled *Victims of a Map,* p. 139. The translation is by Abdullah al-Udhari.

9. See Fouad Ajami, "The Tragedy of Arab Culture," *The New Republic,* April 6, 1987.

10. Khalidi, *The Gulf Crisis: Origins and Consequences,* p. 3.

11. The song which opens with these lines is called "Diktoor" (Doctor). It was composed in 1939 and broadcast that year on Baghdad Radio. The song makes a satirical appeal to a doctor to cure society of its long-term ills.

12. Noam Chomsky, "The Responsibility of Intellectuals," reissued in *The Chomsky Reader* (New York: Pantheon Books, 1987).

13. Oliver Sacks, *Awakenings* (London: Picador, 1991), p. 234.

14. Shklar, *Ordinary Vices,* pp. 8–9. The magnificent phrase "putting cruelty first" was coined by Montaigne, whom I went on to discover after reading Shklar. The worst political vice of them all, she argues in her book, is cruelty.

Index